AF778211

One Europe or Several?

Series Editor: **Helen Wallace**

The One Europe or Several? series examines contemporary processes of political, security, economic, social and cultural change across the European continent, as well as issues of convergence/divergence and prospects for integration and fragmentation. Many of the books in the series are cross-country comparisons; others evaluate the European institutions, in particular the European Union and NATO, in the context of eastern enlargement.

Titles include:

Brian Ardy, Iain Begg, Dermot Hodson, Imelda Maher and David G. Mayes
ADJUSTING TO EMU

Sarah Birch
ELECTORAL SYSTEMS AND POLITICAL TRANSFORMATION IN POST-COMMUNIST EUROPE

Sarah Birch, Frances Millard, Marina Popescu and Kieran Williams
EMBODYING DEMOCRACY
Electoral System Design in Post-Communist Europe

Andrew Cottey, Timothy Edmunds and Anthony Forster (*editors*)
DEMOCRATIC CONTROL OF THE MILITARY IN POSTCOMMUNIST EUROPE
Guarding the Guards

Anthony Forster, Timothy Edmunds and Andrew Cottey (*editors*)
THE CHALLENGE OF MILITARY REFORM IN POSTCOMMUNIST EUROPE
Building Professional Armed Forces

Anthony Forster, Timothy Edmunds and Andrew Cottey (*editors*)
SOLDIERS AND SOCIETIES IN POSTCOMMUNIST EUROPE
Legitimacy and Change

Karen Henderson (*editor*)
THE AREA OF FREEDOM, SECURITY AND JUSTICE IN THE ENLARGED EUROPE

James Hughes, Gwendolyn Sasse and Claire Gordon
EUROPEANIZATION AND REGIONALIZATION IN THE EU'S ENLARGEMENT TO CENTRAL AND EASTERN EUROPE
The Myth of Conditionality

Andrew Jordan
THE EUROPEANIZATION OF BRITISH ENVIRONMENTAL POLICY
A Departmental Perspective

Christopher Lord
A DEMOCRACTIC AUDIT OF THE EUROPEAN UNION

Valsamis Mitsilegas, Jorg Monar and Wyn Rees
THE EUROPEAN UNION AND INTERNAL SECURITY
Guardian of the People?

Helen Wallace (*editor*)
INTERLOCKING DIMENSIONS OF EUROPEAN INTEGRATION

One Europe or Several?
Series Standing Order ISBN 0–333–94630–8
(*outside North America only*)

You can receive future titles in this series as they are published by placing a standing order. Please contact your bookseller or, in case of difficulty, write to us at the address below with your name and address, the title of the series and the ISBN quoted above.

Customer Services Department, Macmillan Distribution Ltd, Houndmills, Basingstoke, Hampshire RG21 6XS, England

---

Also by David G. Mayes

WHO PAYS FOR BANK INSOLVENCY? (*with A. Liuksila*)

IMPROVING BANKING SUPERVISION (*with L. Halme and A. Liuksila*)

PUBLIC INTEREST AND MARKET PRESSURES (*with W. Hager, A. Knight and W. Streeck*)

MODERN PORTFOLIO THEORY AND FINANCIAL INSTITUTIONS (*with D.C. Corner*)

SOCIAL EXCLUSION IN EUROPEAN WELFARE STATES (*with R. Muffels and P. Tsakloglou*)

SOCIAL EXCLUSION AND EUROPEAN POLICY (*with J. Berghman and R. Salais*)

THE EVOLUTION OF THE SINGLE EUROPEAN MARKET

SOURCES OF PRODUCTIVITY GROWTH

THE SINGLE MARKET PROGRAMME AS A STIMULUS TO CHANGE (*with P.E. Hart*)

INEFFICIENCY IN INDUSTRY (*with C. Harris and M. Lansbury*)

THE EVOLUTION OF RULES FOR A SINGLE EUROPEAN MARKET (*editor*)

1. Industry and Finance
2. Rules, Democracy and the Environment
3. Social and International Issues

FOREIGN DIRECT INVESTMENT AND TRANSITION (*editor with G. Csaki and G. Foti*)

THE EXTERNAL IMPLICATIONS OF EUROPEAN INTEGRATION (*with others*)

ACHIEVING MONETARY UNION (*with A. Britton*)

A NEW STRATEGY FOR SOCIAL AND ECONOMIC COHESION AFTER 1992 (*with I Begg*)

THE EUROPEAN CHALLENGE

A STRATEGY FOR THE ECU (*with A. Britton and Ernst & Young*)

SHARPBENDERS (*with P. Grinyer and P. McKiernan*)

INTEGRATION AND EUROPEAN INDUSTRY (*with M. Macmillen and P. van Veen*)

THE EXCHANGE RATE ENVIRONMENT (*with S. Brooks and K. Cuthbertson*)

APPLICATIONS OF ECONOMETRICS

THE PROPERTY BOOM

INTRODUCTORY ECONOMIC STATISTICS (*with A.C. Mayes*)

Also by Iain Begg

INTEGRATION IN AN EXPANDING EUROPE: Reassessing the Fundamentals (*edited with Joseph Weiler and John Peterson*)

EMU AND COHESION: Theory and Policy (*with Brian Ardy, Waltraud Schelkle and Francisco Torres*)

EUROPE, GOVERNMENT AND MONEY: Running EMU – the Challenges of Policy Co-ordination
Paying for Europe (*with Nigel Grimwade*)

APPLIED ECONOMICS AND PUBLIC POLICY (*edited with S.G.B. Henry*)

Adjusting to EMU

Brian Ardy

Iain Begg

Dermot Hodson

Imelda Maher

David G. Mayes

The views expressed in this publication are those of the authors and are not necessarily those of the Bank of Finland, the European Commission or any other organisations that the authors are currently affiliated with.

palgrave macmillan

© Brian Ardy, Iain Begg, Dermot Hodson, Imelda Maher
and David G. Mayes 2006

All rights reserved. No reproduction, copy or transmission of this publication may be made without written permission.

No paragraph of this publication may be reproduced, copied or transmitted save with written permission or in accordance with the provisions of the Copyright, Designs and Patents Act 1988, or under the terms of any licence permitting limited copying issued by the Copyright Licensing Agency, 90 Tottenham Court Road, London W1T 4LP.

Any person who does any unauthorised act in relation to this publication may be liable to criminal prosecution and civil claims for damages.

The authors have asserted their rights to be identified as the authors of this work in accordance with the Copyright, Designs and Patents Act 1988.

First published 2006 by
PALGRAVE MACMILLAN
Houndmills, Basingstoke, Hampshire RG21 6XS and
175 Fifth Avenue, New York, N.Y. 10010
Companies and representatives throughout the world

PALGRAVE MACMILLAN is the global academic imprint of the Palgrave Macmillan division of St. Martin's Press, LLC and of Palgrave Macmillan Ltd. Macmillan® is a registered trademark in the United States, United Kingdom and other countries. Palgrave is a registered trademark in the European Union and other countries.

ISBN-13: 978–0–333–99566–2 hardback
ISBN-10: 0–333–99566–X hardback

This book is printed on paper suitable for recycling and made from fully managed and sustained forest sources.

A catalogue record for this book is available from the British Library.

Library of Congress Cataloging-in-Publication Data
Adjusting to EMU / Brian Ardy . . . [*et al.*].
p. cm. — (One Europe or several?)
Includes bibliographical references and index.
ISBN 0–333–99566–X
1. Economic and Monetary Union. 2. European Union. 3. Europe—Economic integration. 4. European Union countries—Economic conditions. 5. European Union countries—Economic policy. I. Ardy, Brian. II. Series.
HC241.A35 2005
332.4'566—dc22 2005051276

10 9 8 7 6 5 4 3 2 1
15 14 13 12 11 10 09 08 07 06

Printed and bound in Great Britain by
Antony Rowe Ltd, Chippenham and Eastbourne

Contents

List of Tables

List of Figures

List of Boxes

Abbreviations

AMECO	Annual macroeconomic database (DG Ecofin)
APW	Average production worker
BS	Balassa–Samuelson
BEPGs	Broad Economic Policy Guidelines
CEE	Central and Eastern Europe
CEECs	Central and East European Countries
CEPII	Dentre d'Etudes Prospectives et d'Informations Internationales
CEPR	Centre for Economic Policy Research
CEPS	Centre for European Policy Studies
CIS	Commonwealth of Independent States
COREPER	Committee of Permanent Representatives
CPI	Consumer Price Index
CSO	Central Statistical Office (Ireland)
DG	Directorate General (European Commission)
DW	Durbin-Watson (test statitistic)
DM	Deutschmark
EA	Expectations augmented
EC	European Community
ECB	European Central Bank
ECJ	European Court of Justice
Ecofin	Economic and Finance Council
EDP	Excessive Deficit Procedure
EEA	European Economic Area
EES	European Employment Strategy
EFC	Economic and Financial Affairs Committee
EFTA	European Free Trade Area
EIB	European Investment Bank
EIRO	European Industrial Relations Observatory
EITO	European Information Technology Observatory
EMAC	Economic and Monetary Affairs Committee (European Parliament)
EMCO	Employment Committee
EMU	Economic and monetary union
EMS	European Monetary System
EONIA	Euro Over-Night Index Average
EPC	Economic Policy Committee
EPL	Employment protection legislation

ERM	Exchange Rate Mechanism (of the EMS)
ERM I	Exchange Rate Mechanism I (1979–1998)
ERM II	Exchange Rate Mechanism II (1999–)
ESCB	European System of Central Banks
ESRC	Economic and Social Research Council
ESDS	Economic and Social Data Services
ETUC	European Trade Union Confederation
EU	European Union
Eurostat	European Union Statistical Office
FDI	Foreign direct investment
FEDEA	Fundación de Estudios de Economía Aplicada
FRA	Fiscal Responsibility Act (New Zealand)
G7	USA, France, Canada, Italy, Japan, Germany and UK
GDP	Gross domestic product
HICP	Harmonised Index of Consumer Prices
HMSO	Her Majesty's Stationery Office
HMT	HM Treasury
HP	Hodrick-Prescott (filtered trend)
ICT	Information and communications technology
IDC	International Data Corporation
IFO	Institut für Wirtschaftsforschung
IIE	Institute for International Economics
ILO	International Labour Organisation
ILOH	ILO plus hidden (unemployment)
IMF	International Monetary Fund
IT	Information technology
IW	Institut der deutschen Wirtschaft Köln
MPC	Monetary Policy Committee (Bank of England)
MTO	Medium term objective
NAIRU	Non-accelerating inflation rate of unemployment
NARWU	Non-accelerating wages rate of unemployment
NAP	National Action Plan
NBER	National Bureau of Economic Research
NIER	National Institute of Economic Research (Sweden)
NIG	Netherlands Institute of Government
NK	New Keynesian
NRR	Net replacement rate
Obs	Observations
OCA	Optimum currency area
OECD	Organisation for Economic Cooperation and Development
OFCE	Observatoire Français des Conjonctures Economiques
OJ	Official Journal (of the European Union)
OLAF	Office Européen de Lutte Anti-Fraude
OLS	Ordinary Least Squares

OMC	Open method of coordination
ONS	Office of National Statistics (UK)
OOPEC	Office for Official Publication of the European Communities
PNR	Programme for National Recovery
PPS	Purchasing power standard (exchange rate)
QMV	Qualified Majority Voting
R&D	Research and development
REER	Real effective exchange rate
RWI	Rheinisch-Westfälisches Institut für Wirtschaftsforschung
SABL	Statistiche, Ämter des Bundes und der Länder
SEE	standard error of estimate
SGP	Stability and Growth Pact
SPC	Social Protection Committee
SUR	Seemingly-unrelated regressions
SVAR	Structural vector auto-regression
TEPSA	Trans European Policy Association
TEU	Treaty on European Union (Maastricht Treaty)
UA	Unemployment assistance
UI	Unemployment insurance
UACES	University Association for Contemporary European Studies
UNCTAD	United Nations Commission on Trade and Development
WRR	Wetenschappelijke Raad voor het Regeringsbeleid
WTO	World Trade Organization

Acknowledgements

This work was primarily financed by a grant from the Economic and Social Research Council No. L213252034. Without this grant it is unlikely that much of the work would have taken place. David Mayes thanks the Bank of Finland for allowing him to work on this topic and to Matti Vanhala, the Governor, in particular for encouraging the work. Our thanks to all the officials who gave generously of their time in answering our questions and supplying information on the functioning of EMU, and to Helen Wallace and Jim Rollo, who directed the 'One Europe or Several?' programme, for their advice and encouragement. Others were involved in the work whose names do not appear on the cover, particularly Matti Virén, Waltraud Shelkle, Sarah Plant provided sterling assistance in London and Heli Tikkunen and Anu Alander in Helsinki. Janet Mayes and Mihalis Kritikos assisted in the preparation of the typescript.

Preface

This book is one of the products of the 'One Europe or Several?' research programme funded by the ESRC. It is one of a series published by Palgrave Macmillan under the General Editorship of Helen Wallace, who was the first director of the research programme. The programme as a whole was concerned with the way in which the process of integration is developing in Europe. Some facets of integration are characterised by increasing homogeneity across the continent, whereas others highlight the importance of difference or diversity, to use a frequent word in this field. Such diversity can be territorial, related groups in society, policies, institutions, preferences – the list is long. Our concern in this context was with a very specific though substantial issue.

Iain Begg and David Mayes have been working together in addressing aspects of the design and implementation of monetary union in Europe since the 1980s. Right from the outset it has been clear that unless monetary union were perceived to be an arrangement where people right across society benefited, it would fail. Countries would not join it in the first place and if they did, then there would be a strong likelihood of its falling apart under strain, if substantial groups thought they would or were losing out. Our initial focus was on three main facets:

1. Whether the most disadvantaged would lose out and what could be done to assist them. (This work resulted in a major report for the European Parliament, widely seen as a follow up to the MacDougall report of 1977, indeed Sir Donald MacDougall was one of the collaborators in the project.)
2. How firms, regions and industries might be affected, as part of an earlier ESRC research programme, entitled 'The Evolution of Rules for A Single European Market', that first David and then Iain led during the 1990s. One of the great benefits of this programme from a narrow point of view was, *inter alia*, that it brought economists and lawyers together to bring their different expertise to bear on a common problem. The present collaboration with Imelda Maher is a direct result of this appreciation that the impact of what is essentially a rule-driven process of integration cannot be tackled properly without such joint perspectives.
3. How monetary union itself might be structured and introduced to minimise the costs and maximise the gains.

This helped develop many ideas but four in particular led us to want to take on the research described in this book.

1. Quite detailed and locally specific approaches to the process of structural change are required if it is to succeed in reducing poverty, unemployment and inequality to socially acceptable levels. Monetary union may enhance the prospects for overall economic growth but if anything it is likely to make these processes of adjustment more difficult rather than easier by restricting the range of tools available.
2. Successful processes of adaptation cannot be adopted à la carte. They require integrated approaches that take account of institutions, preferences, economic structures and legal frameworks.
3. The EU has made the task of integration difficult for itself by, on the one hand, wanting to provide harsh limits on the ability to transfer resources between member states and, on the other, wanting to integrate great diversity into a single framework.
4. There are some major differences in economic and political philosophy that have to be accommodated for common policies to work.

We have therefore tried to set out the economic principles that have to be addressed, the institutional and legal framework in which it has to operate and most especially the process by which closer integration and structural change can take place. To provide a view of the diversity we look at the specific perspectives of the Anglo-Saxon, Nordic, Continental, 'Southern' and Accession countries.

B.A.
I.B.
D.H.
I.M.
D.G.M.
London, Brussels and Helsinki

Notes on Contributors

Brian Ardy is Senior Lecturer at London South Bank University.

Iain Begg is Visiting Professor in the European Institute at the London School of Economics.

Dermot Hodson recently graduated from the London School of Economics and Political Science with a PhD in European Political Economy.

Imelda Maher is Senior Lecturer in Law at the London School of Economics.

David G. Mayes is Advisor to the Board at the Bank of Finland, Professor of Economics at London South Bank University and Honorary Professor of Banking and Financial Institutions at the University of Stirling.

1
Introduction

Economic and monetary union (EMU) in Europe is a bold and unprecedented development. Although it has long been seen as an obvious extension of the market integration that began in the 1950s, EMU goes significantly further than regional economic arrangements elsewhere in the world by changing the topography of macroeconomic policy-making. Clearly, too, it is more than just the integration of national currencies, encompassing other policy areas that it is not customary to analyse in looking at monetary integration from the perspective purely of creating a common currency. This has profound implications for the processes of economic adjustment. It also raises the question of what the eventual character of economic governance in the European Union (EU) will be, with options ranging from minor tinkering with the present set up to a fully federal system.

Since the pioneering work of Mundell (1961) on optimal currency areas (OCAs), monetary union has had to rise to a relatively simple challenge: Will welfare be enhanced by merging the currencies of the participating nations? So long as the balance of the various criteria – degree of factor mobility, openness, flexibility and so on – is adjudged to be positive, the union is deemed to be worthwhile. Implicit in this way of assessing a proposal for monetary union is the expectation that the mechanisms that allow a national economy to adjust to problems will be replicated in the unified currency area. Critics of EMU such as Feldstein (1997) have stressed that, in practice, EMU lacks most of the adjustment mechanisms on which countries rely and is consequently misconceived. Others (for a good introduction, see De Grauwe, 2003) are more sanguine, believing that once account is taken of the full range of effects, the balance of costs and benefits is positive.

In this volume, we aim to move beyond the cost-benefit calculus and the well-worn question of whether or not countries should join. Instead we ask whether EMU as currently constituted is suitably equipped to allow economic adjustment to shocks – symmetric as well as asymmetric – to take place in a timely and effective manner, and how the policy framework needs to evolve to ensure that it does. Adjusting to EMU and adjusting an economy within EMU involves a dynamic process where prior circumstances and actions in the preceding period have major effects. Since adjustment involves the interaction of people and institutions within a framework of rules that are themselves being developed, its path is only partially predictable from previous experience.

We therefore try to disentangle these different aspects, which can be placed in four groups:

1. How countries' adjustment is influenced by their structures, institutions and conditions.
2. How the rules of EMU have influenced the adjustment process and how institutions and other actors have responded to those rules.
3. How the short-run policy choices over the few years before and since EMU started have affected adjustment in the face of world economic developments over the period.
4. How the rules themselves have adjusted, in the light of experience and as EMU has proceeded.

While monetary union had a fixed starting date and rules of implementation that had been largely developed beforehand, the 'economic' side of EMU has been very much a work in progress, where the plans are much less clearly written. It is not clear when EMU might be 'completed', nor indeed what the concept of completion means in this context. The Lisbon Strategy aimed at revitalising the supply-side of the EU economy set an arbitrary target of 2010 for many of its key variables, but given issues over debt, pensions and structural unemployment, to say nothing of the continuing quest to 'complete the internal market', a longer and somewhat indeterminate process seems a suitable framework for the discussion.

That EMU changes the economic environment is generally accepted and there is broad agreement on several of its expected effects. Equally, there are possible outcomes where neither theory nor evidence provides a solid basis for judgement and no easy way of reconciling the conflicting views. Indeed, despite the large body of research in the OCA tradition and extensive analysis of fiscal and monetary rules as applied to EMU as a macroeconomic framework, the early years of the euro have exhibited a consistent capacity to surprise.

Economic and monetary union not only changes the assignment of competence for monetary policy, but also radically alters the overall system of economic governance in the EU. This may appear to be a statement of the obvious, yet its ramifications are rarely well understood. First, it means that it is a fundamentally flawed conception to view the advent of EMU as little more than a largely technocratic replication of the mechanisms of economic policy employed by Member States at the supranational level, with the latter acting as a quasi-state. Second, it means that when economic adjustment is required, different policy levers have to be pulled and their effects may differ from those that applied for Member States. Certain levers of policy that governments have relied on will lose their effectiveness, while others will need to evolve to play a more extensive role in economic management. Third, economic actors have to adapt to new signals and reaction functions, and may have to go through an extended period of learning and assimilation.

The game, in short, is a different one, played under rules that differ from those to which all sides are accustomed. For countries that participate fully in EMU, the changes may be quite pronounced, especially if the new policy context encompasses features that are far removed from what they are used to. For instance, permanently low inflation is virtually guaranteed by the mandate given to the European Central Bank (ECB) and for many countries this will be a novel experience.

1.1 Outline of the policy framework

The new policy framework in the euro area is complex and, arguably, can be properly appreciated only by viewing it as a very profound regime change (Allsopp, 2002), thereby undermining much of the analysis of its prospects rooted overly narrowly in OCA approaches. It follows that the mechanisms for managing the economy and responding to shocks also have to evolve.

The architecture of demand-side policies[1] under EMU is clear. Monetary policy is assigned the primary task of assuring price stability, leaving fiscal policy and supply-side policies[2] – which remain under the jurisdiction of national governments – to deal with country-specific macroeconomic problems. The approach to policy combines some rule-based procedures with much 'softer' modes of decision-making. For monetary policy, the over-arching rule is the target of price stability which has – so far – been defined operationally by the ECB as a medium-term value for the annual increases in the harmonised index of consumer prices (HICP) of less than but 'close to' 2%. The ECB has adopted a two-pillar strategy (see Issing *et al.*, 2001; ECB, 2004) in which one pillar is a reference value for growth of the money supply (M3), so far of 4.5% a year. But the apparent clarity of the rules is complicated by the other pillar which involves the ECB looking at a range of other economic indicators such as the interplay of supply and demand in the goods, services and factors markets to gauge the trajectory of the economy over the short to medium term. The monetary analysis relates more to the longer-term prospects for inflation and the 'economic' analysis more to the shorter (ECB, 2004: 65–6).

Fiscal policy is constrained by the *Stability and Growth Pact* (SGP), which aims to set a limit of 3% of GDP for the public deficit and initially had a medium-term target of 'close to balance or in surplus' and escalating sanctions to assure compliance. Despite the disarray in the SGP after 2002, leading up to its de facto suspension in November 2003, the reforms agreed in March 2005 broadly retain the 3% limit, though in future the terms on which countries can breach it will be interpreted more flexibly. The rationale for fiscal policy rules is that there are spillover effects amongst decentralised governments in an economically and financially integrated area. Indeed, the spillover arguments appear to have inspired the rules in the Maastricht Treaty and been carried forward into the SGP. The logic is that due to market integration, 'excessive' public deficits in one country will have adverse effects on others through higher interest rates, threats of higher future inflation and so on in a way similar to pollution or any other external effect. Examples are common trends in long-term interest on public debts in federations and, since the inception of monetary union in Europe, the observed trends in, and the narrow band of risk premia on, European governments' debts.

These rules mean that if a country has to deal with more severe economic shocks, it may be unable to do so through demand management while abiding by the terms of the SGP. The Pact has an in-built asymmetry in that it sets limits to national deficits, but imposes no rules on public surpluses. There is, therefore, a co-ordination issue to resolve if the aggregate fiscal policy of the euro area is to be consistent with monetary policy. Moreover, policy co-ordination cannot be seen purely in terms of optimising the conventional policy mix between fiscal and monetary policy, but must also embrace supply-side policies, especially those that bear on the labour market given the political compromise between national and European Council competence.

Agreeing on the virtues of rules to constrain national policies in a multilevel government setting leaves open the question of the nature and content of the rules, and it is by no means obvious that the current institutional mix is optimal (Holzmann, 1996; Creel *et al.*, 2002). Nevertheless, although rules may not fully resolve fiscal policy co-ordination problems in the euro area, there is little doubt that rules are needed to prevent governments from engaging in policies that would be detrimental for the union as a whole.

1.2 Adjustment challenges

As the UK Treasury has shown in its '5 tests' report (HM Treasury, 2003i), there are diverse obstacles to the elaboration of adjustment policies and very disparate strategies can be envisaged. Problems to be confronted not only vary between economies, but are also dependent on the institutional framework and conventions in the Member State, for example in housing finance. As a result, susceptibility to shocks are different, as are the respective roles of the various tiers of government in dealing with the consequences of integration. There are both economic and constitutional dimensions to these issues and it is clear that policy choices have to take account of legal frameworks.

The degree of flexibility any economy exhibits, and thus its capacity to adjust under EMU, will depend, first, on the structure of the labour market and its institutions. This includes not just the bargaining systems in place in the labour market, but also the responsiveness of product markets and the relationship between labour market outcomes and budgetary decisions.

There is very considerable variety across the EU in this regard, and it is for this reason that the present volume assesses a range of national circumstances. Thus, the Nordic 'model' of consensus building and centralised bargaining provides a clear contrast to the more flexible and decentralised system of the UK, and to the more regulated systems of, for instance, France and Germany.

In thinking about the impact of EMU and how it bears on economic adjustment, three general questions arise. First, are stabilisation and growth likely to be at odds with each other for any country that participates fully in EMU? In the right circumstances no such conflict should arise, but it may be a matter of timing: the medium- to longer-term benefits of stabilisation may be uncontested, but if rapid transition is very costly, it is conceivable that the short-term costs may be so great as to make the long-term benefits politically unattainable. Second, if EMU delivers its promise of higher growth in the medium to long term, will it benefit the richer parts of the Union at the expense of the poorer? In similar vein, will the advantages *within* countries be evenly spread or unbalanced? Third is the particular institutional form of EMU suitably configured to facilitate Member States in adjusting their economies, bearing in mind the diversity in their national institutional structures and policy traditions? In this volume, we explore all three dimensions, drawing on the experience and singularities of different Member States.

1.2.1 Stabilisation effects

There is little dissent from the view that there are long-run benefits to be realised from the enhanced stability that EMU is expected to deliver. Instead, the issues surrounding stabilisation are more about the short- to medium-term effects. The expected gains in stabilisation come about because full participation in EMU immediately confers on the country that joins commitment and credibility benefits that it would otherwise find it very difficult to achieve. It is generally accepted that these gains will have to be paid for in the transition to EMU and possibly beyond. The argument about transition costs is straightforward, if empirically contentious. Countries with inflation rates or fiscal ratios above the Maastricht thresholds have had to rein back the economy to attain the required macroeconomic balance and, in so doing, may have lost output growth. The extent of any output loss will depend on a range of influences, such as the magnitude of the adjustment that had to be made, the sequencing of different stages, and whether the main fiscal retrenchment took place in a generally buoyant or stagnating economic environment (both internally and among key trading partners). The degree of internal conflict associated with fiscal consolidation, such as resistance to public expenditure cuts is also an issue.

Certainly, countries that had to travel a long way to achieve nominal convergence had to forgo more growth to attain a stabilised economy than those which only needed to make minor adjustments. Joining EMU prematurely – an issue that the new members who joined the EU in 2004 will have to confront soon – could necessitate the over-riding of other macroeconomic policies while at the same time slowing structural reforms, with heavy costs in terms of output foregone. However, if the pursuit of EMU constitutes a shift from 'bad' to 'good' policy, then the process may well be unambiguously beneficial. A question to pose is, therefore, whether the pre-EMU policy regime was one that favoured growth or, instead, had had a debilitating effect. For example, the Greek economy appeared to pick-up from the mid-1990s onwards as the macroeconomic excesses of the previous decade were replaced by more sensible policies. Ireland, too, rapidly saw benefits as the large deficits and high debt of the decade before were brought under control from the late 1980s onwards. Indeed, the transformation of Irish macroeconomic policy in the late 1980s is regarded as one of the foundations of that country's subsequent spectacular growth (Barry, 1999).

By contrast, both the French and the Italian economies seemed to lose dynamism during the 1980s and 1990s, first through targeting the exchange rate in order to stay in the exchange rate mechanism (ERM) of the EMS, then in making the further adjustment to EMU. It is, perhaps, salient that the small open economies have, on the whole, found it easier to adjust than their larger peers. EMU can also act as an external benchmark cum incentive for policy improvement and there is evidence that it contributed to the recasting of policy in Greece (with results that can be regarded as positive for growth) and Italy (though with, thus far, less encouraging outcomes).

Once in EMU, a country has to adapt to a policy regime that is radically different. In particular, it has to recognise that the ECB will deliver price stability and that resort to inflation as an adjustment mechanism, or to calling on the central bank to print money to finance expenditure are no longer options. Adjustment to shocks, symmetric or asymmetric, will require the creation of room for manoeuvre in fiscal policy, as well as obliging the supply-side to assume a greater share of any burden. Consequently, the fiscal authorities will have to adapt and labour market actors have to recognise that monetary policy can no longer accommodate inflationary pay deals.

1.2.2 Inter-territorial disparities

Even if EMU does fulfil the expectation of its supporters that it will facilitate stable growth in the EU as a whole, there is no guarantee that the resulting growth will be balanced, whether among Member States or regions. Yet there is by no means a consensus in the literature on how the furthering of economic integration by monetary union will affect disparities. In the Delors report (Commission, 1989: paragraph 29) that paved the way for the euro, the fear was expressed that 'historical experience suggests, however, that in the absence of countervailing policies, the overall impact on peripheral regions could be negative'. This statement echoed concerns expressed in the Padoa-Schioppa report (1987) and led directly to the acceptance that there should be some sort of compensatory policy to assure cohesion. The thrust of much of the new economic geography analysis as applied to EMU is that integration will favour core areas at the expense of the periphery through the mechanism of increased trade flows. The evidence on trade creation is indeed that monetary union does give it a sizeable fillip (Rose, 2001, 2004; see also HM Treasury, 2003i), so that the location of activity is affected. But whether it is necessarily to the benefit of core areas will be the result of a balancing of different effects (succinctly summarised in Krugman, 1998) which can only sensibly be assessed empirically.

An alternative view is that EMU will provide a stimulus to the less competitive countries and regions that will enable them to make a leap forward (Barry, 2003), the implication being that separate currencies have acted as a barrier to economic development. Possible explanations for such advances include the overcoming of inhibitions on factor movements that have prevented the optimal allocation of resources, especially investment flows, and the negative effects of markets fragmented in a way that has slowed innovation and the exploitation of economies of scale. The 'Sapir' report notes that 'growth may have a negative effect on cohesion if market forces lead to a widening of the income gaps between regions or between individuals. In the case of economic convergence between regions, there is little evidence of such effects and, on the contrary, lagging regions have provided a boost to overall EU growth' (Sapir *et al.*, 2004: 88). The same report also states that although redistributive policies have helped to assure social cohesion, they may have done so 'at the expense of lower incentives for growth' (Sapir *et al.*, 2004: 89). The inference to draw is, perhaps, that EMU provides a new setting, but that its impact on convergence will depend on the detailed choices made on institutional matters and on supporting policies, rather than there being an unambiguous overall impact of monetary union.

1.2.3 Institutional factors

In contrast to the proposals in the Werner report (1970) for a common fiscal policy as a complement to European monetary integration, the path chosen for EMU leaves economic (as opposed to monetary) policy under the control of Member States. However, if policy anarchy is to be avoided, some form of concertation of these national policies is required. The Delors report (Commission, 1989) that constituted the blueprint for EMU stressed that co-ordination is an essential part of the policy framework, precisely because the choice taken was *not* to introduce a common policy.

The EMU policy regime combines a specific philosophy of economic policy, a novel distribution of responsibility between the national and the supranational levels of economic governance and a reconfiguration of policy instruments and targets. It is easy to forget just how profound the change is. In addition, because of political imperatives that have resulted in a delicate balance of power between Member States and the supranational level, EMU has also had to establish means of co-ordinating a range of national policies. Although co-ordination is explicitly called for in the Treaty (notably in Article

98 EC, given force in Article 99), it comprises a mix of different approaches. Even for fiscal policy, there is a combination of hard law aimed at curbing excessive deficits (adopted for the Stability and Growth Pact) and the much softer provisions for multilateral surveillance and the Broad Economic Policy Guidelines (BEPGs). Amtenbrink and de Haan (2003) suggest the former is a 'closed' method of co-ordination in contrast to the 'open' method employed for the latter. However, the politicised nature of the sanctioning process in the excessive deficit procedure – a key element of the SGP – and the uncertainty which exists over measuring compliance with the SGP give considerable discretion to Member States over the application of EMU's fiscal rules, thus rendering economic policy co-ordination in the euro area primarily soft in character.

A key question is whether what might be called the Artis-Buti policy framework[3] goes far enough in assigning policy roles. In this conceptualisation – to simplify greatly – the role of monetary policy (and thus the ECB) is to deal with system-wide economic effects – including *symmetric* shocks – while national autonomy (fiscal and supply-side policies) is retained to deal with effects specific to the Member State – notably *asymmetric* shocks. At the same time, fiscal and supply-side policies have to be aggregated in a manner that is consistent with supranationally set monetary policy. The challenge for economic policy is to combine these three sets of policies (central monetary, national fiscal, and national and EU-level supply side) into a coherent policy mix.

The difficulty with this framework is that it departs significantly from what is customary within nation-states as currency areas, where there is, typically, also fiscal union. In a fiscal and monetary union, an asymmetric shock hitting a region of the union will be substantially attenuated by net fiscal flows from the centre, predominantly through the operation of automatic stabilisers (see Bayoumi and Masson, 1995; Obstfeld and Peri, 1998; Melitz and Zumer, 2002). The EU budget simply cannot fulfil this function and, although national budgets do provide a substantial degree of stabilisation that diminishes the problem when it manifests itself at the regional level, there remains a gap in the policy framework when it is a whole country that is affected asymmetrically. Finland, for example, suffered a sharp recession in the early 1990s that was largely unrelated to trends elsewhere in the EU.

1.2.4 The constitutional dimension

Economic policy-making is, however, also hemmed-in by legal constraints. The policy/law dynamic is complex in the Community, because policy implementation occurs through a system of multi-level governance where Community rules are generated at the supranational level, yet are mediated through national and sub-national levels of governance. As EMU is consolidated, this interplay of tiers of government and governance raises a number of issues at the EC and national levels.

First, does the Community have the legal competence to develop general economic policies in addition to its powers over monetary policy? While Article 99 TEC clearly signals the 'common interest' in economic policies more generally and requires the Commission and the Council to develop broad guidelines on economic policy, it does not specify how policy is to be pursued. Since the Treaty also stresses the principle of subsidiarity, this leaves open the question of where the boundaries between Community and national policy should lie.

Second, once competence at the Community level is established, how can policy be implemented at the national level? Although legal systems form part of a single social system of law, the jurisdictional differences that exist between the national and EC orders mean that EC law is both internal and external to each national legal order (Maher, 1998). As such, successful integration into the domestic legal order turns in part on the 'fit' between the new Community rule and the existing legal order (Teubner, 1998). If legislation emanating from the Community is confluent with the Member State preferences, it will tend to be assimilated fairly easily, whereas if it requires significant changes in procedures or practices, implementation tends to be much more problematic. Some of the disputes over the Lisbon agenda illustrate the difficulties, with, for example, certain Member States happy to press ahead with liberalisation of network industries and financial services, while others drag their heels.

Third, can a system in which hard law and soft law are inter-mingled be simultaneously robust, flexible and effective? Abbott and Snidal (2000) explain some of the strengths and weaknesses of the hard and soft approaches and many of the points they highlight are exemplified in the EMU setting, not least in the difficulties surrounding the Stability and Growth Pact in 2003. Can formal sanctions be effective, or is it only softer, more political pressures that will induce Member States to change tack?

In short, the relationship between legal rules at the Community and the national level, notably in relation to questions of implementation, is important in establishing the extent to which the policy environment can and will change in the euro area and beyond. It is also essential to distinguish between the formal institutional and regulatory structures and the actual behaviour that occurs: ostensibly harsher regimes may, for example, be characterised by evasion in contrast to apparently softer regimes.

1.2.5 The Stability and Growth Pact

In many ways, the experience of the implementation of the SGP exemplifies the constitutional challenges. The relatively favourable macroeconomic environment of the first two years of the euro and the previous efforts made by many governments to reduce public deficits and debts before entering monetary union, meant that the deficit ceiling in the SGP did not prove excessively binding until 2002. As a result, the fault-lines that subsequently surfaced in the operation of the Pact (Begg and Schelkle, 2004a) remained largely hidden, although it is worth noting that many prominent economists had foreseen some of the difficulties. One of the most visible problems is the SGP's pro-cyclical bias which aggravates business cycle fluctuations and had already become apparent in the decade prior to the launch of monetary union (Fitoussi, 2000). In the good times, several governments (especially the two largest Member States, France and Germany) relaxed their efforts to reduce deficits, preferring to increase expenditures and cut taxes at a time of buoyant economic activity. By 2003, these same governments were under pressure to implement more restrictive fiscal policies at a time of slow growth or even recession.

In November 2003, the SGP was effectively suspended when the Council refused to accept Commission recommendations regarding excessive deficit in France and Germany. The Commission then asked the European Court of Justice to rule on the legality of the Council decision, and the Court provided its answer in July 2004, ruling that the Council was wrong, but also clarifying the procedures (see Chapter 4 for more detail). Implicitly, all parties then accepted that the SGP had to be changed and agreement on a way forward was then reached – not without acrimony – in March 2005.

Amtenbrink and de Haan (2003: 1077) note that calls for reform of the SGP were partly motivated by the quest for a combination of 'long-run sustainability of fiscal policy with short-run fiscal flexibility as a tool for macroeconomic stabilisation'. Solutions may involve changing the rule and moving to a ceiling in terms of a cyclically adjusted public deficit, that is a structural budget deficit (see, for instance, Creel and Sterdyniak, 1995; Eichengreen and Wyplosz, 1998; Buiter and Grafe, 2003a; Begg *et al.*, 2004).

The successive controversies surrounding the SGP have prompted searching questions about whether the current EMU policy framework is appropriate and, although criticisms centre on the SGP, other dimensions of economic policy-making also come under scrutiny (Pisani-Ferry, 2002). In particular, what has become known as the Lisbon Agenda – shorthand for a range of supply-side (or structural) reforms – has come to be seen as an essential complement to EMU (see, for example, Issing *et al.*, 2001), even if the Kok report (2004) bemoans its lack of achievements. At the same time, the ECB has come under fire for adopting an approach to monetary policy that gives too much weight to a low reference value (2%) for inflation, while paying too little heed to output targets. The ECB is also criticised for technical aspects of policy implementation, such as not following an inflation targeting approach and having too unwieldy a decision-making structure.

1.3 The impact of EMU

In assessing how EMU will alter the performance of an economy and thus place demands on policy to establish adequate adjustment mechanisms, three different categories of effects can be delineated (Table 1.1). These are:

Table 1.1 The effects of EMU

Mechanism	Effect	Impact
Macroeconomic shifts, of which:	Change to the new policy regime recasts established policy signals and rules	Affects all members of EMU, but spatial impact uncertain; depends on willingness and capacity to adapt
Acclimatisation in the short term to new policy settings	Low nominal interest rate; impact on asset prices; but disparities in real rates	Previously inflation-prone regions face over-heating. Thus far, positive for less prosperous areas, but increases prospect of macroeconomic imbalances
Adoption of stability-orientated macro policy approach	Alters government and financial market behaviour	Most pronounced for those who have to change most, with need for policy learning; risks from Balassa–Samuelson effect for countries with least developed service sectors
Labour market and transformations of it, of which:	More of the burden of adjustment falls on labour market	Creates problems for least flexible economies. Could aggravate unemployment
Systems for wage setting	Influence wage flexibility and scope for short-term adjustment	Potentially damaging for areas with rigid systems and engenders problems of social cohesion (insiders and outsiders)
Geographical, sectoral and occupational mobility	Affects medium-term scope for labour market adaptability to deal with competitiveness problems	Induced pressures from migration; could lead to brain drain (gain). Possibility of aggravated imbalances within countries
Regulatory setting and institutions under-pinning labour market	Shapes long-term potential for adjustment through supply-side	Adverse for less developed economies that lack training provision, especially where de facto regulation is pronounced
Induced effects on economic structure	Market opening accelerates pace of restructuring	Potential threat to least competitive economies; likely to widen disparities
Regional industrial specialisation	Mix of centripetal and centrifugal 'NEG' consequences	Initially favours core regions; but creates opportunities for low cost areas; ambivalent overall
Concentration of financial services	Lowers intermediation margins; enhances pool of liquidity and supply of risk capital	Economies with weak financial sectors lose activity; ambivalent overall

Source: Adapted from Begg (2003); see also Ardy *et al.* (2002).

- *Macroeconomic changes* resulting from the new policy regime that alter the manner in which policy is conducted and require the country, first, to acclimatise then to develop new accommodations between policy actors and objectives. Thus, a general fall in interest rates (which has occurred as a result of the single currency) favours (relatively) indebted countries. Curbs in public expenditure to meet the SGP may result in lower discretionary public spending.
- *Labour market transformations*. An important consideration in this context is the ease with which countries are likely to be able to render their labour markets more flexible (Nickell, 1997). The difficulties Germany has encountered in pushing forward labour market reforms are in the limelight at the moment, but there is also evidence that there is a lack of adaptability on the part of other lagging countries such as Belgium and France (Algoé and Alphametrics, 2002).
- *Induced effects on economic structure* that shape the longer-term competitive position of the economy by altering the competitive position of different areas and shaping supply-side developments such as backward and forward linkages between intermediate and final producers (Krugman and Venables, 1996).

1.3.1 The timing of EMU effects

In thinking about monetary union, a number of phases can be envisaged for different effects. The first is nominal convergence which, in the EMU model, had to take place before Member States could join the single currency. Second, there is assimilation to the resulting new regime. Then follow the medium- to longer-term real economy effects described in the second and third segments of Table 1.1.

The nominal convergence phase proved to be a testing one for many countries, because the obligation to 'consolidate' public finances tends to mean a combination of tax increases and public spending cuts that dampen demand. In the EU as a whole, public spending fell by some seven percentage points between 1995 and 2002, with most of the change matched by a fall in public deficits (Table 1.2). There are circumstances in which the holy grail of an expansionary fiscal contraction can be achieved, especially if fiscal restraint permits a markedly looser monetary policy, but the consensus is that most Member States lost potential output during the 1990s as they struggled to meet the Maastricht criteria (see Giudice *et al.*, 2003 for an analysis of this debate).

Another major issue is the price level, with marked differences between countries at the start of Stage 3 of EMU. Portugal stands out as having had a much lower price level, but a simple way of calibrating this phenomenon is that countries where GDP measured in terms of purchasing power is higher than GDP measured at current exchange rates have lower price levels and *vice versa*. Moreover, in all the new Member States, the price level is well

Table 1.2 Public finance trends: Selected euro area Member States (% of GDP)

	Gross revenue		Gross expenditure		Interest payments		Expenditure less interest		Net lending		Net lending less interest	
	1995	**2003**	**1995**	**2003**	**1995**	**2003**	**1995**	**2003**	**1995**	**2003**	**1995**	**2003**
Belgium	48.5	51.4	52.8	51.1	9.3	5.6	43.5	45.5	–4.3	0.2	4.9	5.8
Germany	46.1	44.9	49.6	49.1	3.7	3.1	45.9	46.0	–3.5	–4.2	0.2	–1.1
France	49.7	50.5	55.2	54.7	3.8	3.2	51.4	51.5	–5.5	–4.2	–1.8	–0.9
Italy	45.8	45.9	53.4	48.5	11.5	5.3	41.9	43.2	–7.6	–2.6	3.9	2.7
Greece	40.9	44.6	51.0	46.3	12.7	6.0	38.3	40.3	–10.2	–1.7	2.6	4.3
Euro area 12	46.5	46.2	51.6	49.0	5.6	3.6	46.0	45.4	–5.1	–2.8	0.5	0.7

below EU-15 levels; according to a recent report by the OECD (2003), in 2001 it stood at an average of just 51% of the EU-15 level. One potentially disruptive factor is the so-called 'Balassa–Samuelson (BS) effect' which arises because productivity in the tradable sector of the economy rises more rapidly than in the rest of the economy, but relative wages do not adjust. If the effect is substantial, measured inflation will be higher, but the competitiveness of the tradables sector will be scarcely affected. In causing a real exchange rate appreciation, there may be problems. Alesina *et al.* (2001) suggest that the effect may have been quite pronounced for Ireland during the late 1990s, with above-average inflation not detracting from its competitiveness, but possibly perverse for Spain, the implication being that inflation in the trade sector was higher than in the non-traded sector. This problem is likely to be much less important in its impact on the existing Member States, as the combined GDP of the new Members is so small by comparison.

1.4 The challenges of policy co-ordination

Economic policy co-ordination in the EU has made great strides in recent years, yet still finds itself facing uncertainties and awkward choices (Begg, 2002b). Nevertheless, co-ordination is central to the proper functioning of EMU and cannot be seen as just a ritual exercise in which Member States produce reports, the Commission makes some trenchant criticisms, then policy proceeds pretty well unchanged. On the one hand, there is a need to consolidate the policy framework sufficiently to make EMU effective and to ensure that the broader economic and social ambitions of the Union are achieved. On the other hand, subsidiarity in economic policy-making has to be respected and there has been dismay about the conduct of some aspects of policy at the EU level, notably the imbroglio surrounding the application of the SGP in 2003.

Economic policy co-ordination is found in a number of Treaty provisions. These mechanisms have gradually been consolidated since the launch of the euro, yet it has to be stressed that both the EU level and the Member States are in a 'learning phase' with regard to economic modes of governance. The BEPGs provide recommendations for the broad thrust of economic policy. These guidelines comprise general policy aims for the EU as a whole (and not just the euro area), together with specific recommendations for individual Member States. They are both broad and comprehensive, covering macroeconomic policy (for which, read 'fiscal'), a range of labour market and other supply-side policies, and sustainable development. Overlapping with the BEPGs are specific co-ordination 'processes' that try to foster common approaches, for example to employment policy (the Luxembourg process), structural policies (the Cardiff process), pension reform and social inclusion policy. These processes are now streamlined with the Commission reporting on the BEPGs, employment guidelines, social inclusion and internal market strategy at the spring European Council and all guidelines now having a three year rather than an annual cycle. The 2005 re-launch of the Lisbon strategy is intended to achieve further streamlining by bringing the Commission's recommendations on the BEPGs and its proposal on the Employment Guidelines into a single document to be known as the Integrated Guidelines.

However, as noted above, this array of co-ordination machinery does not cover the core of the traditional notion of policy mix, namely how fiscal and monetary policy are combined. Instead, the emphasis is on what might be called *horizontal* co-ordination across individual policy areas, and the only real links between monetary policy and other economic policy domains are consultative, via fora such as the Eurogroup, the Economic and Financial Committee and the macroeconomic dialogue. That monetary policy is not part of the equation is simply explained. An independent central bank with the primary responsibility to assure price stability cannot plausibly engage in the sort of bargaining with other policy actors that would be implicit in co-ordination. If it did, it would open itself to the possibility that the ensuing bargain might mean trading-off higher inflation for other goals, such as faster growth or lower unemployment. The issue is not whether or not such an outcome is *desirable* (the contrast with the Fed's dual mandate is obvious), but whether it is *constitutionally allowed*, and our interpretation of the legal texts is that the room for manoeuvre is very limited.

The status quo is the 'horses for courses' approach that is favoured amongst other by representatives of the ECB (see Issing, 2002). Its essence is that if the authorities or economic agents responsible for a policy area fulfil their obligations, there will be clarity about obligations and no temptation to backslide or compromise. The trouble with this approach, however, is that if the aims of policy are not entirely compatible, the outcomes could be sub-optimal. For Issing, the answer lies in dialogue and careful explanation of policies. Thus, once wage bargainers know and understand that the ECB will be assiduous in assuring price stability, they will take steps to curb inflationary pay settlements. It is, however, less clear how labour market reforms can be informed in this way.

The main alternative is to construct some form of *gouvernement économique* as espoused, notably, by a number of prominent French economists such as Boyer (1999, 2002) and Pisani-Ferry (2002). The rationale for such a body is to act as a fiscal authority, capable of overcoming the fragmentation of both decision-making *and* economic policy that results from separate national decisions. But it could be argued that instead of being constituted largely as a fiscal policy counterpart to a powerful and integrated monetary policy, any new body should have a broader remit to orchestrate policy across a range of supply-side domains. The BEPGs provide a framework within which to develop such an approach – certainly by comparison with the SGP – but have had limited visibility in the policy process, perhaps pointing to shortcomings of 'soft law' forms of economic governance.

There are, clearly, problems of compliance and enforcement. It can also be argued that with so many different co-ordination channels, there is a considerable danger of confusion, not to mention diffusion of effort and purpose. We count no fewer than eight distinct economic co-ordination mechanisms: the Council (above all Ecofin) and the Eurogroup at a political level, the SGP and the Cologne process for macroeconomics, the Luxembourg and Cardiff processes, plus Lisbon for microeconomics (overlapping with internal market), and the BEPGs. There have already been high-profile instances of national governments openly disagreeing with, and ignoring, recommendations derived from soft-law processes: the 'reprimand' to Ireland for its pro-cyclical fiscal policies in 2001 is a case in point. The lack of coercive enforcement mechanisms for soft co-ordination – which relies on the non-coercive mechanisms of peer review, naming and shaming and so on – is compounded by the perceived blandness of many of the recommendations and the sense that excessive detail and overuse diminish their strategic impact.

Nevertheless, although the bulk of economic policy co-ordination is operated under 'soft law' procedures, it does not mean that it cannot be robust, even if it is not immediately obvious how sanctions can be imposed on delinquent Member States. Amtenbrink and de Haan (2003) raise an interesting question, namely whether a Member State that does not conform to the BEPG recommendations or other aspects of surveillance procedures might have formal action taken against it, but conclude that even if there is a theoretical possibility, the issue is politically decided rather than being amenable to a legal decision.[4] Moreover, they note that 'in any event, if the goal is to avoid the emergence of an excessive deficit, the prospect of the application of a lengthy judicial procedure may not be a very appealing one, as it will almost certainly come too late to be meaningful' (Amtenbrink and de Haan, 2003: 1083). The inference to draw is that, other than the political costs for a Member State of being named and shamed, surveillance has no teeth when it comes to preventing the emergence of an excessive deficit. Hence it is only when an excessive deficit actually arises that the Member State will face formal disciplinary procedures and even then the first stages are warnings. It could be argued that, especially for a variable as volatile as the fiscal deficit, the timetable for action is too slow to assure fiscal discipline.

1.4.1 Structural reform

There is a broad consensus that structural reforms in the EU not only continue to be desirable, but also hold the key to medium- to long-term improvements in the performance of the EU economy (HM Treasury, 2004). The more extreme proponents of this view would, indeed, argue that structural reform is the *only* answer to the EU's current economic problems, but we hold the view that however strong the case for such reforms, they do not absolve the demand side of the economy from scrutiny. At the same time, it is evident that the pace of structural reforms has been lethargic and there are growing concerns that the ambitious Lisbon agenda is not only overly-optimistic, but also suffers from inappropriate governance (Kok, 2004; see also Begg, 2005). Inertia and political compromises that have weakened the pace of reform have been evident in countries such as Germany, and there can be a tendency at EU level for lowest common denominator solutions to be reached, resulting in only a slow transformation in areas such as network industries (Pelkmans, 2001).

Structural reform is an expression that embraces a wide range of policies, although there is a fair degree of consensus about the directions structural reform need to take, reflected in the Lisbon agenda and in the current priorities for consolidating the single market. At EU level, the opening up of markets, principally through continuing efforts to complete and enforce the single market, is the principal means by which supply-side improvements are advanced. But it also has to be stressed that the removal of obstacles to economic efficiency and the search for productivity gains is very much a concern of national policies. A key point to note about structural reforms is that they can hurt and may, collectively, have adverse short-term effects on output and employment.

In relation to co-ordination, structural reform has to be looked at from two perspectives. First, with increasing economic integration, if some parts of the Union are very divergent in the performance of their 'real' economies there will be repercussions for others. Divergence might have knock-on effects for the conduct of macroeconomic policy by increasing the range of conditions with which 'one-size-fits-all' policies have to contend. Divergence may also lead to inappropriate responses by vulnerable governments, if they are tempted to reduce well-designed social protection or regulation in a search for competitiveness that leads to a 'race-to-the-bottom'. In the EU context, a second, much more positive, rationale for co-ordination processes is to stimulate policy learning and enhancement. The latter objective lends itself to the soft 'open method of co-ordination' (OMC) approaches that have evolved in recent years. A further question is whether, as the EU itself enlarges, the problems of reaching consensus will be magnified, resulting in a slowing of structural reforms. One way out of this was, as in Sweden, to adjust first then consider joining the single currency, but the signals from many of the new members suggest that they want to be 'in' at the earliest opportunity, though there are signs that some, such as Hungary, are having second thoughts.

1.5 Structure of the volume

The remainder of the book is in three parts. The first describes the legal and constitutional framework and examines the conceptual model underpinning the macroeconomics of EMU. Evidence on key policy areas and how they have evolved in a selection of countries is presented in Part 2. Conclusions are then drawn in Part 3.

Chapter 2 sets the scene for macroeconomic policy in EMU. It identifies the key challenges and how they are being met thus far within the (pervasive) context of the Lisbon Agenda with its call for a quantum leap forward in EU economic performance. The new regime is under pressure with growth slowed and unemployment rising, leading to pressure on the Stability and Growth Pact which so far, correctly, has had minor reforms (see Chapter 4). The macroeconomic policy challenge is explored, noting the diversity as between states necessitating flexibility in the EMU system in general and in policy co-ordination in particular. The degree of difference between states is explored, including whether states are subject to similar shocks and how they respond to them (given states do not have the same social preferences this prompts different responses to the same problems). This phenomenon of asymmetry has been well documented but this chapter contends that asymmetry is not just about inter-country differences but extends to the way the process of growth and economic cycles generate asymmetric problems for macroeconomic policy.

In determining the process of adjustment under EMU, it is clear that monetary policy itself is asymmetric responding to serious threats of inflation more than proportionately and threats of deflation even more strongly. It can counter asymmetry in behaviour and also the asymmetries found in the (decentralised) fiscal policy. The extent to which fiscal policy is asymmetric helps explain the tensions surrounding the SGP. Downturns, such as those currently occurring in the euro zone, worsen employment more than an upturn improves it – a phenomenon compounded by state behaviour in the first years of EMU as states were over-optimistic in the up phase thus creating the controversial deficits seen now. This behaviour has created pressures for the SGP and co-ordination more generally – a theme explored more fully in Chapters 3 and 4. Finally, the extend to which these challenges will exist for the accession states – in particular the risk of higher inflation as a result of catching up – should they look for early entry to EMU are set out.

In Chapter 3 the institutional framework of EMU is examined noting that interdependence is a key characteristic of EMU in relation to both the uniform and highly centralised monetary policy and the de-centralised fiscal policy. This interdependence is manifest even for the ECB with its high levels of independence. The Bank has seen fit to develop higher accountability standards than formally set down in the Treaty, realising the importance of accountability for legitimation of its position and its policies. Interdependence is also important in relation to fiscal policy which is co-ordinated between states through a complex system of Council committees and the Stability and Growth Pact within the context of the Lisbon agenda.

The main compliance mechanism is peer pressure between states based on the shared commitment to the success of EMU. Both fiscal and monetary policies are tightly interrelated – monetary policy cannot be developed in isolation from fiscal policy – a theme developed more fully in Chapter 4. What remains uncertain is what the scope of discretion should be for the states when co-ordinating fiscal policy and in turn, what role the Commission has in that process.

In Chapter 4, the issue of co-ordination of fiscal policy is explored more fully, including an examination of how the issue was addressed in the influential Werner (1970) and Delors (1989) reports. Co ordination is clearly a defining feature of EMU, a common fiscal policy being seen as unrealistic and even undesirable. As suggested in Chapter 3, the co-ordination system is extensive, complex and opaque. All three of these features are in part due to the nature of the legal norms used to frame it. The balance of soft (non-binding) law and hard law (characterised in the fiscal policy domain by the ultimate sanction of a fine) is central to how the system works and critical to the question of reform. Soft law is presented as having merits in and of itself and not necessarily the 'poor relation' of hard law or its precursor. The difficulty is that it is hard to ensure compliance with soft law unless there is a willingness to have regard to the effect of national fiscal policy decisions on the wider euro zone.

Nonetheless, difficulty is not in itself sufficient reason to move to an even less appropriate regime of hard sanctions which are not credible. The Stability and Growth Pact as the centrepiece of fiscal coordination is located within the wider context of the Lisbon Agenda and the parallel coordination of supply-side policies, notably the European Employment Strategy (EES), an issue more fully developed in Chapter 5. The challenges and criticisms of the Pact are addressed as well as the existing piecemeal reforms and proposals for more sweeping reforms including a softer Pact for those states with sustainable debt, providing a much needed carrot to balance the largely symbolic threat of a fine and a suggestion that a form of the 'golden rule' be adopted. The paradoxes of the system remain: that naming and shaming (soft law) is more effective than the 'nuclear option' of a fine; soft law is rendered ineffective without adequate incentives; some of the most difficult structural problems remain outside the scope of co-ordination because states refuse to address them and finally, how a coherent policy mix is to be achieved has yet to be clearly articulated.

Supply-side policies are important to the adjustment process in EMU because they create the conditions that make demand or supply shocks less likely and they have a vital contribution to make to overall macroeconomic policy co-ordination. Chapter 5 discusses structural policy co-ordination within EMU and as part of the Lisbon Agenda. The reasons for co-ordination of employment and labour market policies are explored with primary reference to the Union of 15 (though Chapter 12 examines the impact of EMU on the ten accession states). The main challenge is the level of diversity between the states in policy and in approach. Given this diversity, the OMC is an ideal governance mechanism to encourage policy learning within the context of the targets set by Lisbon. Like fiscal policy, soft law predominates but there are no hard sanctions for failure to meet the guidelines. The emphasis is exclusively on peer pressure.

Effectiveness is hindered by the lack of clearly demarcated responsibility – ownership of the goals is collective but collective responsibility for failure to meet them is not an effective sanction and is a very weak form of accountability. It is difficult to ascribe any job creation to the EES itself after seven years but the procedures of the EES have had some impact on policy formation. The operation of the EES has encouraged the adoption of best (or, at least, better) practice, improving the quality of employment policy in particular. But, just as there has been a failure to articulate how a coherent policy-mix is to be achieved as between fiscal and monetary policy, so too it is unclear how the EES fits with overall policy co-ordination. The 2003 streamlining reforms of the BEPGs may help integrate the EES into the wider policy framework and the 2005 re-launch of the Lisbon strategy promises to go further. There remain the problems at the EU and state level of different ministries co-ordinating their activities. Nonetheless, the EES despite the problems identified is important, as it keeps employment firmly on the agenda and offers one route to greater labour market flexibility.

Part II concentrates on empirical analysis of how countries adjusted to EMU, with five of the chapters focusing on single Member States. To give a more general perspective, we first present an overview of empirical developments in Stage 2 and Stage 3 in Chapter 6. In the mid-1990s, a widely held view was that Germany, the Benelux countries, Austria and France, with Ireland probably also a viable contender, were the Member States most likely to be in the first wave to establish the euro area. Evidence from Bayoumi and Eichengreen (1997) that France and Germany were not, in fact, ideally suited to form a currency area using optimum currency area criteria might have given some reason for caution, but the convergence criteria gave little reason for doubt. In the event, the four geographically peripheral countries were also able to adjust (or be deemed to have adjusted) sufficiently for the euro to be launched with eleven Member States, although the chapter shows that a degree of fudging proved to be necessary.

More surprisingly, as the chapter shows, there have been very diverse experiences in Stage 3. Rather than being the engine of the euro area, Germany has struggled, and in the early years of full EMU the Member States that have had the best economic performances are not those that many would have expected. The chapter presents brief assessments of the contrasting fortunes of three of the largest Member States, France, Italy and Spain, concluding that the challenges of Stage 3 adjustment may well have been under-estimated. The outcomes reveal that acclimatisation to the euro has proved more tricky for some Member States while also offering opportunities to others.

The next two chapters assess the two economies that, so far, appear to have prospered least and most under EMU, Germany and Ireland. That Germany has entered the euro facing a range of economic problems is well known. It has had disappointing growth and has been slow to advance structural reforms. It has also found it difficult to curb its fiscal deficit in line with its commitments under the SGP. Chapter 7 looks in detail at the German economy, especially the problems that have arisen in the labour market. As the largest euro area economy, what happens in Germany clearly has a major impact on other countries in macroeconomic terms.

Chapter 8 presents an analysis of the Irish economy, one which is well accustomed to being part of a monetary union, having been joined to sterling prior to linking to the EMS in 1979. Ireland's phenomenal economic growth in recent years has, plainly, marked it out as a success story. Although Ireland's economy remains strongly linked to that of the UK, potentially exposing it to risks of asymmetric shocks relative to its euro area peers, as a small open economy, it already had to develop appropriate adjustment mechanisms.

Chapters 9 and 10 examine Finland and Sweden, neighbouring countries that opted for starkly contrasting approaches to EMU. Both countries experienced severe economic downturns in the early 1990s, but both have also been among the better performers in the EU in recent years. Finland was quick to embrace Stage 3 and serves as an interesting exemplar of how adjustments needed to enter Stage 3 can be made compatible with a successful economy. As one of the more rapidly growing economies during the early years of Stage 3, Finland could have been discomfited by a euro area that was too loose, but it seems to have avoided problems by other forms of adjustment.

Sweden, by contrast has opted for the slow route to EMU. It meets the budgetary and price stability criteria for membership of the euro area and, unlike the UK and Denmark, does not formally have an opt out, although its non-membership of the ERM provides an escape clause. Essentially, Swedish reluctance to enter Stage 3 owes as much to political factors as to any economic assessment, although as with the UK, the fact that Sweden has appeared to prosper outside the euro area has been telling. If or when Sweden does join, it is not expected to face much of an adjustment problem.

The UK, which is analysed in Chapter 11, has long been among the most euro-cautious members of the EU and has made clear its ambivalence about EMU. In contrast to other countries, the UK has elaborated its own criteria – the five economic tests – for whether or not to end its opt-out and has conducted a very extensive assessment of those tests, coming up with a negative conclusion in 2003. In common with Sweden, the UK would meet the nominal convergence criteria except for exchange rate stability. It has, however, enjoyed a better economic performance than the euro area since the start of Stage 3, and has also developed what many regard as a better macroeconomic policy framework.

For the new members that joined the EU in 2004, how quickly to seek entry to Stage 3 will be a big decision with substantial effects on economic development. A balance has to be struck between preserving flexibility to cope with the challenges of transition and adjustment to the EU internal market, on the one hand, and gaining the macroeconomic stability advantages of full participation in EMU, on the other. The new members are, however, very diverse. Six of them are very small economies that will probably gain from rapid entry and some of them may, indeed, choose to do so at the first opportunity. Reservations have, however, surfaced elsewhere. Chapter 12 discusses the outlook for the new members and focuses on Estonia, which has maintained a currency board since 1992 and has had a stable exchange rate vis-à-vis the euro since day one of Stage 3. The conclusion of the chapter is that Estonia should prosper within Stage 3 and has become sufficiently open to have suitable adjustment mechanisms.

The last part of the book draws together the material in the book and discusses policy issues. It highlights the shortcomings that have become evident in the policy framework, notably with the problems in the SGP, but also in other policy co-ordination processes. A key lesson that emerges from the volume is that not only are there diverse approaches to adjustment under EMU, but also that the experiences of the different Member States show that there is no single best practice. Rather, and this has implication for the new members, it is important to be aware of the choices and how they affect policy strategy.

Part I

Adjustment at the EU Level

2
Macroeconomic Policy in EMU

Our aim in this chapter is to set out the principal challenges facing macroeconomic policy in Stage 3 of EMU and to consider progress in meeting them thus far. The context for this evaluation springs mainly from the 'Lisbon Strategy' that was propounded at the Lisbon special European Council in March 2000 and re-launched at the 2005 spring European Council, which requires a quantum leap forward in the economic performance of the EU. Much of that improvement is expected to come from the closer integration of markets and removal of barriers, which should of itself intensify competition and spur firms to greater innovation, efficiency, effective investment and hence growth. Some of it will stem from co-ordination of policies, particularly in the fields of structural reform and employment through the BEPGs (see Hodson and Maher, 2001). Much of the remainder is expected to arise from Stage 3 of EMU itself, both with the single monetary policy and the enhanced co-ordination of fiscal policy implied by the SGP.

We do not attempt to evaluate the plausibility of the Lisbon Strategy *per se*. There are historical examples of growth being 1% higher over a decade. The Strategy suggests where the extra growth might come from. At the time, the success of the US economy during the 1990s would have suggested that 'new economy' ideas could well have something to them. The key issue in the present context is the coherence of the strategy. If the growth does not emerge then the fiscal requirements of the strategy will come under unsustainable strain. If the strategy does not deliver a sufficient increase in participation in the employment market (or reallocation of working patterns), the burden of the non-employed on the earning capacity of the employed will require considerable changes in behaviour and relative living standards. At the launch of the strategy, the EU had around 10% of the workforce unemployed on current participation rates, but the ageing of the population will start to increase the ratio of the non-employed to the employed strikingly by the end of the period if working patterns do not change.

Thus far the strategy has not produced an obvious pay-off, in the sense that growth in the first five years has been 1% lower than the historical average instead of 1% higher. Unemployment has been persistent. Forecasts for 2006/2007 suggest a return to average growth, but this is still below the Lisbon presumption of 3%. If the aim is still to be fulfilled, not only has all of the gain got to come in the later years of the decade but it has to offset the performance in the first half. This is unlikely, though not wholly impossible, but in any case it is unreasonable to be too literal in dating the improvement in performance. Above all, just looking at actual outcomes tell us nothing about whether the performance is better than it would have been had Stage 3 of EMU not been implemented at the beginning of 1999.

The net result is that we see the system under pressure. Problems always look worse in the downside of the economic cycle, as has been demonstrated in the tortuous processes of reforming the SGP and the weaknesses in the Lisbon strategy exposed by the Kok report (2004). Fiscal requirements are under strain from two directions. The process of restructuring is itself costly and deficits are at their worst. There is therefore pressure for change. The Pact was undoubtedly simplistic and had many flaws (Begg *et al.*, 2004), though the reforms agreed in 2005 are expected to improve matters, but it was also undermined by the failure of some Member States to comply with the letter and spirit of its requirements. It is well-known advice that systems should not be eased when they are under immediate pressure, but in good times, when the motivation is less coloured and the debate can be less passionate. It is equally clear, however, that difficulty makes people more receptive to change. So the ideal is rarely achieved.

The 2003 assessment in the UK of the 'Five Tests' proposed by the Chancellor of the Exchequer for providing an economic case for membership of Stage 3 of EMU provides a lot of useful background for the present discussion (HM Treasury, 2003d). It seeks to isolate the issues relating to membership of EMU, which are applicable to any Member State. In doing so it provides two helpful pointers. By incorporating such a wide range of studies and contributions by academics it indicates appropriate means of analysis. At the same time it shows how dependent any assessments are on what may happen in the future – something that is unverifiable in principle. Thus at the outset we have to admit that while we can paint a picture, the detail is bound to remain fuzzy.

The country studies, which come later in the book, provide a range of viewpoints and evidence for how the problems bite depending upon economic structure – particularly size, institutions and inter-relationships within the EU – economic policy preferences and behaviour, in the sense of how the economy responds to shocks and policy instruments. We begin, however, by exploring the nature of the challenge to macroeconomic policy over the early years of Stage 3 of EMU before going on to explore why the structure of economic behaviour and policy make response difficult, then we appraise the difficulties with the SGP and wider policy co-ordination in the light of that.

2.1 The EU macroeconomic policy challenge

Like other countries or regions the EU is keen to increase the income and wealth of its inhabitants as fast as possible subject to three constraints:

1. It wants to have a high participation rate and low unemployment
2. It values the fairness of the distribution of benefits (cohesion)
3. It wants to avoid too much fluctuation in the real economy along the way.

Macroeconomic policy is set in the light of these objectives.

There are also some presuppositions about the nature of the economic environment that will be best suited for achieving these objectives. Three are particularly relevant to our concerns here:

1. The most efficient system is the proper operation of open and competitive markets unimpeded by government intervention in the form of subsidies to particular industries or interests
2. Price stability
3. Prudent fiscal policy.

This is not an exhaustive list by any means and issues such as consumer protection or sustainable development, to mention just two, could be added to it.

The requirements face three difficulties, which we focus on. The first is that there is a tension between the rapid change that is necessary for maximising income and wealth and the costs that change imposes on society. For example, in the process of shifting production from declining to growing firms or industries, people will lose their jobs and the relative prosperity of some regions will fall. The protection of jobs and support for declining regions can then blunt the incentives for change. Choices and trade-offs have to be made.

The second difficulty is that there are fundamental differences across the Member States in three main regards:

1. Their economic structures in terms of resources, industries and institutions
2. Their policy preferences and cultures
3. How economic agents and economies respond to any given economic measures.

Thus not only may states or regions want to act differently at any given time, but they would be sensible to do so given that they are hit by different shocks, respond differently and have a different balance of objectives.

The third 'difficulty' is that despite the need for flexible and different responses in different states, the EU has chosen to try to achieve these objectives through a number of common policies that limit variation across the Member States. This is not a difficulty stemming from the fact that some of the common policies have been implemented for political rather than economic motives but because the actions of one country have consequences for the others. Such agreements to co-operate are entered into because they tend to increase the economic welfare of the system as a whole not only through avoiding adverse spillovers but also from the lower costs of larger scale and stability.

Although this chapter focuses on the pressures that just one such agreement, namely Stage 3 of EMU, poses on macroeconomic policy, the nature of the pressures depend on all the other issues we have listed. Some of those constraints are themselves alterable but rarely costlessly.

Stage 3 imposes two simple but non-trivial constraints: one on monetary policy and the other on fiscal policy. In the case of monetary policy, it involves adopting the single currency and foregoing the opportunity to use monetary policy as one of the means of adjusting to the three fundamental differences we listed: structures, policies and responses. Adopting such a constraint implies that either it has little consequence or that the benefits, which may be far removed from this immediate concern, are clearly greater. As in any democratic system, EU integration involves trade-offs and participating in Stage 3 could be compensated by issues relating to security, agriculture and so on. Hence in the immediate environment, it may be necessary to consider what offsetting changes need to take place to limit the adverse consequences of foregoing one's own monetary policy.

In the case of monetary policy, there is little conflict about the objective or the means of achieving it. The debate is very much second order, about the technical detail of policy. Thus price stability is accepted as the goal and defined as inflation approaching 2% a year over the medium term with only limited fluctuations round that medium-term value.

In the case of fiscal policy the position is more complicated. For a start, fiscal policy is run separately by the Member States under constraints rather than as a single policy by a single European institution (we do not debate here whether greater European level involvement or indeed a more substantial European level budget would assist with resolving some of the inherent tensions). The framework for reducing adverse spillovers from the actions of one country to another therefore has to be somewhat more complicated. The normal requirement for prudent policy applies. The longer-term outlook for public expenditure has to be consistent with the likely stream of revenues, given the starting debt position. Financial markets are the judge of this consistency or prudence in the interest costs/risk premium they impose on the less plausible plans. However, the sheer size of the debt affects the interest rate as higher ratios increase the risk of default for any given expenditure and tax plan.

The plausibility of any plan also depends upon the enforcement or precommitment arrangements that can be entered into. Here the EU has a great advantage over any individual country as it can enter into an agreement where countries are penalised by their partners for adopting inadequately prudent plans (and has done so). Fiscal Responsibility Acts and fiscal policy principles, as in the UK or New Zealand for example, may be very meritorious in their own right, but if the country itself is the guarantor of their being adhered to in future, their value is more limited. It might be possible to embed such an act into the constitution or require a super-majority in parliament to overturn it, but the suspicion that it will be over-ridden in the first bout of serious difficulty will be very difficult to dispel.

The EU on the other hand can impose some very credible penalties, up to expulsion, if the benefits of membership are thought to be large. The SGP goes some distance down this road through the excessive deficit procedure. However, softening any agreement when it bites weakens the credibility of any future agreement, even (as took place in the 2005 reform of the Pact) one that redresses some of the incongruities of the SGP. With the benefit of hindsight it would have been possible to design the SGP rather better to achieve its purpose. The simplicity and transparency of the deficit rule which was a cornerstone to its credibility proves a problem when a Member State can show that it prohibits prudent policies that would help achieve the balance of macroeconomic objectives.

In the succeeding pages we tackle the main issues in turn. We begin by asking, in Section 2.2, how different the euro area countries really are in the dimensions that matter. We consider not just whether business cycles are similar, as a measure of convergence, but also whether the economies are subject to different shocks and whether they respond in the same way to any given shock. The more different the countries are in these respects, from the general pattern of the euro area, the more they need to find means of adjustment that keep the costs low, as euro area level policy will not address their detailed needs. These concerns can be automatic – often considered in terms of the degree of flexibility of the economy – or through discretionary policy. However, these behavioural differences do not describe the full extent of the problem. The Member States do not have identical social preferences. They may, therefore, want to see different outcomes in the face of the same external circumstances. Again deviation from the average will place more pressure on a Member State. We therefore explore the extent of this source of difference as well, as it helps explain different choices under what otherwise seem common problems.

Many of these sources of difference, particularly in susceptibility to shocks, have been labelled 'asymmetry' in the literature. One of our major tenets in this chapter is that 'asymmetry' is indeed a major cause of the adjustment problems that countries face (both inside and outside Stage 3 of EMU). However, we treat the concept of asymmetry rather more comprehensively than just as intercountry differences. In particular, we consider the degree to which the process of growth and economic cycles generates asymmetric problems for macroeconomic policy. This is the subject of Section 2.3. Monetary policy forms an integral part of the model we use to explore asymmetry. It turns out that monetary policy is itself asymmetric, responding to serious threats of inflation more than proportionately and threats of deflation even more strongly. Monetary policy thus seems to operate in three distinct regimes: threatened deflation, normal times and strong inflationary pressure. This not only helps counter the asymmetry in behaviour but the asymmetries in fiscal policy to which we next turn.

In Section 2.4 we go further and consider the degree to which asymmetry in fiscal policy itself hinders or helps the process of adjustment under EMU. This asymmetry helps explain the problems of the SGP. Not only do downturns worsen unemployment more than a similar size upturn improves it, thereby creating a fiscal tension, but governments in the EU have tended to be over-optimistic about long-term sustainable settings of policy in the up phase of policy, thereby creating excess deficits in downturns. In this section we also touch on the problems of co-ordination of policy.

Enlargement of the EU added to the difficulties as the new members face extra macroeconomic pressures from the process of catch-up or real convergence. We consider this in Section 2.5. If a new member opts for (and obtains) early entry to EMU, it is likely to face considerable pressure on its real exchange rate, as higher inflation is a likely outcome of the catching-up process. Section 2.6 concludes.

2.2 Differences among the EU countries

One of the main difficulties in assessing the degree to which countries are different is that discussions of the past are not necessarily very good indicators of likely behaviour. Typically, discussions about what would constitute optimal currency areas are conducted on the basis of the current regime, whether this involves modelling the consequences of entry to EMU as in Westaway (2003) or in exploring the divergences in the United States (Wynne and Koo, 1997). Typically there is no discussion of how the structure of behaviour might change on entry or indeed on exit. One interesting exception is the (Coleman, 2001) comparison of Queensland and New Zealand as actual and potential members of monetary union. Normally a substantial change in behaviour is not only expected but desired. This is clearly a feature of Finnish membership of EMU described in Chapter 10 and in the Irish decision to leave monetary union with the UK and move into the ERM. The Irish wanted to be viewed as a desirable part of the EU in which to invest and to remove some of the costs of the fluctuations of sterling with respect to the other major EU currencies (Chapter 8).

However, as the rolling estimates in Artis (2003) illustrate, not only does the similarity between economies both in terms of behaviour and in terms of shocks vary very considerably from one time period to another but the most recent five years, which cover the period of actual and virtual EMU, are rather unusual in that the US is more correlated with the larger EU economies than some of the EU countries are with each other. Five years is about as short a period as one could reasonably look at, both for statistical reasons and for coherence of the regime. Even so one could reasonably argue that 1997 onwards is a transition rather than a stable period, so we do not as yet have clear evidence of how EMU will operate over the longer term.

A brief look at Artis's estimates and Figure 2.1 (a–c) shows that there are still considerable variations across the EU and euro area economies with respect to the business cycle, inflation, structure of fiscal policy and debt. Indeed, as far as inflation is concerned, the euro area regime permits more variation than its predecessor. In the convergence process, countries were individually trying to keep inflation close to best performance in the area. Since the onset of the single monetary policy it is only market forces and non-monetary policy that works towards such a convergence. Indeed with differences in price levels at the beginning of 1999 one could expect different inflation rates simply as a result of price convergence.

We can differentiate the countries in three generalised ways: their differences in economic development patterns, their inflation performance and their fiscal position.

- Ireland, Greece and to a lesser extent Spain seem to have come through the latest downturn rather well. However, they and Portugal seem to have been somewhat inflation prone.
- Germany, the Netherlands, Luxembourg and Portugal seemed to have slowed down rather more than the rest. Only in the German case does this seem to be accompanied by very slow growth in prices.
- Denmark, Finland, Luxembourg, Ireland, the UK and to a lesser extent Sweden and Spain seem to be well on top of their fiscal position, although the size of the UK's recent deficits has given rise to questions.
- Belgium, Italy and Greece have substantially larger debt ratios than the target and in the latter two cases are finding serious problems in reducing them.
- France and Germany have clear problems with excessive deficits, as, following the recomputation of its national accounts data in 2004, does Greece.
- Austria has been a middle of the road country in all fiscal features.

Using growth rates rather than output gaps distorts the picture somewhat as it does not consider the sustainability of different growth rates across the countries. As Artis (2003) *inter alia* discusses, the choice of filter for estimating the gap can have important consequences for the outcome. Figure 2.2 uses the OECD estimates, which are based largely on the production function method of estimating potential GDP rather than on the Hodrick-Prescott or Baxter-King (band-pass) filters. With the exception of Greece, these

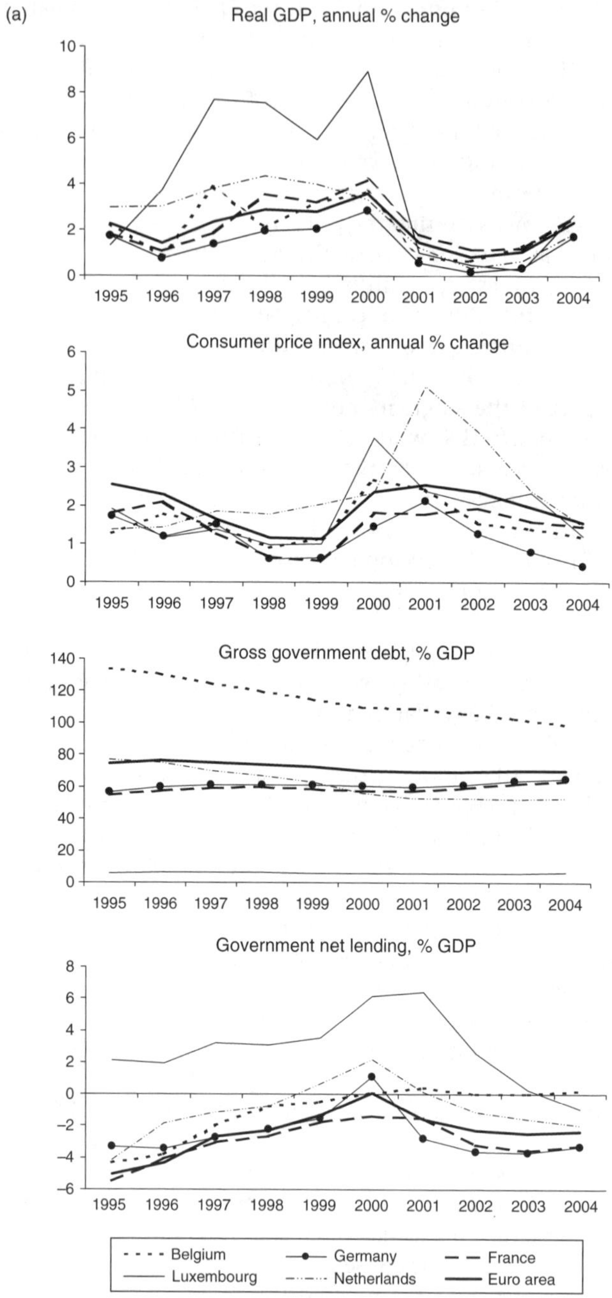

Figure 2.1 EU economic indicators 1995–2004. *Source*: OECD Economic Outlook (2004)

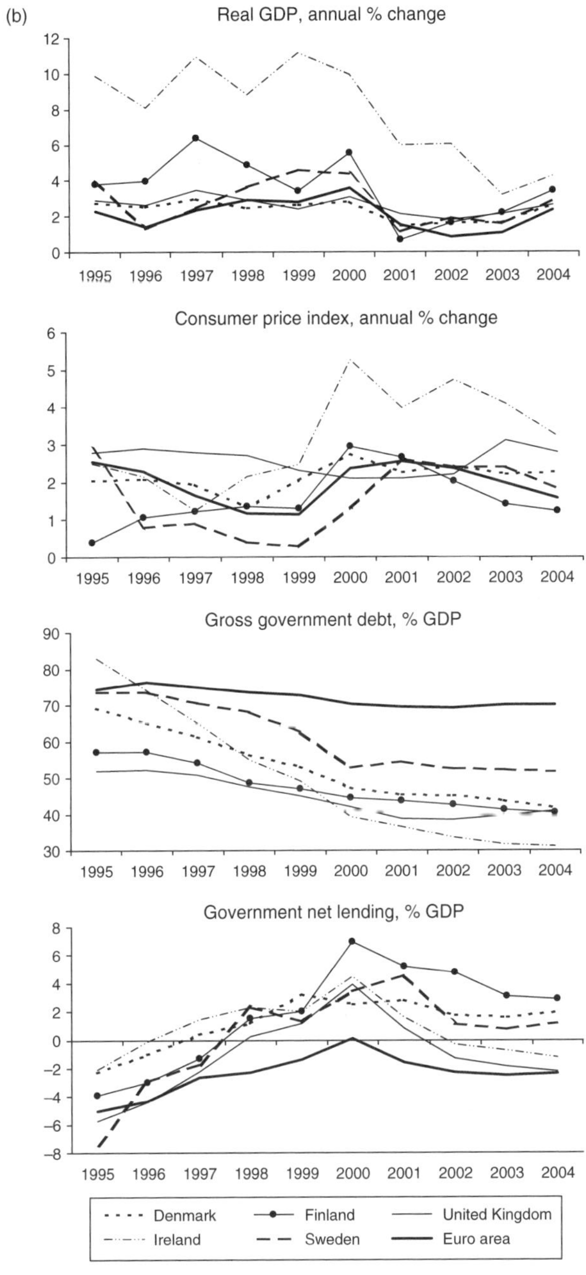

Figure 2.1 (Continued)

(c)

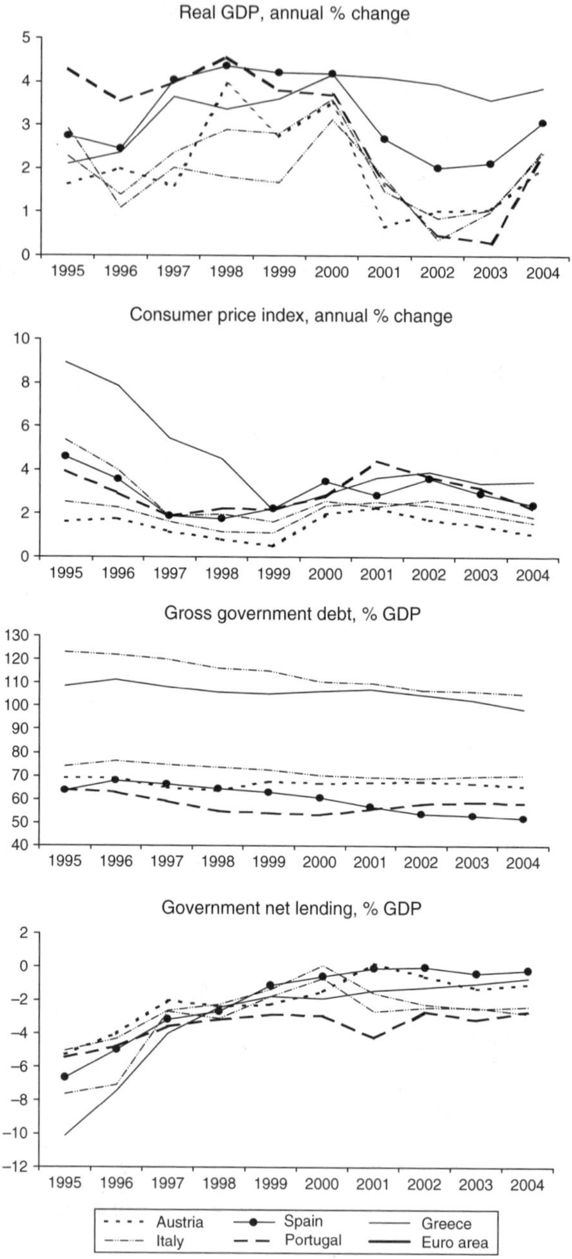

Figure 2.1 (Continued)

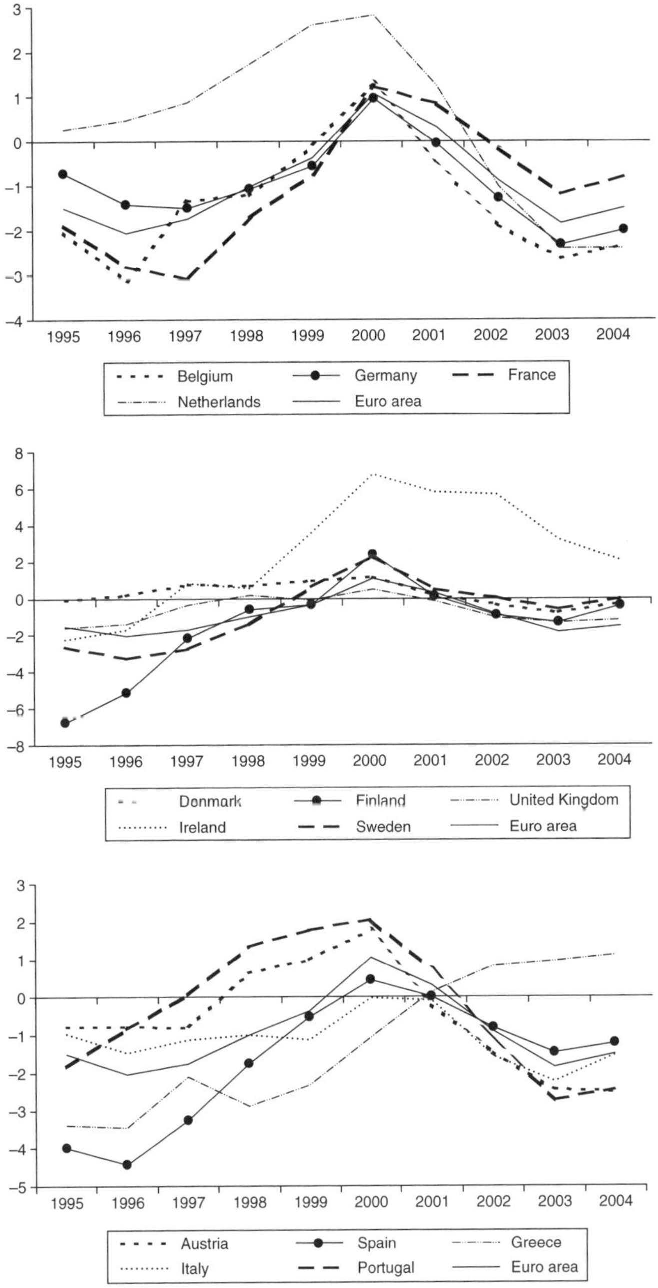

Figure 2.2 Output gaps in per cent. *Source*: OECD Economic Outlook (2004)

measures of output gaps suggest a very considerable convergence of all the EU countries since 2000, including the countries that are not members of Stage 3. The somewhat divergent experience of the Netherlands is noticeable, reflected perhaps in its somewhat different approach to employment and social policy (Muffels and Fouarge, 2001).

However, these characteristics tell us a combination of stories about differences in performance and constraints. Equally important is their apparent responsiveness to shocks, which can only be judged from models of the respective economies. These in turn cannot be estimated satisfactorily on such short runs of data and will be even further from giving a picture of the extent of their likely convergence in the future. We can obtain evidence from the various country models that have been published such as the National Institute's NiGEM and the European Commission's Quest about the differences in properties of the various country models. We can also look at the ESCB's extensive work on the monetary transmission mechanism in the Member States (Angeloni *et al.*, 2002). Here our research has been limited to a simple four-equation model that shows differences across countries in their responsiveness both in terms of size and speed in respect of growth, inflation, unemployment and fiscal policy. However, our focus has been not just on differences across countries but also differences across the economic cycle. Hence if economies are out of phase with each other they will be even more different in their behaviour than if they are in the same general circumstances. We show that ignoring this source of difference considerably underestimates the problem of matching a single monetary policy to the divergent needs and behaviour of the Member States.

We identified three main dimensions in which the Member States of the EU can differ which makes the operation of common macroeconomic policies difficult:

1. policy preferences
2. susceptibility to shocks
3. responsiveness to shocks and policy instruments.

These are not independent, as the economic institutions of a country reflect its preferences and the shocks it has been exposed to. Economic institutions are themselves both a cause of, and a response to, the responsiveness of the economy to external and policy shocks.

However, even if there were to be very considerable similarity between the Member States in the above regards, it would also need to be the case that the position of each Member State in its economic cycle would need to be similar for a common policy to be appropriate. Even given this, the nonlinearities in the economic system mean that the appropriate common policy for the area as a whole needs to take into account the weighted needs of each component and not merely compute the requirements from aggregated variables.

Policy preferences can differ at various levels. Although all the Member States may be interested in maximising the rate of growth in real incomes and wealth, they will impose various provisos as to the characteristics of the process. These may relate to environmental damage, equity of outcome, the importance of participation in the labour market, the extent of various social rights and measures of the quality of life. Building on Esping-Andersen (1999) among others, Muffels and Fouarge (2002) suggest that it is possible to define four main groupings of the EU countries in terms of their employment and related social preferences. They can be variously labelled: 'Nordic', 'Continental', 'Anglo-Saxon' and 'Southern' or 'Social-democrat', 'Corporatist', 'Liberal' and 'Southern'. These groups are not immutable but show clear differences – Madsen *et al.* (2002) in the next chapter of the same book identify 'active', 'intermediate' and 'passive'.

The new members face common problems and will undoubtedly add to the diversity of the EU. It is, of course, anticipated that they will grow faster (and probably inflate faster through the Balassa–Samuelson effect and related concomitants of the process of real convergence). They may also be subject to greater fluctuations. Initially, of course, they will not be in EMU but as they do join they will face greater adjustment pressures, if they are more different.

Treating the new members as a single group is misleading. Some, who are already pegging their exchange rate closely to the euro (completely in the case of currency boards) are already experiencing many of the facets of EMU. Most of the new members are small countries but some are medium size – Czech Republic, Hungary – while Poland, at least in terms of population, is a large country like Spain. Political differences are also wide, ranging from highly flexible, less regulated regimes in countries such as Estonia to much more controlled environments, such as the Czech Republic.

Greater variety adds to the challenge for euro area policy but the challenge is already considerable because the variety among countries runs deeper than we have thus far described. Responses vary over the cycle, as does policy. We therefore move on to consider this 'asymmetry' in more detail.

2.3 Asymmetry

As in Mayes and Virén (2003) we identify six sources of asymmetry in the euro area (and more widely in the EU and OECD) that make the adoption of the single monetary policy more complex. For some reason people seemed to have coined the use of the word 'asymmetric' in the context of macroeconomic adjustment in the EU to mean simply that countries are different. We use it in the more traditional sense that behaviour in any country varies according to the circumstances, particularly that it varies across the business cycle. The upside and downside phases of the cycle are typically different with respect to their depth, length and 'steepness' (downturns tend to be sharper than upturns but not to last for so long nor be so deep as the upturn is high (Diebold and Rudebusch, 1999)). This asymmetry is a result of, and reflects, both asymmetry in the behaviour of households and governments and in the policy response of the authorities. The six aspects we note are in:

1. Discretionary fiscal policy (the authorities are more eager to ease the fiscal stance when they are not under pressure than they are to tighten it when pressure increases).
2. The share of the public sector in economic activity (at low public sector shares, increasing the share tends to go with faster rates of economic growth; beyond a certain point the relationship is reversed).
3. Monetary policy (the authorities react much more strongly to large threats to price stability than to small ones, particularly to the threat of deflation).
4. The influence of unemployment on inflation (pressure from low unemployment on inflation is much greater than that from high unemployment in reducing inflation – this applies both to the tightest labour markets and to the euro area average).
5. The relation between unemployment and output (unemployment rises more for any given fall in output than it recovers for an output increase of the same size).
6. The influence of the real interest rate and real exchange rate on economic growth (while the relative importance of the two varies strikingly across countries – the real exchange rate being much more important for small countries – asset prices, particularly house prices, modify the effect).

Between them these six factors provide considerable difficulty for the running of euro area-wide macroeconomic policies in addition to the problems that stem from the fact that the countries themselves respond differently.

2.3.1 Discretionary fiscal policy

There is a clear discrepancy in the way that fiscal policy appears to behave in the EU countries in periods of better than average economic performance, compared with when performance is below average – see Table 2.1.[1] Deficits appear to expand further in downturns than they shrink (or become surpluses) in upturns. The source of this asymmetry appears to lie not in the automatic stabilisers, which appear to operate in a fairly symmetric manner, but in 'structural' changes both to expenditures and to revenues, particularly to the latter. Discretionary policy appears to be much more counter-cyclical in downturns than upturns, presumably reflecting a willingness to cut taxes when the economy and revenues pick up and a somewhat laxer approach to restraining expenditure.[2]

Table 2.1 Asymmetries in fiscal policy

	Phase of the cycle					
	Down	**Up**	**Down**	**Up**	**Down**	**Up**
Austria	2.115	0.140	1.166	0.279	0.864	–0.032
	(1.04)	(1.21)	(0.60)	(3.10)	(0.40)	(0.33)
Belgium	1.115	0.212	0.816	0.090	–0.238	–0.105
	(2.34)	(1.78)	(1.79)	(0.98)	(0.47)	(1.01)
Denmark	2.084	0.381	2.006	0.494	1.726	–0.229
	(2.01)	(2.51)	(1.78)	(2.92)	(1.79)	(1.56)
Finland	1.158	0.168	0.897	0.177	0.554	–0.359
	(6.01)	(1.55)	(5.66)	(2.33)	(3.17)	(4.31)
France	1.092	0.368	1.329	0.246	0.628	–0.060
	(2.17)	(3.62)	(3.07)	(2.97)	(1.33)	(0.62)
Germany	–	–	1.344	0.106	1.168	–0.321
			(1.86)	(1.05)	(1.52)	(3.02)
Greece	0.021	0.306	0.168	0.145	–0.338	0.061
	(0.09)	(2.51)	(0.79)	(1.90)	(1.47)	(0.75)
Ireland	–8.362	0.048	–7.130	0.041	–7.086	–0.155
	(1.44)	(0.54)	(1.26)	(0.49)	(0.96)	(1.33)
Italy	0.718	0.149	0.861	–0.051	0.258	–0.179
	(1.82)	(1.69)	(1.80)	(0.41)	(0.66)	(1.75)
Netherlands	0.134	0.241	0.404	0.187	–0.293	–0.301
	(0.15)	(1.54)	(0.48)	(1.38)	(0.32)	(2.05)
Portugal	0.155	0.298	0.510	0.210	–0.143	0.079
	(0.43)	(2.39)	(1.59)	(2.12)	(0.41)	(0.75)
Spain	1.757	0.182	1.217	0.206	1.013	–0.216
	(2.67)	(2.67)	(1.94)	(3.12)	(1.45)	(2.88)
Sweden	3.112	0.128	2.852	0.059	2.314	–0.634
	(5.36)	(0.49)	(4.74)	(0.22)	(3.84)	(2.29)
UK	–	–	–0.424	0.309	–0.615	–0.269
			(0.93)	(2.10)	(1.44)	(1.96)
Deficit measure	Net lending 1972–1999		Net lending excluding interest 1961–1999		Structural deficit 1961–1999	

Deficits are relative to trend GDP. SUR estimates.

Most income tax systems contain elements of asymmetry in their structure. For each individual, tax rates are progressive, so that in an unchanged system of rates and allowances, tax revenues will grow faster than incomes. Similarly, in downturns fewer firms have profits which can be taxed. In periods where there is substantial price inflation, these effects will be much stronger. Specific duties on quantities of alcohol, tobacco or fuel behave the other way round, but they tend to form a limited part of the total tax take. Other indirect taxes are fixed rate and hence symmetric. Not only is tax cutting much more popular with electorates than tax increases, whatever the benefits being promised from new expenditures, but tax cuts are required on a regular basis if the share of the public sector in total activity is not to grow. Similarly, increases in spending tend to be politically easier to sell than reductions.

Governments are thus likely to find it more difficult to improve their financial position than worsen it. Compliance with the Maastricht criteria in the run up to qualification for membership of Stage 3 of EMU was therefore a relatively unusual incentive for fiscal prudence both in cutting debt and restraining deficits. It is somewhat akin to the requirements the IMF often lays down for its temporary financial support – politically difficult actions are more acceptable when something is available in return and where the constraint is external and outside the direct control of the government concerned. Both interest rates and debt ratios are included in the analysis and governments do appear to have responded (symmetrically) by restraining deficits as interest rates and debts get higher – market discipline does appear to work.

However, as noted above, this experience necessarily applies to the past and, in order to incorporate sufficient cycles, includes primarily periods where inflation was higher. Some countries, notably the UK, have introduced fiscal 'responsibility' laws constraining their governments to follow prudent and sustainable policies. The quality of the public sector accounting information has also improved making it easier for opponents to detect less prudent measures. (Modern modelling techniques also make it easier for those outside government to compute the results.) This might lead to an expectation of improved behaviour but some of the debate over the SGP and the fiscal decisions of various Member States in the last few years suggest that the problem remains. Nevertheless, it has been specifically recognised in the reform of the SGP and the Member States are now enjoined to improve their underlying fiscal position in 'good times'.

2.3.2 The share of the public sector in economic activity

Since the asymmetry discussed in the previous section runs across the cycle, it could tend to lead to two unwelcome results. First, there could be a tendency to build up debt and, second, there could be a tendency for the share of the public sector in GDP to rise. This is not a necessity, as the result depends both on the mean deficit across the cycle and on the rate of economic growth. Nevertheless, that was the experience for most countries during the period. Clearly neither tendency is sustainable. At some point debt ratios will be high enough to start worrying lenders about the possibility of default and hence ratings will fall and the cost of the debt will rise. The EU has decided that the limit for prudence is 60% of GDP but rating agencies appear to take a rather wider range of factors into account and for smaller open economies AAA ratings normally require somewhat lower debt ratios.

(Note here one of the advantages of EMU membership – that some of the smaller and more vulnerable economies are able to improve their debt rating simply by joining. At some point, however, the union could have an adverse effect. Countries that might individually have the highest sovereign rating could find the rating lowered if too much of the euro area looked somewhat less sound.)

However, we noted in the previous section that increases in interest rates do indeed tend to prompt countries into reducing their deficits. Increasing the relative size of the public sector is a similar natural reaction in that to some extent losses of jobs in the private sector could be replaced by socially useful jobs in the public sector. Here there also appears to be an asymmetry (Table 2.2). Up to a certain point increasing the size of the public sector also seems to have positive effects for the growth of the private sector. Beyond that the sign changes.

In this case the sample is extended to include Iceland, Norway and Switzerland.[3] The data period is somewhat shorter, 1960–1996. The results seem quite robust. The effect on private sector growth is larger below the threshold in all cases. It is negative above the threshold in all cases except France, Italy and Norway, where it is not significantly different from zero.[4] All of the countries are currently operating above the threshold, hence other things being equal, reducing rather than increasing the role of the public sector would appear to be beneficial for growth (these results conform with earlier findings by Barro (1990) and Karras (1996)). However, as already mentioned, the impact of any given level of revenue or expenditure depends on its content. Trying to ease the non-wage taxes on labour, as suggested within the BEPGs, would *inter alia* assist the objective of having employment rich growth, even if other taxes are raised to compensate. Since there are other components to welfare and not just the level of GDP, equity for example, there is no imperative to move the government share in a particular direction. But the nature of the potential conflict of objectives as the Member States seek to invest in the knowledge economy and prepare for the demands of ageing while trying to grow 1% faster is very obvious.

2.3.3 Monetary policy

In Mayes and Virén (2002d) we develop a simple four equation model of the economy to explore the asymmetric interactions between economic behaviour and monetary policy in the Member States. The next three sections deal respectively with the Phillips curve, Okun curve and IS curve components of the model but here we concern ourselves with monetary policy as this (and the exchange rate) represent the main policy constraints inside Stage 3 of EMU.

The issue with monetary policy is straightforward. Under Stage 3 each individual Member State has to accept the monetary policy settings that, in the view of the ECB Governing Council, constitute the best way of maintaining price stability for the area as a whole. This will tend to differ from what

Table 2.2 Thresholds in the role of the public sector

Country	Coefficient		SEE/ DW	FHO	FHT	LM
	Below threshold	Above threshold				
Austria	0.580	–0.568	0.019	20.4	11.52	0.39
	(1.71)	(1.69)	(1.759)	(0.046)	(0.003)	(0.538)
Belgium	0.690	–0.119	0.023	36.7	7.5	0.120
	(2.34)	(0.48)	(2.159)	(0.000)	(0.119)	(0.283)
Denmark	0.113	–0.700	0.024	19.2	7.2	1.63
	(0.80)	(2.86)	(1.833)	(0.046)	(0.167)	(0.212)
Finland	0.458	–1.144	0.032	10.6	3.6	1.25
	(1.68)	(2.25)	(1.648)	(0.308)	(0.876)	(0.274)
France	1.417	0.121	0.017	12.9	8.7	0.002
	(3.23)	(0.25)	(1.961)	(0.270)	(0.028)	(0.966)
Germany	–0.063	–1.537	0.023	14.6	6.3	0.98
	(0.80)	(3.64)	(1.767)	(0.138)	(0.283)	(0.331)
Greece	0.933	–0.354	0.031	26.6	11.6	0.16
	(1.98)	(1.39)	(1.734)	(0.007)	(0.003)	(0.696)
Iceland	0.138	–1.021	0.040	5.25	3.8	0.95
	(0.61)	(1.61)	(1.813)	(0.862)	(0.830)	(0.338)
Ireland	–0.109	–0.941	0.029	7.1	7.2	0.04
	(0.44)	(1.89)	(1.947)	(0.697)	(0.177)	(0.845)
Italy	1.278	0.293	0.022	12.7	5.9	0.89
	(3.28)	(0.99)	(1.785)	(0.221)	(0.415)	(0.354)
Netherlands	0.156	–1.617	0.013	24.6	6.3	0.27
	(0.67)	(4.37)	(1.868)	(0.040)	(0.210)	(0.605)
Norway	0.448	0.159	0.019	7.6	7.3	5.05
	(1.54)	(1.01)	(1.642)	(0.663)	(0.131)	(0.033)
Portugal	0.169	–0.153	0.032	7.7	3.5	0.28
	(1.37)	(1.23)	(2.076)	(0.521)	(0.935)	(0.603)
Spain	0.186	–0.172	0.020	17.6	5.8	0.31
	(1.14)	(1.57)	(2.272)	(0.096)	(0.359)	(0.584)
Sweden	0.330	–0.123	0.022	12.8	7.7	3.99
	(1.90)	(0.88)	(1.673)	(0.222)	(0.117)	(0.055)
Switzerland	0.325	–0.904	0.022	15.2	5.4	7.51
	(1.06)	(2.05)	(1.407)	(0.106)	(0.449)	(0.010)
UK	0.628	–0.131	0.024	7.9	4.6	12.41
	(1.74)	(1.04)	(1.488)	(0.636)	(0.681)	(0.002)

Note: Numbers inside parentheses below the coefficient estimates are t-ratios. SEE is the standard error of estimate and DW the Durbin-Watson test statistic (which here suffers from the bias caused by lagged dependent variable). FHO denotes the LM (F) test for no threshold and FHT the corresponding test for threshold allowing for heteroscedastic errors. Numbers in parentheses below the F statistics are bootstrap probability values. Finally, LM denotes a LM test for first-order autocorrelation of residuals (corresponding marginal significance levels are in parentheses). When computing this LM test we have utilised Chan (1993), in which it is shown that the threshold parameter is superconsistent and can thus be treated as a known parameter.

would be best for each Member State or region (or industry for that matter) at each juncture. We do not attempt to assess net benefits or costs of this result but draw attention to one facet of the policy followed by the Member States over the last decade, namely the Member States have shown an asymmetric importance to different inflation *and output* targets. This has consequences both for the experience of each state in Stage 3 and for the design of the single policy by the Eurosystem.

With respect to inflation, governments have tended to respond more strongly to the threat of deflation and negative output gaps than they have to higher inflation (Table 2.3a). Outside a corridor of inflation of the order of 0–4% a year, governments have responded much more strongly (Table 2.3b). One might expect that with success in controlling inflation that the upper bound of the corridor might have fallen over the period (and indeed the tolerable lower bound may have risen), thereby narrowing the corridor of 'acceptable' variation.

The implication is clear. In Stage 3, individual countries may find themselves outside the acceptable corridor yet monetary policy is not reacting strongly. Substantiating this depends on some major assumptions, first of all that the ECB Governing Council responds for the euro area in a manner similar to the general behaviour of its predecessor authorities. In one respect this may not be a sensible conclusion as the monetary authority institutions set up under the Maastricht Treaty have deliberately strengthened the hand of the central banks relative to the governments in the implementation of policy.

Table 2.3a Reaction function estimates

R_{t-1}	0.771	0.863
	(238.15)	(63.54)
Δp_t	0.391	
	(65.89)	
$\Delta p_t \mid \Delta p_t < 0.005$		0.281*
		(2.30)
$\Delta p_t \mid \Delta p_t > 0.005$		0.164
		(3.30)
∇y_t	0.159	
	(42.13)	
$\nabla y_t \mid \nabla y_t < 0$		0.112*
		(2.65)
$\nabla y_t \mid \nabla y_t > 0$		0.381
		(5.72)

The Wald test result for the equality of the two respective coefficients is 927 (0.009). Thus, the linear model is rejected at the 1% significance level with the chi-square distribution. All estimates are derived from the whole system of equations. Data period is 1993–2001.

Table 2.3b Corridor reaction functions

$\Delta p_t \vert\ \Delta p_t<0$	0.602
	(3.63)
$\Delta p_t \vert\ 0<\Delta p_t<0.01$	0.153
	(3.32)
$\Delta p_t \vert\ \Delta p_t>0.01$	0.230
	(6.60)
$\nabla y_t \vert \nabla y_t<-0.02$	0.249
	(9.32)
$\nabla y_t \vert -0.02<\nabla y_t<0.02$	0.074
	(3.80)
$\nabla y_t \vert \nabla y_t>0.02$	0.147
	(0.41)

Data period is 1993–2001, maximum likelihood, reaction functions only.

This could be expected to increase the willingness to intervene to maintain price stability. Traditionally governments have been thought to have an inflationary bias in policy setting (Rogoff, 1985a), largely as a result of time consistency problems. The institutional change might therefore result both in lowering of the upper bound and in a strengthening of the response of policy when the upper bound is challenged. As is described below, the reaction of the authorities we model is in the form of a Taylor rule (Huang *et al.*, 2001), so they respond in the asymmetric way we describe both to inflation and to the output gap. However, before taking the discussion further it would be helpful to outline the model used.

The model can be summarised as follows:

$$\nabla y_t = a_0 + a_1 \nabla y_{t-1} + a_2 \nabla y_{t-2} + a_3 rr_{t-i} + a_4 re_{t-j} + a_5 \nabla y^*{}_{t-k} \tag{1}$$

$$\Delta p = b_0 + b_1 \Delta p_{t-1} + b_2 \Delta p^e + b_3 \Delta p^* + b_4 u \tag{2}$$

$$\Delta U = c_0 + c_1 \Delta y + c_2 \Delta pop \tag{3}$$

$$r_t = \rho r_{t-1} + (1-\rho)[d_0 + d_1(\Delta p - \Delta p^T)_t + d_2 \nabla y_t] \quad 0 \le \rho \le 1 \tag{4}$$

where the variables in order of appearance are defined as:

∇y is the deviation of output y from its Hodrick-Prescott filtered trend
rr is the real 3-month interest rate (i.e. the nominal rate of interest r less the annual rate of consumer price inflation Δp)
re the real exchange rate with the US dollar (in logs)
∇y^* the deviation of OECD output from its HP trend (lag lengths i, j and k typically vary from 1 to 3 quarters in estimation)

Δp^e is expected inflation
Δp^* is the foreign price (in domestic currency)
u is the deviation of unemployment, U, from its trend[5]
pop is the population of working age
Δp^T is the target for inflation.

Thus (1) is a simple IS curve along the lines of Duguay (1994) and Goodhart and Hofmann (2000). Equation (2) is a version of the standard expectations augmented Phillips curve, (3) the Okun curve (which is augmented in some of the discussion in Section 2.3.5 and (4) is a monetary reaction function in the form of a Taylor rule, where the parameter ρ permits an element of interest rate smoothing (Huang *et al.*, 2001).

This set of equations determines inflation, output, unemployment and the rate of interest. Foreign prices, foreign output and the exchange rate are treated as exogenous to the system. Data constraints led us to modify (2) in some of the estimation and price expectations are represented by the OECD forecast a year ahead. The model is estimated using a panel of quarterly data for the period 1985Q1 to 2001Q3 for all the euro area countries except Greece and Luxembourg, for which the information was not available. This gives a potential 770 observations. The initial truncation date of 1985Q1 is determined partly by availability of data but mainly because it is difficult to sustain the idea that there is a single regime applied over the period as a whole. Prior to 1985 there was considerable realignment of exchange rates within the ERM of the European Monetary System (EMS) and in some cases we find we cannot use the first two years because the data are incomplete or show indications of a regime shift. We also found that there were substantial problems in handling the monetary policy reaction function (4) across the exchange rate crisis of 1992/1993. The period since the beginning of 1999 lies within Stage 3 of EMU although in practical terms that probably began earlier in 1998.

The model thus treats all the Member States together as a panel. Changes in monetary policy were too infrequent for many of the Member States individually. In any case, some followed the Bundesbank lead so closely that it was not clear whether they were adding information to the discussion.

As discussed at the beginning of section, this asymmetry will tend to mean that the Member States will become particularly concerned about monetary policy at the extremes, especially when they are threatened by actual decline. Under normal circumstances any discrepancies will not be so important. However, this neglects one feature of the targeting regime implied by the model and by Eurosystem policy, namely the cumulation of pressures. Under conventional inflation targeting, past 'errors' are set aside and policy focuses on getting the future right, not on correcting the past. In a monetary union this does not apply. There is much less of a mechanism for correcting pricing errors, with a fixed exchange rate with the other Member States and no opportunity to vary independently with respect to the outside world.

The same asymmetry poses a problem for the Eurosystem itself as it cannot operate simply from aggregate statistics about the output gap or inflationary pressure. However, unlike the way in which this is posed by De Grauwe and Sénégas (2003) and others, this is not best seen as a problem about asymmetric policy requirements or preferences across countries. The members of the Governing Council of the ECB are only supposed to have a regard for the policy needs of the area as a whole. The aggregation is of their differing views about the euro area, not of their individual views about their part of the area as national central bank governors. In the coming sections we therefore show the problem the asymmetry poses for decision-making about the aggregate. Here we merely note that asymmetric preferences, in the sense of being much more than proportionately concerned by deflationary or inflationary outcomes will increase the chance of conflict when countries face substantial asymmetric difficulties.

2.3.4 The influence of unemployment on inflation

The classic relation in the determination of inflation is the Phillips curve (2). Not only does the fact that it is a curve mean that aggregation is more complex, but asymmetry occurs in three respects: how much inflation responds to changes in unemployment; how fast it responds and how sharply curved the relationship is. If we abstract for the moment from the problems of curvature initially, we can see from Figure 2.3 (drawn from

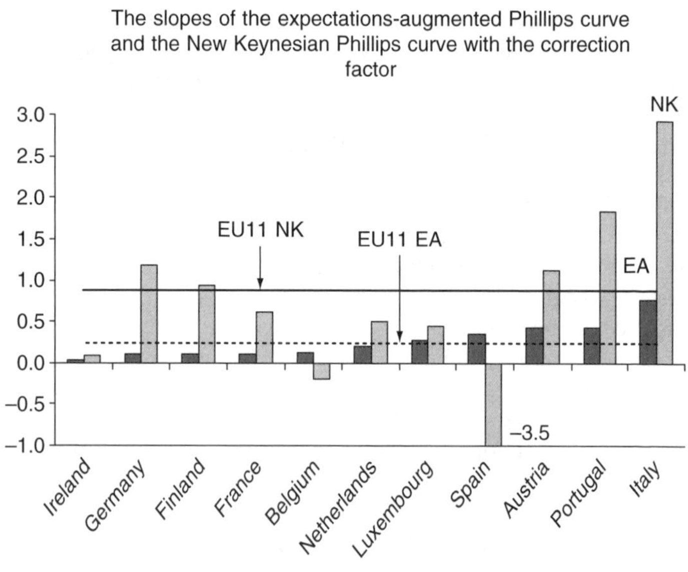

Figure 2.3 Effect of the output gap on inflation in the euro area

Paloviita and Mayes, 2003) that there is wide range in the slopes of the Phillips curve across the Member States, whether the curve is formulated in its traditional expectations augmented version (EA) as in (2) or in its New Keynesian equivalent (NK) (Fuhrer and Moore, 1995). Portugal, Italy and Spain show considerable discrepancies from the EU average in the NK case, but even in the less volatile EA framework the response is around four times as large in Spain, Austria, Portugal and Italy as it is in Ireland, Germany, Finland, France and Belgium.[6] (These models are estimated using annual data for the period 1984–2002, drawn from the OECD *Economic Outlook* database. Data were not available for Greece. Expectations are represented by the OECD forecasts published in June each year for the next calendar year.)

Persistence does not vary quite as much (Figure 2.4), especially for the output gap, but it is still clear that the dynamics will vary markedly from one country to another. This is emphasised when it comes to the appropriateness of the two different expectations formulation schemes illustrated. In the EA scheme, it is last year's expectation of this year that influences inflation. In the NK scheme, it is this year's expectation of next year, a much more forward-looking approach. Paloviita and Mayes (2003) find that while the EA formulation is preferred for four countries and for the

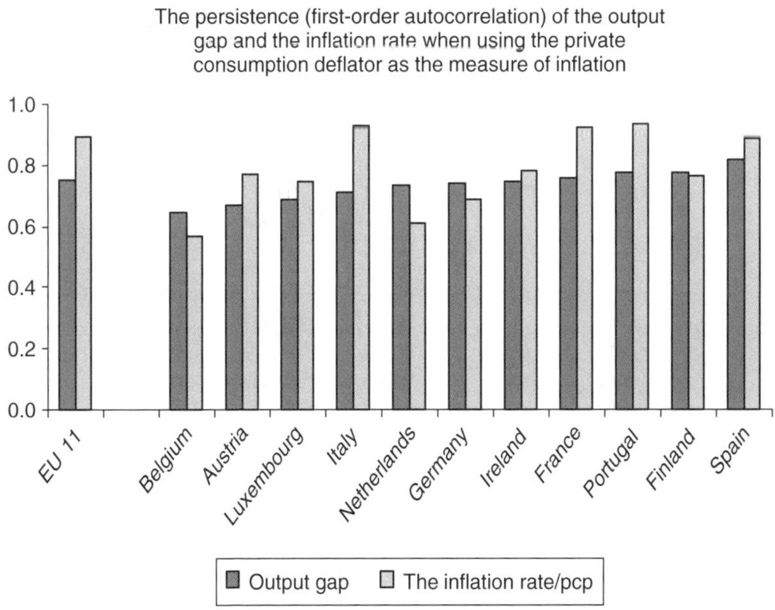

Figure 2.4 Persistence in inflation and the output gap in the euro area

aggregate EU11 data, as opposed to only two for the NK specification, five show mixed results on the basis of non-nested tests.[7]

We thus see two obvious consequences:

1. It matters for the policy reaction where the problem lies as the same size shock has very different result in both size and timing across the euro area.
2. Some countries will be much more affected than others by common shocks.

When we add the problem of curvature, Table 2.4 (drawn from Mayes and Virén, 2003), we can see that in the case of the output gap, negative gaps have almost no influence on inflation. There is a clear difference between the influence of unemployment above and below the mean, so assuming a linear relationship in that case would also lead to incorrect policy inferences. The spread of output gaps across the euro area thus matters for policy. If the countries had converged then the problem is trivial, but if some have positive and some negative gaps, one has to be clear where the shocks fall in assessing the response of monetary policy.

Table 2.4 Phillips curve estimates from panel data

	OLS	GLS	SUR	OLS	GLS	SUR
Δp_{-1}	0.199	0.173	0.147	0.195	0.178	0.158
	(5.05)	(5.23)	(4.11)	(5.11)	(5.32)	(4.88)
Δp_{-2}	0.249	0.256	0.208	0.239	0.247	0.201
	(5.68)	(7.29)	(6.03)	(5.49)	(7.14)	(5.90)
Δm	0.013	0.007	0.006	0.019	0.014	0.009
	(1.46)	(2.00)	(1.26)	(2.12)	(2.69)	(1.96)
Δm_{-1}	0.020	0.013	0.011	0.020	0.013	0.015
	(2.54)	(3.95)	(2.38)	(2.66)	(3.29)	(3.13)
∇x^-	–0.022	–0.034	0.006	–0.177	–0.145	–0.081
	(0.60)	(1.48)	(0.22)	(2.58)	(2.78)	(1.96)
∇x^+	0.163	0.159	0.099	–0.078	–0.072	–0.060
	(4.12)	(5.20)	(4.29)	(1.71)	(1.87)	(1.59)
R^2	0.373	0.373	0.373	0.365	0.363	0.355
SEE	0.006	0.006	0.006	0.006	0.006	0.006
DW	1.967	2.027	1.907	2.042	2.012	1.935
N	732	732	732	770	770	770
Wald	8.15	19.51	5.12	0.75	0.084	0.109
	(0.004)	(0.000)	(0.024)	(0.401)	(0.357)	(0.741)
Defn. of ∇x	∇y	∇y	∇y	∇u	∇u	∇u

p denotes consumer prices, m import prices, ∇y the HP output gap for GDP, ∇u is the deviation of unemployment from the mean level of unemployment over the sample. The data period stretches from 1985Q1 to 2001Q3. t values in parentheses using heteroscedasticity consistent standard errors. Wald test for equality of coefficients on ∇x^- and ∇x^+. p-value in parenthesis.

2.3.5 The relation between unemployment and output

It was noticeable in the previous section that unemployment had a rather less well-defined relation with inflation even though it conformed to the traditional Phillips curve. A major reason is that aggregate unemployment alone is not a very good representation of the effect. It is necessary to look at the spread of unemployment across the regions of the EU (Table 2.5). The more spread out the experience of unemployment across the EU, the greater the inflationary impact of any given level of unemployment on aggregate inflation. The reasoning follows from the shape of the Phillips curve. Tight labour markets have a strongly inflationary effect while slack markets have little effect. The overall impact therefore tends to be driven by the tighter markets (see Buxton and Mayes, 1986, for the example of the UK where it was the tightest regional and industrial labour markets that had the major influence on inflation).

These discrepancies have important implications for EU macroeconomic policy because the Lisbon strategy has clear requirements for employment

Table 2.5 Estimates of the Phillips curve with regional EU data

	(1)	(2)	(3)	(4)	(5)	(6)
Δp^e	0.655	0.649	0.513	0.488		0.522
	(12.42)	(10.17)	(12.72)	(11.77)		(13.76)
Δp_{-1}	0.254	0.214	0.191	0.143	0.567	0.187
	(5.72)	(3.92)	(5.26)	(3.66)	(23.89)	(5.31)
Δm	0.058	0.056	0.063	0.068	0.085	0.065
	(6.56)	(5.43)	(10.14)	(9.25)	(13.19)	(10.54)
U	0.053	–0.003	–256	–248	–290	–306/–0.260
	(3.36)	(0.23)	(10.06)	(12.84)	(11.82)	(11.66/12.00)
Umax-Umin	0.068		0.147		0.154	0.130
	(4.81)		(6.47)		(6.86)	(5.91)
Usd		0.103		0.192		
		(2.32)		(2.93)		
t	–0.016	–0.001	–0.112	–0.108	–0.112	–0.110
	(1.82)	(0.45)	(10.06)	(9.05)	(9.25)	(10.57)
R^2	0.868	0.866	0.914	0.918	0.885	0.918
SEE	0.963	1.073	0.816	0.878	0.938	0.797
DW	1.526	1.289	1.800	1.590	1.928	1.822
Dummies	No	No	Yes	Yes	Yes	Yes
Obs	153	143	153	143	153	153

Note: All estimates are SUR estimates. Δp^e denotes expected inflation (OECD forecasts), *m* import prices, Δp is inflation in consumption prices, *U* the aggregate unemployment rate, *Umax-Umin* the range of regional unemployment rates, *Usd* the corresponding standard deviation and *t* time trend. Column (6) is estimated using a threshold model specification and allowing the coefficient of the unemployment rate to vary depending on whether the rate is below (first coefficient) or above (second coefficient) the 10.8% threshold. The hypothesis that the coefficients are equal can be rejected with marginal probability of 0.0013% using the F-test.

and not just for economic growth. Labour shortages in the knowledge-based sectors, if they drive the growth process, would tend to generate inflation even if other sectors were relatively slack.

Our main point in the introduction was, however, about the asymmetry in the relationship between output and unemployment over the course of the economic cycle – more people lost their jobs in the down-phase than regained them when output returned to its previous level. This is clear from Table 2.6, which shows estimates of (3) across the EU countries (except Luxembourg) plus Iceland and Norway. Twelve out of the sixteen cases considered (annual OECD data 1961–97) show the expected asymmetry if zero growth is used as the threshold. Finland shows no asymmetry, Greece and Italy are perverse but insignificant. Only the UK shows a perverse and significant relationship. The position is slightly improved if, as in the second pair of columns in the table, the threshold is chosen endogenously (Mayes and Virén, 2003). Thus if there are negative shocks the problem of maintaining or indeed increasing employment and participation is made more difficult. We also experimented with exploring whether it is the error-correction mechanism that is different above and below the trend, with unemployment returning to equilibrium more slowly in the case of a negative shock. This result was borne out and is shown in Harris and Silverstone (1999).

2.3.6 The influence of the real interest rate and real exchange rate on economic growth

We end this discussion with a brief consideration of (1), which describes some of the elements of the monetary transmission mechanism in a manner that emphasises both the relative importance of the exchange and the role of asset prices in the process of economic adjustment. As is clear from Table 2.7, last column, the relative importance of the real exchange rate to the real interest rate varies by a factor of at least two across the EU countries in the period before the start of Stage 3 (Mayes and Virén, 2000). Many of the countries appear decidedly open to influences through the US dollar exchange rate as indicated by values of λ, the ratio of the two effects, of three or less. Indeed, Mayes and Virén (2000) suggested that a reasonable starting value for estimating the openness of the euro area as a whole in terms of this ratio would be 3.5. This would be a decidedly open economy, with a rather higher influence of external prices than would appear to be the case from a simple analysis of trade shares, which would imply a ratio twice as large.

While Mayes and Virén opined at the time that the euro area would become increasingly closed as the euro became more important in international pricing and the market became more integrated, the early years suggest that the exchange rate channel has remained important. There is a well-known debate (HM Treasury, 2003c) as to whether the exchange rate is more

Table 2.6 Estimates of a nonlinear Okun curve

	$\Delta y^+(0)$	$\Delta y^-(0)$	$\Delta y^+(c)$	$\Delta y^-(c)$	F
Austria	–0.039	–0.512	–0.050	–0.075	14.53
	(3.76)	(–0.047)	(5.03)	(3.93)	
Belgium	–0.026	–0.125	–0.038	–0.070	18.29
	(2.33)	(2.85)	(4.42)	(4.66)	
Denmark	–0.022	–0.451	–0.030	–0.392	18.45
	(1.03)	(3.36)	(1.48)	(3.52)	
Finland	–0.071	–0.070	–0.066	–0.079	16.82
	(5.29)	(3.07)	(6.15)	(6.28)	
France	–0.019	–0.050	–0.028	–0.080	15.75
	(1.15)	(0.43)	(2.00)	(2.48)	
Germany	–0.096	–0.135	–	–	–
	(4.56)	(0.93)			
Greece	–0.023	0.024	–0.027	0.038	21.67
	(3.03)	(0.67)	(3.58)	(1.19)	
Iceland	–0.072	–0.119	–0.076	–0.121	15.67
	(4.84)	(2.81)	(5.76)	(3.35)	
Ireland	–0.019	–0.088	–0.025	–0.050	5.20
	(2.17)	(0.35)	(3.31)	(2.86)	
Italy	–0.026	0.021	–0.019	–0.043	14.05
	(2.27)	(0.34)	(1.81)	(2.82)	
Netherlands	–0.023	–0.182	–0.048	–0.123	112.86
	(0.95)	(1.22)	(2.73)	(4.07)	
Norway	–0.043	–0.185	–0.059	–0.094	6.79
	(2.14)	(0.49)	(3.00)	(2.95)	
Portugal	–0.044	–0.250	–0.055	–0.094	16.11
	(2.47)	(0.71)	(3.19)	(3.60)	
Spain	–0.019	0.062	–0.026	–0.013	29.24
	(3.49)	(0.79)	(5.09)	(1.61)	
Sweden	–0.064	–0.122	–0.062	–0.110	13.11
	(2.72)	(1.92)	(3.65)	(5.05)	
UK	–0.032	0.095	–0.031	0.102	21.08
	(1.50)	(1.83)	(1.51)	(1.97)	

Note: Numbers in parentheses are t-ratios. $\Delta y^+(0)$ and $\Delta y^-(0)$ denote estimates with zero threshold and $\Delta y^+(c)$ and $\Delta y^-(c)$ estimates with nonzero (estimated) threshold value. The parameters are derived from the following estimating equation $\Delta u_t = a_0 + a_1\Delta y^+_t + a_2\Delta y^-_t + a_3\Delta pop_t + a_4\varepsilon_{t-1} + \eta_t$, where u denotes the (log) number of unemployed, Δy the growth rate of output, *pop* the (log) working-age population, ε an error-correction term in terms of u, *pop* and time trend and η the error term. In the nonlinear case, Δy is replaced by Δy^+ and Δy^- so that Δy^+ corresponds to positive values of Δy and Δy^- to negative values. F is the F(1,31) test for the equality of the coefficients of Δy^+ and Δy^- in the case of nonzero threshold. Estimates are based on annual OECD data for 1961–1997.

important as a buffer to ease shocks or as a cause of the shocks themselves. Certainly with the euro–dollar exchange rate fluctuating by more than a third, first down and then up, between the beginning of 1999 and early 2003, external stability has been no greater. Indeed, the more closed an economy

Table 2.7 OLS estimation results for the 1987Q1–1997Q4 period

Name lags	Δy_{t-1}	Δy_{t-2}	rr_{t-i}	re_{t-j}	$\Delta oecd_{t-k}$	R^2 (SEE)	DW	λ
Austria 2,2,2	0.729	–0.095	–0.021	0.009	0.338	0.660	1.90	2.4
	(6.39)	(0.74)	(0.91)	(0.65)	(0.65)	(0.58)		
Belgium 4,3,2	1.145	–0.457	–0.046	0.001	0.334	0.882	1.81	41.7
	(6.60)	(2.85)	(1.28)	(0.08)	(1.55)	(0.40)		
Denmark 1,3,1	0.105		–0.152	0.018	0.065	0.261	1.96	8.3
	(1.02)		(1.77)	(1.51)	(1.12)	(0.84)		
Finland 3,2,2	0.773	–0.158	–0.152	0.048	0.406	0.881	1.99	3.1
	(5.36)	(1.00)	(2.36)	(3.90)	(0.83)	(1.19)		
France 4,2,2	0.960	–0.274	–0.069	0.027	0.305	0.871	1.94	2.5
	(6.64)	(1.56)	(2.06)	(1.99)	(1.35)	(0.44)		
Germany 7,3,2	0.545	0.181	–0.072	0.020	0.123	0.911	1.53	3.6
	(2.73)	(1.23)	(0.87)	(0.84)	(0.57)	(0.81)		
Ireland 1,3,2	0.970	–0.298	–0.056	0.028	0.788	0.867	1.81	2.0
	(7.18)	(2.63)	(1.73)	(1.56)	(3.09)	(0.72)		
Italy 3,2,1	0.701		–0.095	0.012	0.332	0.767	1.97	7.8
	(8.88)		(1.90)	(1.43)	(2.35)	(0.50)		
Neths 1,2,2	1.077	–0.381	–0.037	0.016	0.259	0.824	1.86	2.3
	(11.41)	(4.72)	(1.53)	(1.76)	(2.34)	(0.39)		
Port 3,1,1	0.447	0.135	–0.081	0.007	0.747	0.901	1.95	11.6
	(3.47)	(1.30)	(2.87)	(1.24)	(3.74)	(0.48)		
Spain 1,2,1	1.518	–0.595	–0.008	0.009	0.115	0.982	1.44	0.8
	(15.98)	(6.53)	(1.16)	(3.01)	(1.85)	(0.18)		
Sweden 1,2,2	0.537	0.226	–0.065	0.052	0.604	0.809	2.33	1.2
	(5.21)	(1.70)	(5.21)	(4.05)	(2.30)	(0.77)		
UK 1,1,1	0.981	–0.175	–0.033	0.022	0.262	0.950	1.83	1.5
	(10.50)	(1.86)	(1.84)	(2.96)	(4.34)	(0.40)		

Note: The dependent variable ∇y is the output gap constructed by the HP filter. *rr* is the real interest rate, *re* the real exchange rate with respect to US dollar. $\nabla oecd$ denotes the output gap for OECD GDP. λ is the ratio between interest rate and exchange rate elasticities. The numbers after the country names give the lag length for *rr*, *re*, $\nabla oecd$ (in this order), respectively. The data are quarterly and cover the period 1987Q1–1997Q4. For the UK, the US output gap is used instead of the OECD output gap. The German equation includes a level and one period dummies for the unification period (1991Q1–1997Q4). All estimates are OLS estimates.

the more its exchange rate has to fluctuate for price effects to have an impact on correcting imbalances. Thus the more externally exposed members of the euro area, such as Finland, may have found themselves more exposed to exchange rate fluctuations than would have been the case outside the area. However, the comparison between Sweden and Finland in Chapters 9 and 10 suggests that it would be difficult to give a definitive answer. There is some irony here. In 1992–1993 Finland and Sweden found the exchange rate an extremely helpful buffer to ease the real impact of their banking crises. A fall in their exchange rates of a third enabled a rapid recovery in their economies and an export boom (and subsequent rise in the exchange rate as circumstances improved). Since the start of Stage 3 Finland has benefited from the failure of the exchange rate to appreciate despite a major trade surplus and growth on the back of the technology boom and the performance of Nokia in particular.

The exchange rate acts as a helpful buffer to adverse asymmetric shocks. However, it reduces the impact of favourable asymmetric shocks. While there is in general no reason to expect anything other than a symmetric distribution of shocks over the long run, the particular nature of shocks over the first few years inside or outside a monetary union will have a considerable impact on the perceived success of the policy choice. Having a string of adverse shocks early on would be unfortunate for a country that had not yet managed to make its labour market more flexible and to achieve relative price adjustments at a relatively low cost HM Treasury (2003g).

The picture is complicated by the role of asset prices. All the equations in the model including (1) are relatively simple compared to the complexities of the world they seek to describe and there is no role in the model, as set up, for other channels of monetary policy (Mayes, 2003). One aspect of the transmission mechanism that is of particular importance in recent years given the fluctuations experienced, both up in the second half of the 1990s and down since then, is asset prices. Using a model similar to Goodhart and Hofmann (2000), Mayes and Virén (2002d) consider the addition of house prices and stock market prices to (1), see Table 2.8.[8]

It is immediately clear that house prices play an important role in the transmission mechanism, although Goodhart and Hofmann (2000) suggest that it varies considerably across the EU countries, affected in part by the nature of the prevailing systems of tenure and housing finance. Stock prices on the other hand seem to have played a rather limited role despite the importance that has been attached to them, particularly in the United States. The role of financial wealth and the ability to diversify shocks both across different markets and across time is an important characteristic of the way an economy is affected inside a monetary union. In general, cross-country wealth holding is reasonably limited in the EU, although it is practised more by pension funds acting on behalf of households rather than directly by the households themselves. It is of course also practised extensively by large companies and indeed the first few years of Stage 3 were characterised by extensive diversification outside the euro area.

Taken together, therefore, these six sections suggest that there are considerable tensions in trying to meet the demands of the Lisbon strategy of the present decade, only some of which relate to the existence of Stage 3 of EMU. The fiscal constraints and the labour market constraints apply whatever monetary policy framework is chosen, as do the challenges from the increasing longevity of the population. The most important feature of the foregoing is the two sides to asymmetry that it reveals. First, the asymmetry across the economic cycle, particularly on the part of government, will tend to ensure that the pressure on the system emerges in the downturn, to an

Table 2.8 Alternative estimates of the impact of house and stock market prices with European cross-country panel data

Data/estimator/*N*	(λ)	House prices	Stock prices	R^2/DW
Output gap	1.97	0.043	0.002	0.729
SUR, 540	(0.002)	(4.60)	(0.68)	2.036
Output gap	3.28	–	–	0.694
SUR, 612	(0.000)			1.950
Output gap	2.94	0.042	–0.006	0.700
SUR, 402*	(0.000)	(4.50)	(1.61)	1.961
Output gap	2.97	0.047	–	0.699
SUR, 402*	(0.000)	(3.99)		1.962
Output gap	3.17	–	–	0.692
SUR, 417*	(0.000)			1.934
$\Delta\log(y)$	2.34	0.060	0.007	0.247
SUR, 540	(0.000)	(6.13)	(2.27)	2.009
$\Delta\log(y)$	3.55	–	–	0.174
SUR, 611	(0.000)			1.863
$\Delta\log(y)$	4.44	0.107	0.004	0.231
SUR, 402*	(0.000)	(3.23)	(1.02)	1.921
$\Delta\log(y)$	4.15	–	–	0.206
SUR, 416*	(0.000)			1.954

Note: The equations also include the lagged dependent variable and the (lagged) OECD output variable.
* The sample period is 1991Q1–2000Q3. Otherwise, it is 1985Q1–2000Q3. *N* denotes the number of observations. $\Delta\log(y)$ indicates that log differences are used instead of the output gap variables.

important degree because governments are over-optimistic about sustainable fiscal structures in the upturn. Easing the constraints in the downturn is not a solution but then 'voluntarily' increasing the short-run real cost will not appear desirable either. Second, the structure of the Member State economies is clearly still substantially different and their degree of convergence only partial. This poses a bi-directional challenge to the Member States to adjust to a single policy that may not suit their individual needs at the time closely, and to macroeconomic policy-makers who need to consider not just the aggregate euro area but how the shocks and their impact are distributed across Member States with different output gaps and macroeconomic tensions. Policy-making is thus clearly different from that in more homogeneous and flexible economies like the US.

2.4 Fiscal policy and the SGP

The SGP has two main provisions that impinge on our analysis. The first is that EU countries need to bring their finances into a form that is sustainable over the longer term. Currently there are two difficulties in that regard.

Some countries have rather high debt levels compared to their GDP and would have difficulty coping with any large shocks (see Figure 2.1a–c). The consequences of actual or threatened default would rebound on the other Member States and would indeed put pressure on them to bail out the country in difficulty, thereby creating the usual moral hazard problems. Second, there are some predictable problems already in the system, most importantly that entailed by the ageing of the population. Unless something is done many of the Member States will find they have unsustainably generous pension systems. One or more of three things needs to change. Benefits will have to fall relative to average incomes, contributions will have to rise as a proportion of income or the length of time for which people are dependent will have to fall, that is they will have to work longer.

Unfortunately it seems politically difficult in many countries to make these changes rapidly. It therefore seems likely that to some extent the extra costs will have to be borne by an increase in debt, that is by shifting some of the cost towards future generations. Both of these problems therefore imply that in total the debt ratios of the EU countries need to fall if fiscal policy is to be sustainable. This has resulted in the requirement that budgets should be in surplus or near balance over the course of the cycle (and that those countries that have not yet reached that position should do so at the rate of at least half a per cent of GDP per year). If this result can be achieved, debt ratios will fall steadily in the face of GDP growth of around 2 to 3% a year and should on average be sufficiently low that they can withstand substantial predicted and unexpected pressures in ten to fifteen years' time. Unfortunately, if anything, the reform of the SGP results in a weakening of the resolve to reduce the debt burden, as some mitigating circumstances are now permitted.

However, a major problem is that, while the euro area as a whole may need this debt reduction, the needs of the individual countries vary markedly. Some, such as Luxembourg, have no such need, as they have little debt to speak of. Others, such as Italy and Belgium, have major problems that are only slowly being resolved. The Maastricht Treaty has built into the discussion a simple guideline, that the debt ratio should be below 60% of GDP. Such a number is arbitrary but it does represent the approximate average of the Member States at the time and also is quite a close approximation to what would be required if all public sector investment were to be debt financed (at prevailing growth and real interest rates). Despite its arbitrary nature such a ratio would enable the EU to obtain finance at the lowest commercial rates (AAA rating) and be generally thought to be prudent.

There is clearly little incentive for countries that have got their finances approximately in line with the longer-term requirements to want to reduce their debt further, purely to compensate the higher debt ratios and greater problems in effecting debt reductions that some of their partners face.

Running across this discussion is a second requirement and the one that attracts the penalties within the SGP, namely that in the absence of a severe downturn the deficit to GDP ratio should always be below 3%. This is a simple device to stop the debt ratio worsening beyond 60% at current growth rates. It faces two straightforward problems. The first is that a country whose debt ratio is well below 60% of GDP faces a much lower chance of either going above 60% with a 3% deficit ratio or running a policy that markets find unsustainable. The UK is a case in point at present. The second is that this is a difficult constraint to meet in a technical sense, as it requires good forecasting. A Member State's budget has to be such in good (or average) times that the deficit will not exceed 3% in a downturn. The operation of automatic stabilisers will result in countercyclical deficits and surpluses. Most tax systems are progressive so as real incomes grow the share of tax receipts in GDP will rise. Thus to keep tax revenues constant relative to GDP would require periodic 'discretionary' reductions in tax rates. Tax rates are set at the beginning of the year based on the forecast of activity during the year. Over-forecasting will result both in a tax shortfall and in an expenditure increase relative to plans.

Deficits are quite sensitive to growth rates, so that a country anywhere near the 3% boundary could find itself tipped over the top if its forecasting is awry – or indeed simply within the normal bounds of error.[9] Once such a mistake has been made, the country is then faced with a very difficult decision – it needs to cut back expenditure and/or raise taxes just at the time when growth rates are low and where the normal expectation is for a greater rather than a lower contribution from public spending. Failure to recognise that sustainable growth rates may have fallen would exacerbate the problem, particularly since the reform of the SGP now permits a prolonged period of low growth as a mitigating factor for slower adjustment.

Both France and Germany faced aspects of this dilemma in the period leading up to the de facto suspension of the SGP in November 2003, and other euro area members have since joined them in 'the dock'. German growth has been unexpectedly low and fiscal reform has been politically difficult to introduce. France on the other hand has wanted to make a greater public sector contribution to reinvigorating the economy than the 3% limit permits. However, it anticipates being able to do this within the 60% debt ratio limit. However, as Section 2.3.1 shows, this sort of problem has been endemic in the EU countries over recent years. While policy may be fairly balanced when conditions get difficult, there has been a general failure to make adequate improvements in the longer-term fiscal position when the economy has been doing well. Thus when surpluses or low deficits are observed, governments have been inclined to cut tax rates too fast or allow expenditures to rise faster than is consistent with the longer-term pattern.

Countries do however face a problem with the SGP if they wish to use the automatic stabilisers vigorously and do not simultaneously wish to reduce their debt ratio. Both Finland and to an even greater extent Sweden want to make vigorous use of automatic stabilisers (see Chapters 9 and 10). Sweden is not currently inside Stage 3 so the discussion there (Johansson, 2002) has been in terms of what they would do if they join. To do so they need to run their budgetary stance in normal times with a sufficient surplus to stop the deficit breaching 3% of GDP in a bad year. In both cases this suits their policy preferences for their debt at present, as they wish to run the debt ratio down.

Interestingly enough they both also wish to set up the arrangements in a sustainable manner by using buffer funds. In that way the resources are already set aside for the extra expenditure in bad years. The funds will then have to be replenished after the event so that they are ready for the next shock. This automatically entails that not only are expenditures counter-cyclical, but so also are revenues. Thus the problem of not making sufficient allowance in good times does not apply. Indeed Finland has already built its buffer funds up to the full amount. Despite a couple of quarters of actual decline in GDP, Finland has not as yet triggered the use of the funds.

Two further issues reflecting the accounting and real aspects of these funds are worth noting. There was some debate that, because of the particular nature of the social benefit system in the two countries, the buffer funds could be regarded as being in the private sector and hence not subject to the limits of the excessive deficit procedure. The funds are administered by employers and trade unions on an industry-by-industry basis, subject to rules laid down by the state. Hence even though the funds are collected through the normal tax system and perform the same function when spent as a state-run fund, they would be placed differently in the country's accounts. Finland decided early on that making use of such an accounting technicality would not be in the spirit of the SGP, as the need to raise revenue for the funds would be identical under the two schemes. The second is that in most respects this is a matter of labelling rather than strict 'funding'. The government could admit a contingent liability for future payments and simply repay debt faster in the earlier period rather than having entries on both sides of the balance sheet, namely the buffer fund and the extra debt necessary to cover it. The difference in this approach is simply that tax revenues are higher earlier. Some of the cost of the next downturn is paid in advance rather than being loaded on the future. However, this is largely a once and for all step change. The pattern of net revenue/net expenditure once the funds have been accumulated for the first time need not be very different over the cycle, depending on whether the expenditure is technically paid for in advance or in arrears. Even the debt level need not be different as the government could run up a matching debt for other purposes.

However, what can be achieved with fiscal policy is heavily debated. Generally there is opposition to the use of 'active' (discretionary) fiscal policy as a smoothing or stabilisation device. These points are certainly emphasised in the UK government paper on fiscal policy in the context of the Five Tests (HM Treasury, 2003h). The main lines of argument are simply that it is difficult to decide in advance how extensive the policy should be and in any case the decision-making and implementation lags are likely to be sufficient that there is a good chance that the policy will end up being pro-cyclical rather than counter-cyclical. Furthermore a symmetric active policy involves cutting expenditures or raising taxes, neither of which tend to be attractive to governments. When inflation was higher, doing nothing for a while would quite rapidly restore the real position of public finances, as inflation would erode the real value of expenditures and increase revenues through the progressivity of the tax system.

It is, however, mistaken just to look at the totals in assessing the impact of policy, as the speed and scale of impact of tax and expenditure measures depend on their specific nature. The traditional route of public sector projects is not merely an expensive way of maintaining employment, but the projects themselves tend to take a long time to have an impact on economic activity (a new bridge has to be completed before it can be used). Short-run means of easing the taxation of labour, on the other hand, as implied by the Nordic buffer funds are more likely to have an immediate effect in easing the downward pressure on employment.

2.4.1 Alternatives to fiscal policy

Prima facie, real fluctuations inside a monetary union will be greater than those outside it on the basis of common policies. Inside it two adjustment mechanisms to specific shocks are lost, monetary policy and the nominal exchange rate. Hence the dampening mechanism for shocks is reduced. However, it is unrealistic to believe that nothing else changes. Countries inside a monetary union tend to become more similar and more related, hence the extent of specific shocks falls (Frankel and Rose, 1997). As a result the single monetary policy will become somewhat more appropriate for each Member State's needs. Second, economies will tend to develop greater flexibility in the face of potentially greater shocks. As discussed in Chapter 9, Finland has shown much greater wage flexibility since the onset of monetary union. There has been no change in the bargaining structures over wages but the nature of the outcomes from the same system has changed (Kilponen *et al.*, 2000). Wage bargainers seem to be more alert to the competitive threat now that any excess wage inflation cannot be offset by a subsequent devaluation. Hence productivity fluctuations have not been translated so readily into real wage changes and the benefits of productivity growth have accrued to employees in a smoother manner across the cycle.

To some extent it has been easier to spread the benefits through having a centralised bargaining system, which could in effect offer greater wage restraint in return for the increased buffers and strengthened automatic stabilisation. To some extent the greater financial deepening of economies and the reduction in uncertainty about the future path of inflation have made it easier for the private sector to do its own smoothing and hence reduce the immediate consequences of unfavourable shocks.[10] Some of this may be at one remove in that their investment funds may hold securities in other parts of the union and elsewhere, thereby reducing the impact of shocks that are specific to one country region or industry. At the same time, fiscal policy itself may be losing its bite – for example, through Ricardian equivalence, where households offset fiscal expansions by increasing their saving to be able to meet the inevitable increase in taxation later on. However, within the union, fiscal policy can become more effective as the offsetting mechanism though the exchange rate is smaller in a more closed economy. Smaller Member States in particular can be beneficiaries in this regard.

Furthermore, in addition to the small gains through reduced transactions costs and more transparent prices, small countries and previously inflation prone countries may reap the benefit from lower real interest rates. Thus even if there are some losses through increased fluctuations these may be more than offset by a higher rate of growth.

2.4.2 Is there a bias towards contraction?

Some authors have been very concerned that EMU has a contractionary bias (Arestis and Sawyer, 2003) for example. We have already noted that the reduction in debt required by the SGP is something implied by the dictates of prudence and not by the SGP *per se*. In any case, as the results of Section 2.3.2 suggest, this reduction in the activities of the private sector is if anything likely to be expansionary, assuming that there has been some degree of crowding out in the economy. However, the more important concern is that, inside EMU, fiscal policy and monetary policy may tend to work against each other rather than in supporting roles.

Much of the argument is based on the institutional structure (see the next two chapters). First of all there is no explicit mechanism for co-ordination between the social partners, the Council and the ECB outside the macroeconomic dialogue, the 'Cologne process'. Even within that process the ECB is not obliged to respond to any 'offers' made by the fiscal authorities. Indeed the treaty requires the ECB to be independent of political pressure. However, given the over-riding requirement of price stability, the treaty also requires the ECB to have regard for the economic policies of the EU. Furthermore, the other 'soft' co-ordination processes, particularly the BEPGs, the Luxembourg process on employment policy and the Cardiff process on structural policy represent a substantial attempt to get the Member States to implement, innovate and learn from each other, policies supporting the Lisbon strategy (Begg *et al.*, 2003).

Second, because the Member States are responsible individually for the fiscal policy (within the confines of the SGP), there is no guarantee that they could keep a bargain as well as the unitary and independent monetary authority can. Thus an unfortunate cycle could develop. The monetary authority could be sceptical of the commitments that the fiscal authorities have made and hence hold policy tighter than they would under a credible commitment. This argument is conducted in terms of relative tightness as the process is normally regarded as being asymmetric – examples of governments voluntarily holding the fiscal stance tighter than their initial commitments are relatively difficult to find. Since the monetary stance is tighter than expected, the fiscal authorities ease even more followed by a second relative tightening by the monetary authority.

Issing (1999) disputes this view, arguing that having a highly predictable monetary authority, which is not able to commit to contingent bargains actually makes co-ordination of policy easier (see also Mayes and Virén, 2002c). The fiscal authorities can be very clear what the monetary authority is going to do. With a clear inflation target, the monetary authority is not merely limited to saying what fiscal stance it is assuming in its current setting of policy, but it can also set out how it will react if deviations from that setting seem likely. Ironically, some of the criticism of ECB monetary policy has been on the basis that the target is not that transparent (Alesina *et al.*, 2001). A wide variety of policy settings would be consistent with achieving inflation below 2% a year on average over the medium term, even after the clarification of policy in the 2003 review by the ECB (ECB, 2003a). It is a different issue whether inflation in the HICP of less than but close to 2% a year over the medium term is in some sense 'too low' – say because it encounters the 'lower bound problem' (De Grauwe, 2002a).[11] The problem is that, even though the monetary authority can make credible commitments, the Member State governments cannot. This leads some people to advocate the establishment of an economic authority (gouvernement économique) to provide the necessary co-ordination (Fitoussi and Creel, 2002).[12] There are, however, gains within EMU from voluntary co-ordination, especially for smaller states (Virén, 2001).

Similar concerns apply to commitments by the Member States to make structural changes that will enable their economies to be more flexible in response to shocks. Membership of EMU enhances the pressure to make such changes and even though many of them may only be encouraged through the Open Method of Co-ordination (Hodson and Maher, 2001) progress has been noticeable. Of course membership has much less incentive for a country that already regards itself as being flexible. Nevertheless, one of the continuing complaints of the ECB is that the lack of flexibility in the euro area as a whole puts too great a burden on monetary policy. There is thus a trade-off here. A country that is highly flexible and credible might face an increase in average interest rates through joining EMU while one that is less flexible or has less credible macroeconomic policies might on balance face a noticeable reduction. This creates a potential divergence, as those keenest to join the euro area would be those with the greatest problems.

Their membership would thereby worsen the aggregate performance of the euro area. The current convergence criteria for membership of Stage 3, even as amended (slightly) in the new constitutional treaty which is, at the time of writing, still not ratified, would not prevent membership by many such states. Such a prospect would harden the position of current EU members that have not joined Stage 3 and heighten the discontent of some of the current smaller states that have made greater progress in fiscal responsibility and structural flexibility.

2.5 Expanding EMU

The discussion thus far has been largely in terms of the existing members of the EU, whether or not in Stage 3 of EMU. With the expansion of the EU in May 2004, not only is the picture complicated somewhat, but 10 more countries are faced with making a decision about when to join Stage 3. In their case it is 'when' rather than 'whether' as the accession agreements allow only a temporary derogation from full participation. Effectively the decision about when to try to join will be made by the countries themselves, although technically speaking it will be made by the Council of Ministers on the basis of the Convergence Reports by the Commission and the ECB. Since the rules for such membership are laid out in advance, the scope for discretion is relatively limited, provided that there is no great change in the fiscal position of the countries concerned and they are not pushing the edges of qualification at the time.

In this book we have only examined one of the new members in any detail, namely Estonia, though Chapter 12 elaborates the arguments laid out here. The reason for doing this was simply that in running a currency board it is already facing most of the constraints of membership of Stage 3. It is hence of value to explore how fixing the exchange rate and hence following the single ECB monetary policy affects a country whose GDP per head is so far below the EU average. For such a transition economy the rates of growth and hence pace of change would tend to be much faster than for any existing Member State. Furthermore most of the new members, Estonia in particular, do not have debt problems as severe as those that affect some of the existing members. Estonia is very aware of the example of Argentina that a currency board will not be sustainable if the government cannot control the accumulation of debt.

It seems unlikely that the process of rapid transition is going to be without difficulty. After the initial stabilisation, Estonia experienced problems in the wake of the Russian crisis and default in 1998 and it has had a high, though rapidly improving current account deficit that reached an unsustainable 13% of GDP in 2003 and 2004. While current account deficits are to be expected as consumers access durable goods from western manufacturers and firms import equipment in the process of developing local manufacture, this has to be balanced by the inflow of FDI and other funds seeking to purchase assets. Currently the scale of the net inflow is being enabled in Estonia by lending by the banks for construction and on mortgages against real estate. As the banks are foreign owned, they can readily draw on external funds, which are virtually without a risk premium within the euro area and with the EONIA interest rate around 2% at present are extremely cheap by the standards outside the advanced countries. In the same way that FDI has slowed, so will this source of lending, if the collateral is to provide adequate cover. It is not normally possible to borrow more than about 70% of the value of the collateral at present.

Typically asset prices overshoot and there is no reason to think that the new member countries will be immune from this experience. However, the nominal exchange rate cannot adjust in the case of a currency board. Hence closing the gap will have to come from a relative reduction in demand, which could, in part, be through the real exchange rate. The consequences will be much more painful if it has to be imports that contract rather than exports expanding. The new members may thus have to make larger real adjustments than the existing Member States. If that becomes politically difficult then there will a real challenge to the exchange rate and monetary policy regimes.

The new members already face the challenge of needing to see the relative price of domestically produced services and other non-tradeables rise substantially as increasing wages elsewhere in the labour market filter through. Service sectors almost by definition have more limited opportunities for productivity increases than their manufacturing counterparts. Hence with tradeables prices being largely determined in international markets the new members will tend to show faster inflation rates. This 'Balassa–Samuelson effect' has been variously estimated to be relatively small, and hence not a challenge to euro area monetary policy, even if the new members were to join Stage 3 early on (Björksten 2000). In any case the weight of these countries in the area-wide price index will be small initially (but rising along with relative incomes). Nevertheless it would be remarkable if the convergence process were smooth and did not at some stage result in an overvalued exchange rate.

2.6 Concluding comments

In recent remarks, Wood (2003) has pointed out that one should perhaps pay more attention to the lessons of history when considering the development of EMU. He argues that there is a lack of examples of successful monetary unions without political union (forced political unions have also unwound as illustrated by the former Soviet Union). The main basis for his argument is that monetary unions alone lack the mechanisms for coping with extreme shocks or persistent disadvantage to some of the members. In wider unions there are more extensive mechanisms in place to compensate the losers, whether through fiscal federalism as in Germany, through extensive public procurement as in the US or through the redistributive nature of the tax system as in the UK or Canada. Indeed one of the most enduring monetary unions that between Ireland and the UK relied for its success on the free movement of labour, even though the Irish had no say at all in the setting of monetary policy and no particular attention was paid to their plight in the setting of fiscal or other policies by the UK. The same lack of concern by the UK authorities about the substantial income flows to Ireland meant that the monetary union could endure with substantial political disagreement particularly during 1939–1945. Similarly, labour mobility has been one of the key features that has characterised the US market.

Such mechanisms do not exist to a strong extent in the EU. Not only is the EU budget small by comparison with that of the Member States, at around 1.1% of GDP, but even within that budget the redistributive effect is limited as the strong agricultural component (Begg and Grimwade, 1998) is in many respects perverse in its expenditure and revenue pattern. While the free flow of labour is one of the four fundamental freedoms of the EU single market, it does not result in substantial flows across borders (Kilponen and Mayes, 2003) and where it has appeared that these might occur, particularly with the accession of new members (Chassard, 2001), the flows have been inhibited.

Although exit from the EU will formally be countenanced if the constitutional treaty is ratified, exit from Stage 3 of EMU is something for which there are no provisions. That is part of the design intended to impart credibility by making the change seem 'irrevocable'. If exit is very costly then members know that they will have to be prepared to endure very considerable costs under membership before they are prepared to withdraw. The history of the United States is not exactly helpful in this regard. These provisions in themselves act as a deterrent to membership where the potential upside is limited but the chances of a very expensive downside are not zero. In the case of the EU, however, the implicit expectation is that the process of integration will continue. Hence the hope would be that before any part of the EU becomes a loser to the extent that would be politically intolerable, mechanisms will be in place for automatic compensation so that circumstances never become that bad. It is one thing to legislate for compensation where no such possibility seems imminent and quite another to try to implement such a change when one particular part of the union has an immediate need. However, it worth recalling that one of the reasons why the MacDougall (1977) proposals were never taken further forward was that there was an expectation that such transfers would be made to Southern Italy under conditions suspected of corruption (see Levitt's contribution to Begg and Mayes, 1991). An ex ante commitment to such automatic transfers will not be made if the contributors expect that others will 'free-ride' on the system.

We have not attempted to evaluate the merits of euro area membership for those who have not yet joined nor how they might be assessed in this chapter. This is followed up in Chapter 11 on the UK in the context of the Five Tests and for Estonia as a likely member of the next group of entrants in Chapter 12. It is, however, noticeable that all three existing EU members that have chosen to stay out of the euro area have followed different reasoning and strategies. The strategies of the new members are different again. In some cases it will be some time before they comply with the Maastricht criteria even if this is their prime intention. The Czech Republic, for example, does not expect to meet the deficit criterion until 2006 and has signalled that it will not seek to move quickly to Stage 3. Others such as Poland are concerned to make more progress in real convergence. These decisions lie rather outside the case studies we move on to, but the same principles apply.

3
The EMU Constitution

A constitution has two key functions: structurally it defines the institutions and the powers that they can exercise and substantively, it sets out key values and goals according to which those powers are exercised (Walker, 1996: 270). The articulation of values and goals institutionalises the underlying normative vision, but that vision alone cannot control and constrain the way power is exercised. It is the structural elements of the constitution that both allocate powers and control their exercise, and it is these structural elements that are the focus of this chapter.

While the text of a constitution may be constant, the constitutional settlement remains a dynamic process where there is ongoing bargaining. This bargaining allows for changes in institutional set up, values and goals over time. As North and Weingast (1989: 806) point out, the incentives for compliance with an existing constitution are not the same as those for entering into the constitutional bargain in the first place and hence the constitution must address future compliance problems for all the parties. While repeat games help in reenforcing the constitutional bargain where reputation is an issue, they are not sufficient to prevent reneging. This creates the need for institutional arrangements, especially at times when Member States might face asymmetric shocks. These arrangements are critical for ensuring a credible commitment by the constituents to the bargain and hence to the stability of the system underpinned by the constitutional arrangement.

While there is a vast literature on the vexed question of whether there is an EU constitution (e.g. McCormick, 1993; Weiler, 1997), this chapter does not enter into that debate. Instead it takes as a given that insofar as there is an institutional framework, powers exercised and key values and goals, the notion of a constitution is a powerful conceptual device for understanding how power is exercised and rendered accountable within EMU. This chapter discusses the structures of EMU in relation to economic and monetary policy. It first sets out the institutional structure and how power is allocated between the ECB, the Council and the Commission, before exploring the control of those powers by focusing on accountability via the European

Parliament and the European Court in particular. It concludes that in relation to monetary policy, while independence is a key value in the constitutional framework, it must be seen as relative rather than absolute. The interdependence of the ECB is particularly apparent in the context of the interdependence of monetary and fiscal policy. In relation to economic policy, the chapter concludes that while interdependence is explicitly recognised through the requirement of Member State co-ordination, accountability mechanisms are weak, mainly relying on reputational damage as a mechanism for securing compliance. As the debacle surrounding the failure to move towards sanctions against France and Germany in November 2003 indicated, the issue of the credibility of the commitment of the Member States to fiscal stability is crucial. Damage to reputation is not enough to ensure economic policy co-ordination: first, if the credibility of the mechanisms for co-ordination is called into question as inappropriate and even 'stupid';[1] second, if states' priorities prove to be substantially different from those previously agreed to; third, if there is a marked divergence in the rhetoric of all states being treated the same and the reality of more lenient treatment for larger states and fourth if criticism of a Member State by the Commission or Ecofin generates little or no opposition at the domestic level against the government's economic policies. In these circumstances, reform of the Stability and Growth Pact is desirable to ensure that its goals are once again seen as credible and its sanctioning mechanisms productive, and thus that the stability of economic policy co-ordination and, in turn, of monetary policy are underpinned.

3.1 Institutions

3.1.1 The European system of central banks

Under the EMU constitutional arrangement, the objective is to establish a common currency with monetary policy defined by the uniform value of price stability. While regard is also to general economic policies in the Union,[2] this is secondary to that of price stability. The institutional arrangements emphasise price stability as the key objective, with the ECB having responsibility for securing it, while the European System of Central Banks (ESCB) is the structure within which the ECB and national central banks conduct monetary policy. The Bank, while not an EU institution in the existing Treaty, is in the new constitutional treaty (Art. I-30(3)), has full legal personality, the power to issue general and specific legislative measures without reference to any other institution and the power to fine undertakings that fail to comply with them.[3] It must also be consulted and can give an opinion on both EC and national legislative proposals in its field of competence.[4] The ESCB controls the issuance of currency,[5] holds and manages foreign reserves, promotes smooth operation of the payments system[6] and of prudential supervision, and shares responsibility for external policy in a complex manner with the Council (also, constitutional treaty Art. III-185).[7] Decisions relating to monetary policy are taken by the ECB Governing Council, which consists of the heads of the national central banks of the 12 Member States[8] and the six member ECB executive (Louis, 1998: 55; Usher, 2000: ch. 10).[9] The ECB Executive Board then implements those decisions. The heads of all the central banks, including those states not in the euro area, meet with the President and Vice President, as the General Council, but this body has no decision-making powers other than the fixing of exchange rates for new entrants (Bini Smaghi and Casini, 2000: 380). This power is of some significance in the light of the accession of the ten new Member States all of which participate in EMU since accession but will not join the euro area until at least 2007. This is because they have to be members of the ERM for two years before they can adopt the euro – and membership of the ERM was not available before accession. Substantively, they have to show that their public finances are sustainable and that their inflation is close to the three best performing Member States before they can join the euro area.[10]

The ECB is an institution formally defined by its independence, independence being seen as essential for the credibility of central bank decisions and the objective of price stability (Hadjiemmanuil, 2000: 153; Jayasuriya, 2001: 113; De Grauwe, 2003: ch. 7). Independence is reinforced through the precondition of independence for national central banks.[11] The voting model in the Governing Council means national central bankers are in a clear majority over the ECB executive, but in practice the Board dominates the decision-making of the Council. This domination by the Board will be retained as the euro area enlarges (Allsopp and Artis, 2003: 11). To ensure the Governing Council can continue to function after enlargement, the one-person–one-vote model is broken in so far as voting rights for national bankers are capped at 15 votes and will be rotated among two or three groups with rotation determined objectively by size of economy and importance of financial sector.[12] At the moment each member is notionally equal with consensus rather than voting being the standard practice (Dyson, 2000: 33). After the creation of groups of members, some with votes and some without, all will be entitled to attend meetings but only some will have votes, changing the symbolic importance of one-member–one-vote while attempting to ensure the Council is representative of the larger economies (Paczyński, 2003). Irrespective of the formal position, larger states are arithmetically more important in the assessment of monetary conditions in the overall euro area (Levitt and Lord, 2000: 124) and the influence of the central bankers of the larger states may be greater than that of smaller economies (Favero *et al.*, 2000: 30). For smaller economies, the credibility of their economic argument is more contingent on their reputation for sound economic management and on the quality of their economic arguments (Goodfriend, 1999: 10).

The criteria for appointment of members of the Executive Board underline the independence of its personnel, but the process shows the extent to which it is a political and hence highly interdependent process with Member State governments in charge. The criteria for appointment are that members must be of high standing and have expertise in monetary and banking matters,[13] and they are appointed for eight years. Appointment is by the EC (euro area members) on the basis of Council recommendations after consulting the parliament and Governing Council.[14] National interests are underlined in this appointment process by the fact the Commission plays no formal role. This could be seen in practice in the 'horse trading' over the nationality of the first President, Wim Duisenberg and the fudge over whether or not he would retire after four years to make way for a French national (Levitt and Lord, 2000: 204). It was also seen in the subsequent replacement of a Spaniard by a Spaniard (in 2004) and of an Italian by an Italian (in 2005), paving the way for the last of the original appointees (Otmar Issing, a German) also to be replaced by a compatriot. In contrast, the removal of a member of the Executive Board is effectively insulated from political influence. A member of the Executive Board can be compulsorily retired by the European Court of Justice if they no longer fulfil the conditions required for the performance of their duties or for gross misconduct but only the Executive Board or the Governing Council can apply to the Court.[15]

3.1.2 The Council

European monetary union is organised asymmetrically (Verdun, 1996). There is a uniform monetary policy, co-ordination of fiscal policy and other aspects of economic policy through binding rules and the open method (Hodson and Maher, 2001). Formal responsibility for all aspects of economic policy remains with the Member States. Yet, price stability does not exist in a vacuum and its achievement is contingent on the overall economic policy-mix (Begg *et al.*, 2003) and the extent to which it supports the sound money, sound finance paradigm (Chapter 4). The main challenge facing the constitutional bargain for EMU is how to design an institutional framework that supports and signifies state commitment to price stability through the operation of economic policy that promotes balanced economic growth and allows sufficient flexibility so that discretion can be exercised to take account of variations between state economies, and thus avoid an inappropriate 'one-size-fits-all' approach to economic policy (Begg and Schelkle, 2004b). With the current emphasis on co-ordination, a plethora of committees and policy-making processes has emerged under the ambit of the Council. This is in sharp contract to monetary policy where there is a single institution, the ECB, responsible.

The European Council

In addition to its role as the body that oversees revision of the Treaty, including the provisions relating to EMU, the EC keeps economic policy under ongoing review, with questions of system design, timetabling and objectives to the fore (European Council, 2001b, 2002; Hodson and Maher, 2001: 729). The policy cycle culminates annually with the 'Spring Economic Summit' at which the Council meets to discuss economic, social and environmental policies of the Union (European Council, 2002). It reviews performance in the previous year in the light of the Lisbon objectives, sets out future policy objectives for the EU and endorses specific recommendations for each state in the BEPGs that now run for three years (Commission, 2003a). Since the decisions taken at the 2005 spring European Council, the BEPGs will be more closely integrated with the Lisbon strategy, implying closer co-ordination across policy domains. Nevertheless, responsibility for policy remains firmly at the national level with co-ordination facilitated ultimately through peer pressure, the idea being that states will be anxious to adopt best practice and to avoid loss of face with the benefit of repeat plays creating further momentum for co-ordination. The weakness in this bargain is that there are no institutional mechanisms to address conflict or an unwillingness to work towards benchmarks.

The Economic and Finance Ministers (Ecofin)

Article 99EC requires the Member States to coordinate their economic policies through the Council of Ministers. Ecofin is thus the central coordinating body for economic policy (European Council, 1997: para. 44; Dyson, 2000: 73), but its role in monetary policy is limited to its President having the power to attend the meetings of the Governing Council of the ESCB to present a motion, participate in discussions but not to vote.[16] In practice, the President rarely attends these meetings.

One of the consequences of EMU has been an increase in the power and influence of Ecofin, with it developing a network of committees, which report primarily, if not exclusively, to it. Ecofin is mainly responsible for the operation of the BEPGs – the key co-ordinating mechanism for economic policy. It both reports to the spring Economic Summit of the EC on the BEPGs and gives effect to any Summit conclusions on them. In order to evaluate the operation of the guidelines, and to ensure closer co-ordination, the Council monitors economic developments in each state and the Union through multilateral surveillance[17] (Harden *et al.*, 1999: 155). The states submit annual stability programmes to Ecofin (convergence programmes are submitted for states outside the euro area, including the new states that submitted their first convergence programmes in May 2004, Commission, 2003d), so that it can form a picture of the overall state of economic development within each state, and throughout the Union (Hodson and Maher, 2002). Where Ecofin believes there is a significant divergence from the medium-term budgetary objective, it issues a recommendation to the state concerned to make the necessary adjustment mechanisms, in order to avoid an excessive deficit. Under the constitutional treaty, the maverick state will not have a vote, an improvement on current arrangements

(European Convention, 2003: Art. III-179(4)).[18] Multilateral surveillance with its emphasis on an early warning system, non-binding recommendations and peer pressure, leads to the more formal Stability and Growth Pact, which requires states to maintain a sound budgetary position of close to balance or in surplus as a means of dealing with nominal cyclical budgetary fluctuations and in order to support price stability. The aim is to avoid excessive deficits of more than 3% of GDP. If the Commission triggers the excessive deficit procedure,[19] then Ecofin makes recommendations to the state concerned, threatening to go public if the state fails to comply. The states being investigated can vote as to the existence of the EDP but not on any other step in the procedure. The Draft Constitution, however, would no longer allow the state under review to vote (Draft Constitution, 2004: Art. III-184). Voting is by qualified majority which is defined as at least 55% of the other states representing Member States comprising at least 65% of the population of the euro area states. (A blocking minority must include at least the minimum number of states representing more than 35% of the population of the euro area states, and one other member. If this blocking minority cannot be achieved, then the qualified majority shall be deemed attained.) In practice, recommendations have been made public immediately, it being politically useful for national governments to be able to point to them either as a way of justifying changes to economic policy or as a way of showing how the government is willing to 'stand up to Europe' in order to protect national interests. If non-compliance is persistent over time, Ecofin can take a number of measures culminating in a fine of up to 0.5% of GDP. It is only within the excessive deficit procedure that Ecofin can take binding measures and then only after several intermediate steps, designed to secure voluntary compliance.

The operation of multilateral surveillance and of the EDP is controversial. Ireland was the first state to receive a recommendation under multilateral surveillance when its budget was seen as pro-cyclical and inflationary. The recommendation was controversial because of doubts over the accuracy of the economic forecasting and analysis, with the OECD favouring the Irish position (OECD, 2001; Hodson and Maher, 2001: 736). Subsequent experience of multilateral surveillance has failed to quell concerns. Ecofin failed to issue a warning against Germany in 2002 even though the Commission deemed its deficit to be approaching excessive levels (Ecofin, 2002a: 9). Ecofin did not want to censure Germany in an election year – showing that multilateral surveillance is seen as having some political impact (*The Economist*, 2002; Begg *et al.*, 2003; Maher, 2004). Portugal was spared a warning being able to piggyback on Germany's predicament (Ecofin, 2002a: 22; Buti and Giudice, 2002: 841). Recommendations were issued about both Portugal in November (see Ecofin, 2002b) and Germany in January 2003 (see Ecofin, 2003a). Concerns about delay and consistency in the operation of multilateral surveillance (House of Lords Select

Committee on the EU, 2003: 18) have been overshadowed by the operation of the EDP.

The Ecofin has shown itself singularly unwilling to trigger the pecuniary stages of the Pact. In November 2003, recommendations of the Commission to set time limits for France and Germany to take specified steps to reduce their deficits did not receive the required number of votes, voting being by qualified majority of euro area states excluding the recalcitrant state (Ecofin, 2003b).[20] Instead, Ecofin adopted conclusions by a two-thirds majority vote setting out agreed steps to be taken by France and Germany explicitly stating that the EDP was in abeyance with no decision under Article 104(9). A decision under Article 104(9) triggers the setting of targets and time limits constituting the first formal steps towards sanctions. Ecofin clearly wanted to avoid fixed deadlines and the path to sanctions, as it did not simply amend the Commission recommendations to introduce softer targets and longer time limits. At the same time, a majority of states wanted to ensure there were some benchmarks and deadlines (however soft) for Germany and France to commit to, with the threat that the EDP could be[21] re-activated against them if they did not work to reduce their deficits (Bandilla, 2004: 3) – hence the conclusions. The conclusions of Ecofin were successfully challenged before the European Court of Justice by the Commission with the Court indicating that while failure to vote in favour of a Commission recommendation leaves it in abeyance, Ecofin cannot then unilaterally agree new terms and conditions with the recalcitrant states.[22]

Despite the enhanced status of Ecofin following EMU, there remain serious concerns as to the effectiveness of economic policy co-ordination where there is such a strong emphasis on voluntariness and peer pressure and a clear unwillingness to move to more formal sanctions. While Ecofin stressed that all states remained committed to sound economic policies as a common goal even as it refused to move to the next stage with France and Germany (Ecofin, 2003b: 21), the nature of that commitment is not clear. The threshold of a deficit of 3% of GDP triggering the EDP is no longer credible and the issue is whether or not a very firm commitment to such a measure is necessary for the overall objective of price stability. The consensus is that there is a need to place greater emphasis on the medium-term budgetary target of close to balance or in surplus rather than the short-term (but more visible) target of a budget deficit. The Commission has suggested (2002b) and Ecofin accepted (2003a) a series of reforms of the Pact including allowing for the assessment of national budgets in cyclically adjusted terms; an emphasis on the medium-term rule of close to balance or in surplus and regard to the sustainability of public finances so as to allow temporary deficits in excess of 3%. These proposals were eventually agreed by Ecofin in March 2005 and subsequently endorsed by the EC (see Chapter 4).

The mechanisms designed to address compliance problems with the economic policy rules in the Pact also lack credibility. It is difficult to advance any argument as to how a fine will assist a state to secure sound finances and not further exacerbate them. More prosaically but almost as important, the lack of common statistical methods meant the system for evaluating budget deficits lacked transparency and varied between states. A code of conduct on statistical practice has now been agreed and should improve transparency allowing for better surveillance and early detection (Commission, 2002c), but the revelations (only) in 2004 that the Greek government had 'cooked the books' in the run-up to euro area accession shows that the problem remains a difficult one.

The states, at least on some level, remain committed to economic co-ordination as they clearly engage with the process even if operating contrary to its spirit. A more worrying trend is where states fail to engage; for example, the Italian government released revised budget plans in July 2001 two days after the Eurogroup meeting, without having mentioned them at that meeting (Hodson and Maher, 2002). Such behaviour is indicative of how domestic politics can trump economic co-ordination (Norman, 2001) and is likely to continue to do so. The July 2004 court ruling, however, has allowed tempers to cool and has provided some clarity as to the respective roles of the Commission and Council, and the limits on the scope of Council discretion. In doing so, it has provided the impetus for further reform.

The Eurogroup

The main constraint on this newfound status of Ecofin is that, because not all Member States are in EMU, matters relating to the euro area are discussed in the Euro-group, an informal, monthly meeting of euro area ministers, which then reports to Ecofin. Informality is reinforced by the fact the meetings are attended only by the minister and an adviser and meetings are confidential, although it is standard practice now to issue a press release after each meeting. Dialogue with the ECB is secured by the regular attendance of the ECB President while the Commission attends as an observer, occasionally providing background discussion papers (Lemierre, 1999: 50; Bini Smaghi and Casini, 2000: 383). Meetings are held immediately prior to those of Ecofin, which is the final decision-making body. The 'outs' can participate in discussions either by invitation or at their own request save in relation to single currency matters (Levitt and Lord, 2000: 218). Despite its absence from the Treaty, the Eurogroup is a very important body which addresses an institutional gap viz. co-ordination between states where not all Member States have joined EMU. Its informality is a strength, facilitating frank exchanges and consensus building, thereby providing a key co-ordinating mechanism especially over the medium term (Peutter, 2003: 1). That status is, however, also problematic in that there is a risk that, despite the formal legal position, Ecofin as the official decision-making body merely rubber-stamps its decisions (Levitt and Lord, 2000: 76; Paczyński, 2003: 21). The Commission has called for its status to be formalised within Ecofin so the

EC institutions can fully participate. This formal argument does not address the functional nature of the Eurogroup nor does it address the impact formalisation would have on the way states currently participate and engage within it. The Commission's preference highlights its unease with new forms of governance where it is being sidelined (Commission, 2001b: 7; Scott, 2002a).

The proposed constitution includes specific provisions and a protocol on the Eurogroup (Draft Constitution, 2004: III-195) thus giving the group formal status but without any constraint. Indeed, the protocol states that the group shall meet informally the aim being to improve co-ordination through enhanced dialogue. The only clarification of any real substance is that the eurogroup members must appoint a President for a two and half year term. The draft constitution also expressly reserves to euro area members meeting in Council the power to adopt measures to strengthen fiscal co-ordination and the adoption of economic guidelines, which are to be consistent with the BEPGs (2004: Art. III-194). This further underlines the separation of the euro area states from all Member States – a demarcation that has become necessary since the 2004 enlargement. Now that there are more states in Stage 2 of EMU than in Stage 3 and hence given the way voting currently operates in Ecofin, the euro area states cannot secure a qualified majority and those outside the euro area could constitute a blocking minority. The constitution redefines what constitutes a qualified majority, but even if adopted, it will not come into force until 2009 leaving the existing system in operation until then (Paczyński, 2003: 22).

The tension between an absence of formal power and consensus building (the Eurogroup), on the one hand, and formal power constrained by more formal discussions and adoption of national positions (Ecofin), on the other, goes to the heart of the tension in the asymmetry of the EMU constitution. The need for repeat games to develop consensus over common goals and to embed them so they are not reneged on is central to this new constitutional project. At the same time, this policy learning and bargaining process needs to be supported by more formal structures which secure the fundamental bargains that emerge so as to ensure the credibility of the system as seen in the commitment of the states to it especially at times of asymmetric shock. The limited reforms in the proposed constitution seek to strike a balance between these tensions by giving the Eurogroup a place in the constitution and ring-fencing the powers of the euro area members while at the same time expressly endorsing the informal operation of the group.

3.1.3 The Council committees

The Economic and Financial Committee

Of the three main committees that support Ecofin, the most important is the Economic and Financial Committee (EFC), the successor of the Monetary Committee (Hanny and Wessels, 1998; Verdun, 2000). This 54-member committee with two members (strictly, 'no more than two') from the Commission, the ECB and each Member State[23] consists of senior finance or central bank officials who are appointed as experts, not national representatives. This emphasis on expertise combined with the continuity of membership, the atmosphere of confidence in the committee and the fact members also have the confidence of the relevant national Minister, means that there is sufficient leeway in discussion for consensus to be the modus operandi with areas of disagreement being referred back to Ecofin for further guidance (Verdun, 2000). These characteristics also give it a level of influence that belies its formal advisory role. It prepares the work of the Council, its reports often being accepted by Ecofin and it also provides the forum within which the Commission, ECB and Member States engage in dialogue. It is akin to the Committee of Permanent Representatives (COREPER) in that it prepares the work of the Council but differs in that its members are not appointed as national representatives. It is required to act without prejudice to COREPER.[24] In practice, the fact the EFC Chair attends Ecofin meetings and the undoubted expertise of its members, means that it dominates monetary and financial policy (Hanny and Wessels, 1998: 119). It has several functions specified by the Treaty itself[25] including an important consultative and review function in relation to the economic and financial situation of the EU and the Member States as co-ordinated through the Pact. It tempers the extent to which the Commission can shape the agenda, for example, in relation to the excessive deficit procedure. If the EFC is of the opinion that there is an excessive deficit but the Commission thinks there is not, then the latter must give reasons for its conclusions to the Council, leaving it to arbitrate between the differing opinions with the burden of proof on the Commission.[26] Overall, it is a joint forum in relation to horizontal co-ordination across policy sectors especially monetary and fiscal policy (Padoa-Schioppa, 1999: 21).

Now that there are 25 rather than 15 EU Member States, that the EFC works in two formations to ensure the ongoing smooth operation of the Committee. The restricted formation excludes members from national central banks, leaving it to the ECB representative to ensure that its position on monetary policy is not undermined. There is also a full formation that includes the national central bankers (Commission, 2003b).

Economic Policy Committee

This Committee long predates EMU, having been set up in 1974.[27] It consists of two members each from the Commission, the ECB and the Member States. It promotes co-ordination of national short- and medium-term economic policies and analyses developments in national economies to discover reasons for divergence. Its main policy concern is with structural policy and it implements the Cardiff process, reviewing national reports and drawing up benchmarks and guidelines for states. It helps formulate the BEPGs as well as contributing to multilateral surveillance (Hodson and

Maher, 2001: 729).[28] It organises the macroeconomic dialogue set up at the Cologne Summit. This meeting between the social partners and ministers, the ECB and the Commission is of some importance to neo-corporatist states where it provides a high level forum for the social partners to discuss with ministers and the ECB economic policy and the scope and direction of co-ordination. The EPC takes a broader and more long-term view than the more senior committee of the EFC. This is because of the range of its tasks, the fact that its members are relatively free to bring up matters for discussion and the scope for reports to be prepared on its own motion or at the request of the Council. This relatively broad remit means it sometimes reports to Council formations other than Ecofin. The flexibility of the committee to analyse and explore a wide range of macroeconomic issues may create tensions between committees as to jurisdiction. There are no formal mechanisms for resolving such differences, with the chairs of each of the committees having a role to play in ensuring there is complimentarity rather than overlap between the committees.

Employment Committee

This more recent committee[29] replaces the Employment and Labour Market Committee and monitors employment policy under the Luxembourg Process reviewing tri-annual national action plans (NAPs) and formulating a Joint Employment Report for the Union with the Commission (Chapter 5). It also contributes to framing major economic policy guidelines in order to ensure consistency with the employment guidelines. It facilitates information exchange between Member States and the Commission and participates in the macroeconomic dialogue. As with structural policy, the emphasis is on action at the national level and enabling national policy initiatives. The increased emphasis on the structural dimension to unemployment has brought the Economic Policy Committee and Employment Committee into close proximity with one another in recent years. Membership consists of two senior bureaucrats from each state (usually from the department responsible for employment policy) and the Commission who are appointed for their expertise. Members on the Economic and Financial Committee and the Economic Policy Committee are generally based at the government department with responsibility for finance. As a result, where tensions exist at national level between government departments, these can resurface between the Committees. In those Member States that have separate Economic and Finance Ministries, the possibility for inter-jurisdictional tension is greater still.

Social Protection Committee

The Social Protection Committee (SPC) was established on the basis of a Council decision in June 2000[30] and its status has since been enhanced by its inclusion in the EC Treaty following the Treaty of Nice (Commission,

2003c).[31] The SPC is charged with promoting and advising on co-operation in the field of social protection. It is to monitor the social situation and the development of social protection policies in the Member States and to provide an annual report of its activities. The bulk of its work is reactive to the mandates given to it by the Council in the light of the Lisbon agenda with four areas of particular importance: social inclusion, pensions, health care and making work pay (Chapter 5). The Committee consists of two representatives and two alternates from each Member State and from the Commission – with membership much increased since enlargement and without any change proposed in the draft constitution (Art. III-217).

3.1.4 Commission

Despite the centrality of the ECB in monetary policy and the emphasis on intensive transgovernmentalism in relation to economic policy with a primary role for the Council and its related committees (Wallace, 2000: 33; Hodson and Maher, 2001: 735), the Commission still retains some formal functions in relation to economic policy in particular. It retains its overall role as representative of the Union interest and as such attends most Council and committee meetings. Attendance at these meetings ensures it is well informed of economic trends and developments among states. In addition, it also provides administrative and technical support to the Economic and Financial Committee, the Economic Policy Committee, the Employment Committee and the Social Protection Committee. Its involvement with these committees gives it some role in the open method that it identifies as providing analysis, neutrality (presumably as between states only, given its role as guardian of the Treaty) and synopsis (Commission, 2001a: para. 13). Overall, the OMC is state centred with the Commission and the European Parliament both marginalised to varying degrees.

Formally, the Commission plays two key roles of providing information and gate keeping, both of which give it an important agenda-setting role (Pollack, 1997), a role that is however tempered by the powerful Economic and Financial Committee. One of its key roles is the provision of information. Significantly, its data are used for assessing whether the budget deficit threshold has been breached under the excessive deficit procedure. This circumvents the ambiguity that could arise of deficits being measured by a number of parties according to a variety of methodologies. The Commission's reports also form the basis of the Ecofin's assessment of national stability programmes.[32]

The Commission also has an important gatekeeper function at a number of junctures. The BEPGs are drawn up or revised on the basis of its recommendation to Ecofin.[33] Opinions of Ecofin on national stability and convergence programmes are adopted on the basis of a Commission recommendation[34] and where national policies are deemed inconsistent with the guidelines or risk the proper functioning of EMU, the Council can make recommendations to the state concerned on the basis of Commission recommendations.[35] Under the proposed constitution, the powers of the Commission will be increased in that it will be able to issue a warning to the state concerned. This represents a compromise as a warning does not seem to have the status of a recommendation and the Council still retains the power to issue a recommendation with both powers more or less freestanding (Draft Constitution, 2004: Art. III-179(4)). The excessive deficit procedure (EDP) can be triggered only by a recommendation from the Commission. Even if the state does not have a budgetary deficit exceeding the threshold in the Treaty, the Commission can trigger the procedure if it thinks that there is a risk of such a deficit, giving it considerable discretion.[36] The Council can request a Commission recommendation and while the Council Resolution says such a request will be granted as a rule, the Treaty places no such obligation on the Commission simply requiring it to examine the request and submit its conclusions without delay (Harden, 1999: 81).[37] The Council resolution, while politically important, formally cannot override the Treaty that is at the top of the EC hierarchy of rules. Since the introduction of the Pact the issue has not been one of the Commission being slow to act, but of the unwillingness of the states to reprimand peers in breach of the 3% budget deficit rule, highlighting the difference between the economic and political climate in which the Pact was drawn up and in which it now operates.

Unlike Article 249(1), the Commission recommends rather than proposes action under the EDP; consequently, a qualified majority in Ecofin rather than unanimity is all that is necessary to amend the Commission position (Harden, 1999: 81). The fact that the Commission's recommendations are delivered to Ecofin in the form of an open letter, however, means that the former can make its views felt whether the latter supports them or not. By the time Germany escaped censure at the hands of Ecofin in February 2002 it had been named and to a certain degree shamed at the hands of the Commission (Commission, 2002a), and there was extensive media coverage of the Ecofin meeting of 25 November 2003 when it refused to follow the Commission recommendation to start the process leading to formal censure and sanction of France and Germany. Two changes have been made increasing the power of the Commission in the proposed constitution. First, if the Commission considers that there is, or may be, an excessive deficit, it shall address an opinion to the Member State concerned (Draft Constitution, 2004: Art. III-184(5)). Second, as suggested by the Commission, its recommendations to Ecofin that there is an excessive deficit will be replaced by proposals (Commission, 2002a: 7; Draft Constitution, 2004: Art. III-184(6)).

3.2 Accountability

In order to ensure that power is exercised within the scope of competence and in a manner consistent with the agreed values and goals of EMU, institutional arrangements are built into the system. Accountability can follow traditional hierarchical forms where there are reporting obligations, for example, to Parliament and through judicial review (Scott, 2000: 40). It can be managerial – through the internal administration of the agency, and a form of broader public accountability through dissemination of reasoned decisions taken (Hadjiemmanuil, 2000: 158). Broader public accountability can be a matter of practice by an institution whereby it provides greater transparency in its procedures and decision-making. These traditional hierarchical forms of accountability have been extended in the light of new governance methods such as that found in economic co-ordination. Where governance is fragmented, policy actors are interdependent on each other for information, authority, expertise and legitimacy (Scott, 2000: 50). Because of this interdependence, they depend on each other for legitimation in relation to shared constituencies, such as the markets in the context of monetary and fiscal policy. One of the weaknesses in economic co-ordination is that constituencies are fractured between the state and European levels. Thus, where a national constituency is deemed more important than the collective European constituencies of other states, EMU institutions and the rest of the population, the commitment to the constitutional bargain and fear of loss of reputation among the supra-national constituencies will be diminished if not lost. Even where there is consensus as to policy beliefs, this is not the same as convergence in policy outcomes (McNamara, 1999: 458). It is this disjunction between beliefs and outcomes that highlights the need for formal mechanisms to lock in, where necessary, the bargain that articulates agreed policy beliefs.

Within EMU, there are two main tensions in the institutional framework in relation to formal accountability. First, the independence of the ECB, which is a keystone of its credibility and of the price stability objective, leaves few formal accountability mechanisms. Yet accountability is vital for legitimising independence within a democratic political structure, because independence imposes an obligation to explain to the public and not just the markets (Dyson, 2000: 238). Second, the co-ordination of economic policy, with responsibility remaining at the national level, means formal accountability mechanisms are also left at the national level. At the Union level, there is a plethora of institutions and processes with little formal accountability. Outside the sphere of monetary policy, accountability depends primarily on peer pressure between Member States and their overall commitment to EMU. The convergence criteria in the Maastricht Treaty were very effective incentives for restrained fiscal policies, because membership of EMU is dependent upon compliance with them. Once membership is achieved, however, there is no corresponding threat of ejection for non-compliance with the fiscal criteria in the Pact. Instead, the threat of a deposit convertible to a fine against the recalcitrant state is regarded as weak or, at best, can be described as symbolic (Wessels and Linsenmann, 2002). Nonetheless, the presence of fiscal criteria backed by sanctions is an incentive for co-ordination, as it provides a framework within which information exchange at the national level with guidelines at the European level may lead to policy formation backed by peer pressure. The question that remains is whether or not that peer pressure will be sufficient to ensure the sort of budgetary restraint necessary to ensure low inflation, especially when approaching a national general election or in the light of an asymmetric shock. The architects of EMU placed considerably more weight on monetary policy and its credibility rather than economic developments. This emphasis could ultimately be self-defeating since even if the ECB earns credibility in the eyes of the markets, the policy landscape within which the ECB makes its decisions – and the commitment of Member States to securing an appropriate policy-mix – could lack credibility.

3.2.1 The ECB

Accountability is important not only to ensure power is exercised appropriately, but also in order to ensure legitimacy of the Bank as an agent of government (Majone, 1998: 24). The ECB enjoys a higher level of independence than the Federal Reserve of the United States and the German Bundesbank but is formally less accountable than either of these two institutions (De Grauwe, 2003: 162). Its independence is underpinned by the fact it has separate legal personality, its members and those of national central banks are immune from political interference[38] and its statute is contained in a protocol to the Treaty and hence can only be amended by the EC, meeting at an intergovernmental conference.[39] While it is charged with ensuring price stability in the Treaty, the Bank – further underlying its autonomy – defines price stability.

On a formal level, the ECB reports annually to the EU institutions and may be heard by committees of the European Parliament.[40] The extent to which these mechanisms go beyond the superficial depends on the goodwill of the ECB as the Treaty does not, for example, specify the content of the ECB reports (Taylor, 2000: 181). In practice, the ECB President has volunteered to appear before the Economic and Monetary Affairs Committee four times a year (Dyson, 2000: 239). These appearances render the monetary policy and the workings of the ECB more transparent and may generate media interest. However, because the statutes of the ECB can only be amended by Treaty revision, requiring the agreement of all the Member States, formally the overview function of the Parliament is limited (De Grauwe, 2000: 162).

As the ECB has adopted informal accountability mechanisms primarily designed to improve transparency, these practices will become difficult to depart from, even though not formally required. For example, it publishes monthly reports and its President holds monthly briefings with the Press after the meeting of the Governing Council. Nonetheless, these measures do not go far enough for some (notably Buiter, 1999), as minutes outlining reasons for decisions at the monthly meetings are not published, although

Issing (1999) mounts a staunch defence (see also, de Haan and Eijffinger, 2000). The argument against providing such information is the collective responsibility of the ECB (Dyson, 2000: 239) and the avoidance of inappropriate national government influence on members of the Council. The independence of the Bank and its members is given greater weight than the need for accountability through the sort of transparency found in the Bank of England. Arguably, the very high level of personnel independence (de Haan and Eijffinger, 2000: 44) would allow for transparency. The members of the Governing Council are top professionals in their field, and their professional integrity is such that they should be willing and able to defend themselves in the light of criticisms of any decisions they take. Similarly, it can be argued that there would be less inappropriate pressure if voting were made public (even if it is just to show that decisions are taken by consensus), as any member would have to explain any unusual change of position. At the moment, should a state wish to exercise influence, it would be difficult to establish whether it had done so or not given the opacity of the ECB decision-making procedures. The constitutional treaty does little to change the accountability of the Bank save to subject it (and the European Court) to a general requirement of transparency when exercising its administrative tasks (Art. III-399). Transparency however has a role to play over and above any constitutional value in ensuring the legitimacy of the eurosystem. If the way the bank is likely to react is understood and can be anticipated by the private sector and other policy actors, then this in itself renders the system more stable in the light of any economic shocks. Thus transparency is important not just as a constitutional value but also in substantive terms in ensuring the effective operation of the eurosystem.

Using principal/agent analysis, the scope of delegation of power to the ECB and the potential for securing accountability (or control) become apparent (Elgie, 2002). Under this theory, a principal delegates to an agent with the expectation that the agent will act in a manner consistent with the preferences of the principal, the motivation being a reduction in transaction costs – the agent being better equipped to carry out the relevant tasks(s) than the principal. One of the hazards for the principal in this arrangement is that there may be shirking or slippage by the agent that is deliberate or structurally induced departures from the preferences of the principal. In order to limit this, controls (including accountability mechanisms) are necessary. These controls can be *ex ante*, for example the criteria for appointment of personnel, competence and institutional design. *Ex post* controls are oversight and even sanctions. There are no sanctions for the ECB, although the Treaty could, in principle, be amended to allow for them.

Oversight can be hierarchical through centralised mechanisms such as reporting to parliament. Informal oversight can also develop over time. The institutional design of the ECB is such that its independence necessarily allows it to depart from the policy beliefs and preferences of its principals (the states), other than price stability – the only goal articulated in the Treaty. This is seen as essential for its credibility. As Elgie (2002) notes, the ECB has been criticised for not using its discretion to give sufficient weight to the secondary objectives in the Treaty (to support the general economic objectives of the Union), especially as the policy priorities of the states have changed since the Treaty was drafted. While this criticism is probably exaggerated and the evidence suggests that ECB decisions have, in fact been more balanced than is generally appreciated (Surico, 2003), there is a strong case for it paying more attention to developments in the real economy. If its sole focus is on the inflation aspect of inflation targeting, this risks downplaying its role in stabilisation more generally (Allsopp and Artis, 2003: 9). Elgie argues that *ex post* controls can be increased, in particular non-standard oversight. For example, the role of the European Parliament has grown in importance and there is potential scope for the Eurogroup to exert indirect influence over the ECB thus bringing the preferences of the states (the principals) and the ECB (as agent) closer together. This may, though, assume that there are clear preferences in the Eurogroup when the failure to trigger the EDP shows a degree of equivocation, with the states still seeking to rely on peer pressure rather than bringing the full force of the EDP to bear (Elgie, 2002: 197).

Interdependence is manifest *inter alia* through information flows. The ECB has a presence on the myriad of committees that have emerged in the economic policy sphere: it can and does attend the meetings of the Ecofin, the Eurogroup, the EFC and the EPC, as well as participating in the macroeconomic dialogue. Even where it has no vote, it is in a position to ensure that the agreed sound money–sound finance paradigm is not forgotten and is even advanced. It also gleans a fairly comprehensive picture of the economic landscape within which it has to develop and apply its monetary policy through the information flows that arise from its attendance at these committees. Information is also acquired from the meetings of the Governing Council of the ECB and the ESCB. The Commission is also represented on these committees (and at the ECB Governing Council) ensuring that it too has a wide range of information. On the other hand while the Ecofin President can also attend meetings of the ECB Governing Council,[41] he has thus far not always chosen to do so.

On a managerial level, the ECB is accountable to the Court of Auditors (Amtenbrink, 1999: 359). It asserted managerial independence when it set up an anti-fraud regime so that it would not be subject to review by OLAF (the EU's anti-fraud office), but the Commission successfully challenged this. The European Court of Justice (an institution also sensitive to the importance of its political independence, but which had been willing to be subject to OLAF), found the Bank should be subject to OLAF. It applied a functional test to the Bank's independence, examining whether review by OLAF would undermine its ability to perform independently the specific tasks conferred on it by the Treaty. Because OLAF was itself an independent body meeting high standards of confidentiality, being subject to it would not threaten the Bank's independence. It also drew a distinction between independence (necessary for Treaty conferred tasks) and separateness. The ECB, like other EC institutions, is independent but not separate from the rest of the Community. Finally, the Bank had pointed to the fact that economic operators saw it being subject to OLAF as a threat to its independence. The Court rejected this argument saying that such concerns were based on either a lack of information or a failure to see the full picture.[42] The concerns of such constituencies are not paramount in the eyes of the Court and cannot override the application of Community law to the Bank. Thus the Bank is subject to managerial accountability mechanisms, and its independence is defined by the Court as functional vis-à-vis its Treaty tasks and inclusive within the overall treaty framework.

3.2.2 The European Parliament

The Economic and Monetary Affairs Committee (EMAC) of the European Parliament has responsibility for monetary and economic policy planning and the ECB President (and/or a senior member of the Executive Council) appears before it at least four times a year. While these encounters have not yet attracted the same sort of close attention as their equivalent in the US context, both parties take them seriously and the committee has appointed a number of experts to assist it in preparing its members and their questioning. The Committee can issue influential reports, but its powers are limited given the insularity of the Bank, the voluntariness of its appearances before the committee and the fact Parliament lacks formal powers over the ECB. Nevertheless, there is scrutiny and Parliament is adept at maximising whatever power it does have. The Bank for its part is sensitive to criticisms as to the extent of its independence and has taken its need to account to the Parliament seriously.

Outside of monetary policy, the Parliament's role is primarily receipt of information. It is informed of the BEPGs by the Council President[43] and receives a report from the Commission and Council Presidents on the results of multilateral surveillance.[44] Where a recommendation has been made to a Member State and this has been published then the Council President can be invited before EMAC.[45] The rules for multilateral surveillance were adopted under the old co-operation procedure, which gives the Parliament a greater say than mere consultation, but not as much as it would have with co-decision. The co-operation procedure was retained for these provisions under the Treaty of Amsterdam because of unwillingness to re-open any aspect of EMU (Beaumont and Walker, 1999: 181). The macroeconomic dialogue – a framework designed to be inclusive (of the social partners) and to encourage dialogue – does not include the Parliament. This reflects the extent to which the Parliament is sidelined from policy discussions in the economic sphere. The Commission in its Governance White Paper expressed concern that the exclusion of the Parliament from the open method, and hence from economic policy formation, would lead to an institutional imbalance – presumably reducing accountability and creating legitimacy problems (Commission, 2001a: 21; Commission, 2002d: 7). The rather limited role of the European Parliament also can be seen in the response of Ecofin to the lack of transparency and accountability in economic policy; this was to suggest improved information and dialogue with national parliaments, thus further underlining the intensive transgovernmental nature of economic policy (Ecofin, 1999). The assumption that lies behind this proposal is that, because responsibility lies at the national level, there can be no role for the European Parliament. A better view is that at a minimum, the Parliament could conduct an overview function as the recipient of annual reports from each of the committees involved that could then be discussed within EMAC. The main purpose of such a system would be to render the open method more transparent (given the number of committees and policy areas involved). It would also put EMAC in a better position to evaluate the overall economic policy of the Union.

The reforms of the Stability Pact accepted by the EC in March 2005 make no reference to the European Parliament instead seeking to once again involve national parliaments more closely in the process.

3.2.3 National parliaments

When it comes to the exercise of monetary policy, national central banks, like the ECB, enjoy considerable freedom from political control. National parliaments nonetheless continue to play an important monitoring role with respect to monetary policy, although the strength of accountability mechanisms differs from one Member State to the next. The Finnish Parliament, for example, appoints a Parliamentary Supervisory Council to monitor the policies, procedures and activities of the Bank of Finland. The Governor of the Central Bank of Ireland can be called before the joint committees of the Oireachtas (Parliament) to account for monetary policy developments. The accountability of national central banks is limited by their lack of autonomy outside the context of the Eurosystem, but parliamentary debates can help to improve the transparency of monetary policy.

National parliaments have a greater role to play, however, when it comes to the economic dimension of EMU, where differentiated policies are formulated and delivered at the national level. A recent survey by the Trans European Policy Studies Association (TEPSA, 2002) reveals uneven interest in economic policy co-ordination amongst national parliaments. In the case of the UK, the European Scrutiny Committee of the House of Commons discusses the BEPGs economic policy guidelines, although the committee's reports are 'largely a summary of the guidelines and the UK Government's response to them' (TESPA, 2002: 22). The Austrians too pay scant regard to economic policy co-ordination, with just one reference to the guidelines recorded in parliamentary debates during 2001. Accountability mechanisms are perhaps greatest in the Netherlands, where the guidelines are discussed in a parliamentary session, prior to each meeting of Ecofin. A more detailed discussion of domestic policy action under the guidelines in particular and the economic situation in the EU more generally is conducted by a 'domestic' rather than a 'European' committee, the Standing Parliamentary Commission on Finance (TEPSA, 2002). Improved scrutiny at national level could arguably improve co-ordination between government departments, as turf wars would be more transparent providing an incentive for resolution and, more fundamentally, the extent to which there is co-ordination between national employment, structural and fiscal policies could be rendered more conspicuous. Improved co-ordination at the national level creates a stronger base for co-ordination at the Union level. The transparency engendered by some scrutiny also reduces the risk of lip-service to the open method. The constitutional treaty contains a protocol on the role of national parliaments with the aim of encouraging greater involvement of national parliaments in the activities of the Union. Under paragraph five, the agendas and outcomes of Council of Ministers meetings will be sent to national parliaments as well as national governments. Given the primary role the Council plays in economic policy co-ordination this has the potential to alert national parliaments as to the nature and scope of co-ordination at the EU level. There is no reference to the ECB in the protocol, which will not be in any way accountable directly – even to the limited extent of providing agendas for meetings – to national parliaments.

The reforms of the Stability Pact agreed in March 2005 invite national governments to present their stability/convergence programmes and the Council opinions on them to their national parliaments who may then wish to discuss the follow-up recommendations given under the early warning system of the EDP.

3.2.4 The European Court of Justice

The legal personality of the Bank means it can appear before the European Court (Louis, 1998: 55) and can be either a litigant or defendant. Thus far, employees of the Bank have brought a small number of cases[46] and the Commission successfully challenged the Bank's parallel fraud regime that would have excluded OLAF.[47]

The Court would seem to have a very limited role to play in relation to economic policy, given the lack of formal mechanisms. The BEPGs and multilateral surveillance are not sufficiently juridified to provide a legal basis for judicial review, save where there is a failure to follow procedures, for example, by failing to consult the EFC or the Parliament (Chapter 1; Amtenbrink and de Haan, 2003: 1083). The excessive deficit procedure is the most formal mechanism, yet judicial review is expressly excluded until the Council has set down a time limit for the introduction of measures to reduce the budget deficit following the failure of the recalcitrant state to meet the earlier recommendations of the Council.[48] It is only when the Council proceeds to a decision to intensify or to apply measures including the imposition of a fine that the Court is deemed to have jurisdiction, as the decision creates an obligation with which the state must comply.

The Court reviewed the legality of the outcomes of the controversial November 2003 Ecofin meeting at the behest of the Commission whose recommendation had been substituted by the Council in an attempt to suspend the EDP and set new conditions of compliance for France and Germany. The Court rejected a Commission argument that Ecofin's failure to adopt the Commission recommendations constituted a decision. It did regard the Ecofin conclusions as intended to have legal effects and hence worthy of judicial review. The Court went onto annul the conclusions on three grounds. The EDP can only be put into abeyance for the very limited grounds (not applicable in this case) given in Article 9 of Regulation 1467/1497. Nonetheless, the Court recognised that if there is not sufficient support for recommendations in the Council, then de facto the EDP is put into abeyance. The disputed conclusions went considerably further by saying the EDP would only be left in abeyance as long as France and Germany complied with the new conditions set down therein. The Council did not have the power to suspend the EDP in this way and hence the conclusions were void.

The conclusions were also void because the Council did not have the power to modify the original conditions recommended to France and Germany in January and June of that year by the Council on the heels of a Commission recommendation. Such modification could only take place if the Commission recommended it and that had not happened here. The Council cannot substitute new conditions for those agreed earlier unless invited to do so by the Commission. Finally, on a procedural ground the conclusions were void. They had been adopted only by the euro area states in accordance with Article 104(9), but because – in the eyes of the Court – they were modifying the original recommendations, they should have been adopted under Article 104(7) which requires all the states to have a vote.

Thus the Court confirmed the agenda-setting role of the Commission which cannot be sidestepped by the Council. The Council can however leave the EDP in abeyance if there is not sufficient votes to adopt a recommendation. What should happen if there is deadlock between the Commission and the Council? The Court expressly noted that it was not ruling on such a scenario in this case – in effect inviting another visit to it should it arise. The effect of the judgment was to push further reform up the agenda. It is also likely to re-emphasise the role of the early warning system as Ecofin is going to be even less likely to agree to the existence of a deficit (as currently defined) if it clearly has less control over the procedure than it thought, given the role of the Commission in it. The Court expressly ruled on the roles of the

Council and Commission in the case, but its own role – which would prior to this case have been seen as marginal in the extreme – has proved important, both in defining the scope of the EDP and advancing the reform agenda.

3.3 Concluding comments

Whatever new forms of governance there are within EMU, it is important that the commitment of states to the EMU project is secured. The question of how to embed such state commitment turns on two related issues. First, it relies on a balance being struck between flexible policy-making arrangements where there is sufficient discretion to secure an appropriate response to current economic developments nationally, within the Union, and globally. This is the balance between policy co-ordination through soft law measures where there are no legally binding measures that can be issued against defecting states, and hard law where policy-making occurs within the shadow of the law, with the implication in the latter case that states that fail to comply with certain policy prescriptions face the prospect of sanctions (Begg *et al.*, 2003). On the one hand, the co-ordination of economic policy through the open method is entirely dependent on peer pressure, repeat games and fear of loss of face to secure some consistency in approach across the euro area. Consequently, it lacks any credible sanction. On the other hand, the stability pact is criticised for failing to provide sufficient flexibility for states faced with downturns in their economies (Eichengreen and Wyplosz, 1998).

Second, and related to the first, the credibility of EMU turns on the extent to which each institution is accountable so as to prevent an abuse of power. The ECB is responsible for monetary policy and, although it has very high safeguards to secure its independence, the high level of discretion it has in relation to, for example, the content of reports and appearances before the European Parliament is being eroded by its practices that recognise the importance of accountability. In relation to economic policy, responsibility primarily remains at the national level, but with an obligation to co-ordinate, given the importance of economic policy to the common objective of price stability. Because of decentralisation of policy-making, accountability mechanisms are also primarily national.

In short, the current constitutional arrangement is one where the states are ostensibly responsible only for their own economies, yet for EMU to operate effectively, they must be committed to the overall EMU project and be aware of the role their economic policy decisions will play within that context. They must recognise the interdependence of those policies and the centrality of that interdependence to the success of the EMU. This means that they must be willing to make difficult decisions in the interests of the euro-area public generally, rather than just their own public because membership of EMU requires the states to take account of the other members and the overall economic picture (Joerges, 1996). Evaluating which interest to prioritise may require carrying out an assessment of the weight of each of the national and Union interests at stake (Chalmers, 1998: 326; Maduro, 1998: 169). Member States must develop their policies in a manner consistent with Union law, including the need to provide a policy environment that will lead to price stability (Scharpf, 1999: 197).

While they cannot pursue a common, uniform economic policy, the duty to co-ordinate and the commitment to price stability extend that obligation so as to avoid any reaction that would jeopardise the joint enterprise. The duty of loyalty provision[49] applies to the co-ordination of economic policy, as it does to other areas of Union law, and arguably provides a basis for developing accountability mechanisms for states at the Union level which will help to ensure consistency even in the light of domestic political and/or economic pressures. There are strong economic reasons – the success of EMU – why co-ordination of policy necessarily involves consideration of interests beyond those of the state. The challenge for the current constitutional arrangement is to secure a sufficient counterweight to a narrow definition of economic interests at times of crisis which fails to give due regard to the overall context of EMU, by underpinning the policy-learning and peer pressure of the open method with a rarely to be invoked but nonetheless credible threat of sanction, such as to ensure that even under pressure, the commitment of states to the overall, long-term project is assured. This can be achieved through recognising the interdependence of the institutions of EMU both in terms of achieving policy outcomes and in relation to the credibility and legitimacy of the current constitutional arrangement.

4
Policy Co-ordination under EMU

One of the most important and novel features of EMU as a policy system is the extent to which it relies on policy co-ordination. As explained in Chapter 1, this is a deliberate choice, motivated by a reluctance to push more powers upwards to the Community level in the wake of monetary union. EMU, however, means not just integration of the currency, but also a furthering of the single market and the reduction or elimination of barriers that segment factor markets. It follows that economic policies implemented by one Member State increasingly affect those in others, so that the common interest in the impact of national policies is evident, as is the need to ensure that policies are mutually consistent. Co-ordination therefore has to steer a course between allowing Member States to exercise their discretion, while restricting disruptive policy divergences. Initially, the focus was on co-ordination of fiscal policies and on ensuring the smooth functioning of the single market, but subsequently, machinery for co-ordination has developed for a range of other policies, notably employment.

There are many questions about economic policy co-ordination and strongly held views about its extent or form (see the contributions to, the special issue of *Empirica*, vol. 26(3), published in September 1999; Brunila *et al.*, 2001; Begg, 2002b; Buti *et al.*, 2002; Buti, 2003b). How much co-ordination should there be? Should it be confined to individual policy areas or have a wider remit to cut across policy borders, perhaps even leading to outcomes where bargaining occurs on the settings of different policies? Should it be formal or tacit? What legal and institutional framework is needed if co-ordination is to function well, and can there be effective enforcement, including use of sanctions? How these questions are answered will shape the scope for adjustment and it follows that the character and effectiveness of co-ordination under EMU will, in turn, bear on the prospects for successful economic governance of the euro area.

This chapter assesses the case for co-ordination as opposed to alternative means of economic governance and describes the system for co-ordination that has been put in place for EMU. The first section discusses the advantages and drawbacks of co-ordination and looks back at the evolution of the approaches to it in the EU context. Section 4.2 outlines the co-ordination machinery, then Section 4.3 discusses the system in practice. Concluding comments complete the chapter.

4.1 Why have co-ordination?

Management of any economy requires action by the authorities on a wide range of policies and extensive concertation between different policy actors. Most obviously, macroeconomic steering requires the fiscal and monetary authorities to take account of one another's policy positions in setting their own priorities. Traditionally, this was done within powerful finance ministries which were able to determine fiscal policy and to instruct central banks on monetary policy. However, this institutional arrangement was widely found to impart an inflationary bias to policy-making and the response was to give central banks the task of combating inflation, along with the power and independence to have a credible chance of success. Thus, once central bank independence became the norm, the game changed in so far as the central bank tended to be assigned specific objectives (typically, price stability with some regard for output) and had to focus on these, leaving fiscal policy to pursue its own designated objectives. Nevertheless, the two authorities could be regarded as having equivalent powers and could be expected to work out procedures for reconciling differences of opinion to arrive at a coherent policy mix. These accommodations did not always work, and there are well-documented examples of clashes, such as in Germany in the early 1990s when rising Federal government expenditure associated with unification provoked the Bundesbank to react by raising interest rates.

Under EMU, however, the problem became more complex because the single monetary authority has multiple fiscal authority counterparts. This potentially alters the balance of power between fiscal and monetary policy, as well as making it more difficult to set a coherent fiscal policy for the Union as a whole. Macroeconomic policy in the Keynesian tradition, as articulated by the likes of James Meade and Jan Tinbergen, conceived of the policy mix as a means of assigning the available policy instruments to a range of macroeconomic target variables. In the simplified systems of simultaneous equations used to model this mix, the number of instruments had to be at least as great as the number of targets. But with a system in which co-ordination is much more important, and in which competence for economic decision-making is shared between many authorities, such simple characterisations cannot adequately describe the processes played out in setting policy. Complex game theory is required. By extension, much the same issues arise in other policy areas that bear on the supply-side of the economy.

Co-ordination must, however, be seen from different vantage points. It can relate straightforwardly to achieving a common approach to a particular policy area (fiscal policy or employment policy, for instance), such that the principal challenge is to devise procedures or rules for constraining national discretion. This might be called *horizontal* co-ordination. A more ambitious and demanding form of co-ordination (*vertical* co-ordination) would involve efforts to reach common positions across policy boundaries. In practice, EMU contains elements of both, but the system is still evolving.

4.1.1 The objectives of co-ordination

There is an intense debate about whether more extensive macroeconomic policy co-ordination in the EU is desirable. It is useful to clarify what the end goal of economic policy co-ordination (particularly as proposed in the euro area) is. In political economy terms, it can be thought of as a means of resolving two dilemmas. The first can be understood as a problem of social cost and concerns the difficulties of implementing disparate fiscal and supply-side policies within a single monetary union. The second is essentially a problem of collective action and concerns the 'provision' of central bank credibility in a decentralised fiscal regime. Co-ordination aims to achieve a harmonious macroeconomic policy mix comprising fiscal and other policies that are both mutually compatible and consistent with the objectives of the ECB's monetary policy. The worth of the euro area's policy architecture should, consequently, be assessed on its ability to support both aims.

4.1.2 Economic policy co-ordination and the problem of social cost

Under EMU, social costs may arise when Member States act in an uncoordinated fashion which mean that what one Member State does produces an adverse effect on economic stability or growth prospects in other Member States. If euro-area fiscal policies can be co-ordinated so as to deal with the common concern of all Member States, the side effects of fiscal profligacy will be re-internalised (Commission Working Group 4a on Governance, 2001). From a Mundell–Fleming open macro economy perspective, if exchange rates are able to float freely, deficit spending by a domestic government would have 'crowded out' private investors in the domestic economy through a higher domestic interest rate. Aggregate demand would have been depressed still further by the appreciation of the domestic exchange rate in the face of monetary tightening. Under these circumstances, a government had little incentive to pursue a loose fiscal policy since this would cause only tighter monetary conditions and a loss of international competitiveness.

Within a supranational monetary union, however, internal exchange rates are fixed and there is a single interest rate for all members. A Member State running a deficit will no longer face a higher real exchange rate vis-à-vis the rest of the currency zone, while the burden of crowding out will be shifted onto the currency zone as a whole in the form of a higher unified interest rate. Thus, Member States can externalise the costs of excessive deficits and to exercise fiscal restraint is, by implication, diminished (Aizenman,

1994; Allsopp and Vines, 1996; Beetsma and Bovenberg, 1999). If all Member States are free to act on this incentive – and this is clearly the case in a decentralised fiscal regime – then a retaliatory and discordant mix of fiscal policies will lead to a deterioration in the aggregate fiscal position (Agell *et al.*, 1996; Collignon, 2001). Assuming that the single currency has a flexible exchange rate vis-à-vis the rest of the world, the effect will be a higher currency-zone interest rate and a loss of international competitiveness. This outcome is socially sub-optimal for the currency zone and we argue that a similar logic applies to supply-side policies.

4.1.3 Economic policy co-ordination and the problem of collective action

Independence from unwanted political influence and clear and unambiguous policy preferences are widely regarded as the cornerstone of credible monetary policy (Cukierman, 1992). Even with such measures in place, however, fiscal policy – as Sargent and Wallace (1981) famously noted – must be consistent with the objectives of monetary policy if the credibility of the central bank is to be maintained. However conservative or independent the central bank might be, a fiscal authority that runs excessive budget deficits over a prolonged period will place the bank under mounting pressure to monetise the public debt and hence compromise its commitment to stable prices. In EMU, a Member State that defaults on its public debt will lead to capital impairment amongst its creditors, not least the commercial banking system. The risk that this banking crisis will spread to the rest of the euro area would place the authorities (both the ECB and national fiscal authorities) under intense pressure to bail out the profligate Member State, even if this destabilised euro-area prices in the process (Eichengreen and Wyplosz, 1998). So long as private agents believe that the ECB would succumb to this pressure and providing that Member States retain the right to behave in a profligate manner, the central bank will ultimately lack credibility. Again, much the same logic applies to various supply-side policies. Consider, for example, the prospect of inflationary wage settlements. Wage bargaining that pushes the Phillips' curve outwards will arguably engender pressures for the bank to accommodate the resulting inflation to avoid industrial unrest.

This can be interpreted as a problem of collective action, if the credibility of monetary policy in a federal union is viewed as a public good. The good is non-rival in the sense that each Member State will benefit in terms of price stability and a lower cost of disinflation once the central bank policy is perceived as being credible (Blinder, 1999) and non-excludable in so much as no member can be excluded from these benefits once credibility can be achieved (Jacquet and Pisani-Ferry, 2001). As with all public goods, there is the risk that some Member States might free ride on the fiscal prudence of their peers and still enjoy the benefits of credibility. But if too many do, the aggregate stances of other policies will be inconsistent with the objectives of monetary policy, thus eroding the credibility of the central bank. The end goal of economic policy co-ordination is, in this instance, to borrow a second phrase from the Commission's White Paper on European Governance (Working Group 4a, 2001), to promote consistency between national policies and the Community's objective of monetary credibility.

4.1.4 The case against co-ordination

The core of the argument against co-ordination is the fear that an arrangement under which monetary authorities seek instruction from fiscal authorities (and vice versa) would directly compromise Article 108EC, confuse the roles of fiscal and monetary policies (Issing, 2002) and jeopardise the credibility of the ECB. Even if the institutional ties between fiscal and monetary authorities remain unchanged under co-ordination, the mere fact that centralisation reduces the number of independent fiscal players in the euro area will increase the (potential) pressure on the ECB to monetise excessive public debt. If the bank shows signs that it would capitulate to this pressure and permits Member States to externalise the costs of excessive deficits then the prior constraints on fiscal profligacy will have been removed (Beetsma and Uhlig, 1999). Under these circumstances, the common policy approach to co-ordination contradicts its primary purpose by generating greater inconsistency in the macroeconomic policy mix.

Some protagonists are unequivocal. Alesina *et al.* (2001) and Issing (2002) are adamant that it is not necessary, arguing that although a case can just about be made on theoretical grounds for a 'policy mix' approach in which fiscal and monetary policy are set jointly, any possible benefits are heavily out-weighed by political economy considerations. This echoes the warning of Rogoff (1985b) that international macroeconomic policy co-ordination will endanger the credibility of stability-orientated monetary policy – see also the survey by Muscatelli and Trecroci (2000). The essence of the Alesina *et al.* case is that if the respective authorities 'keep their houses in order', all will be well. In terms of who does what, it falls to monetary policy (and thus the ECB) to deal with symmetric shocks or adjustments, while fiscal policy (national finance ministries) has the primary responsibility for asymmetric shocks (see Buti and Giudice, 2002). Policy co-ordination might help to solve the problems of social choice and collective action, but in doing so it jeopardises the credibility of monetary policy. Since monetary credibility is an overarching principle in the design of EMU, politicians and economists alike have largely discounted common policy as a realistic cure for the euro area's ills.

4.1.5 Preparing the way for EMU: Approaches to co-ordination in the Werner and Delors reports

The road to EMU was a long one[1] and along the way views of how it should function have, themselves, evolved markedly. Two key documents in the development of EMU are the Werner report (1970) and the Delors report

(1989). The Werner report set out a roadmap for EMU by 1980, and was written at a time when there was a greater disposition to transfer power to EU institutions than was the case by the time of the 1989 Delors report. This is visible in the nature of the proposals for policy co-ordination. The Werner report noted that integration meant that it inevitably became more difficult for national economic policy-making to remain autonomous. Efforts to compensate for this loss of autonomy had made 'partial progress but they have not in fact led to the co-ordination or effective harmonisation of economic policies in the Community' (Section II). The report set out proposals for the minimum action needed to achieve an effective economic and monetary union.

> For influencing the general development of the economy 'budget policy' assumes great importance. The Community budget will undoubtedly be more important at the beginning of the final stage than it is today, but its economic significance will still be weak compared with that of the national budgets, the harmonised management of which will be an essential feature of cohesion in the union (Section III).

While stressing the need to avoid excessive centralisation, the report calls for a

> centre of decision for economic policy [that] will exercise independently, in accordance with the Community interest, a decisive influence over the general economic policy of the Community. In view of the fact that the role of the Community budget as an economic instrument will be insufficient, the Community's centre of decision must be in a position to influence the national budgets, especially as regards the level and the direction of the balances and the methods for financing the deficits or utilising the surpluses (Section III).

As the programme to complete the single market was in full swing in the late 1980s, a blueprint for taking integration further by progressive realisation of economic and monetary union was put forward in the Delors report (1989). This report had, according to the terms of reference given to it by the 1988 Hanover European Council, 'the task of studying and proposing concrete stages leading towards this union'. It argued that co-ordination is needed, in part, because:

> By greatly strengthening economic interdependence between member countries, the single market will reduce the room for independent policy manoeuvre and amplify the cross-border effects of developments originating in each member country. It will, therefore, necessitate a more effective coordination of policy between separate national authorities. (Paragraph 10)

The report also stresses the necessity of more closely co-ordinated policies if exchange rates are unable to change, especially in a context of free capital movements (Paragraph 12) and elaborates on the reasons:

> An economic and monetary union could only operate on the basis of mutually consistent and sound behaviour by governments and other economic agents in all member countries. In particular, uncoordinated and divergent national budgetary policies would undermine monetary stability and generate imbalances in the real and financial sectors of the Community. Moreover, the fact that the centrally managed Community budget is likely to remain a very small part of total public-sector spending and that much of this budget will not be available for cyclical adjustments will mean that the task of setting a Community-wide fiscal policy stance will have to be performed through the coordination of national budgetary policies. Without such coordination it would be impossible for the Community as a whole to establish a fiscal/monetary policy mix appropriate for the preservation of internal balance, or for the Community to play its part in the international adjustment process. Monetary policy alone cannot be expected to perform these functions. Moreover, strong divergences in wage levels and developments, not justified by different trends in productivity, would produce economic tensions and pressures for monetary expansion. (Paragraph 30)

Although the reasons for opting for co-ordination rather than the economic government advocated in the Werner plan are not discussed in detail, the report notes that many of the factors that affect macroeconomic conditions will continue to be specific to Member States. To respect national autonomy and preferences in public finances, 'the level and composition of government spending, as well as many revenue measures, would remain the preserve of Member States even at the final stage of economic and monetary union' (Paragraph 30). Implicitly, therefore, the form of macroeconomic union envisaged is one in which the political imperative of subsidiarity over-rides any advantages that might accrue from having a centralised fiscal policy body. The rejection of the Werner approach may have reflected growing misgivings about the benefits of policy co-ordination alongside doubts amongst certain Member States about the true motives for further fiscal integration. Germany, most notably, feared that a supranational fiscal authority would become a Trojan Horse from which politicians could emerge to attack the independence of the ECB (Dyson, 2000).

Nevertheless, and notwithstanding the strong independence conferred on the ECB, the Delors report emphasises that procedures would have to be set up to allow for effective *coordination between budgetary and monetary policy*. This might involve attendance by the President of the Council and the President of the Commission at meetings of the ESCB Council, without power to vote or to block decisions taken in accordance with the rules laid down by the ESCB Council. Equally, the Chairman of the ESCB Council might attend meetings of the Council of Ministers, especially on matters of relevance to the conduct of monetary policy. Consideration would also have to be given to the role of the European Parliament, especially in relation to the new policy functions exercised by various Community bodies. (Paragraph 33)

4.2 The EMU co-ordination system

In practice, and despite impressions to the contrary, the procedures for policy co-ordination in the EU are quite extensive (for an overview, see Chapter 3 of this book, Commission, 2002e; and Hodson and Maher, 2002; Amtenbrink and de Haan, 2003). It functions through a range of committees and mechanisms, and the economic governance of the euro area (and the EU as a whole) has progressively been fleshed out with a view to achieving, *inter alia*, stable and non-inflationary growth. It is, however, sometimes hard to ascertain where effective control lies in a system that involves so many players and the various reforms to the process agreed at the spring 2005 European Council that re-launched the Lisbon strategy have the ostensible purpose of achieving a better focus. Moreover, some facets of co-ordination apply identically to all EU Member States, while others are only applicable to the euro-area members.

In the Maastricht Treaty, co-ordination is explicitly provided for, with Member States enjoined to 'conduct their economic policies with a view to contributing to the achievement of the objectives of the Community, as defined in Article 2' (Article 98, EC). Member States are to 'regard their economic policies as a matter of common concern and shall co-ordinate them within the Council' (Article 99, EC). The framework for co-ordination is the BEPGs, to be agreed by qualified majority by the Council on a recommendation from the Commission. It is worth noting that the BEPGs are intended to cover all economic policy and are, consequently, upstream of specific co-ordination processes described below, including the Stability and Growth Pact. However, it is also noteworthy that the Guidelines have only soft law status, so that their ability to shape Member State policy relies on the acquiescence and commitment of the respective national authorities responsible for different facets of economic policy. As the Kok report (2004) notes, this conjunction has resulted in a reluctance to take 'ownership' of the processes, undermining the policy aims.

4.2.1 The legal framework underpinning economic policy co-ordination

Policy co-ordination has traditionally taken place under the auspices of international organisations such as the OECD or the IMF, with goals set by the likes of the G7. Its aim tended to be to deal with global problems of economic management, examples being misaligned currencies, macroeconomic imbalances or sluggish global growth. The commitments entered into were, necessarily, informal and unenforceable. By contrast, the co-ordination mechanisms in the EU rely on a variety of legal provisions, spanning the range from hard law embodied in Treaty articles to soft law. The distinction is explored by Abbott *et al.* (2000) who define hard law as law that creates legally binding obligations, is precise and delegates authority for interpretation and implementation. They define *legalisation* as a spectrum and the strength to which each factor is present determines the extent to which legalisation is hard or soft.[2]

There is no presumption that hard law is superior to soft law or that soft law always act as precursor for hard law. In some situations, soft law may be the best legal tool available. In short, hard and soft law are part of a continuum, rather than a dichotomy. Legalisation of commitments signifies the expectation of governments that they intend to comply. It goes towards making the commitment to the articulated policy credible especially to the market (Simmons, 2000: 573). At the same time, legalisation of commitments does not occur in a political vacuum and the creation of legal arrangements and their subsequent modification is a highly political process (Abbott *et al.*, 2000: 419). The emphasis on the interplay of law and politics and the conceptualisation of legalisation as a continuum are particularly valuable. First, it re-introduces a normative dimension into the debates on economic policy co-ordination that are dominated by instrumental concerns (Hodson and Maher, 2004). Second, an analysis of the type of rules used sheds light on the nature of the commitments made by the states in relation to economic policy co-ordination and on the character of reform at this juncture in EMU.

Abbott and Snidel (2000: 429) identify conditions that lead states to use hard law. A first is where assurance is required, for example where there are reciprocal commitments but non-simultaneous performance and where violation of the rules will impose significant externalities on others. Second, it can be to increase the credibility of commitments where non-compliance is difficult to detect and the legal norms allow for monitoring. Third, hard law is more likely where individuals are members of a 'club'. They already have experience of negotiating with each other. In addition, reneging costs increase where an agreement is part of a regime as the costs may be borne by all members. This makes the need for commitment greater. Fourth, executive officials may look for hard law commitments where their preferences differ from other competing power centres in the state. Firm external obligations can be important for pushing through particular policy agendas at the national level. The softer or less precise the obligation, the more difficult it can be to use it as leverage at the national level. This can be particularly important in federalised or regionalised states. Finally, legal commitments should be more credible when made by states with particular characteristics whose reputation is enhanced by participation and whose strong domestic institutions enhance credibility also. Hard law provides consistency and prevents the re-opening of bargains. Here, the idea of law as a continuum with hard law in the form of legal obligations or pecuniary sanctions at one end and soft law in the form of non-binding declarations of intent and enforcement by peer pressure at the other is pertinent. Even if hard law does not prevent re-opening of bargains, it can shape the basis for that re-opening and limit the number of options that are available.

Soft law

Snyder (1995: 64) defines soft law as 'rules of conduct which in principle have no legally binding force but which nevertheless may have practical effects' (House of Lords Select Committee on the EU, 2003: 12). Soft law is not new in EU law, the Commission having made wide use of communications and guidelines in well-established policy spheres such as competition (Scott, 2002a: 70). Soft law can become hard law, but it is not an inevitable trajectory. This can come about in two ways. Soft law measures can be transformed formally through enactment of legislation or, less predictably, through judicial recognition where a court holds that the supposedly soft law measure has hard legal consequences and hence creates legal rights and obligations which the court is willing to enforce (Baldwin, 1995: 227; Snyder, 1995: 65). The European Court, for example, is not guided by the form of the measure but will look to content and context.[3] Thus soft law may cross the boundary between negotiation and legislation where precision and the strength of obligation is such as to mark out the measure as further along the spectrum of legalisation than may have been thought. Such a shift can only occur where a court is given jurisdiction and hence the importance of not delegating interpretation in order to keep some controls over the status of the measures.

Abbott and Snidel provide a thorough analysis of where soft law measures may be the most appropriate rule type (2000: 436). First, soft law reduces negotiating costs. Because the commitments made in hard law are precise and may involve delegation of interpretation, greater care is taken over negotiation with lawyers concerned about every word. If the levels of obligation, delegation or precision are reduced, then the costs of negotiation are similarly reduced making agreement possible. Second, soft legalisation may also reduce sovereignty costs while still allowing for some sort of agreement. Rather than accepting external authority over significant decisions in relation to economic policy, for example, states protect their sovereignty by choosing to co-ordinate through political structures where there are few specific obligations and little delegation. Third, where there is considerable uncertainty because the consequences of agreement are difficult to predict or the targets of an agreement are unavoidably imprecise then soft law may be the most appropriate method of legalisation. Fourth, such an agreement can ease bargaining problems and thus may represent a compromise. Divergent national circumstances that cannot be accommodated in a single text are instead addressed through flexible implementation. The main problem with such flexibility is that it can be correspondingly difficult to evaluate whether or not there is appropriate implementation. Soft law may also facilitate compromise over time. The fact that a bargain has been achieved makes it easier to work towards future bargains. A soft arrangement can give states the opportunity to learn about the consequences of what they have agreed to, opening the way for further negotiation and greater commitment after the learning curve when information asymmetry has been reduced and with it the levels of risk associated with uncertainty. Thus the use of soft law measures may itself signify an expectation of reform and change over time, so, where frequent negotiation is expected, the use of soft law is preferable, with the capacity for re-negotiation built-in. Change *per se* is not, in these circumstances, indicative of failure. In fact, the use of a particular combination of measures may be designed to facilitate change after a limited time, especially where there is considerable uncertainty entering into the bargain. As well as allowing for change over time, soft law measures can also shape the parameters of reform and change – emphasising some issues and removing others from the agenda. Similarly hard law can completely remove some issues from debate, particularly where agreement has been hard won. States can be extremely unwilling to re-open the bargain, leaving reform to the arena of soft law and areas of political discretion contained in the original bargain.

Cini (2001: 194) notes that soft law can provide guidance, for example, through the use of codes of practice. Such guidance can encourage consistency in bureaucratic decision-making and inform the wider public of official attitudes. Measures like opinions can set out broad policy positions that cannot be contained in more precise legal documents and through this combination of greater specificity and flexibility in form, soft law can contribute to governance and have a regulatory effect where otherwise one would not be possible. At the same time, these same characteristics can be seen as problematic. Soft law can be vague and opaque – drafted by bureaucrats with no democratic input. There can be a complete bypassing of accountability mechanisms with no judicial review and no parliamentary input or scrutiny. In short, the less legalised policy development is, the greater the focus on instrumentalism and less on any normative agenda, with the concomitant loss of the benefit of legal autonomy and the rule of law.

Sanctions

The nature of sanctions that can apply is indicative of the scope of legalisation. Sanctions also range across a spectrum with peer pressure at one end and punitive fines and imprisonment at the other (Maher, 2004). Where the only sanction envisaged is soft, for example, a declaration that a state has breached its legal obligations (for example, in the context of the BEPGs or a Council recommendation), then the effectiveness of that sanction is dependent on a number of factors (Hodson and Maher, 2004). First, the obligation must be sufficiently precisely drawn so that it is clear that a breach has occurred, to minimise denials and counterclaims by the state. Second, the state sanctioned must have a strong regard for the rule of law, such that a declaration of breach carries with it a diminution in credibility with peers and the possibility of censure by political elites, the media and public opinion within the state. Third, the body issuing the declaration must be credible. This means that it must be shown to be impartial, consistent and committed to upholding the legal obligations entered into. For example, this would require even-handed dealing with all states, without preference being given to more powerful states. Where there is discretion, it should be exercised transparently so the basis for the decision can be seen to be consistent. Finally, and linked in particular to the previous point, declarations of breach of obligation depend on the behaviour of peers for their effectiveness. If peers are unconcerned about breach, for example, because they wish to be treated leniently if and when they are in breach, then the sanction is rendered useless. In short, where political ownership of the arrangement is absent, then its very existence can be called into question.

A fine is found at the hard law end of the continuum of legalisation. The question of who imposes the fine raises questions of how far along the continuum is the particular arrangement. Where peers in their absolute discretion levy a sanction, then political commitment to the process leading to the fine is critical to its success as a deterrent against recalcitrant behaviour. If states control the process such that they can decide whether or not to impose a time limit, the process is kept within the political domain and does not create legal obligations sufficiently hard to allow for an enforcement action through the courts. Where states sign up to an arrangement that allows for the imposition of punitive sanctions, they signify a high level of commitment to that obligation. The assumption is that they want to avoid the financial and reputational costs of a fine, but if they control if and when a sanction is imposed, the sanction remains symbolic. Even if the power to fine is seen as purely symbolic, its removal would act as another symbol of a change in political commitment to the underlying policy and hence, once created it can be counter-productive to remove it (House of Lords Select Committee on the EU, 2003: 37).

The use of sanctions – even a soft one like a recommendation – can also backfire politically if used inappropriately (Goldstein and Martin, 2000: 621). This is because enforcement arises in a political as well as a legal context. Flexibility in enforcement is important particularly where there is uncertainty. If sanctions are triggered without any get out clause, there is the risk that the rules themselves will get stretched where there is an unanticipated shock so as to avoid the trigger, undermining the credibility of the self-same rules. Finally, if fear of the penalty is such as to lead to compliance even if that imposes high costs domestically, then general support for the policy can be lost. The corollary of this is that if compliance will impose high domestic costs, then the threat of even a large fine may not be enough. If this is apparent at the time of legalisation, then the credibility of the arrangement is undermined leaving the sanction as little more than symbolic.

4.2.2 Fiscal policy co-ordination: The SGP

The SGP is rooted in the provisions on excessive deficits and multilateral surveillance in Article 104EC and given substance by two regulations formally agreed in 1997 (1466 and 1467), which flesh out the excessive deficit procedure and how surveillance is to be conducted (Chapter 1, Table 1.1). In March 2005, agreement was reached on reforms to the Pact which will eventually mean that new regulations will have to be agreed, but at the time of writing these were still to be put forward.

It is important, at the outset, to note that there are significant differences between the convergence criteria for entry into Stage 3 of EMU and the SGP. First, the former had two fiscal tests, the current deficit ratio (which had to be under 3% of GDP) and the debt ratio (which was not supposed to exceed 60%). By contrast, the SGP only refers to the current deficit. Second, the SGP has a medium-term target of a deficit 'close to balance or in surplus', together with a definition of an excessive deficit of 3%, other than in exceptional circumstances. As Buti and Giudice (2002) show, these are far from trivial differences that give rise to quite distinct political economy consequences for the conduct of policy.

The rationale for the medium-term target under the SGP is straightforward because deficits rise as automatic stabilisers are allowed to work in periods when the economy is below trend, a margin is needed. A medium-term fiscal position of balance means that the deficit can inch up to 3% without difficulties when there is a slowdown, whereas if the deficit is already close to the SGP limit, there is little scope for it to do so. In addition, if governments are to provide for long-term obligations, especially the anticipated pensions bill, it is argued that the public sector needs to take action now to bolster its balance sheet. Sweden, for example, already targets a 2.5% surplus for just this reason. It should be noted that, by maintaining fiscal balance, the ratio of debt to GDP will fall asymptotically towards zero so long as nominal GDP grows. But there are also occasions when increased public expenditure is required in the short to medium term for other than cyclical reasons or today's geopolitical imperatives. The new members of the EU, for example, are bound to have substantial public investment needs, just as Spain and Portugal had after they joined the Union. More generally, the ambitions articulated at the Lisbon European Council to effect a transformation of the EU economy will have expenditure implications. The problem with the current policy framework is that such aims cannot easily be accommodated.

The SGP does not, however, work in isolation. On the one hand, it is just one component in the increasingly elaborate machinery for policy co-ordination at EU level (Figure 4.1). Policy co-ordination can be defined in this context as supranational rules or norms which are agreed by all Member States, leave primary responsibility for the policy area with national authorities, but set limits on their discretion. The most comprehensive of these is the BEPGs through which the EU level sets out a series of recommendations for the broad thrust of economic policy. These guidelines comprise general policy aims for the EU as a whole (and not just the euro area), together with specific recommendations for individual Member States. They are both broad and comprehensive, covering macroeconomic policy (for which, read fiscal), a range of labour market and other supply-side policies, and sustainable development. Overlapping with the BEPGs are specific co-ordination 'processes' that try to foster common approaches to employment policy (the Luxembourg process), structural policies (the Cardiff process), pension

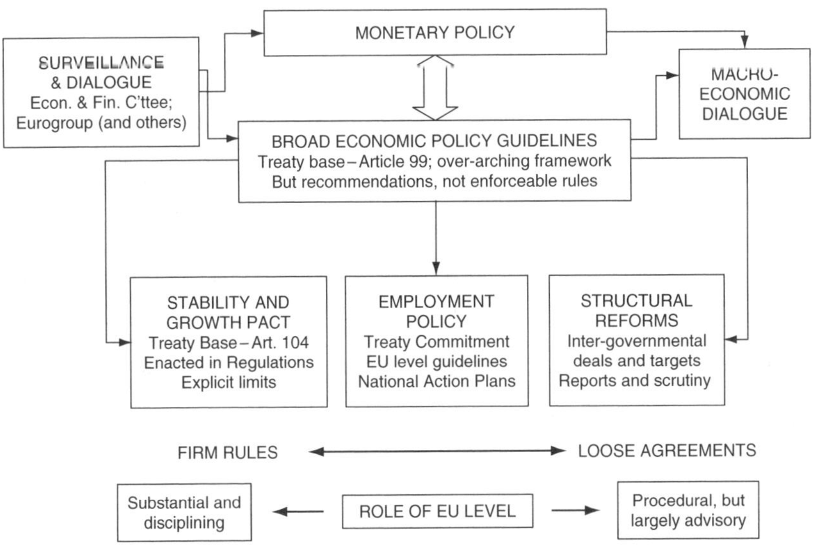

Figure 4.1 Policy co-ordination in the EU

reform and social inclusion policy. Provision has also been made for a forum – the macroeconomic dialogue (the Cologne process) through which the social partners meet representatives of the finance ministries, of the Commission and of the ECB to discuss the macroeconomic policy stance. There is, too, the agenda set at the Lisbon European Council held in March 2000 that sought to promote the EU as 'the most dynamic knowledge-based society in the world', while also paving the way for a modernisation of the European social model. 'Lisbon' has, since, become institutionalised through the holding of a special meeting of the EC (i.e. the heads of state and of government) each spring, the primary purpose of which is to discuss economic reform. Figure 4.1, adapted from Commission (2002f), summarises the current system.

What is conspicuously missing, however, is any formal means of co-ordination between fiscal and monetary policy, the conventional notion of the policy mix. As the chart shows, there is provision for dialogue between monetary policy and other policy domains but no overt channels for joint decision-making although there are the two mechanisms shown for exchanges of views, including the political forum of the Eurogroup.[4] Thus, on one of the key issues of policy management, it is soft procedures which dominate and which, in practice, represent the sole means of arriving at an overall macroeconomic policy orientation. One consequence of this arrangement is that opportunities for normative input into the choice of policy are severely circumscribed, so that the underlying 'stability' model is not subject to challenge.

When it comes to peer pressure and multilateral surveillance the EU has more elaborate review procedures and involves higher-level national decision makers than either the IMF or the OECD. It also has a more developed political input into decision-making and policy formulation, mainly through the Council of Ministers – for macroeconomic policy (Ecofin) and parallel councils for employment or for social affairs. It is, however, apparent that these formal councils are rather cumbersome for agreeing policy. By contrast, the informal *Eurogroup* comprising just one official and one politician from each member of the Eurosystem is reported to be much more political in its deliberations and to offer means of debating policy options more overtly.[5] Whether this informality and its apparent effectiveness will be able to continue if, or when, the constitutional treaty provisions on economic governance of the euro area come into force remains to be seen.

4.2.3 Supply-side co-ordination

On the face of it, the supply-side is well covered in the policy framework, with explicit processes covering employment (Luxembourg) and product market reform (Cardiff), topped up by the looser ambitions agreed at the 2000 Lisbon European Council. The EES has, arguably, contributed to a general rethinking of how labour market adjustment can be achieved, although it is open to the criticism that too many of the guidelines are tangential to a genuine adjustment strategy, with their focus more on activation and equity related aims. This is, in part, because the focus of the EES has been on employment policies *per se* and not on the broader contribution that they might make to steering the economy. But it is also because the links from the Luxembourg process to other structural reform measures have been inadequately developed in the institutional framework. In particular, the hard parts of labour market reform, notably the flexibility of wages and of the regulatory framework, are only tangentially affected by the Luxembourg process and outside the scope of the Cardiff process, even though the BEPGs have, for several years, ritually called on Member States to speed-up labour market reform; thus, Chapter 3 of the guidelines in 2002 was headed *Invigorate labour markets*. Yet even here, the detailed recommendations stop short of confronting these two dimensions of flexibility convincingly.

The most developed forms of supply-side co-ordination in the EU are the EES – discussed in Chapter 5 – and the more diffuse ambitions to achieve the structural reforms encapsulated in the 'Lisbon' agenda. The latter, to a considerable extent, is an extension of the drive to complete the EU's internal market launched in the mid-1980s. Liberalisation of markets for financial services, enhancing the provision of risk capital and rendering network industries more competitive are current preoccupations, all of which have as an underlying aim boosting the EU's competitiveness, especially in knowledge-intensive industries. The procedures for moving towards common policy include the conventional 'hard law' Community method of directives and regulations, and 'Action Plans' and commitments by governments that are softer forms of inter-governmental co-ordination. In addition, the Lisbon agenda comprises initiatives to promote social inclusion that have also now been institutionalised through NAPs, while pensions have also now been brought within the ambit of the OMC.

Indeed, it sometimes seems as though there are so many different actions plans and processes that they detract from the objectives. The Kok (2004) review of the Lisbon strategy was critical of the governance of the process noting the lack of focus and calling for more 'ownership' and commitment by Member States. In particular, Kok advocated a more effective form of naming and shaming as a key part of the way forward, and might, therefore have been a means of pushing governments to act. However, amid metaphors about not being treated as naughty schoolchildren, even such moderate reprimands were rejected. Instead, the proposals endorsed in March 2005 will leave the onus largely on Member States and the workings of domestic politics.

There are three stages in the EU's 'guided' policy co-ordination cycles. First, Member States agree collectively on economic policy objectives for the EU as a whole: typically, proposals are put forward by the Commission, then adopted by the Council of Ministers. Second, each Member State formulates a NAP to deliver these objectives in a manner that takes into account the specific structure of the national economy. Third, the design and implementation of the NAP is monitored through a system of multilateral surveillance, which involves the European Commission, Council of Ministers and individual Member States. If a Member State deviates from the NAP (or if the plan is deemed inadequate to begin with) the Council can issue a public recommendation for corrective action. However, there is neither a legal obligation to conform (as in the case of Community legislation) nor the threat of financial sanction (as in the case of the Excessive Deficit Procedure); instead it operates through a combination of pressure from the Commission and other countries, benchmarking and deliberation.

Yet without the anchor of simple rules enshrined in hard law, policy anarchy is much more probable. The nature of the rules may be doubtful or at variance with the inferences drawn from the economic reasoning, but as political economy devices which help to keep policy-makers on course, they can have a pragmatic impact that belies their questionable theoretical rationale.

4.3 The system assessed

Advocates of firm rules, drawing on the seminal contributions of Kydland and Prescott (1977) and Rogoff (1985b), appeared to have won the battle to shape the EU policy system by tying the hands of both fiscal and monetary policy-makers. If the logic of Rogoff (1985b) is reflected in the absence of a centralised approach to fiscal policy within the institutional architecture of EMU then the Kydland and Prescott (1977) approach to economic policy is reflected in the presence of two distinct modes of decentralised coordination. It nevertheless has to be stressed that in opting for a system relying heavily on co-ordination, the architects of EMU made a choice that balances competing aims rather than being the most economically efficient. As Buti (2003a: 7) notes, 'the existence of spillovers between monetary and fiscal policies implies that co-ordination can, in principle, be welfare-improving. Co-ordination, however, also implies costs, in particular in the presence of numerous players as in EMU'.

That monetary policy is not part of the equation is simply explained: an independent central bank with the primary responsibility to assure price stability cannot plausibly engage in the sort of bargaining with other policy actors that would be implicit in co-ordination. If it did, it would open itself to the possibility that the ensuing bargain might mean trading-off higher inflation for other goals, such as faster growth or lower unemployment. The issue is not whether or not such an outcome is desirable (the contrast with the Fed's dual mandate is obvious), but whether it is constitutionally allowed, and our interpretation of the legal texts is that the room for manoeuvre is very limited.

A second broad observation about the present system is that it embraces both formal obligations rooted in hard law and very soft guidelines and recommendations, with the latter as enforceable as these two words imply. Indeed, there have already been high-profile instances of national governments openly disagreeing with, and ignoring, recommendations: the 'reprimand' to Ireland for its pro-cyclical fiscal policies – issued under the BEPGs and not the SGP as is sometimes mistakenly assumed – is a case in point. The 'Brussels' recommendation were not only at odds with Irish preferences, but also predicated on competing economic analyses (Chapter 2). In the event, the Irish Finance Minister was able to fend off the attempted reprimand, though not without some political embarrassment and, with hindsight, it is a moot point who was correct, but what is clear is that the soft co-ordination of the BEPGs was unable to discipline the Member State policy.

In principle, the 'hard' co-ordination of the SGP, with its escalating sanctions, should avoid this difficulty. There is a clear policy rule – that countries should aim for a budgetary position 'close to balance or in surplus' – and explicit procedures for issuing warnings to delinquent Member States and (though almost certainly never to be used) the ultimate sanction of financial penalties. Yet the practice in 2002 and 2003 was for Ecofin to overturn properly constituted Commission recommendations for sanctions to encourage Member States to conform. This happened in 2002 when Ecofin refused to issue an early warning of an impending 'excessive deficit' in Germany and Portugal and again in the now notorious meeting in November 2003 when the Commission's recommendation against France and Germany was sidestepped. An *ex-post* rationalisation is that the German government, in particular, had signalled that it would deal with the problem, so that the desired outcome would be achieved without resorting to the formal machinery. Cynics might interpret Ecofin's demurral as other members of the club not wanting to upset a peer who might subsequently sit in judgement on them.

The question is not whether the fiscal policy being urged on Germany and France is appropriate – indeed, many would argue that it is not – but whether the system for co-ordination works, or can be made to work, as intended. The answer to this question must now take account of the European Court of Justice judgment overturning the conclusions of the November 2003 Ecofin meeting (C-27/04, 13 July 2004). With Ecofin able to suspend but not ignore Commission recommendations, its discretion is more circumscribed than previous practice implied and with the Commission as gate-keeper, more negotiation between the two institutions is likely in the operation of the EDP. With Ecofin having to operate within the parameters set in the EDP, one outcome is that even greater emphasis will be placed on using soft law under multilateral surveillance, making resort to even the early – but defining – stages of the EDP less likely. Reform is also more likely given the shift in the institutional balance that has occurred as a result of the judgment and the realisation that soft law is not just politics but even recommendations – non-binding soft law instruments – can have some legal effects by curtailing the exercise of discretion.

Amtenbrink and de Haan (2003) ask whether a Member State that does not conform to the BEPG recommendations or other aspects of surveillance procedures might be subject to sanctions, but conclude that even if there is a theoretical possibility, the issue is politically decided rather than being amenable to a legal decision. Moreover, they note that 'in any event, if the goal is to avoid the emergence of an excessive deficit, the prospect of the application of a lengthy judicial procedure may not be a very appealing one, as it will almost certainly come too late to be meaningful' (Amtenbrink and de Haan, 2003: 1083). The July 2004 judgment shows that the delay in fact may be politically desirable. In that case, political tempers had cooled considerably by the time the judgment was handed down, creating the opportunity for compromise and change on the parts of both institutions and allowing for fresh consideration of further reform. What the judgment did not, and arguably could not, do was to prevent the excessive deficits of France and Germany or even provoke a change in their conduct.

The difficulties surrounding the SGP in 2003 suggest that it is overly rigid application of firm rules rather than the principle that there should be rules that is causing problems. Equally, although the precise threshold (the 3% limit) may not hold, the degree to which it is breached is likely only to be minimal. The difficulties are, however, more acute in relation to the second aim of the SGP: the requirement to keep public finances in the medium term 'close to balance or in surplus'. Overall, what seems to bedevil the system is that political decisions on policy are dominated by national interest considerations, rather than the interests of the euro area as a whole. This highlights the lack of a coherent counterpart to the supranational monetary authority. With the reforms agreed in March 2005, it is clear that the Member States are bowing to the inevitable by introducing much more political discretion, much to the dismay of the ECB. Now that the full details of the new system are clear, a provisional verdict is that the worst features of the SGP probably have been corrected, but that it may be at the price of a system that lacks real bite.

4.3.1 Challenges and criticisms confronting co-ordination

The key challenge for co-ordination, plainly, is to deliver integrated policy in an institutional setting in which monetary policy stands on a pedestal. If it did not, Issing (2002) believes that it would lead to confusion in responsibilities and objectives, and could undermine the credibility of monetary policy. Indeed, it could be argued that if any central bank is genuinely to be independent, then it simply cannot countenance any form of co-ordination that might lead it to compromise its mandate. The alternative view is that piecemeal co-ordination – a range of procedures and co-ordinating bodies, with fiscal policies under one set, employment under another and very loose means of achieving 'Lisbon' aims – is not enough and that they should be reinforced by a powerful counter-weight to the ECB, fulfilling functions similar to those of the finance minister in a Member State. The Eurogroup, in a limited way, does this at present, but is an informal body with limited authority. It is, perhaps, indicative of how sensitive the whole issue is that the working group on economic governance of the Convention on the Future of Europe, chaired by Hänsch, could only agree on very limited reforms (Working Group on Economic Governance, 2002) and the constitutional treaty changes little in this arena, other than formalising the euro group.

Six main strands of criticism of the economic governance system that was in place by 2003 can be enumerated, some of which have been at least partly remedied since:

1. First, both monetary policy and fiscal policy were considered to be too focused on stability and not enough on growth. This was, in part, the result of the dominance of a single 'model' of how the economy works, but it also reflected the institutional separation of policy-making and the dominant position of the single monetary policy vis-à-vis fragmented fiscal policy, and is compounded (Pisani-Ferry, 2002) by the uncertainty about what macroeconomic policy should try to do.
2. Second, the rules governing fiscal policy have been pro-cyclical to the extent that governments (e.g. Germany at present) are pushed to engage in fiscal tightening in a downturn, but do not face pressures for fiscal consolidation in good times and consequently lack incentives to do so. Thus, fiscal policy is too tight in a downturn and too loose in an upturn and the overall impact is destabilising. The SGP reforms will ease, but not eliminate this criticism.
3. A third concern is that the policy machinery relies too much on rules that have no evident economic logic to them and that the underlying objectives become lost. The reference value for monetary policy and the use of concurrent fiscal ratios irrespective of the point in the cycle can be considered too crude, and conceivably lead to ill-judged responses. Moreover, the underlying purpose of fiscal restraint – sound public finances – is not easily captured in simple rules. As Pisani-Ferry (2002) points out, 'there is wide agreement on the need for fiscal discipline in a monetary union, but there are several problems with our current definition of it'. He refers especially to the use of current rather than cyclically adjusted ratios, the neglect of public debt and of off balance-sheet public liabilities. In addition, the comment in a Commission communication on reform of the SGP that 'the process of budgetary consolidation has ground to a halt since 1999, and in some cases has reversed' (Commission, 2002b) is symptomatic of a broader concern that the Pact does not (and cannot) promote fiscal discipline effectively. Again, the proposed reforms will diminish, rather than remove this criticism.
4. The fourth criticism was that it did not make sense for all Member States to be subject to the same rules. In particular, a heavily indebted country

that runs a deficit is at much greater risk of fiscal instability or indeed solvency problems. Equally, if a country has a good case for raising public spending – most obviously to bolster investment – the rules ostensibly inhibit such spending. Here, the reforms that have been agreed of the SGP are more convincing, because they effectively customise the Pact for each Member State, though arguably still within too tight a straitjacket.

5. Fifth, it is evident that demand-side and supply-side policies are inadequately integrated, and also that there are gaps within the supply-side 'processes'. The re-launched Lisbon strategy may offer a solution here, but for now it has to be 'wait and see'.
6. Finally, the ease with which some (especially larger) Member States have been able to flout (or at least appear to flout) the fiscal rules undermines their credibility. France, most prominently, has asserted its right to choose when to meet the medium-term targets of the SGP and, in so doing, has inflamed an already delicate dispute between larger and smaller Member States. The reluctance to comply is exacerbated by the nature of the enforcement mechanisms and sanctions. Giving Ecofin discretion to determine when early warnings should be issued – and ducking the hard choice at virtually the first time of asking – suggests that asking a peer group to judge a potentially delinquent Member State is unlikely to work. The more flexible reformed SGP will help in this regard by cutting the frequency with which the excessive deficits procedure is triggered, and that in itself should help to restore its credibility. Equally, the risk is that credibility is achieved only at the expense of a less effective disciplining device.

These problems point to a number of obvious potential directions for reform, with the emphasis on rethinking the system of governance rather than the rules themselves. They also highlight the importance of optimising between hard and soft approaches, and reform will also need to take heed of a number of apparent paradoxes in the functioning of the system.

4.3.2 Paradoxes

EMU, as an economic system, clearly has to have economic co-ordination, as provided for in Article 99 of the Treaty, if policy anarchy is to be avoided. But there are several inconsistencies or, indeed, paradoxes inherent in the system. First, the supposedly hard rules are regularly breached by both the monetary and the fiscal authorities. Yet it is generally agreed that the ultimate sanctions in the SGP (fines for delinquent Member States) are designed not to be used. Instead, it seems to be soft sanctions (e.g. 'naming and shaming') and the political problems – above all domestically – of being seen to be in the wrong that force governments to change course.

A second paradox is that the soft processes cannot be enforced and it will be all too easy for Member States to opt out of co-ordination precisely when it becomes most necessary. This may be the result of a lack of credible incentives as much as prospective sanctions; it can be argued that the strong target of entry into Stage 3 of EMU provided substantial incentives to governments to conform to a co-ordination system, but in the current system, the rewards are lesser. As the Kok report (2004) shows, some of the shortcomings in the Lisbon strategy arise for precisely this reason.

Third, the least tractable structural problems are regarded as off-limits for policy co-ordination, not because co-ordinated action, as such, is adjudged to be the wrong approach, but because the governments have been loath to take the first steps. Thus, in employment policy, modernisation of the regulatory framework has been very timid, while wage flexibility is scarcely confronted.

A further paradox is that a supposedly rule-based system, with hard law provisions governing both fiscal and monetary policy, relies so heavily on soft procedures – dialogue and consultation – to achieve a coherent policy mix. Despite the aim, articulated in the 2003 spring Presidency conclusions, of achieving 'a more comprehensive, efficient and coherent approach' within which 'sound macroeconomic policies must be pursued in order to restore confidence and economic growth', the means of achieving both the horizontal co-ordination of fiscal policy and the mix with monetary policy are not spelt out. In the 2003 BEPGs, the aim is 'stabilising output around a higher and sustainable growth trend', yet when it comes to *how*, the emphasis is predominantly on fiscal and supply-side policies, with no reference to monetary policy.

4.3.3 Reform of the SGP

The reform of the SGP and the re-launch of the Lisbon strategy agreed in March 2005 go some way to address these criticisms but do not entirely deal with the paradoxes identified above, in particular the balance and role of hard and soft norms and the exclusion of the most intractable structural reforms from policy co-ordination. One of the key changes agreed in March 2005 was to emphasise the medium-term objective (MTO) of sustainable public finances, while allowing more leeway for states facing special circumstances. Although no compromise is envisaged in the treaty-based parameters of the 3% deficit and the 60% debt, these will not be implemented as rigidly as hitherto.

The core rule will become that each Member State will have an MTO that reflects its needs, prospects and debt levels. The agreement envisages a range from a medium-term deficit of 1% of GDP for countries described as 'low debt/high potential growth countries' to an (unspecified) surplus for those that are 'high debt/low potential growth'. The limit of a 3% deficit is to be maintained, although all the calculations will, in future, relate to the cyclically adjusted budgetary balance.

Some flexibility will be built into the system insofar as 'medium-term budgetary objectives could be revised when a major reform is implemented and in any case every four years, in order to reflect developments in government debt, potential growth and fiscal sustainability'. The agreement also stresses that more should be done to achieve fiscal consolidation in good times, but does not specify how this is to be enforced. Countries are, however, given a benchmark of 0.5% of GDP as the annual improvement to be sought where the current deficit is above the MTO. An exception may be granted if a country is engaging in structural reforms which involve outlays today in order to save on public expenditure or boost growth tomorrow. As regards enforcement, an intriguing statement is that 'the purpose of the excessive deficit procedure is to assist rather than to punish, and therefore to provide incentives for Member States to pursue budgetary discipline'. Nevertheless, sanctions are to remain available. A severe downturn will, in future, be where there is negative growth rather a 2% fall in GDP, a further softening.

Throughout, a far greater role is envisaged for political decision-making by the Council in, for example, assessing special circumstances or extending deadlines for complying with a decision that an excessive deficit needs to be corrected. The aim seems to be pragmatic and reform is limited in that there will be amendment rather than wholesale replacement of the formal legal rules (the two contrasting regulations: 1466/1497 that emphasises the use of the early warning procedure and 1467/1497 that sets a tight time frame for the formal part of the EDP once initiated). Instead reform is in the realm of soft law re-defining where the emphasis should be in the assessment of fiscal policy and, by introducing some flexibility, removing the inappropriate stricture of a one-size-fits-all rule for all states. By softening the rigidity of the 3% rule and the MTO some account will be taken of the quality and sustainability of public finances across Member States. However, despite allowing for country-specific circumstances in relation to long-term sustainability of public finances, the maintenance of safety margins to avoid a breach of the 3% ceiling continues to be stressed, as is the maintenance of coherence between the evolution and quality of public finances and the medium-term rule. Member States with healthy budgetary positions and low levels of public debt should be able to run deliberate but temporary deficits, provided the additional resources generate economic and budgetary benefits. This addresses one of the key concerns in the UK position where a planned deficit due to an increase in public spending would not meet the objective of being close to balance or in surplus even though the UK debt levels are well below the 60% threshold and it remains within the 3% budgetary debt figure also (Begg *et al.*, 2003: 75).

Finally, Ecofin agreed on a code of conduct for improving the quality of budgetary statistics, which re-emphasised the Commission's role as statistical authority within the context of the EDP, and the responsibility of the states to provide timely and accurate data.

The limited nature of the reform is due in part to the difficulty of securing agreement to a more profound change that would necessitate a renegotiation of the governing regulations. The draft constitution does no more than tinker with the EDP and the BEPGs by removing the anomaly of the maverick state having a vote in the early stages of the EDP and by increasing the Commission's role to a limited degree so it can issue a warning under multilateral surveillance and changing its recommendation to a proposal under the EDP (Convention, 2003: Art. III-71(4); Art. III-76(6); Chapter 3). This latter change is institutionally significant as it makes it more difficult for the sort of outcome seen in November 2003 in relation to France and Germany.

Although the increased political discretion should both reduce the frequency with which the EDP is formally triggered and help to defuse the political tensions when it is, there remains the difficult question of how to control and discipline states to ensure compliance with the Pact. Proposals for reform here are more limited given that conventional legal sanctions such as fines are largely symbolic rather than effective for a state with a problematic budget deficit. Lacking a credible sanction, compliance must be secured through peer pressure in the form of naming and shaming. This requires commitment from the states to the Pact and its targets and to the operation of EMU as a whole. Such commitment is there in principle, but the difficulty is for states to have regard to the effect of their fiscal policy on all the euro-zone even though their electorate is more geographically limited – a problem that is relevant for EU policy-making generally but more immediate and conspicuous in relation to fiscal policy. Enforcing soft law is not easy, but that does not necessarily imply that it is not the most appropriate legal tool in the context – particularly if backed up by a system with relatively high levels of transparency and accountability. If these two mechanisms could be adequately institutionalised, for example through codes of conduct and independent review of fiscal policy by independent expert committees (Wyplosz, 2002: 16), the risk of actually being shamed within the state if named is more likely. Soft law works best where the values and norms contained within it are internalised by policy-makers and by electorates, that is where there is ownership. This is partly a function of time. Until that point, it will remain difficult to control compliance with the Pact irrespective of how it is reformed.

4.4 Concluding comments

An examination of how policy is being co-ordinated in the EU shows not only that there is much of it going on, but also that it is being done through an eclectic range of approaches. The underlying question, however, is whether current arrangements provide a policy framework that is robust enough for what EMU will become five, ten or twenty years hence. Economic policy co-ordination under EMU is motivated by the fact that monetary integration has created fresh channels of interdependence between the euro area economies. Under such circumstances, a discretionary and decentralised approach to national economic policies could produce a set of fiscal policies which are incompatible with one another, an aggregate fiscal stance that is inconsistent with the objectives of the ECB, and competition in supply-side policies that could be damagingly disruptive. In so far as a centralisation of fiscal policy within the euro area is politically unacceptable, a harmonious macroeconomic policy mix can be pursued through either hard or soft modes of co-ordination or a combination of both.

In particular, can the present reliance on the OMC for so many important areas of supply-side policy survive and prosper? On this, the jury is out, but there are other facets of policy co-ordination that also warrant more thought. At the heart of the matter is what the EU has become, or is moving towards, as a system for economic governance. If the *finalité économique* is to become and create a substantially integrated European economy as is implicit in Article 2 of the Treaty on European Union (Article I-3 of the constitutional treaty), not to mention the rhetoric surrounding the single market and the necessity for it of a single currency, then Member State economic policies will have to be more closely aligned. If they are not, tensions in the system will inevitably grow, making it more difficult to maintain the integrity of the single market.

An obvious resolution of the first two paradoxes outlined above would be simultaneously to soften the hard processes and to harden the soft processes. Emphasising the BEPGs rather than the SGP at the core of co-ordination would be an important start. Their thrust is less on fiscal discipline, narrowly defined, and more on the overall conduct of economic policy, including better integration of the supply-side. One key development was the establishment in 2002, in the context of rationalising – or perhaps re-weighting – the Council formations, of the Competitiveness Council. While it should give greater coherence to the supply-side, it remains to be seen whether the gaps in supply-side co-ordination can be bridged.

4.4.1 The way forward

Although the introduction of the euro went well, the economic management of the EU as a whole, and the euro area in particular, has been subject to increasing condemnation. Awkward questions are being asked about the rationale and arrangements for economic policy co-ordination (see, for example, Pisani-Ferry, 2002). Indeed, since the inception of the euro in 1999 and even during the period of convergence that preceded it, there has been a steady stream of criticism about the EU's emerging system of economic governance (Buiter *etal.*, 1993; Eichengreen and Wyplosz, 1998; Boyer, 2002). The troubles of the Stability and Growth Pact – never loved – highlight the underlying *malaise*, not least because of the reluctance to abide by its terms on the part of large Member States, one of which is Germany, the very country that demanded it. Despite generally supporting fiscal discipline, many economists regard the SGP as an ill-conceived, blunt and ultimately counter-productive set of rules that encourage pro-cyclical fiscal policy, inhibit economic recovery and damage the long-term growth potential of the EU economy (Begg *et al.*, 2004). The charge sheet also cites the inability of the policy system to deliver a coherent policy mix and bemoans the lack of flexibility in the conduct of policy. Moreover, Hughes Hallett *et al.* (2004) come to the view that it is those countries which have achieved growth that have been able to improve their fiscal positions, and that the SGP has, in practice, had no effective disciplining impact.

Can better, more effective co-ordination, possibly with a fresh approach to the implementation of hard and soft mechanisms, be achieved? It can be argued that what distinguishes hard co-ordination is its disciplining role and the fact that it seeks to impose an agreed model of how the economy functions. It nevertheless combines wide discretion for national authorities within the context of a common commitment to co-ordination backed up by more specific legal rules. By contrast, soft policy co-ordination now entails a multi-annual approach to economic policy-making, which publicly pre-commits Member States to deliver agreed policy objectives. Soft policy co-ordination also goes beyond the coercive logic of Kydland and Prescott (1977) by placing greater emphasis on policy learning and consensus building. Hence, it has the positive aim of improving the quality of policy, rather than constraining discretion. It also, to some extent (and this is especially true of the supply-side), provides incentives to governments to stick to agreed approaches so as to lessen the spillover effects of divergent policy. In regulating, for example, governments may have a collective interest in avoiding the so-called 'race to the bottom'. Moreover, as Hughes Hallett *et al.* (2000) show, effective labour market reforms can ease the macroeconomic co-ordination problem.

Although the SGP was the main focus of attention in late 2003, major changes were made in the functioning of the BEPGs which shifted from an annual to a triennial cycle (albeit with provision for annual updates), while the Employment Guidelines not only have been reorientated towards medium-term 'Lisbon' objectives (2010), but have also been significantly remodelled. The March 2005 re-launch of Lisbon consolidates these new directions, yet key co-ordination challenges are likely to remain unresolved. A crucial question is whether the political will, not to mention the means, exists to assure compliance with the agreements. For hard policy co-ordination one test will be whether the re-forumated SGP can be made to fulfil its designated role, failing which a different approach to fiscal policy co-ordination may be needed. Much of the rationale for soft co-ordination is that it encourages policy learning and enhancement, and can thus be portrayed as having positive rather than disciplining functions. But to the extent that soft processes also have to constrain Member State discretion in the pursuit of common aims, can they be effective, and if so, how?

Maintaining coherence and discipline will never be easy and there are no easy answers for delinquent Member States. Compliance is more likely to be assured if there is, first, a minimum of ambiguity and if targets make economic sense. Attention to the logic and definition of rules and targets would help, so that in relation to fiscal policy, a shift to cyclically or structurally adjusted deficits would be an obvious first step. The adoption of a 'golden-rule' for fiscal policy under which higher levels of public investment could well be justified on 'Lisbon' grounds (Creel *et al.*, 2002). Although such a rule would require careful definition and monitoring of eligible investments, the problems are not insuperable. Moreover, a golden rule need not be a loose rule; if necessary the benchmark could be set at a figure below zero, and there might well be scope for setting differentiated targets depending on national circumstances, for example impending pensions obligations. But there also has to be a political commitment to act responsibly, with the corollary of a political price to be paid for transgression. Giving the Commission or an independent fiscal council (Wyplosz, 2002), rather than Ecofin, the authority to issue warnings would be an improvement.

It can be argued that the new 'streamlined' systems integrating the procedures for the BEPGs, the EES and (since March 2005) Lisbon will go some way towards ensuring that co-ordination itself is better co-ordinated (Begg, 2002a). Reform has also meant the BEPGs becoming less detailed, while the move to a triennial rather than annual cycle, albeit with scope for annual updating should help continuity.

Perhaps the most intractable aspect of co-ordination is that it is caught in a political no-man's-land between the Member States and the supranational level. The nub of the problem is that if a Member State chooses not to play the game, there is little that can be done to chastise it, even under the (relatively) hard law provisions of the SGP. Sanctions might be an answer, but not (as in the SGP) when their strict application would exacerbate the problem that triggers them. Rather, the answer lies in the progressive building of a common understanding and commitment. It is in this regard that some of the arguments against co-ordination fail to reflect what happens in the EU: co-ordination as a disciplining device will inevitably provoke resistance but, where its function is to improve the quality of policy, national authorities are less likely to approach it in a largely defensive manner. However, it also has to be seen to work to achieve legitimacy (Hodson and Maher, 2002) and this is where the politics becomes more tricky.

Although the success of fiscal consolidation in the late 1990s bodes well for the potential of hard co-ordination, the subsequent deterioration of fiscal balances in several Member States highlights weaknesses. Somewhat paradoxically, the SGP has been criticised for the perverse impact of its fiscal policy rules in the face of a global economic slowdown and at the same time for the failure of Member States to implement these rules. The pro-cyclical focus of fiscal policy rules should diminish with the new SGP, but the reluctance of some Member States to abide by the terms of the pact is a cause for concern. Experience suggests that Member States, which themselves face the risk of running excessive deficits in this or subsequent periods, have a strategic incentive to tolerate fiscal profligacy in others. This implies that a stronger enforcement role should be given in the process of hard co-ordination to an independent arbiter such as the European Commission.

It could be inferred from the experience of the BEPGs in operation that soft co-ordination should not be regarded as a substitute for hard co-ordination because it cannot, by definition, impose discipline. However, this would be to misunderstand the purpose of the BEPGs and other forms of soft co-ordination which have helped to generate a broad consensus amongst policy-makers over the goals of policy action. Peer pressure has proved to be useful as an auxiliary mechanism of coercion with Member States keen to seek approval and avoid punishment from the Council and European Commission, not least in an election year. At the same time, however, policy-makers have illustrated a preference for widening and loosening the remit of soft co-ordination rather than deepening it, giving rise to the much looser and, arguably, rather empty targets that have emerged in relation to the EU as a knowledge intensive economy. The risk, as the debate around the 2005 reform of the Lisbon strategy showed, is that there are now too many policies and co-ordination processes and that they have become unwieldy.

More radical proposals should, nevertheless, be explored. Means of toughening up the BEPGs have to be sought so as to enhance their disciplining role. 'Punishments' such as withholding of structural funds' payments have been mentioned, but would probably poison relationships rather than help. Instead, it is important to look beyond a narrow, disciplining view of economic governance both to ensure that the underlying economic policy aims are not forgotten and that political commitment to successful policy – even if it is awkward in the short term – is reinforced. The broad shape of the economic governance system, and the role of co-ordination within it, are set to remain. As Buti (2003a: 24) observes, 'what can safely be predicted is that EMU's monetary policy will remain a rules-based macroeconomic framework. The way the current rules will evolve is, however, unclear.' It is easy to forget that this is a new system that is still feeling its way.

5
Structural Policies as Means of Adjusting under EMU

A Member State that has adopted the euro, and which subsequently encounters macroeconomic imbalances that monetary policy cannot resolve, has to rethink its mix of fiscal and supply-side responses in the light of expectations about the stance of monetary policy. A key element of this is that policy has to adapt to a low inflation environment. If fiscal policy, too, is unable to deal adequately with demand shocks, the onus will then be on supply-side measures to effect the adjustment. In particular, this will put pressure for change on to the labour market, although it is important to recognise that other supply-side policies can also play a part.

A problem, however, is that supply-side policies have not been seen as capable of acting quickly enough to deal with asymmetric shocks. Rather, their function in the policy armoury has been to enhance longer-term performance by acting on productivity and the employment rate. Under EMU, however, it can be argued that supply-side policies can help to meet the challenges of adjustment in two ways. First, they can help to create conditions under which either demand or supply shocks are less likely. Second, there may be scope for changes on the supply-side to ease the adjustment process. In particular, while labour market initiatives contained in the EES have an important microeconomic function in boosting employment levels and in assisting the reform of the labour market, they also have a vital contribution to make to overall macroeconomic policy co-ordination.[1]

The chapter starts by looking briefly at selected indicators of, first, labour market performance, then other structural variables. The next two sections explore why integration of employment policies matters and provide a concise description of the Luxembourg process and its evolution. The chapter then turns to the question of whether the OMC is proving to be a cogent means of delivering more coherent labour market policy in the EU or, instead, has major flaws. Concluding remarks complete the chapter.

5.1 Labour market and structural indicators

There is considerable diversity in labour market performance in the EU as a whole, as well as among the members of the euro area (Table 5.1). Yet, perhaps surprisingly, it is difficult to identify coherent groupings, as some Member States exhibit favourable values on certain indicators, but disappoint on others. Employment growth in the four-year period before and after the start of EMU is especially divergent. Germany is the clear laggard with the lowest rate of increase of all over the eight years, but employment growth in Italy and France was quite robust after the advent of the euro, substantially above the EU and euro area averages, while Spain has created jobs at more than twice the rate of its peers. Among the smaller Member States, too, there is great diversity. Austria has lagged well behind, but in the period since the euro, both Greece and Denmark have created jobs at a lower rate. The Netherlands has seen a rapid turnaround with its impressive job creation in the 1990s running out of steam in the last three years and has been overtaken latterly by Belgium. Ireland, Finland and Luxembourg have continued to be substantial net job creators, while Portugal's well-known fiscal problems have been reflected in the slow rate of job creation since the advent of the euro.

Figure 5.1 shows that Spain made the largest aggregate contribution to EU employment creation between 1998 and 2003, accounting for nearly a quarter of the total of some 8 million new full-time equivalent jobs, but Germany managed only to chip in one job for every four in Spain. Interestingly, the three outs, between them, only generated 18% of new EU jobs, some way below their share of total employment in 2003 of 22%. By contrast, job creation in Italy and France was higher than their 2003 shares although in Italy's case, it is important to bear in mind the low employment rate. Moreover, there is the further problem in the Italian labour market, especially, of the very pronounced regional disparities in employment rates. The lowest employment rates in the EU are in the Southern Italian regions which achieve just half the rate of the most employment friendly regions in the Nordic countries, a disparity even more pronounced for female employment rates (Commission, 2004b).

Unemployment remains high in four of the five larger EU countries, the exception being the UK. It is also still high in Belgium and Finland (though having declined markedly as the country has sustained its recovery from the deep recession of the early 1990s), and has crept up in Greece. Only a minority of countries currently have low unemployment. There are also big differences in the composition of unemployment, with high rates of long-term unemployment still affecting Italy, Greece and Germany, but comparatively low in what might be described as social democratic welfare states (Denmark, Sweden and the Netherlands). Employment rates also exhibit marked differences, with a gap of 20 percentage points between Italy (the lowest) and Denmark.

Table 5.1 Labour market indicators

	Employment growth, full-time equivalents % cumulative		Unemployment rate % labour force			Employment rate % of labour force	
	Total (1995–1999)	Total (1999–2003)	Aged 15–64		Aged 15–24	Total, aged 15–64 (2003)	Older, aged 55–64 (2003)
			Total (2004)	Long term (2003)	Youth (Sept 2003)		
Belgium	4.5	2.9	7.8	3.7	22.2	59.6	28.1
Denmark	5.2	−0.3	5.8	1.1	10.6	75.1	60.2
Germany	1.8	0.0	9.5	4.7	10.0	65.1	39.5
Greece	4.7	1.0	9.7 (2003)	5.1	26.5	57.8	42.1
Spain	12.7	9.5	10.8	3.9	22.4	59.7	40.8
France	3.2	5.0	9.6	3.5	20.3	63.2	36.8
Ireland	25.9	10.1	4.5	1.5	8.4	65.4	49.0
Italy	2.3	5.4	8.0	4.9	26.7	56.1	30.3
Luxembourg	16.0	17.1	4.2	0.9	10.6	62.7	30.0
Netherlands	11.4	2.2	4.7	1.0	6.8	73.5	44.8
Austria	2.9	1.7	4.5	1.2	7.4	69.0	30.1
Portugal	7.9	2.7	6.7	2.2	15.1	68.1	51.6
Finland	9.5	3.9	8.8	2.3	22.1	67.7	49.6
Sweden	1.5	4.4	6.3	1.0	13.2	72.9	68.6
UK	6.3	2.5	4.7	1.1	12.3	71.8	55.5
EU-15	4.9	3.4	8.0	3.3	15.5	64.4	41.7
Euro area	4.7	3.7	8.8	3.9	16.7	62.6	37.8

Source: Eurostat structural indicators database, Commission (2004a).

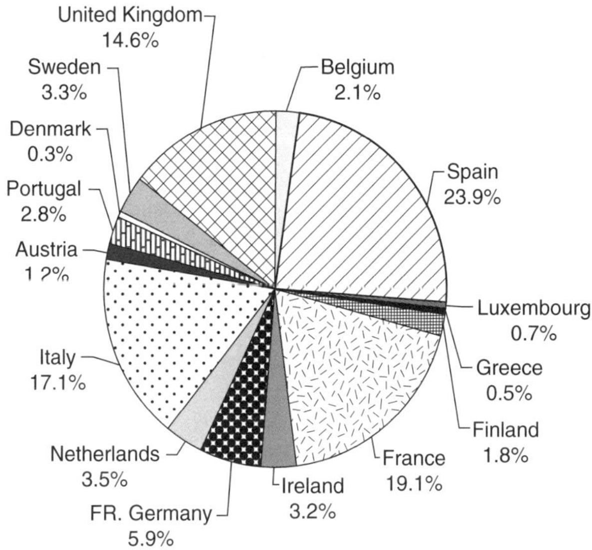

Figure 5.1 Contributions to EU employment growth (Share of FTE jobs created, 1998–2003, %). *Source*: Eurostat: Cronos database

Turning to other structural indicators (Table 5.2), the picture is again very mixed. High levels of labour productivity are attained in Belgium, France, Ireland, Luxembourg and, to a lesser extent, in Italy. Portugal is the clear laggard, attaining under two thirds of the EU average. To a degree, these differences are a mirror image of employment rates and tougher welfare conditions, with the implication that the Member States with higher employment rates opt to keep people unproductively employed, rather than unemployed. Thus, the Netherlands has actually seen productivity fall over the last four years as its economy has slowed. Greece, by contrast, has had a productivity surge.

A key Lisbon target is to raise investment in R&D to 3% of GDP, a target met only by Finland and Sweden. Of the other countries, Germany is closest to the target, largely because it has a number of very research intensive regions, as shown by the 3rd Cohesion Report (Commission, 2004b). The other countries fall into two groups: those with R&D ratios around the 2% mark, and the others – mainly in the South – which lag a long way behind. Indeed, in Portugal and Greece, the R&D indicator is just 0.6%, which may foreshadow medium-term difficulties in staying competitive within EMU. Total business investment as a proportion of GDP, by contrast, tells a more encouraging story for Greece, Portugal and Spain, though less so for Italy.

Table 5.2 Performance on key structural indicators

	Labour productivity per person employed		Business investment	R&D spending	Comparative price level	At risk of poverty rate
	Level, EU25 = 100 (2004f)	Annual % change (1999–2003)	% of GDP (2004)	% of GDP (2003)	EU-15 = 100 (2001)	% (2001)
Belgium	128.2	0.6	17.0	2.3	99	13.0
Denmark	103.8	1.6	17.9	2.6	131	10.0
Germany	100.2	0.8	16.0	2.5	104	15.0
Greece	97.2	3.9	21.4	0.6 (2001)	80	20.0
Spain	102.5	0.6	22.9	1.1	82	19.0
France	119.4	0.4	16.4	2.2	100	12.0
Ireland	127.7	3.5	20.7	1.1	118	21.0
Italy	108.1	−0.1	16.9	1.2 (2002)	95	19.0
Luxembourg	142.4	−0.7	15.3	1.7 (1999)	100	12.0
Netherlands	103.0	−0.1	17.0	1.9 (2001)	102	12.0
Austria	102.5	1.2	20.7	2.2	102	12.0
Portugal	66.8	0.0	19.3	0.8	74	20.0
Finland	110.5	1.4	15.8	3.5	123	11.0
Sweden	105.0	1.0	13.0	4.3 (2001)	117	11.0
UK	109.2	1.7	15.1	1.9 (2002)	107	19.0
EU-15	106.4	0.7	16.9	2.0	100	15.0

Source: Eurostat structural indicators database.

On this indicator, Sweden lags furthest, although an explanation may simply be the size of the public sector in Sweden. But the UK too is at the lower end of the range, despite its slimmer public sector.

Two other indicators shown in Table 5.2 provide insights into future prospects. First, the data on the price levels in the different Member States show the extent of the disparities confronting the smaller countries. Prices in Ireland (after relatively higher inflation over several years) and in Finland are some 50% higher than in the two Iberian countries and Greece. More encouragingly for the conduct of policy, price levels in the three largest euro area Member States are much closer to one another. The implication, nevertheless, is that monetary policy could dole out some unpleasant shocks for the divergent smaller countries that will have implications for how they engage in adjustment.

The 'at risk of poverty' indicator can be interpreted as a way of calibrating social problems, but is also a measure of likely future demands on social expenditure. It is clearly higher in the two Iberian countries and in Greece, which accords with evidence from research on social exclusion – see Muffels *et al.* (2002). By contrast, the poverty risk is low in those countries with well-developed social programmes, notably the Nordic countries, Germany, Austria and the Netherlands. However, in some of these countries, the social protection systems are under challenge, partly as part of the recasting of policy induced by EMU, so that tensions can be anticipated.

5.2 Why co-ordinate employment and/or labour market policies?

The social dimension of European integration has, on the whole, been less developed than market integration, in spite of the efforts of its champions, notably Jacques Delors. In recent years, however, it has made progress. The addition of the Employment Title in the Amsterdam Treaty was followed by a breaking of the logjam (at Nice) on integration of policies to promote social inclusion, with the adoption of the Social Agenda. Since the launch of the EES in 1997, ten million new jobs have been created in the EU; there are also four million fewer unemployed persons and the active population contains an extra five million people. Nevertheless, unemployment in the EU remains persistently high and progress has stalled in the aftermath of the 2001 downturn.

The headlines from the Lisbon European Council in March 2000 reflected the agreed goal of making the EU the most dynamic and knowledge-based economy in the world, yet a key thrust of Lisbon was the target of raising the employment rate to 70% by 2010 and modernising rather than dismantling the welfare state. These developments reflect a political commitment by Member States to reassert many of the fundamental values of the European social model (see Begg and Berghman, 2002), but also a recognition that there are common problems.

The 70% targets as well as interim targets and a parallel target for the female employment rate apply to all Member States, even though the means of attaining them are left to national policy. But from the perspective of adjustment, there are several facets of labour market policy that warrant co-ordination and a shared purpose in doing so. First, for the efficient conduct of monetary policy, wage bargaining matters. If the character and behaviour of bargaining institutions results in inflationary pay settlements, the ECB will be forced to respond, so that it is no surprise that ECB representatives regularly call on labour markets to exercise restraint (Issing, 2002, for example). Indeed, wage bargaining can be seen as a third ingredient of the EMU policy mix along with fiscal and monetary policy. Social dialogue is seen as part of the answer and is formally embodied as a co-ordination mechanism in the macroeconomic dialogue or 'Cologne' process, a key purpose of which is for representatives of the three policy areas to exchange views and to understand each others' intentions.

Second, the labour market matters for growth. An inadequate employment rate means un- or under-used factors of production and even in the simplest Solow-type growth model restricts potential output. As a result, the unemployment/inflation trade-off is likely to be worse. As Chapter 2 indicates, operating with high unemployment places an extra, 'deadweight', burden on the economy in having to transfer resources from the employed.

Third, there is a problem of mismatch. The complexity and structural nature of the EU's unemployment problem is demonstrated by the fact that it persists at the same time as acute skilled-labour shortages in many of the economy's fastest growing sectors. On one level, the coincidence of labour surpluses and shortages reflects simple cross-national differences in labour markets. The skills-differential is greatest in the three Member States that have unemployment rates below 5%: Luxembourg, the Netherlands and the United Kingdom. This tells only part of the story, however, since the skills-differential is also acute in Germany, France and Italy, each of which has an unemployment rate in excess of 8%. At the sectoral level, the excess demand for labour has been driven in part by developments in information and communications technology (ICT). A study by IDC/EITO in 2001 found a skills shortage of 1.2 million extra workers in ICT in 2000.[2] In addition, as the 3rd Cohesion Report (Commission, 2004b) shows, there is still a major regional problem of mismatch, as well as the differences in regional employment rates noted above.

All Member States bar Luxembourg have pockets of persistent unemployment, a significant proportion of which results from EU-wide structural changes. Thus, although there is evident national diversity in forms of employment problems, it is clear that it is something that European society as a whole has to face. There are many reasons for this lacklustre record, the causes of which have been extensively studied (see, for example, Vinals and Jimeno, 1998; Calmfors, 2001). The salient point, however, is that to attain the Lisbon aim of creating some 16 million jobs by 2010, the rate of increase of employment will have to accelerate significantly. The challenge was captured in the title of the report of the Employment Task Force chaired by Wim Kok that sought to review the EU's employment performance and found much amiss (Employment Task Force, 2003). This group argued that the EU will only be able to boost employment and productivity if four key requirements are met:

1. Increasing adaptability of workers and enterprises.
2. Attracting more people to the labour market.
3. Investing more and more effectively in human capital.
4. Ensuring effective implementation of reforms through better governance.

It also puts forward more detailed proposals on topics such as regional differentiation in pay rates and a range of other reforms designed to make the labour market more flexible. The report then enjoined governments to 'make better use of the many examples of good practice that exist'. Implicitly, therefore, it endorses the OMC approach to Europeanisation.

The deepening of European integration could itself justify a rethinking of the assignment of policy competencies, even though there are arguments suggesting that the need for employment policy lessens with the degree of integration if local shocks are buffered by more extensive market interaction. The latter logic is that the elimination of exchange rate variability may diminish fluctuations in the demand for labour because financial market integration makes it possible to reduce local risk as a result of portfolio diversification and cross-border credit. Estimates suggest that this is the most important means of cushioning regional specific shocks in the USA (Asdrubali *et al.*, 1996; Mélitz and Zumer, 1999). However, market integration, particularly financial market integration, is far from complete in the EU, hence this mechanism is largely absent in EMU.

The step increase in economic integration implied by EMU thus provides a strong case for further Europeanisation of employment policy. The fundamental problem, though, is how to develop European policy in an area where national differences in policy and approach were, and are, so great. The limits of the Community method are clearly shown in the Social Agreement reached at Maastricht. Here the less controversial areas largely deriving from earlier Treaty commitments, such as equal opportunities, the health and safety of workers and equal pay between men and women are subject to QMV. But new, more controversial, areas including social security and employment protection require unanimity. With Europe's unemployment problem and the new challenges of EMU a new approach was needed.

The form of policy co-ordination adopted for the EES is, manifestly, very different from that of the Stability and Growth Pact. As noted in the previous chapter, the EES follows a 'soft law' procedure, subject to the OMC, in which there are no firm rules or sanctions. Nevertheless, the experience of the first few years of the Luxembourg process suggests that Member States have both adapted their own approaches and achieved a degree of co-ordination that, arguably, might have been implausible through the Community method (Zeitlin and Pochet, 2005).

5.3 An overview of the Luxembourg process

The contours of the EES as it has functioned up to now are now fairly well known and will, therefore, only be briefly summarised here.[3] The core of what had become an established annual process by 2003 is the Employment Guidelines, a decision of the Council based on a proposal from the Commission. These provide the foundation upon which each Member State draws up its NAP describing how these Guidelines are to be put into practice in the way judged to be best suited to that country. The NAPs are also part of a political process where different actors try to influence the national and EU agenda and policy (Goetschy, 1999; Jacobsson, 1999; Teague, 1999). From a political economy standpoint, one of the strengths of the Luxembourg process is that it has allowed labour ministries and the social partners to have a more effective input. Indeed, one (probably fortuitous) interpretation of the word 'open' in the OMC is that it has promoted broader consultation on policy. In contrast, the Cologne process of macroeconomic dialogue is held by a number of participants to have been somewhat disappointing.[4]

5.3.1 The EU employment guidelines

The employment strategy is encapsulated in the guidelines, which serve as a template for the development of the NAPs. Until the procedure was changed in 2003, these guidelines evolved from year to year in response to changing economic circumstances and decisions taken at the European Council. Following the March 2000 Lisbon European Council, Member States were asked, for example, to develop policies to raise the aggregate employment rate and to support the transition to a 'knowledge-based society'. The 2002 guidelines (Council, 2002) have 18 clauses that cover the four pillars of policy, with a series of objectives under each. The four pillars were:

1. *Employability*, which is about supporting workers to gain initial employment, maintain employment and obtain new jobs, with particular emphasis given to lifelong learning and preventative measures. Specific guidelines cover areas such as action to reduce youth and long-term unemployment, and to provide pathways into employment.
2. *Entrepreneurship* concerns the ease with which a new business can be started and enabled to employ people. Because of the higher potential for employment in many service industries, governments are asked to focus particularly on these industries.

3. *Adaptability* is about developing more flexible ways of working and of organising work, so that firms can be more competitive and responsive to demand. As part of this, plans are expected to include proposals for improved training.
4. *Equal opportunities* refers to measures to make it easier for women, especially, to obtain access to jobs and training, as well as equal treatment at work. This last group of guidelines is advocated, in part, to maintain the essence of the European social model. The French emphasis on rights is, clearly, prominent in this respect, but so too are many of the Nordic traditions.

In addition, the Member States have to take into account 'Lisbon' issues such as the development of the information society, the need to bring undeclared work into the open, and the promotion of local and social employment. An innovation in 2002 compared with previous years is a focus on the quality of work. As part of the procedure, quantitative targets and indicators have to be developed, while a key expectation is that EU resources such as the Structural Funds should support the EES.

In 2003, taking heed of a five-year review, the EES was re-launched with three new overarching objectives and a revised planning cycle of three years (though subject to annual updating). The new focus of the Luxembourg process was to be on three objectives (Commission, 2003e), even if the detailed plans retain many of the same targets. They are:

1. *Achieving full employment*, an aim that is explicitly linked to the Lisbon and Stockholm employment rate targets: reaching a 70% rate (in steps) by 2010, with complementary targets for the female (60% by 2010) and older-workers (50% by 2010) employment targets.
2. *Improving the quality of jobs* and, in so doing, stimulating higher productivity.
3. *Making the labour market more inclusive*, an aim which emphasises links to the parallel policy initiatives to promote social inclusion.

At first sight, these new aims seem to differ substantially from the existing four pillars, but the Commission also identifies eleven priorities intended 'to support the above mentioned three overarching objectives [which] would be most relevant for the future guidelines' (Commission, 2003e: 12). Reading between the lines, these priorities regroup much of what was in the previous four pillars and the upshot is reasonable continuity, albeit with less repetitive procedures and demand on Member States. Part of the aim of the 2003 reforms was to link the EES more closely to the Lisbon strategy and to assure greater coherence with the BEPGs and this trend was taken further in the decisions taken at the spring 2005 European Council that re-launched the Lisbon strategy.

Key points to note about the Luxembourg process prior to the 2005 changes are that:

- Member States of the EU are expected, in their NAPs, to indicate how they plan to make progress on the four pillars of the employment strategy. These are then subject to scrutiny both by the Commission and, in the Council, by other Member States.
- This 'peer review' and 'peer pressure' could be said to improve the prospects for policy co-ordination and might assist the search for gains in policy efficiency.
- It also draws attention to governments that do not achieve much by exposing them to scrutiny and the prospect of being given an adverse rating in 'league tables'.
- The pressures to adopt common statistical tools and to use benchmarking could help to improve national monitoring and adaptation of policy.
- The EES does not include sanctions against states that do not conform to the guidelines or fail to achieve what they promise, and has no financial resources directly at its disposal from the EU level,[5] prompting the question of whether it can hope to achieve much impact. Its potential impact is, therefore, likely to be qualitative in nature and its focus on improving national policy-making by means of a common framework and processes.
- There is a potential for confusion about where ultimate responsibility for job creation lies and this could both weaken the coherence of the EES and call the legitimacy of the policy into question.
- While the Commission has an important role, it is more technocratic and enabling than strategic. It does not have the same sort of disciplining and surveillance role as in the SGP; instead, the Commission's input is much more about stimulating policy learning.

Prior to their entry into the EU in 2004, to enable the new Member States to participate in the EES, each state and the Commission agreed a joint assessment of employment policy priorities implementation of which were then monitored in part to see where the European Social Fund and Structural Funds could be best used and where progress was needed for the implementation of the new Employment Guidelines (Commission, 2003e). A series of national seminars were held aimed at reviewing policy developments and administrative capacity within each state. These pre-accession measures were designed to ensure that the new members would be in a position to submit their first NAP under the EES in October 2004. The new members also attended EMCO and its committee meetings as observers for a year before accession. As expected, the new members face major challenges (Chapter 12). In most, labour market participation had stagnated or decreased in the period 2000–March 2002. The employment pattern of growth was driven by increases in productivity while employment growth remains stagnant or at best moderate (Chapter 2). Increasing employment of older workers particularly women, remains problematic. With rapid restructuring, labour markets are becoming segmented with labour shortages in the newer economies centred on major urban centres and growing unemployment in the regions. Administrative capacity also needs to be addressed and the participation of the social partners in policy development improved. Overall, the new members are developing employment strategies using the EES model, but there is clearly a learning process.

5.3.2 The OMC and employment policy

The EU encompasses such a wide array of labour market models that it is hard in present circumstances to see an alternative to the OMC. The Anglo-Saxon model implies decentralised labour markets with bargaining at company or plant level, low levels of legal employment protection, low benefit levels and tough eligibility criteria. Continental European countries such as Austria, Belgium, France and Germany have more centralised wage determination, high levels of legal employment protection, quite generous benefit levels and more liberal eligibility criteria. Scandinavia and Southern Europe are different again. Within each grouping there is considerable variability.

OMC's principal advantages are that it provides the means to move towards common solutions to common problems without demanding the sort of harmonisation that would be anathema to many governments, and that it can be implemented by governments without recourse to major and potentially contested legislative change. Moreover, by allowing countries to shape national programmes within common guidelines, OMC allows governments to weight their policy packages appropriately. Such *differentiated policy harmonisation* represents an artful compromise between policy integration and subsidiarity. Politically, the mere fact of being seen to 'do something' is likely to be appealing to governments. The question that then arises is whether this outcome is one which goes far enough to resolve problems common to all Member States.

The legitimacy of OMC is, however, dubious. This is despite the fact that the intimate involvement of national government in the process seems to invest the process with the legitimacy of the nation state (Zeitlin and Pochet, 2005). This, it can be argued, is little more than a veneer. The OMC does not answer the fundamental criticisms of EU governance, elitism and opacity, even if it does allow for the participation of the social partners to some degree (Hodson and Maher, 2001; Barnard, 2002). The democratic legitimacy of guidelines drawn up by unaccountable officials and agreed by representatives of national government in closed session is questionable, especially in so politically sensitive a policy area, however well intentioned the proposals and the underlying diagnoses. Decisions in areas like employment have always been reached through a delicate process of mediation between interests within a country, so that if guidelines are issued by 'Brussels' that call for unpopular or controversial reforms, they risk being seen as unacceptable (Chassard, 2001). A risk in this regard is that the EU could be used as a scapegoat. Indeed it might be argued that this could provide part of the motivation for Europeanisation for governments keen to push through unpopular measures such as agreeing to pension reforms at the European level in order to circumvent a lack of domestic support.

The issue of monitoring and enforcement of policy is also important. Here, there is a tension at the heart of OMC. The more strictly any targets are monitored, the less the discretion available to a Member State in shaping programmes. At the same time, if there is no sanction (or, as was the case for the EMU convergence criteria, a reward) for failing to adopt suitable measures, let alone meeting targets, the attempt to co-ordinate could prove to be empty. The degree to which the OMC genuinely leads to policy innovation rather than repackaging of existing policies is germane. More generally, the OMC could be used as a pretext for avoiding hard decisions about the appropriate recasting of policy competencies in the EU policy framework, bearing in mind the salience of the integration of monetary policy.

Given the very limited extent of convergence of employment policy and the differing politics and institutional character of national systems of labour relations, agreement is never going to be easy to achieve on the ideological basis for policy. This shows in the EES guidelines for employment policies which contain a mixture of approaches from reform of tax and benefit systems to reducing poverty traps and providing incentives, to promotion of career breaks and parental leave. These problems of differentiation, lack of consensus and absence of an agreed ideological basis of employment policy are compounded by the interventionism necessary to create a European employment policy. The broad remit of employment policy means its reform is contentious, particularly as at its heart is the social welfare system and the redistributive policies of the state. Yet, as Andersen and Rasmussen (1999) show, a country like Denmark has been able to transform the capacity of the economy to employ people through a series of structural reforms. These initiatives may not translate directly into what others can do and there is no single magic solution, but the opportunities for learning are not to be dismissed.

5.4 How well is the process functioning?

The main difficulty in assessing the effectiveness of the EES is that its outcomes in terms of the employment rate or a reduction in unemployment cannot convincingly be attributed to the strategy alone. Macroeconomic volatility since the first year of the strategy (1998) has been considerable, with above average growth in 1999 and 2000, followed by a sharp slowdown in 2001 then only gradual recovery. Although there has been net job creation in most Member States since the Luxembourg process was launched and some progress towards the Lisbon employment rate target, a causal link cannot plausibly be demonstrated. Instead, the issue from the perspective of co-ordination is whether the process itself is working well. This raises a number of questions at different levels. First, have the procedures been implemented as intended? Second, is there evidence that the process has led to significant changes in policy? Third, do any changes appear to have improved the quality of policy intervention? Finally, does the EES represent a successful mode of co-ordination that ensures not only that microeconomic objectives are fulfilled but also that the macroeconomic dimension of employment policy is enhanced in a way that promotes adjustment under EMU? These are addressed in turn.

5.4.1 Procedures in the EES

The cycle of guidelines, plans, reports and delivery appears to have become well entrenched in the policy calendar up to 2003 and to be taken seriously by the various actors involved. The guidelines compiled year by year evolved, as intended, took account of experience, and were accepted by Member States as broadly reasonable. The substantial revision that took place after the Lisbon European Council was followed by a relatively minor change for the 2002 guidelines, although the broad thrust (i.e. the four pillar structure) remained. A comparison between the first employment report in 1998 and the 2003 version suggests that Member States have become much more attuned to what is expected and have been willing to conform, rather than just playing along. All Member States produce substantial NAPs that set out credible strategies. However, following the switch to a three-year cycle and the closer integration of the EES with the Lisbon strategy, it remains to be seen whether this enthusiasm will be maintained.

Moreover, there is a grey area between, as Jacobsson (2002: 2) puts it, 'the superficial adaptation of fulfilling the reporting procedures' and having a long-term (beneficial) impact on policy practice. Where the procedures still warrant some criticism is in the lack of enforcement and in situations where recommendations challenge national preferences. Thus, Jacobsson (2002: 6) notes, for Sweden, that both the BEPGs and the employment recommendations have urged the government to lower taxes on

> labour particularly for low and middle-income earners and to review tax and benefit systems to improve job incentives. The position of the Swedish government is that taxation is an issue of national competence. To have European goals for the level of taxation is not considered to be in line with the subsidiarity principle. However, so far, the recommendations on tax reductions on labour have been acceptable for Sweden (but

not the setting of a specific target for the tax reductions, a recommendation from 2001 to which the government has not responded).

5.4.2 Policy evolution

Studies commissioned by Member States for the five-year review of the EES confirmed that, although it was too early to observe much tangible impact on employment from the EES, the procedural changes were having an impact (for a summary, see EMCO, 2002). In Germany, for instance, the effect has been marked in pushing the authorities, on the one hand, to pay more attention to stimulating employability policies, with greater focus on the disabled, and on the other, that equal opportunities have been taken more seriously (RWI, 2002). The authors also conclude that the pay-off in terms of jobs will become greater in the medium term. Changes in other countries suggest similar detailed changes that point to policy learning.

The evolution of the Employment Guidelines themselves was partly the result of pressures for simplification, but also seems to reflect certain policies becoming routine in the national armoury, whereas certain additional areas have been added to help to refocus effort. Lisbon, to some extent, was a significant development that added new tasks and priorities.

Visser (2002), citing interviews on how the EES has functioned in the Netherlands, found that 'the EES receives broad political support in the Netherlands. Our respondents argue that they take the EES seriously, and we believe they do. The largest benefit is that employment policy is being discussed at the highest European level, Ministers and national civil servants are kept alert, and an activating approach towards social policy is more widely diffused.' Visser also found some evidence that the EES had led to policy innovation notably helping 'the national discussion in the Netherlands on some issues (such as long-term unemployment) out of a blind alley. It also helped the introduction of some new instruments of labour market policy.' Visser also expresses some scepticism about the process, remarking that 'the EES served as an additional justification for policies that would have been introduced anyway'. This highlights one of the fundamental dilemmas about the OMC generally and its application specifically in the field of employment policy, namely whether it genuinely leads to policy innovation or is simply a re-packaging of existing policies with no more than a veneer of co-ordination.

Change has, however, been evident in the philosophies of different countries' approaches. As an illustration, France, initially, was uncomfortable with the notion of employability, seeing it as a neo-liberal approach at odds with French traditions (a reaction that has, ironically, resurfaced in 2005 in the discourse around the services directive – often labelled 'Bolkestein' after its progenitor in the Prodi Commission – and the referendum on the constitutional treaty). But examination of the 1999 and 2000 NAPs by Madsen *et al.* (2002) suggests that the French plans (at least on paper – execution is another issue) have rather more in common with the UK than might have been anticipated. These and other examples (see, notably, some of the national chapters in Zeitlin and Pochet, 2005) demonstrate that policy learning has taken place within the Luxembourg process.

5.4.3 Quality of policy

Assessments of the quality of policy are more problematic. Successive employment (subsequently 'joint') reports from the Commission, written as part of the monitoring of the Luxembourg process, provide some insights into the changing character of policy and generally suggest that overall quality has improved. Plainly, though, the changes depend on respective national starting-points and are more convincing in some areas than in others. The point, however, is that as a co-ordination process, the EES *has* been instrumental in stimulating qualitative changes in policy.

On the whole, the NAPs show a willingness to adapt and to draw on best practice or lessons from others. In this respect, there is evidence that the learning that is supposed to be promoted by the process and is central to the open method is happening. It is also evident from national reports and research done by commentators on the EES that worthwhile changes in Member State approaches have been induced by the EES. Visser, for example, cites better statistical monitoring, while most of the national reports that feed into the five-year review cite similar improvements in policy practice.

The Italian report for the five years is, however, less sanguine than some others. It acknowledges the worthiness of the aims, but suggests that the extent of the focus on activation in the guidelines may not be appropriate in Italy. In contrast, the Danish report is very positive in drawing attention to how closely Danish policy conforms to the guidelines. An interpretation might be that where the guidelines are confluent with national policy preferences they work better, an inference that could presage problems for the EES as a co-ordination mechanism.

One area in which qualitative change can be noted is in policy debate and the broadening of policy input. Even in Sweden, a country in which social dialogue is well entrenched, Jacobsson (2002: 6) reports that the EES 'has contributed, *inter alia*, to new dynamics in social partner dialogue, improvement of policy integration and a more comprehensive perspective on employment policy, and better coordination between policy areas within their own organisations'. Again, evidence from elsewhere points to similar shifts in behaviour, although whether there will be tangible benefits in terms of output variables is necessarily unproven.

Nevertheless, there is evidence that the Luxembourg process has given a higher profile to employment policy and that it has resulted in a less Balkanised approach to dealing with the policy area within national administrations.

In an assessment of the impact of the EES, the Employment Committee cites, and praises examples of such enhanced intra-governmental co-operation in several Member States. It concludes that 'the integrated employment policy approach embedded in the employment guidelines has forced national governments to strengthen the coherence of their policies. The jury remains out, however, on whether the changes are the direct result of the EES or merely the natural evolution of policy-making. The EMCO report, for example, draws attention to the greater involvement of national parliaments in employment policy, yet waters down its finding by observing that 'this better quality of involvement does not yet extend beyond the institutional circles of employment and social affairs committees' (EMCO, 2002: 6). Moreover, observers of the debate in Germany on labour market reform would be hard pressed to find EU processes behind the successive 'Hartz' initiatives or the elaboration of the Agenda 2010 strategy (Ardy and Umbach, 2004).

5.5 Integration with core macroeconomic policy

Although the EES appears to be working tolerably well in its own terms, what is less clear is how it fits into the overall conduct of macroeconomic policy and policy co-ordination more generally. There are three distinct issues here: first, the success of the EES in stimulating employment in the EU; second, whether the content of the strategy assists macroeconomic adjustment and third, whether it is adequately co-ordinated with demand-side policies and other supply-side measures. A reasonably sanguine view can be taken of the first, since the evidence of employment trends suggests that there has been some improvement in the underlying rate of job creation, although the lacklustre recovery from the downturn of 2001 was a disappointment, suggesting that it is the second half of the current decade (following the 2005 re-launch of the Lisbon strategy) that will be the real test. So far, the indications are that unemployment has not risen as it might have done, although the corollary (borne out by the data in the Commission's structural indicators database) is that productivity growth has been sluggish.

The EES has, arguably, contributed to a general rethinking of how labour market adjustment can be achieved, although it is open to the criticism that too many of the guidelines are tangential to a genuine adjustment strategy. In particular, the EES does not deal with the politically most awkward dimensions of the labour market, such as wage flexibility and labour market regulation. This is, in part, because the focus of the EES has been on employment policies *per se* and not on the broader contribution that they might make to steering the economy. But it is also because the links from the Luxembourg process to other structural reform measures have – so far – been inadequately developed in the institutional framework. Here, again, the 2005 re-launch of the Lisbon strategy ostensibly promises improvements by requiring a closer integration of policies.

Some critics, such as Visser (2002), argue that there has also been an undue concentration on what he identifies as the OECD (as in the 1994 'jobs study') viewpoint in which liberalisation and deregulation of labour markets is crucial. While there is undoubtedly truth in this, it can also be argued that the EES encompasses more, especially in the degree to which it has stressed, and continues to stress, employability and adaptability, yet does not, in fact, engage with the liberalisation agenda. The question turns on what constitutes flexibility in the labour market and three possible orientations can be put forward:

1. The first is to let the market function much more freely, with less rigidity in conditions of employment and much more scope for wage adjustment.
2. Second, flexibility can imply greater mobility, whether across sectoral, gender, occupational or geographical boundaries.
3. A third route to flexibility is to 'invest' in labour by giving workers attributes that facilitate redeployment and help to avoid bottlenecks.

In practice, the Luxembourg process affects the third of these routes unambiguously and contributes to the second, but has little relevance for the first. The Cardiff process is ostensibly about improving the functioning of markets, but is principally concerned with product markets and consequently has little resonance for labour markets. Although 'Lisbon 2' (from 2005) represents a sensible attempt to bring together the competitive and cohesion aspects of economic policy co-ordination, there remains a gap in supply-side co-ordination processes around some of the harder dimensions of labour market change. Moreover, in the overall co-ordination of policy, further problems can be identified that aggravate the supply-side difficulties. The shortcomings were highlighted in a submission by the ETUC (2002) in which it was noted that:

> ETUC-supported Commission attempts to make a direct link within the first Guidelines to the overall economic policy-mix were defeated in the Council and, despite significant improvements having been made since, the EES became essentially a labour market rather than a broader employment strategy.

The challenge now is how to ensure that the reforms of the co-ordination machinery introduced in 2003 and the 2005 re-launch of the Lisbon strategy can assure better outcomes for employment as well as integrating labour market and employment policies more comprehensively in the overall policy framework. The BEPGs, in principle, provide a mechanism to co-ordinate co-ordination across policy boundaries, but the record to date has been patchy, though probably explicable by the sheer scale of change ushered in by the move to Stage 3 of EMU. The EES and the BEPGs followed separate timetables until 2003 and, institutionally, have been 'owned' by different DGs of the Commission and Councils of Ministers (and their counterpart ministries in Member States). The key changes introduced in 2003 are, first, to synchronise the timetables for the BEPG and EES procedures and, second, to move away from a strictly annual procedure towards a multi-annual programme by foreseeing a full review only every three years (with opportunities for updating in intervening years. The 2005 Lisbon re-launch, in principle, consolidates these changes.

What is less clear is how easy it will be either at EU level or at Member State level for co-ordination across different policy areas to take place, and especially for the sponsoring ministries to concert their activities. In many countries (and, arguably, the Commission), the finance ministries (DG Economic and Financial Affairs) tend to be the custodians of economic orthodoxy and thus to favour stability-orientated policies, whereas labour ministries (DG Employment and Social Affairs) are apt to be regarded as more concerned with full employment aims and redistributive policies. Social affairs ministries, meanwhile, often see themselves as the guardians of the welfare state. Marked and genuine differences in policy outlooks may therefore arise and will not easily be reconciled.

Two sorts of alternatives can be envisaged. The first would be greatly to enhance the upstream role of the BEPGs such that they set the general tone for employment policy, with the EES then being much more about the tactics rather than the strategy. On some readings of the nature of the co-ordination machinery, this is indeed how it is supposed to function (see notably, Commission 2002e) and implies a degree of subordination of employment policy which would imply, almost certainly, Ecofin having the decisive role. Some of the rhetoric around the 2005 Lisbon re-launch also goes in this direction (Commission, 2005a). If this lexicographic ordering of roles is enhanced, the trade-off is that gains in coherence would risk being offset by the loss of the creative tension of having the issue addressed by policy-makers with different outlooks and priorities.

The second resolution is a variant on the notion of a gouvernement économique as espoused, notably, by French economists such as Boyer (1999) and Pisani-Ferry (2002). But instead of being constituted largely as a fiscal counterpart to a powerful and integrated monetary policy, any new body should have a broader remit to orchestrate policy across a range of supply-side domains.

5.6 Concluding comments

Economic policy co-ordination in the EU has made great strides in recent years, yet still finds itself facing uncertainties and awkward choices. On the one hand, there is a need to consolidate the policy framework sufficiently to make EMU effective and to ensure that the broader economic and social ambitions of the Union are achieved. This calls for fresh thinking about who does what in the policy framework and about the interplay between, and importance of coherence in, different policy areas. Co-ordination has largely been seen as a disciplining device (as in the SGP), yet it is clear that this is not a central aim of the Luxembourg process, nor of the other supply-side reforms under the Lisbon umbrella.

On the other hand, political imperatives combined with dismay about the conduct of some aspects of policy at the supranational level result in a reluctance to countenance the conferring of further competence on supranational bodies. As a means of resolving this dilemma, the OMC – as used now for eight years in the EES and adopted subsequently for social inclusion and pensions policy as well as more generally for the Lisbon strategy – offers a promising way forward precisely because it reconciles these conflicting elements.

That said, what should the Luxembourg process be expected to deliver as part of the integrated, post-EMU policy system? First, it ensures that employment remains firmly on the agenda, a political advantage not to be under-estimated. Second, it offers a route towards greater labour market flexibility from perspectives other than variations in wages, especially in providing for various means of enhancing the attributes of the labour force. The importance of this contribution is that it means that labour market responses are not confined to pressures that might be perceived purely negatively, such as lowering wages or lowering conditions of employment.

The Luxembourg process has, moreover, exhibited a capacity to evolve – as shown in the reform post-Lisbon in 2000, the major changes that were implemented in 2003, and the new approach from 2005 – while also maintaining a degree of consistency and continuity as can be seen in the proposed constitutional treaty where change is minimal. In all these respects, it has functioned pragmatically. An awkward question is, nevertheless, where it goes from here. It could be argued that the stimulus to change from the array of benchmarking and peer review processes will start to suffer from diminishing returns, with the risk that the administrative weight of the process becomes unacceptable.

As the new streamlined machinery for policy co-ordination is replaced by the more integrated post-2005 'Lisbon 2', therefore, it is to be hoped that the Luxembourg process will be seen as valuable not just in its own right, but also in terms of its scope for contributing to an improved EU policy system. The analyses in Zeitlin and Pochet (2005) show that it has had its successes, though it can be difficult to trace change directly to the EES. The broader question of whether the OMC offers a worthwhile approach to policy co-ordination, however, elicits a less positive answer, as in the Kok report (2004). But in both cases, there is a question of where next? Kok's criticism turns, above all on the reluctance in many Member States to make a strong commitment to the specific reforms required to enact the Lisbon strategy, despite paying lip-service to the aims. The requirement, as part of the 2005 re-launch, to adopt National Reform Plans somewhat hardens the Lisbon approach, and in so doing follows the EES path. Ultimately, though it still requires that actors at the national level take it seriously, that governments invest enough political capital in it to create momentum, and that back-sliding engenders a political cost that acts as a deterrent.

A tentative conclusion is that 'soft' co-ordination has an important role to play in the economic governance of the EU, and should not be seen as a mode of governance that is just transitional, or somehow of lesser importance. But it has to be properly integrated with other facets and forms of co-ordination and that is the challenge for the coming years. It also has to be capable of motivating policy-makers to take bold decisions. If it cannot, then hard questions may have to be asked about whether a European dimension to co-ordination is needed or how it can be made to support adjustment under EMU.

Part II

Adjustment at the National Level

6

The Early Years of EMU: Convergence, but Uneven Adjustment?

Although a vast amount of research went into prior assessments of how EMU would function and there was an abundance of theoretical work on what would shape outcomes, the empirical picture is, in some respects, quite surprising. From the vantage point of the early 1990s, for example, it might have been expected that Germany and its close neighbours – notably the Benelux countries and Austria – would be the countries most comfortable with monetary union. Germany's dominance of the EMS implied that it would also be the core of monetary union and would not have to change much, especially with the European Central Bank having been set up, apparently, in the image of the Bundesbank.

In the event, Germany has proved to be one of the countries least at ease with EMU. It has struggled to recover from the 2001 slowdown, found it difficult to keep its deficit below the 3% of GDP threshold and has yet to realise the benefits of its piecemeal labour market reforms. Germany also presents paradoxes that go to the heart of the economic governance challenges confronting EMU. It entered Stage 3 with an exchange rate which, by common consensus, was probably too high (Deroose *et al.*, 2004), yet appears to be internationally competitive if its strong performance in export markets is the benchmark. Germany's fiscal problems have been well documented, but it has had one of the lower inflation rates, so that any blame for inflationary pressures in the euro area cannot plausibly be laid at Germany's door, even though such a link was part of the rationale for the SGP. Germany would have been expected to be the anchor of EMU, but correcting its slow growth and fiscal difficulties have come to define one of the core challenges for the EMU framework.

Greece, Italy, Portugal and (to a lesser extent) Spain, by contrast, had a very different background, characterised notably by persistently high rates of inflation that appeared to be incompatible with those in Germany and the other core EMS countries. Indeed a common interpretation of Theo Waigel's insistence on a tough Stability and Growth Pact was that it was needed to assuage fears in German public opinion by forestalling any possibility of stable macroeconomic policies being compromised or contaminated by inflation-prone partners. For the southern European countries, the distance that had to be travelled to conform was greater and it might have been expected that they would struggle within EMU. So far the outcome has been very varied. Greece and Spain seem to have gained from the EMU framework, whereas Italy and Portugal are struggling.

Much of this book is concerned with the questions of adjustment in Stage 3 of EMU, though for many Member States there was a much greater problem of adjustment in qualifying for Stage 3 in the first place. Several of the new Member States face the same issue. At the root of these questions is how easily the different EU economies would find it to live together in a monetary union. While the optimum currency area (OCA) approach can offer some answers, Bayoumi and Eichengreen (1997: 761) are surely correct in their judgement that 'many economists do not like it very much. OCA theory, with its focus on asymmetric shocks, labor mobility and the transactions value of a single currency, subsumes but a subset of considerations relevant to the decision of whether to fix the exchange rate or form a monetary union.' The theory does not even consider political motivations for EMU, even though these are manifestly central to the EU 'project'.

In this chapter, we first review what was expected from EMU, notably in empirical assessments of the 'optimality' of the EU Member States as a currency area and in the convergence process. We then present an overview of macroeconomic trends in Stage 2 and Stage 3 and of the experience since the launch of the euro, notably with regard to the Stability and Growth Pact. Section 6.3 consists of brief case studies of three of the larger countries – France, Italy and Spain – in the Stage 2 convergence period and since, highlighting the contrasts between them. Subsequent empirical chapters look in much greater detail at developments in individual Member States. Chapter 7 is on Germany, the country long seen as the anchor of monetary integration in Europe, but which has encountered considerable difficulties in recent years. The chapter highlights the problems of adjustment and concentrates on the supply-side reforms that are regarded as a necessary complement to EMU. Ireland, the runaway success story of recent years, is the subject of Chapter 8. Chapters 9 and 10 look, respectively, at two of the Nordic countries – Finland and Sweden – that have adopted strategies towards EMU that are in marked contrast to each other. Finland has embraced EMU enthusiastically and has proved to be one of the better performers within the euro area, whereas Swedish doubts about EMU culminated in the rejection of the euro in the September 2003 referendum. The UK, which has consistently been the least enthusiastic about EMU, yet which has also, perhaps paradoxically, conducted the most thorough empirical assessment of the case for membership, is the subject of Chapter 11. In Chapter 12 we explore the prospects for the new members, focusing especially on Estonia, which is hoping to be in the first group of new euro area members to participate fully in EMU, possibly as early as 2007.

6.1 What was expected of EMU?

The EMU's very long gestation meant that the likely empirical consequences of forming a monetary union among the EU's Member States had been extensively analysed (see, for example, De Grauwe, 2003, and the series of studies produced by HM Treasury in 2003). On the whole, the literature tended to the view that EMU would be beneficial to the core countries such as Germany and France, but might prove more challenging for others such as Italy and the southern European countries which joined the EU in the 1980s.

A successful convergence process, in effect, requires the ability to mimic membership of the monetary union, without obvious strain, for one or two years. But it is by no means the only consideration, not least because it says little about the likely impact on the real economy, nor was it the only pathway to membership. In the debate around joining EMU at the time of the negotiation and ratification of the Maastricht treaty, two schools of thought emerged about how to proceed. One favoured prior convergence by ensuring that the participants in the monetary union had similar inflation rates and other nominal indicators. As Wyplosz (1997: 10) notes, this approach came to be known 'as the "economist's view," although it does not seem to have been fully articulated in the professional literature'. Indeed an irony of the labelling is that this economists' view was most heartily endorsed by central bankers; for example, Wyplosz (1997: 10) draws attention to the fact that 'the Bundesbank championed it under the name of "coronation approach," ... EMU is to be born in a land dedicated to a culture of price stability'.

The other school of thought – again with some irony – came to be known as the 'monetarist' approach, in spite of being the one mainly espoused by academic economists of diverse persuasions. Its main thesis was that once countries entered a monetary union, economic agents would rapidly adapt their behaviour, a corollary of which is that their history would have only a marginal bearing on how they conducted themselves under EMU. The logic of this position was that a 'big bang' move to EMU would be the most attractive route, partly because it would avoid the potential damage to the real economy from an extended period of restraint aimed at achieving the required limits for the nominal indicators.

6.1.1 Optimum currency area indicators

In considering what might have been expected of EMU, it is useful to start by considering whether insights can be gleaned from research in the optimum currency area tradition. Though many have argued, in the spirit of Feldstein (1997), that the EU lacked – and still lacks – many of the necessary attributes to justify forming a currency area, these judgements have mainly been conceptual rather than empirical. An important exception is the OCA index developed by Bayoumi and Eichengreen (1997) which provides a measure of how easy it was likely to be for other Member States to live in monetary union with Germany. This index captures the effects of asymmetries between pairs of countries in the trend of output, linkages between countries via trade, and the usefulness of money for transactions.

Perhaps surprisingly, after the lengthy period during which France and Germany pursued similar policies following the adoption of the *franc fort* policy after the major policy shift in 1983, the index shows France and Germany as not being that close. As prospective partners for Germany in a monetary union, Finland and Spain score even worse in contrast to the relatively favourable scores for Germany's other immediate neighbours (and Ireland). Bayoumi and Eichengreen distinguish between three groups of countries as regards their compatibility with Germany on the OCA index, which they compute for 1987, 1991 and 1995. They noted (p. 769) that 'the make-up of the groups tends to coincide with popular handicapping of the Maastricht stakes with one notable exception: France', although their assessment of France is explained more by the third observation than the first two. In Table 6.1 their findings are summarised, with countries ranked by the 1991 value.

These groupings differ slightly from those presented by Bayoumi and Eichengreen in that we have placed France at the bottom of what we define as the 'ambivalent' group, rather than with the 'least likelys'. France, in 1991, achieved a score similar to Italy's, but only drifted away subsequently. The table also highlights the substantial difference between the last group and the first, the implication (ironically with hindsight) being that Spain and Finland would have the greatest difficulties in a monetary union with Germany.

Table 6.1 Compatibility of monetary union with Germany (OCA index, 0 = compatible)

	1987	1991	1995
Closest to Germany			
Belgium	0.003	–0.008	0.013
Netherlands	0.003	–0.008	0.007
Austria	0.008	–0.004	0.008
Ireland	0.043	0.036	0.021
Ambivalent			
Greece	0.053	0.054	0.054
Denmark	0.063	0.060	0.074
Sweden	0.068	0.063	0.056
Portugal	0.068	0.066	0.062
Italy	0.070	0.065	0.059
France	0.068	0.067	0.074
Least likely			
Spain	0.088	0.082	0.073
U.K.	0.099	0.094	0.089
Finland	0.098	0.095	0.087

Source: Bayoumi and Eichengreen (1997).

6.1.2 The formal convergence criteria

A different perspective on what was expected to happen during Stage 2 of EMU is attained by looking at the nominal indicators incorporated in the Treaty to measure convergence. Formally, as is well known, eligibility for full participation in EMU is conditional on fulfilling the Maastricht convergence criteria described in earlier chapters.

Meeting the convergence criteria was not easy for several of the eleven countries that were, subsequently, to become the first wave. Excessive deficits had been endemic throughout Stage 1 of EMU in the early 1990s and much of Stage 2. Indeed in 1997, one year before the assessments on eligibility for Stage 3, the Council decision (based on 1996 indicators) was that only Ireland, Luxembourg, the Netherlands and Finland *did not* have excessive deficits. Five years earlier, the divergences among EU Member States were substantial (Table 6.2), with deficits ranging from 1% in Finland to double figures in Italy and Greece.

At the start of Stage 2, in 1994, deficits had jumped in several countries, though it is noteworthy that Germany – still then regarded as the model – only had marginal slippage above the 3% threshold during the 1990s, despite the well-publicised costs of supporting unification. The lure of Stage 3 clearly galvanised national governments, because there was a pronounced fiscal consolidation between 1994 and 1997.

Inflation convergence had, perhaps surprisingly given the history of some Member States, been attained rather more easily, although still in 1996, all four southern European countries were just above the reference value. Table 6.3 summarises the positions on the Maastricht convergence criteria that formed the basis for the decisions on which countries would enter Stage 3 in the

Table 6.2 General government deficits of euro area members

	1991	1994	1997
Austria	–2.3	–4.7	–2.0
Belgium	–7.5	–5.1	–2.0
Finland	–1.0	–5.7	–1.3
France	–2.4	–5.5	–3.0
Germany	–2.9	–2.4	–2.7
Greece	–11.0	–9.3	–4.0
Ireland	–2.9	–2.0	1.5
Italy	11.7	–9.3	–2.7
Luxembourg	1.2	2.7	3.2
Netherlands	–2.7	–3.5	–1.1
Portugal	–7.6	–7.7	–3.6
Spain	–4.6	–6.5	–3.2
Euro area	–5.0	–5.1	–2.6

Source: OECD *Economic Outlook*, Volume 2004/2, No. 76, December.

Table 6.3 The Council decision on the first wave of euro area members

Reference value	Inflation (2.7% HICP)	Long-term interest rate (7.8%)	Budget deficit (3% of GDP)	Public debt (60% of GDP)	Exchange rate (In ERM for 2 years +)
Belgium	1.4	5.7	2.1	122.2	Yes
Germany	1.4	5.6	2.7	61.3	Yes
Spain	1.8	6.3	2.6	68.8	Yes
France	1.2	5.5	3.0	58.0	Yes
Ireland	1.2	6.2	0.9	66.3	Yes
Italy	1.8	6.7	2.7	121.6	No, but stable exchange rate for 2 years
Luxembourg	1.4	5.6	–1.7	6.7	Yes
Netherlands	1.8	5.5	1.4	72.1	Yes
Austria	1.1	5.6	2.5	66.1	Yes
Portugal	1.8	6.2	2.5	62.0	Yes
Finland	1.3	5.9	0.9	55.8	No, but stable exchange rate for 2 years
Greece	5.2	9.8	4.0	108.7	No

Source: European Monetary Institute (1998).

first wave. The table shows that all were comfortably in line with the inflation criterion, reflecting the steady price stabilisation that had taken place during the 1990s. All eleven were also comfortably within the long-run interest rate limit, with only Italy looking at all vulnerable.

However, it is in relation to the two fiscal criteria that the fineness of the judgements about eligibility become more evident. Only three of the countries were actually under the threshold for public debt, which meant that the other eight had to rely on the subsidiary test of moving sufficiently rapidly towards it. Even then, Germany was not only above the level (though by a tiny margin), but its debt was also rising. Finland and Italy had not been in the ERM for the stipulated two years, though they were adjudged to have had stable exchange rates. Greece failed all the tests in 1998, though it was able (with what proved subsequently to be creative accounting) to do so by 2000, though with the same dispensation as Italy and Belgium on its very high debt.

On price stability, the EMI report notes that there had been very rapid progress in the two years preceding the assessment in Italy, Portugal and Spain, with all three shaving 2–3 percentage points off their inflation rates. The report (p. 7) also contains carefully phrased warnings about future prospects, especially as regards fiscal positions: 'Notwithstanding recent achievements, further substantial consolidation is warranted in most Member States in order to achieve lasting compliance with the fiscal criteria and the medium-term objective of having a budgetary position that is close to balance or in surplus.' Indeed, in a foretaste of problems to come, only Ireland and Luxembourg were left off the list of countries to which this advice is addressed, though the warnings about the heavily indebted countries are strongest. Despite the use of dry and careful language, the EMI manages to convey a greater degree of concern about fiscal policy in Italy than in other Member States. Doubts are expressed about whether fiscal sustainability had been achieved, and the authorities are enjoined to make further fiscal consolidation a priority.

In summary, even on the apparently strict convergence criteria, the evidence used to assess the first participants in Stage 3 was, at least in part, fudged. Moreover, although there had obviously been considerable convergence, it could not be guaranteed that an interest rate set for the euro area as a whole would be well suited to prevailing conditions in all of the euro-area economies. Mayes and Virén (2000) argue that differences in the speed and extent of national monetary transmission mechanisms could lead to divergent responses to common euro area monetary policy, even in the presence of convergent national business cycles. Their findings, which are summarised in Figure 6.1,

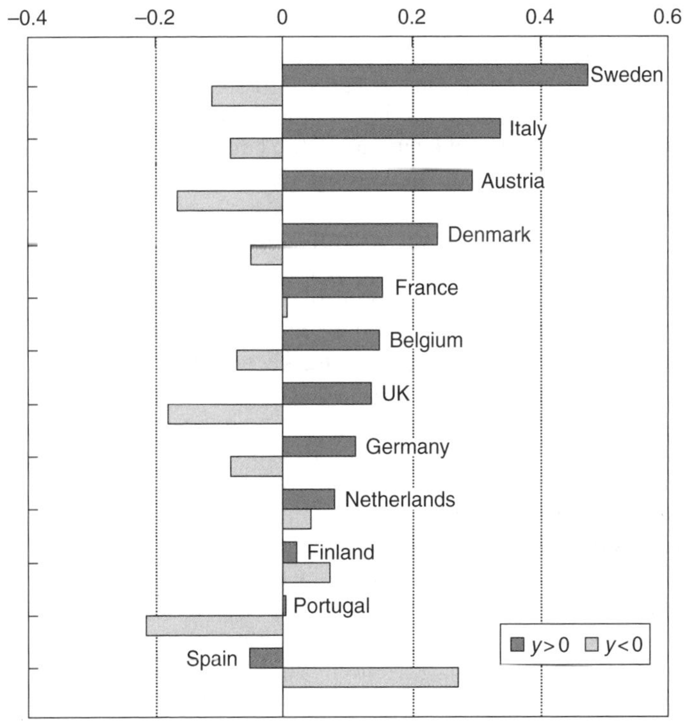

Figure 6.1 Responsiveness of inflation to positive ($y>0$) and negative ($y<0$) output gaps EU countries 1987–1998. *Source*: Mayes and Virén (2000)

are that there is significant asymmetry in the Phillips curves of individual Member States over the period 1975–1998.

In general terms, these results indicate that the disinflationary consequences of a negative output gap are likely to be less intensive than the inflationary consequences of growth. Moreover, the fundamental differences in national inflationary processes means that those Member States with high unemployment could face a higher interest rate to alleviate the inflationary consequences of high growth elsewhere in the euro area. Spain, in this regard, is a case in point. Mayes and Virén find that the impact of disinflationary policy is comparatively slower and milder in Spain than in the other countries. This evidence is supported by the findings of Artis *et al.* (1999) who show that the inflationary response to booms in Spain is considerably quicker than its reaction to recessions.

6.1.3 Supply-side considerations, especially the labour market

EMU changes the scope for using different policy instruments in adjusting the economy, reducing the importance of conventional demand management and putting more of the burden of adjustment on supply-side polices, notably those that bear on the labour market. A further empirical issue is, therefore, how suited the labour markets of the Member States were for monetary integration. The data show that the EU Member States had very different labour market characteristics in the run up to Stage 3 not only in terms of unemployment, but also in the employment rate and in the underlying dynamics and flexibility. For example, in the late 1970s, Spanish unemployment began to diverge from the European average and has since remained the highest in the Union.

Long-term unemployment was a significant problem in several countries, such as Greece, Germany, Italy, Belgium and Spain. One of the consequences of long-term unemployment is to increase the proportion of the labour force that becomes detached from the labour market (known as *hysteresis*). This explains in part why economic growth quickly reaches the economy's output capacity despite the existence of considerable labour market capacity. The unemployment problem, especially in Italy and in Spain, is compounded by relatively low levels of labour participation, hence the emphasis in the Lisbon strategy on raising the employment rate. In the light of this evidence it is hardly surprising that a significant reduction in the rate of unemployment is a primary objective for several governments.

One particularly contentious issue is the form of regulation of the labour market. As discussed in earlier chapters, labour market flexibility is considered to be an important alternative to demand-side adjustment in a monetary union. Table 6.4 summarises the position on the eve of monetary union. The table shows that several of the first wave of members of the euro area had characteristics that can be considered inimical to flexibility. As emphasised in HM Treasury (2003a), this absence of flexibility was expected to be an obstacle

Table 6.4 Labour market institutions and regulation

	Unemployment rate %	Employment protection legislation 1998						Summary measure of centralisation/ co-ordination, 1998			Net replacement rates, 1997[c]		Active labour market policies, 1997[d]		Minimum wage/average earnings,[e] 1997	
		Overall index[a]		Permanent contract[b]		Temporary contract[b]										
	1997–1999 average	Index	Rank	Index	Rank	Index	Rank	Cent	Coor	Cent/ coor	Index	Rank	Index	Rank	Index	Rank
Spain	18.4	3.2	4	2.8	4	3.7	2	2	2	2	74	4	0.56	5	32.4	6
Italy	12.2	3.3	3	3.0	3	3.6	3	3	3	3	54	11	1.08	7		
France	11.9	3.1	5	2.5	6	3.7	2	2	2	2	74	4	1.37	10	57.4	1
Finland	11.6	2.1	8	2.3	7	1.9	9	2	2	2	84	2	1.57	11		
Greece	9.5	3.5	2	2.6	5	4.5	1				46	12	0.35	3	51.4	2
Germany	9.4	2.8	6	3.0	3	2.5	6	2	3	3	74	4	1.25	8		
Belgium	8.8	2.1	8	1.6	9	2.6	5	2	2	2	60	9	1.29	9		
Sweden	8.5	2.4	7	3.3	3	1.8	10	2	1	2	84	2	2.09	14		
Ireland	8.0	1.0	10	1.7	8	0.3	13	2	3	3	62	7	1.66	13		
UK	6.2	0.5	11	0.7	10	0.3	13	1	1	1	64	6				
Portugal	5.5	3.7	1	4.3	1	3.2	4	2	2	2	77	3	0.87	6	32.4	6
Denmark	5.2	2.4	7	2.8	4	2.0	8	2	3	3	73	5	0.45	4		
Austria	4.4	2.4	7	2.8	4	2.0	8	2	3	3	73	5	0.45	12	49.4	4
Nether	4.4	2.4	7	3.2	2	1.5	11	2	3	3	85	1	1.65	12	49.4	4
Euro area	11.7	2.9		2.8		3.0		2	2–3	2–3	70		1.20			
US	4.65	0.2	12	0.1	11	0.3	14	1	1	1	61	8	0.18	2	38.1	5
Japan	4.1	2.6	6	3.0	3	2.3	7	1	3	1	56	10	0.10	1	30.8	7

[a] Average of the indices for permanent and temporary contracts.
[b] For permanent contracts, the main aspects of legislation covered are those related to regular procedural inconveniences, notice and severance pay and difficulty of dismissal. For temporary workers, the index is a function of the number and tightness of the restrictions imposed on the use of fixed-term contracts (maximum number of successive contracts allowed or maximum cumulated duration) and temporary work agencies (type of work authorised).
[c] For a married couple with two children.
[d] In % of GDP. 1996 for Ireland and Italy.
[e] Mean hourly pay in manufacturing for Greece and Portugal and full-time median earnings including pay and bonuses for all other countries. Several EU countries do not have statutory minimum wages but have wage floors set by collective agreements.
Source: OECD (2000c), p. 98.

to efficient adjustment to shocks, as well being a source of incompatibility between Member States.

Other supply-side concerns include the impact of EMU on public investment, though it can be argued that the problem in this regard is more about the medium-term consequences of Stage 2 adjustment rather than a longer-term one. Evidence on this is provided by Turrini (2004) who reports that during Stage 2, public investment may have been disproportionately cut as countries sought to consolidate their public finances, but also finds some indications that after the initial adjustment, there may have been a recovery in public investment. He therefore concludes that it may be unfair to blame sub-optimal public investment purely on fiscal rules. Nevertheless, the slowdown may have aggravated the adverse effects of Stage 2 on a number of Member States as they then sought to make Stage 3 work.

6.1.4 Business cycle indicators

One of the simplest aspects of the 'economists' view of convergence is simply to see if the shape and characteristics of the 'business cycle' are similar. This enables all of the various facets that lead to differences to be summarised under a single heading. Thus not just the stream of shocks that hit the economy but the structure of responses given the nature of the supply side and other aspects of the institutional structure of the economy as well as any policy reactions are taken into account. On this count the evidence suggests (Crowley *et al.*, 2005) that the relationship among the euro area countries and the way it has been changing over the last 30 years is quite complex.

Just focusing on France, Germany and Italy, it is clear that at the normal business cycle frequency of four to eight years the countries have indeed been moving closer together, with a marked shift in the case of France, contemporaneous with the change in policy direction in the 1980s. However, at higher or lower frequencies there has been some divergence in addition to the obvious impact of German unification. These divergencies could pose problems both for the common monetary policy and for fiscal and structural policies which can be country specific (within bounds). Since 1997, the longer-term trends in France have been diverging from those in Germany and Italy. At higher frequencies, France has moved from lagging Germany to leading it. It also leads Italy.[1]

These are stylised facts and do not tell us whether it is the French economy that has become more flexible, the policy that has become more volatile or simply the shocks that have become different. Nevertheless, since the normal horizon for monetary policy is between one and three years, this divergence at a policy-relevant frequency suggests that a story of increasing convergence is over simplistic.

6.2 EMU during Stage 3

With Stage 3 of EMU now in its seventh year and a reasonable degree of consensus around the forecasts for 2005 and 2006, an assessment of how it has functioned can now be undertaken based on eight data points: six observations of actual data and two of forecasts. This section draws mainly on the European Commission's spring 2005 forecasts, published in April 2005 (Commission, 2005a). For the EU as a whole and for the euro area, three main phases can be distinguished:

1. The period 1999–2000 when growth was reasonably robust.
2. The period 2001–2003 when most Member States experienced a cyclical downturn.
3. The period 2004–2006 when growth rates recovered, though in a rather weak manner in a majority of euro area members.

Over the whole period, as Figures 6.2 and 6.3 show, there has been a huge dispersion in growth rates. Taking the forecasts for 2005 and 2006 to be accurate, Ireland's economy will have expanded by a staggering 64% in the eight years of Stage 3, more than six times as much as Germany – the laggard – which will have posted a cumulative growth of just 10.1%. There is no obvious pattern to the performances of the other ten euro area members. Two of the lower-income countries – Greece and Spain – have grown pretty robustly, but Portugal has languished near to the bottom of the table. Of the

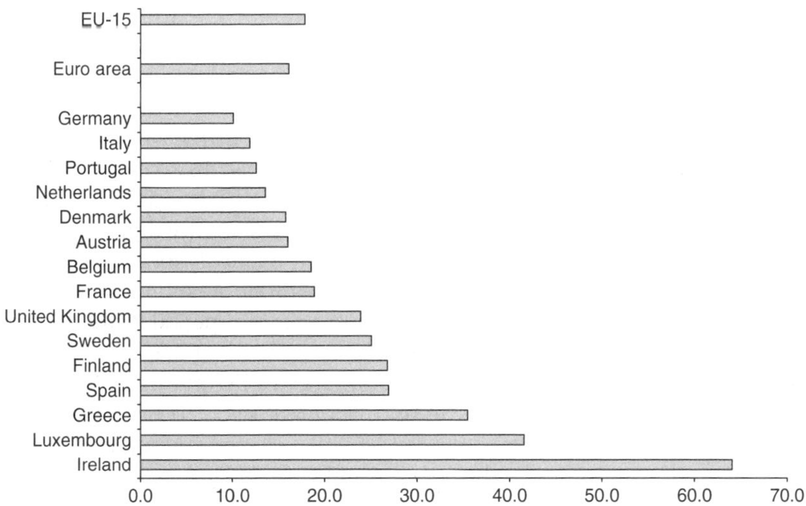

Figure 6.2 Cumulative growth in GDP, 1999–2006 (forecast), %

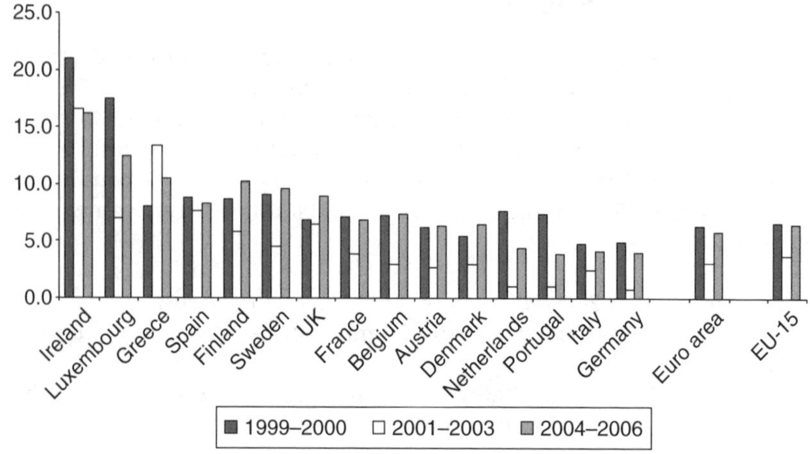

Figure 6.3 Growth since the launch of Stage 3, cumulative % over sub-period

larger economies, France has comfortably outpaced Italy, but lags significantly behind Spain. Most of the countries identified in the Bayoumi and Eichengreen index shown in Table 6.1 as being closest to Germany have grown relatively slowly, though the comparably slow growth of Italy and Portugal suggests this may not be a convincing explanation, especially in the light of Ireland's performance. Of the three 'outs', the UK and Sweden seem to have done well by staying out of Stage 3, but Denmark is almost exactly on the euro area average.

The three sub-periods – though obviously arbitrary – also reveal some intriguing differences. The Netherlands and Portugal were hit especially hard during the 2001–2003 recession, having been in line with EU average growth in the first two years of Stage 3, with their GDP growth stagnating, as did that of Germany. In the third period, these same three countries, along with Italy have become the back-markers. Greece, by contrast, had an acceleration of its already healthy growth rate in 2003 (helped by the substantial investment in the 2004 Olympics), while Spain's economic growth only dipped and has remained at a comfortable rate throughout, albeit markedly lower than in the first two years of the euro. France has continued to grow more rapidly than its two largest neighbours, but its growth over the third period is not enough to make inroads into its persistent unemployment. Among the 'outs', Sweden has maintained above average growth at a rate just behind that of Finland, its Nordic neighbour, while the UK and Denmark seem to have improved their relative positions.

Problems in conforming to the Stability and Growth Pact generally affected the slower growing countries most, though Greece (for more idiosyncratic reasons) is an exception. Table 6.5 summarises the record on the progressive increase in countries subject to the excessive deficit procedure, revealing the

Table 6.5 Member States subject to the excessive deficit procedure

	2002	2003	2004
New measures	Germany, Portugal	France	Greece, Netherlands, UK, Czech Rep., Cyprus, Hungary, Malta, Poland, Slovakia
Continuing		Germany, Portugal	France, Germany

weaknesses that led to the *de facto* suspension of the SGP in November 2003 and the reforms that were agreed in March 2005.

The shortcomings in the Pact as a framework for adjustment under EMU are, to a degree, chicken and egg in character: the effects of slow growth and the kicking-in of automatic stabilisers meant that deficits increased, but the capacity to adjust was itself diminished because the necessary correction prolonged the slowdown. In France, especially, this conjunction was regarded as damaging (see, for example, Le Cacheux, 2004; Fitoussi and Le Cacheux, 2005). The upshot was a classic example of the aphorism 'you wouldn't start from here'.

While the answer – namely that more should be done to consolidate public finances in good times so as to provide room for manoeuvre – is not only obvious, but also implicit in the SGP's medium-term close to balance rule, it proved to be ineffective. The main difficulty in this regard is that what look like good times after the event may not at the time, as can be seen by considering the circumstances of France and Germany, since demonised as serial delinquents in relation to the SGP. With hindsight, 1999 and 2000 can be regarded as 'good times' insofar as growth rates reached their highest levels in recent years in both countries. In Germany it reached 2.9% in 2000, well above the average of 2.1% recorded over the previous two decades, while in France growth surged to 3.8% in 2000, compared with a 20-year average of 2.2%. But unemployment was still regarded as alarmingly high in both countries at 7.8% in Germany (above the 20-year average of 6.9%) and 9.3% in France (a little below the long-term trend, but at a politically sensitive rate). It is important to recall that the political discourse at the time was about how to cut unemployment, not how to guard against slippage in fiscal ratios.

Turning to inflation rates, the magnitude of the change that has taken place for the previously inflation prone countries can readily be discerned from Table 6.6. Although there has been a little slippage in some countries since 1998 and there have been specific problems of asset inflation in some countries, the most striking phenomenon is that price stability seems to have become entrenched.

Table 6.6 Harmonised consumer price index: The long-term picture

	1961–1990	1991–1995	1996–2000	2000	2001	2002	2003	2004	2005f	2006f
Germany	3.5	3.1	1.1	1.4	1.9	1.3	1.0	1.8	1.3	1.1
Long-term low										
Austria	4.5	3.2	1.2	2.0	2.3	1.7	1.3	2.0	2.3	1.7
Luxembourg	4.6	2.8	1.7	3.8	2.4	2.1	2.5	3.2	3.1	1.9
Netherlands	4.7	2.9	1.9	2.3	5.1	3.9	2.2	1.4	1.3	–3.0
Belgium	5.1	2.4	1.6	2.7	2.4	1.6	1.5	1.9	2.0	1.8
Converged										
France	6.7	2.2	1.3	1.8	1.8	1.9	2.2	2.3	1.9	1.8
Finland	7.6	2.3	1.6	3.0	2.7	2.0	1.3	0.1	1.1	1.4
Ireland	8.6	2.5	2.6	5.3	4.0	4.7	4.0	2.3	2.1	2.4
Inflation prone										
Italy	9.1	5.0	2.4	2.6	2.3	2.6	2.8	2.3	2.0	1.9
Greece	11.6	13.9	4.6	2.9	3.7	3.9	3.4	3.0	3.2	3.2
Spain	10.1	5.2	2.6	3.5	2.8	3.6	3.1	3.1	2.9	2.7
Portugal	13.2	7.1	2.4	2.8	4.4	3.7	3.3	2.5	2.3	2.1
Euro area	6.8	3.5	1.7	2.1	2.4	2.3	2.1	2.1	1.9	1.5
Sweden	6.9	4.2	1.1	1.3	2.7	2.0	2.3	1.0	0.4	1.4
Denmark	7.2	2.0	2.0	2.7	2.3	2.4	2.0	0.9	1.4	1.7
United Kingdom	8.0	3.4	1.6	0.8	1.2	1.3	1.4	1.3	1.7	2.0
EU-15	7.1	3.7	1.7	1.9	2.2	2.1	2.0	2.0	1.8	1.6

Source: Commission (2005a).
Note: 'f' denotes forecasts.

6.3 The experience of Germany's three largest partners

France was pivotal to the development of EMU. Indeed, it can be argued that the process that ended with the establishment of the euro in 1999 began with the French government's decision in 1983 to switch its economic policy completely. By contrast, Italy was regarded, from the vantage point of 1991, as one about the Member States most likely to remain out when the decisions on Stage 3 were due to be taken in either 1996 or 1998. Indeed, a latent concern about Italian fiscal and monetary laxity was generally believed to be behind German fears about monetary union, and provided a key part of the rationale for the SGP. France had comparatively little need for adjustment to meet the Maastricht criteria and it would have been difficult to envisage EMU without it. Italy, however, had been forced to leave the ERM in 1992, at the same time as the UK, and had to deal with high inflation and unsustainable public finances. Spain, too, was seen as a marginal candidate for first wave membership of Stage 3, although it started without the millstone of very high debt that afflicted Italy, so that its principal challenge was to achieve inflation convergence. Yet it is also important to recognise that both Spain and Italy saw membership of Stage 3 as a vital national goal and they showed great determination not only to be included, but also to push through the reforms that were required to be eligible. According to Dyson and Featherstone (1999) 'for Italy, EMU was a test of external credibility: domestic weakness limited her overall influence on the progress of the initiative, whilst EMU was seized upon by a small leadership group as a new *vincolo esterno* (external constraint) to secure otherwise difficult domestic reforms'.

In the event, all three countries were among the first wave of euro area members. France fulfilled the convergence criteria easily and Spain was able to adjust fairly comfortably during Stage 2. Italy, however, had to rely on a combination of one-off measures to bring the deficit down to the 3% threshold and met the debt criterion only because it was deemed to be declining sufficiently (Commission, 1998).

The three cases are, therefore, very different in character and provide interesting insights into Stage 2 adjustment strategies that may have lessons for the new members. Section 6.3.1 looks at how France adjusted itself for the euro during the convergence phase. The following sections examine Italy first, then Spain. A concluding sub-section attempts to draw out broader implications.

6.3.1 France

Franco-German co-operation has been central to the process of European Integration in general, and monetary integration in particular. The European Monetary System (EMS) developed as a result of an initiative of Helmut Schmidt and Valerie Giscard d'Estaing and has been sustained by their successors, with Mitterrand and Kohl as the fathers of EMU. The two countries have also pursued broadly similar policies since the end of the French 'dash for growth' that rapidly ran into such trouble that the government had to change course in 1983. It had to choose between the political opprobrium associated with leaving the EMS while maintaining its growth policies, or stick with the EMS and abandon its economic programme in favour of deflationary policies to protect the exchange rate (Favier and Martin-Roland, 1990). The decision to remain inside the EMS and to pursue the *franc fort* policy became the central tenet of French economic policy for the 1980s and 1990s. It was this change of policy that, arguably, set in train the events that were to lead sixteen years later to EMU.

The decisive nature of this change in economic policy is illustrated by the exchange rate between the Franc and the Deutschmark which, from 1983 to 1998, was extremely stable. There were three relatively small realignments in the period 1985–1987 (de Haan and Eijffinger, 2000: 13), but since 1987 the central rate has been maintained. In practice, since 1987 the French economy has effectively had the same monetary policy as Germany.[2] Since there was no period of convergence, no structural adjustment, the continuance of a monetary policy based on Germany's requirements and none of the gains from imported credibility or reduced transactions costs, this represented a 'cold turkey' approach to EMU. The operation of the French economy under this regime provides a unique insight into the implications of membership of a monetary union.

The macroeconomic policy which France pursued prior to Stage 3 has been termed 'competitive disinflation' by one of its architects (Trichet, 1992) and had two key phases. The first involved reducing inflation by the exchange rate peg and fiscal consolidation and saw a sharp fall in inflation as early as 1983–1984. The second required keeping inflation low to make France more competitive and thereby to increase the demand for French goods and services. This seems to have been the result of a successful wages policy, but apart from this interlude, the shift in policy does not seem to have affected wage setting and inflation processes in France (Blanchard and Sevestre, 1989; Poret, 1990; Ralle and Toujas-Bernate, 1990; Onofri and Tomasini, 1992). Inflation was reduced, though at the costs of a high level of unemployment (Lecointe *et al.*, 1989; Confais and Muet, 1994). In the absence of negotiated disinflation, as has been achieved in the Netherlands and Ireland, the French way was through unemployment (Jobert and Théret, 1994). Although France achieved its aim of becoming a low inflation paragon, the results were disappointing (Blanchard and Muet, 1993) with little impact on stubborn unemployment and, by the standards of previous decades, slow growth. French growth has been highly correlated with that of the EU-15[3] for many years. It was a little higher than the EU average in the early 1980s and a little lower in the late 1980s, but the differences were small. Generally the cycles in economic activity have also been very similar.

Inflation in France has been close to the EU-15 average for many years. Having been a relatively inflation-prone country in the 1970s, France's shift from inflation sinner to saint illustrates the change in economic policy wrought since 1983 and it became a lower inflation country than Germany in the late 1990s. As one would expect, this price stability was reflected in falling interest rates which gradually converged to German rates, though it was not until 1993 that the interest rate differential was largely eliminated.

France's external balance also improved strikingly in the 1990s. After 1990, improving competitiveness and more rapid growth in export markets led to the development of a current account surplus, which was very large by French standards. Both inflows and outflows of foreign direct investment for France have been very stable compared to the other 10 members of the euro area.

Stage 2 adjustment

Because of the legacy of the adjustments effected during the 1980s, France did not face a great challenge in fulfilling the Maastricht criteria, although in common with many other countries it saw a deterioration in its budgetary position in the early 1990s. The response was, initially, to raise taxes which jumped from a low of 47.7% of GDP in 1988 to 50.4% in 1999, well above the average for the euro area of 45.6%. These increasing receipts made it possible to reduce the public sector deficit from 6.0% of GDP in 1993 to 1.8% in 1999. Debt, however, proved to be more difficult and, although France was just on the limit of 60% in 1997, it then rose and stayed above 60%.

The major weakness in the French economy in recent years has been the persistence of high unemployment which peaked in 1997. From having unemployment below or equal to the EU-15 average, France has moved to a situation where it is above average. Labour market shortcomings are also apparent in the employment rate which is below the EU-15 average.

As in many other countries, youth unemployment is very high in France, while recorded unemployment among older workers is around the EU average, but because of the legacy of early retirement schemes, participation and employment rates for 55–64 year olds in France are well below the EU-15 average.

Although there are some differences between the geographical pattern of France's trade and that of the euro area, these seem unlikely to present very significant problems for asymmetric shocks. Differences in geographical composition of trade are not very large. France is not that heavily dependent upon trade and most of that trade is with the EU-15. Services are more important for the French economy than the EU average, especially tourism and travel.

Stage 3

Despite having achieved the Stage 3 entry criteria, relatively straightforwardly, France has not (so far) reaped much reward since 1999. Growth has remained low and unemployment has barely fallen. As noted above, France did, however, achieve quite high growth in 1999–2000 and has continued to be more or less in the middle of the spectrum of euro area members as regards its macroeconomic performance. The inference to draw is that, unlike Germany, France has had a monetary policy that matches its macroeconomic circumstances pretty well.

Two main adjustment problems have, nevertheless, arisen. The first is that France has proved unable to consolidate its public finances any further than it had in Stage 2. Although the deficit fell below 2% in 1999 and went as low as 1.4% in 2000, it rebounded in 2002 since when it has remained above the 3% threshold. With hindsight, the failure to reduce debt and deficits in the early years of Stage 3 curtailed the room for fiscal stabilisers to work in more difficult times. This duly contributed to France breaking the terms of the SGP in 2003 leading to the political disputes surrounding the implementation of the Pact described in earlier chapters. Equally, it is important to stress that although the deficits have been above the 3% threshold, they have not exceeded it by much, having peaked at 4.1% in 2003. An implication is that France's public finances are not that vulnerable. France, in contrast perhaps to Germany, has taken a more robust view as to the validity of the SGP constraints and it will therefore be interesting to see whether the reformed Pact is better received in Paris. It is also noteworthy that many leading French economists such as Pisani-Ferry, Blanchard, Fitoussi, Wyplosz and Le Cacheux have led calls for reform of the euro area's fiscal framework (see for example, the views expressed in Conseil d'Analyse Economique, 2004).

The second area in which France has encountered difficulties during Stage 3 is in accelerating structural reform, again something it has in common with Germany. On the face of it, France has a rather heavily regulated labour market (Table 6.4). Contracts of employment, particularly temporary contracts, are quite restrictive. The net replacement rate is high at 74% and there is a high level of employers' social security contributions to pay for these benefits. This made the tax wedge for France among the highest for the OECD, with a single worker, on 66% of the average production worker's income, having an average rate of tax of 47% and marginal rate of over 50% (OECD, 1997a: 72). The minimum wage relative to average earnings is the highest among the countries shown. In addition, working time is now restricted, with a statutory working week of 35 hours, although the current administration is taking measures to undo this decision.

Government policy reform and the practical operation of these measures mean that in reality there is considerably more flexibility than looks to be the case. Social contributions for low-wage workers are reduced by a panoply of exemptions and rebates. Unemployment benefit remains relatively generous, but changes are being introduced to tighten the rules and to reduce the incidence of the unemployment trap. What has been happening has been that statutory working time has been superseded by decentralised collective agreements. These agreements have made working time increasingly flexible with weekend working and annualisation of hours. The picture of the French labour market that emerges is mixed. Despite an apparently restrictive regulatory environment, employers are in a strong bargaining position in firm-level negotiations because of the very low level of unionisation of French labour.

Assessment

France demonstrated that a fixed exchange rate with the Deutsche Mark (DM) is reconcilable with a reasonable performance by its economy and it is arguable that it should find the economic conditions of EMU more benign than those that existed between 1983 and 1998. Nor is there much concern that the structure of the French economy should leave it especially vulnerable to asymmetric shocks.

Although the rhetoric of the French government's opposition to flexibility in labour markets continues, the reality is rather different. Considerable decentralisation of wage bargaining has taken place and this has led to flexible opting out from national agreements and there has been a growth of flexible forms of work. Unemployment benefits remain high and the pension system remains largely unreformed, so considerable impediments to flexibility remain. The French economy also seems to be more dynamic, with considerable interest in the new economy and signs of resurgence in the more traditional industrial sectors.[4] The early rapid economic growth and the decline in unemployment did not presage a period of greater economic success associated with the euro. It was more a cyclical upturn utilising spare capacity and was associated with the low value of the euro. Given its past performance, however, there is little doubt that France could adjust to the new conditions caused by the creation of the euro.

It remains an open question whether France's low-inflation zeal will be rewarded. Relatively slow growth since 1983 could be blamed on the de facto monetary union with Germany and may have had a more insidious effect in damaging the long-term dynamism of the economy. But most of the other countries in EU-15 and the euro area have also maintained relatively fixed exchange rates against the DM, with the implication that the deterioration of French economic performance against these countries is largely the result of factors other than the exchange rate. It could be argued that the failure to combine competitive disinflation with more fundamental structural reform was the reason for the relatively poor performance.

6.3.2 Italy: Virtue or conjuring trick?

In no other country was popular support for joining EMU higher than in Italy which, in 1997 polls conducted by the European Commission, recorded an 80:20 majority in favour. In a survey of Italy published in the

6 November 1997 issue of *The Economist,* Matthew Bishop summed up the imperative:

> For Italian politicians and businessmen especially, being part of EMU from day one has become a project of almost mythical proportions. This is not just about trying to give the country a hard, low-inflation-risk, low-interest-rate currency. Despite its prosperity, Italy has never quite managed to be taken seriously as an advanced market economy and democratic state. Acceptance into the single currency would mark Italy's coming of age as a modern nation.

Equally, no other country seemed less likely to fulfil the convergence criteria. As late as 1996, Italy's nominal indicators were all awry and a survey in *The Economist* of the 29th May that year argued that EMU would go ahead, but without Italy. Yet the extent of change in Italy may have been under-estimated, as is signalled in the rhetorical question in the title of a paper by Chiorazzo and Spaventa (1999): 'The prodigal son or a confidence trickster?'. These two authors suggest that although there was some disquiet about the special 'EMU' tax introduced by the Prodi government at virtually the last minute, it was accompanied by quite radical reform measures.

Stage 2

Nevertheless, the background had been inauspicious. Italy's public debt rose markedly in the early 1990s, jumping from 98% in 1990 to 125% in 1994, and only stabilising thereafter. This was above all because of the high burden of debt service, given that there was a primary surplus and that the deficit was brought down sharply from 11% in 1990 to under 3% in the assessment year of 1997. The EMI (1998) points out that temporary measures in 1997 helped to reduce the deficit by one percentage point and drew attention to what it calls 'self-reversing measures' that were worth 0.3% of GDP in 1997 and would be unwound subsequently. Regular surveys of financial market practitioners by Reuters in the early part of 1997 put the chances of Italy being in the first wave at under 20%.

How then did Italy manage to confound the data, the sceptics and the entrenched opponents to be in the first wave? According to Battocchi (2003), it was a combination of political commitment, diplomacy and a wider public concern not to be left out. Maes and Quaglia (2004: 25) suggest that a key part of the political equation was that 'Belgium and Italy both played an active role in the debate on European monetary integration in policy-makers' circles, be it to different degrees'. Hallerberg (2000), in a comparison of how Italy and Belgium managed to be in the first wave despite seemingly intractable obstacles, attributes their success to a combination of external incentives and national institutional adaptation. He argues that the threat of exclusion from Stage 3, while an important and necessary condition for the turnaround in both countries, was not sufficient. For both countries, the complementary factor was institutional reform. In Italy, the key change was the centralisation of power in the hands of a powerful treasury minister who was able to push through tough decisions. In Belgium, the creation of a High Council of Finance was crucial because it was able effectively to depoliticise budgetary decisions and thus ensure that its recommendations for assuring sustainable public finances were followed. In both cases, the institutional changes dovetailed well with the external pressures (the 3% deficit target as a goal) to modify behaviour and expectations.

The Prodi government, in which the respected figure of Carlo Ciampi was appointed Treasury Minister, engaged in assiduous diplomatic activity to persuade its EU partners of the political importance of Italy's participation. Italy rapidly re-joined the ERM, though (as discussed above) it still required a benign interpretation to be able to fulfil the exchange rate criterion. In the domestic arena, support from the unions for structural reforms was crucial, while public opinion was prepared to accept pretty draconian changes in public finances, including a special tax, designed to bring the deficit under the 3% limit by 1997. In short, Italy underwent shock therapy from the mid-1990s onwards.

Stage 3

Having made the cut, Italy has struggled and, since 1999, has been among the worst performing economies. In its 2003 survey of the Italian economy, the OECD (2003) observes that 'Italy faces two major medium-term challenges at present: how to raise the underlying growth rate, and managing public finances so as to reduce high debt levels and keep the deficit under the 3% of GDP Stability and Growth Pact obligation'. Noting that these two aims are not necessarily in conflict in the longer term because the many different supply-side reforms can be expected to boost growth, the OECD nevertheless draws attention to the fact that 'implementing them will have significant up-front budgetary costs'. In this respect, Italy finds itself on the horns of the same sort of dilemma as Germany in having to pay more in the short run against a backdrop of low growth and high unemployment, yet being subject to criticism from its peers. Indeed, in Italy's case, these criticisms are all the sharper because they relate not only to the budgetary position, but also to its lack of progress on the Lisbon agenda.

The OECD also observes, that Italy still faces awkward challenges in macroeconomic management: 'as regards fiscal policy, room for manoeuvre has now been greatly reduced by tax cuts – desirable in themselves – and significant additional corrective measures will be required for some years to come, if medium-term targets are to be achieved and long-term fiscal sustainability is to be assured...The ambitious programme of structural reforms over the past decade allowed Italy to join the EMU and to improve macroeconomic fundamentals, but has not been enough to spare the country from a disappointing performance in 2002, when the deceleration of growth was one of the sharpest among OECD countries' (OECD, 2003: 2).

Although the public debt has remained above 100% of GDP, Italy is estimated to have substantial public assets earning comparatively low rates of return that could potentially create room for manoeuvre. The debt maturity has also increased and, coupled with the lower debt servicing requirement from being subject to euro area rather than national interest rates, the burden of debt servicing has fallen markedly. Nevertheless, Italy faces an uphill struggle in putting in place Stage 3 adjustment mechanisms. Growth has consistently undershot projections and this has inevitably put pressure on the budget deficit, with the result (in 2003) that Italy became subject to the EDP.

Assessment

Some of the reforms initiated in Italy during the 1990s illustrate the problems of achieving a viable armoury of policies to achieve adjustment under EMU. Several steps were taken to alter the pension system which had become a heavy burden on both social budgets and on labour costs. In the short term, these reforms proved to be costly to the public finances, although they will bring substantial benefits subsequently.

What this assessment suggests is that entry to Stage 3 in the first wave may have been *politically* vital not only for the national self-esteem of one of the six founder members of the EEC, but also to reinforce the momentum for structural change imposed by external obligations – the *vincolo esterno* identified by Dyson and Featherstone (1999). Italy has embarked on a wide array of structural reforms, partly because, to live within EMU, it has little option and the expectation must be that these will, in time, bear fruit. But to the extent that early entry happened without having achieved full nominal convergence, above all of the public debt (exacerbated by the use of creative accounting to massage the deficit downwards), the more immediate *economic* impact may have been negative.

6.3.3 Spain

In contrast to the three largest euro area members, Spain has, so far, been one of the star pupils of EMU. It embarked on an adjustment trajectory in the mid-1990s that allowed it to achieve the Maastricht convergence criteria comfortably and has since successfully weathered the slowdown that hit in 2001. A recent study of the Spanish economy by the European Commission notes that during Stage 2 and Stage 3 of EMU, 'Spain has enjoyed a virtuous economic cycle of high GDP growth, outstanding job creation, and relatively low inflation' (Commission, 2005b).

A number of elements in the Spanish success story are worthy of mention. First, the economy has experienced a period of uninterrupted growth since recovering from a recession in 1993. Spain's annual growth rate has outstripped that of the euro area by a margin of 0.5–2.0 percentage points since 1996. Second, the labour market has witnessed a remarkable improvement. Although Spanish unemployment remains amongst the highest in the euro area (just over 10% of the euro area labour force), it has fallen by nearly 8 percentage points since the mid-1990s. Total employment in Spain grew at twice the euro area rate over the same period and has stayed comparatively buoyant in spite of the 2001 slowdown. Finally, the country has experienced a sustained process of real convergence with the rest of the EU. In the decade prior to EU accession (in 1986) Spain had been through a period of stagnation that had seen its GDP per head fall from 80% of the EU average to just over 72%, but has since climbed back to 86%.

Stage 2

Spain's adjustment to life in the euro area is all the more remarkable when it is remembered that few commentators had initially expected it to qualify for EMU. The Spanish economy entered Stage 2 of EMU with long-term interest rates of 10%, a budget deficit of 7% and an inflation rate of 5%. Under such circumstances, it is hardly surprising that the financial markets put Spain's probability of joining the euro area at 'close to zero' (Balmaseda *et al.*, 2002: 198). In the end, however, Spain has confounded its critics by qualifying for EMU with an inflation rate of 2%, a budget deficit of 1% and long-term interest rates that were almost 1.5 percentage points below the Maastricht target.

The means by which Spain achieved nominal convergence in the run up to EMU is the subject of debate in the literature. Jarocinski (2003), for example, argues that budgetary reforms and the government's political commitment to euro-entry triggered a decline in its long-term interest rate differential. Balmaseda *et al.* (2002), on the other hand, attribute Spain's turnaround to a process of painful disinflation built on wage moderation, central bank independence, fiscal austerity and an economic policy that put qualifying for EMU above all other priorities.

Stage 3

Although it is somewhat premature to explain Spain's strong economic performance under Stage 3 of EMU, the resilience of the economy in the face of shocks and a virtuous combination of sound budgetary policies and structural reforms appear to have played a role.

Spain's economic resilience is linked to the fact that domestic demand has remained robust since the 2001 economic slowdown thanks to buoyant consumer demand and a surge in the demand for housing, with the latter being linked to, *inter alia*, historically low interest rates and net inward migration. The strength of domestic demand is a comparatively new phenomenon for the Spanish economy and it suggests that it has reduced its reliance on external demand as a catalyst for economic recoveries (Commission, 2005b).

Spanish budgetary policy has been a model of conformity with the Stability and Growth Pact. Whereas the 2001 slowdown triggered rising deficits in the large euro area Member States, Spain maintained a position of close to balance, while at the same time reducing cyclically adjusted borrowing towards a position of balance. Spain's commitment to fiscal discipline is further reflected in the 2001 General Law of Budgetary Stability, which *de facto* codifies the EU's budgetary rules into domestic legislation. More specifically, the law makes the close to balance or in surplus rule binding on all government sectors and regions. It also threatens to pass on any fines incurred under the excessive deficit procedure to profligate sectors and regions, while at the same time setting up a contingency fund to cover government expenditure under unforeseen economic circumstances (Kingdom of Spain, 2001).

Sound budgetary policies have been matched by a continued commitment to structural reforms. For the European Commission, a number of factors can explain Spain's improved unemployment and employment performance, including the increased stability of the financial system under EMU, reduced labour shortages during the economic upturn thanks to increased female labour participation and high net inward migration, and the trade unions' acceptance of wage moderation and competitive unit labour costs (Commission, 2005b: 47). At the same time, the Commission highlights the positive impact of a raft of labour market reforms, including a revision of employment protection legislation for permanent and part-time contracts and the tightening of eligibility conditions for unemployment benefits (see Commission, 2005b: 49–50).

Assessment

The success of the Spanish economy under EMU lies in the speed of its recovery from a starting point of low growth, high inflation and unbalanced macroeconomic policy. The process of recovery is far from complete, however. Two challenges loom large on the horizon. The first is to prolong the downward trend of the unemployment rate. For Blanchard and Jimeno (1995) this means, in part, that Spain must continue to grow faster than the rest of the euro area, while at the same time reorienting this growth towards investment. For others, it means that further structural reforms are unavoidable. The OECD (2005) attaches particular importance to reducing the degree of labour market segmentation in Spain between over-protected permanent workers and under-protected temporary workers. To this end, it recommends a further easing of employment protection legislation for the former and a better enforcement of employment law for the latter.

A second major challenge for the Spanish economy is to tackle the persistent inflation differential that has developed vis-à-vis the rest of the euro area. The effect of this differential, which has remained above 1 percentage point since 2003, is to erode the external competitiveness of the economy. Whereas in the past, a depreciation of the nominal exchange may have offset such effects, a positive inflation differential directly translates into a real exchange rate appreciation under EMU.

An important question is whether Spanish inflation can be explained by the Balassa–Samuelson effect, whereby price increases in the higher-productivity traded sector generate higher prices in the economy as a whole. Sinn and Reutter (2001) find this explanation to be intuitively plausible for high-growth euro area countries, and estimate that productivity growth differentials should lead to an inflation rate of around 3% in Spain. Alesina *et al.* (2001) are more sceptical of this viewpoint. The fact that productivity growth in Spain has lagged behind that of the euro area, they argue, means that if anything the Balassa–Samuelson effect is working in reverse. The European Commission shares this scepticism and argues that Spanish inflation is the result of structural rigidities, particular in services like transport, restaurants and hotels and health care (Commission, 2005: 75).

6.3.4 Conclusions from the French, Italian and Spanish experience

Unlike France, which has found fiscal discipline and structural reform difficult, Spain has shown a capacity to achieve not only rapid adjustment on the way to EMU, but also in Stage 3. Italy was able to achieve entry in the first wave, after a surprisingly determined adjustment strategy (given the country's tradition of relatively weak governance), but may now be paying the bill. France has been able to achieve a sustainable balance of payments and low inflation, but without especially strong growth. Indeed the lack of growth has pushed it into an unsustainable fiscal position, and both France and Italy would find their position immensely improved by faster growth. In the French case the decision to converge was taken well in advance of Stage 3 of EMU.

Spain had experienced real convergence, strongly in the years before EU membership and then again more recently in the run up to EMU. There is a contrast, in this regard, with the French and Italian experience. Structural problems remain, notably in relation to some of the Lisbon targets such as the low rate of spending on R&D, but to some extent potential and actual membership of the euro area have been a motivation for the change. It is not clear how much membership *per se* alters behaviour, except through the improved credibility resulting in lower real interest rates for countries with prior inflation or fiscal problems.

There is, therefore, is a mixed message for the countries still to join the euro area. Spain itself was able to meet the criteria and change noticeably and managed adjustment both in Stage 2 and Stage 3, though challenges remain. The experience of France and Italy offers less encouragement. France converged easily during Stage 2, but in Stage 3 it has struggled (as has Germany) more than might have been expected. Italy achieved Stage 2 adjustment with much more of a struggle and arguably belied expectations, but its experience in Stage 3 has been more predictable.

6.4 What can we infer about EMU so far?

In some respects, EMU has exceeded expectations. At an institutional level, monetary policy has functioned as intended and although the recorded inflation rate has yet to fall below the reference value of 2% set by the ECB, it would be hard to argue that prices have not been stable. The major institutional failing is in policy co-ordination, with both the SGP and the ambitious Lisbon aims falling into disrepute.

For some of the current members of the euro area, the adjustment challenges in Stage 2 may well have been more demanding than those they have had to cope with since. For example, inside Stage 3 there is no requirement for inflation in a Member State to be at any specific level. Yet in other respects, life within EMU has become more demanding, with the SGP setting stricter fiscal conditions than the Maastricht convergence criteria. Being prepared for EMU also necessitated adaptation to ECB monetary policy and the fixed nominal exchange rate with the other members.

As Hughes Hallett *et al.* (2004) show, significant fiscal 'consolidation' – markedly lower deficits and falling public debt – took place during the 1990s, notably during 'Stage 2' of EMU, as Member States sought to qualify for full participation in the monetary union. In the first two years of full EMU (1999 and 2000), a period of relatively rapid growth, all members of the euro area stayed comfortably within the 3% of GDP deficit threshold stipulated for the SGP. However, the larger countries, especially, did not consolidate their public finances sufficiently to attain the position of 'close to balance or in surplus' that constitutes the medium-term rule at the heart of the SGP. With hindsight, the lack of fiscal tightening in this period is at the root of the deficit problems that surfaced in 2002. Then, as the slowdown became more prolonged than was generally forecast, the French and German deficits breached the 3% limit, triggering the EDP.

Flores *et al.* (2005: 6), similarly, suggest that although the fiscal framework was reasonably successful in curbing excessive deficits, discipline was relaxed in the early years of Stage 3. They observe that 'while several smaller Member States did in fact complete the transition to budget positions of "close to balance or in surplus", most large countries in the euro area failed to improve their cyclically-adjusted budget positions'. A possible reason is that there are systematic differences between large and small countries that derive from different incentives and salience for the ECB monetary policy stance (Buti and Pench, 2004).

The main explanation for many of the problems has to be that economic growth simply has not achieved rates that were either expected or necessary to allow the euro area to achieve its ambitions. It makes little sense to pass judgement on a project that is likely to accumulate microeconomic gains from increased price transparency and macroeconomic certainty over the long run, on the basis of its initial growth performance. However, the disappointing performance of the euro area economy since 2001 underlines the fact that macroeconomic policies to keep output in and around its growth potential, coupled with structural reforms to raise this growth potential over time, are necessary for EMU to realise its ambitions. Figure 6.4 shows that through the three stages of EMU (1991–1994, 1994–1999 and since 1999), euro area GDP growth has exceeded the 1980–1990 average (itself not that impressive) only in the four year period of 1997–2000 and is forecast only in 2006 to creep above that reference rate. In March 2000, when the Lisbon strategy was launched, the annual growth rate on which the strategy was predicated was 3.0%, so that with growth barely attaining half that rate in the first half of the present decade, it is no surprise that the strategy is in such trouble.

Hoeller *et al.* (2004: 5) show that the euro area has been less successful than its peers among the OECD countries in coping with common shocks and also note that it is the three largest euro area countries that have fared worst, whereas the smaller euro area members have been able to adjust more effectively. They argue that this outcome is 'paradoxical as it is at odds with optimum currency area theory which suggests that in monetary union core countries should suffer less from cyclical divergence and benefit more from the common currency than the periphery'. They find, in particular, that in smaller countries there is greater product and factor market flexibility and that the extent of their integration in the euro area market reinforces this market discipline. The larger countries are found to have greater scope for adjustment using fiscal policy, but have been unable to make much use of this adjustment channel because they have not succeeded in managing fiscal policy so as to have room for manoeuvre. An inference to draw from their work is that Germany, Italy and (less so) France are in a sort of Catch-22 in which, if only they had been able to create space for fiscal policy to work, it would solve many of their adjustment problems.

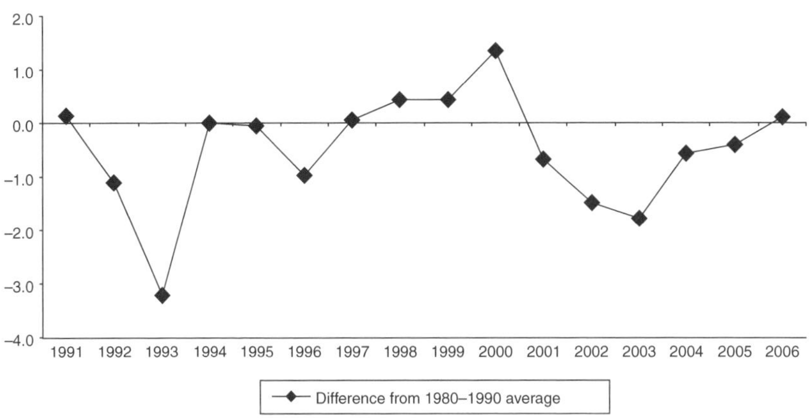

Figure 6.4 Euro area growth during stages 1–3. *Source*: OECD *Economic Outlook*, Volume 2004/2, No. 76, December

Monetary conditions have also contributed a little to asymmetric adjustment to common shocks. Calculations by Hoeller *et al.* (2004: 8) indicate that 'short-term interest rates were below the equilibrium rate consistent with a Taylor rule in the majority of euro area countries, and substantially so in Ireland, Greece, the Netherlands, Spain, Portugal and Italy, but exceeded it in Germany and Belgium'. France, on the whole has been in the middle of the pack. As regards improvements in competitiveness, there are divergent effects among euro area countries according to Hoeller *et al.* (2004) who find that Finland and Ireland have benefited from strong productivity gains, whereas in the larger Member States, such gains are small (and non-existent in Italy). External demand has, however, had a marginal impact in that the slower growing euro area economies have gained a little in competitiveness at the expense of the faster growing ones.

EMU's record on price stability is clearly much better. During the 1980s, double-digit price inflation was observed in eight of the twelve euro area countries in the early part of the decade. Since then, inflation rates have generally dropped, initially under the impulse of the German-led EMS, and subsequently under EMU. As Figure 6.5 shows, not only has the average rate fallen progressively, but so too has the range. Greece, for a long time was the most inflation prone euro area member, then it was Ireland in 2000, 2002 and 2003, with the Netherlands intervening in 2001. Finland has recorded the lowest inflation rate most often over the last decade, but the forecasts for Germany suggest that it will have the lowest rate in 2005–2006, possibly courting deflation. It is an interesting reflection on the euro area's price stability that, at the time of writing, the ECB repo rate has remained unchanged at 2% for fully 24 months.

Looking forward, the obligation to reduce consumer price inflation to within 1.5 percentage of the inflation of the average of the lowest three *EU*

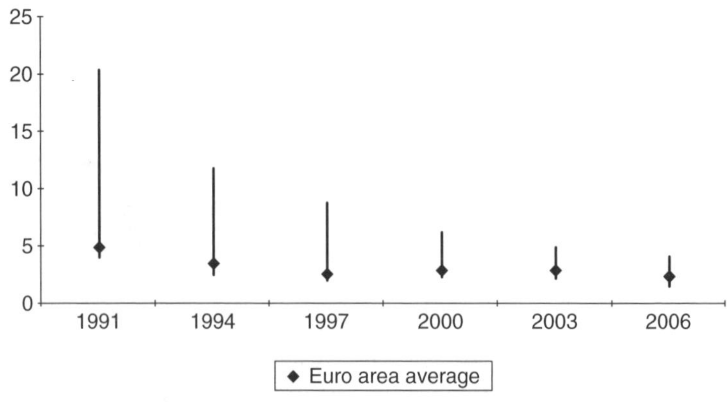

Figure 6.5 Range of euro area inflation during stages 1–3 of EMU (Harmonised index of consumer prices, annual % change). *Source*: OECD *Economic Outlook*, Volume 2004/2, No. 76, December; ECB (2005) *Statistics Pocket Book Database*

countries is likely to be harsh for the new members. It would be easy for asymmetric factors to depress the inflation of three countries well below the general run of euro area experience and not impossible for the euro area inflation rate to be above the reference value that will be used. Indeed, the Commission forecast (published in April 2005) for the Dutch HICP for 2006, a possible reference year, is –3.0%,[5] although other forecasts are less dramatic.

What, finally, can be made of Germany's experience in EMU, given its pivotal role? Jansen (2005) sketches a number of the contradictions that have come to the surface during Germany's recent growth predicament. Hourly labour costs in Western Germany are the highest in Europe, yet the country's unit labour costs relative to its key trading partners have fallen considerably since the mid-1990s, thus boosting the country's external competitiveness. Germany's statutory corporate tax rates are at the top of the European league table, yet, due to the prevalence of escape-clauses, implicit corporate tax rates (the associated revenues as a percentage of GDP) are among the lowest. Overall, Jansen (2005) judges expectations to be a key explanatory factor in the German case, in so far as the country's stuttering performance in recent years has led to high savings amongst consumers and caution amongst investors, in spite of the government's labour market reforms and the external competitiveness of the economy. Deroose *et al.* (2004) draw attention to the importance of entering EMU at a suitable exchange rate, stressing that in a low inflation environment, it may be especially difficult to alter the real exchange rate subsequently, and that it will be a slow process. They contrast the effects of demand and competitiveness shocks. The arithmetic is salient. Gustav Horn[6] has stressed that Germany's competitiveness gains, though welcome, have been offset by stagnating domestic demand. Hence, because it is the larger countries, generally, which have been slower growing, the spillover effect has also been asymmetric. The next chapter looks in more depth at Germany's economy.

However, there is a limit to which the past is a good indicator of the future. The problems experienced by Germany, insofar as they stem from unification may well be transitory. This experience shows how difficult it is to make a downward adjustment in the price level inside a monetary union under low inflation. However, Germany's continuing competitiveness outside the euro area suggests that the economy is basically sound and hence could resume its longer-term trends in due course. Countries such as Spain, on the other hand, which have adjusted their relative price levels upwards quite rapidly may face the same problems that Germany has experienced if it turns out that they have overshot. Indeed, overshooting is the normal experience, particularly in asset prices such as housing. At that point, the Spanish economy would continue to be in phase with its partners at business cycle frequencies but longer-term trends would change as would the higher frequency dynamics, if excessive deficits emerged.

An evolving pattern seems a more likely outcome than simple monotonic convergence in the euro area, particularly if its membership changes.

7
Germany: Painfully Adjusting to EMU?

Without Germany there simply would have been no monetary union. The pre-eminence of its economic policy framework during the post-war period made the Deutschmark the natural anchor currency for the Exchange Rate Mechanism and the Bundesbank provided the institutional blueprints for the ECB. Today Germany is much the largest economy in the euro area, accounting for roughly one-third of its domestic product. Although the advantages to other Member States of adopting Germany's credibility and stability approach to monetary policy are well documented, it is a little more difficult to pinpoint what Germany took from the bargain. There were few macroeconomic advantages and some potential disadvantages for Germany, which would be trading-in a stable macroeconomic policy tailored to the needs of the German economy, for one based on the needs of the euro area as a whole. The effect of this change would dominate in the short term over the microeconomic advantages, which relate to the improvement in efficiency stemming from permanently fixed exchange rates and a common currency.

As the dominant economy in the EMS, Germany was in privileged position, enjoying a considerable degree of monetary autonomy in the system,[1] so that monetary policy was suited to its economic conditions. The Bundesbank in combination with the German Federal Government had achieved the macroeconomic stability to which other EMS members aspired. The credibility of the Bundesbank and the history of low inflation ensured low nominal and real interest rates. Germany's commitment to EMU was not narrowly based on economic advantages so much as on the politics of a wider European policy which 'did not involve the question of whether in principle EMU was desirable' (Dyson and Featherstone, 1999: 261).[2] Given these circumstances, the problems Germany has had with EMU are, therefore, not surprising.

This chapter assesses the particular difficulties that Germany has had with the EMU, in relation to the characteristics and past performance of the economy, and examines the adjustments it has made. The analysis is in six sections. The first section begins with the role that Germany has played in European monetary integration. The second considers the state of the German economy on its entry to EMU. Of particular interest here is the appropriateness of the entry rate chosen for the Deutschmark. The third assesses Germany's economic performance under EMU, particularly the extent to which Germany's recent slow growth is a new phenomenon. This leads to consideration in the fourth section of the extent to which German adjustment to EMU is necessary and possible. This section concentrates on the processes of acclimatisation and labour market adjustment. Germany entered EMU while still adjusting to the economic shock of unification, and the fifth section considers the extent and effects of this problem and the degree to which they may have contributed to the weak overall performance. We end in the sixth section by evaluating, given these difficulties, the potential risk of deflation or at least slow growth in Germany, and its ramifications for EMU.

7.1 Germany and European monetary integration

Germany and the Deutschmark had been at the centre of both the Snake, in the early 1970s, and the EMS from its inception in 1979. The economic institutions of Germany, together with an anti-inflationary culture, meant that Germany consistently achieved low inflation. This, together with the success of German industry, especially in export markets, meant that the Deutschmark was the strongest EC currency. After the establishment of the Snake in 1972, following the break-up of the Bretton Woods system of fixed peg exchange rates, this strength of the German currency put the system under pressure and it quickly collapsed into a Deutschmark zone. A more widely based system was re-established as a result of an initiative by the German Chancellor, Helmut Schmidt, and the French President, Valery Giscard d'Estaing, to restore exchange rate stability in the EC with the European Monetary System. German preferences were also decisive in the structure of the system. For example, the proposal to fix exchange rates to the ECU was replaced by a parity grid of bilateral exchange rates. With the Deutschmark tending to strengthen in value relative to other currencies, other countries had to respond to German monetary policy to maintain the parity grid.[3] Germany inevitably became the centre of the system, with the Deutschmark as the currency against which other countries tried to maintain their parity. Paradoxically, German unification provided both a political and economic impetus for EMU, but compromised Germany's ability to participate successfully. The political impetus – especially for France – came from the desire to tie Germany more closely into the European integration project. The economic impetus was Germany's macroeconomic policy response to the asymmetric shock of unification, which made German policy unsuitable for other members of the ERM, provoking the 1992–1993 crises of the EMS.[4] The system survived but only in a weakened form.[5] Nevertheless, Germany remained central to the EMS and entered EMU as a founding member without realigning its exchange rate. Unification and the burdens it placed on the economy, reduced Germany's ability to adjust to the new system.

7.2 German transition to EMU

Germany satisfied the inflation, general government deficit, long-term interest rate and ERM participation criteria for entry to EMU in 1998, but it failed by a small margin to satisfy the debt criterion, an omission that the twin assessments of eligibility found it expedient to overlook. Moreover, Germany was the only country that both exceeded the formal test of a ratio to GDP greater than 60%, and had a level of debt which was rising rather than falling, flouting the let-out clause that permitted a debt level above the benchmark if the ratio is diminishing sufficiently and approaching the reference value at a satisfactory pace (Article 104b). In the Commission recommendation (Commission, 1998c) and the Council Decision (Council of the EU, 1998), debt was effectively ignored, with government finances being judged sound because of the absence of an excessive deficit (see Table 7.1). While Germany did not resort to some of the more dubious fiscal manoeuvres employed by certain other countries, the closeness of the deficit to the 3% limit and the rising level of debt could, with the benefit of hindsight be seen to have presaged the subsequent German problems with the Stability and Growth Pact (SGP).

Germany's fiscal position at this time was still being influenced by recovery from the post unification collapse in the East German economy. Slow growth and fiscal problems have persisted, and one factor that could have contributed to these problems is an overvalued exchange rate. The currency appreciated with unification, enabling resources to be transferred to the new Länder and the issue is whether this temporary overvaluation was locked in as a result of membership of EMU. There certainly was a sharp

Table 7.1 Germany and the convergence criteria 1997/98 (in %)

	Germany	Criterion	EU-15 average
Inflation (HICP)[a]	1.4	2.7	1.6
General Government Deficit[b]	2.7	3.0	2.4
Public Debt[b]	61.3	60.0	72.1
Long-term interest rates[a]	5.6	7.8	6.1
ERM participation[c]	yes	yes	

[a] January 1998; [b] 1997; [c] March 1998.
Source: Commission (1998c).

rise in the Deutschmark real exchange rate, with a peak occurring in 1995. There was some fall from this peak in 1996–1998, but from 1999, the falling value of the euro and low rate of increase in wage costs reduced the overvaluation relative to third countries (Commission, 2002h: 52–63, 53–4; IMF, 2002b: 65–74; Sinn, 2003: 13–17). However, there was little improvement within the euro area, because of the fixed exchange rates and the generally low rate of increase of wages. Indeed, according to Hancké and Soskice (2003) Germany is in a bind, because if (as they imply has been happening) other Member States regard German wage inflation as the benchmark, it becomes much more difficult under EMU for Germany to use wage restraint as a means of improving its competitiveness. This is significant for Germany because intra-EU exports of goods are more important than for other large EMU economies.[6] In addition, the rise after late 2000 in the value of the euro reversed some of the gains in external competitiveness.

7.3 Germany's economic performance in the euro area

German economic performance since the start of Stage 3 of EMU has been disappointing. After the unification boom, its annual GDP growth has fallen below the euro area average and has aggravated an already deteriorating employment situation. After a brief period of falling unemployment from 1998 to 2000, unemployment started rising again in 2002. Slow growth and high unemployment have contributed to a low rate of inflation, the lowest in the euro area. This is improving German competitiveness but the process is painfully slow. Although, as argued above, the exchange rate in EMU has been broadly in line with past levels of competitiveness, this does not mean that Germany has emerged from its competitiveness problem. A rapid increase in real hourly labour costs since the 1980s led to West German labour costs being amongst the highest in the world (Table 7.2), with non-wage labour costs especially high. This was associated with slow growth in hours worked in the economy, although the effect on employment and unemployment was masked by reductions in average hours of work and early retirement. The burden of transfers to East Germany also tended to undermine overall German competitiveness. The shift of Germany's fortunes in the 1990s is shown clearly in the balance of payments statistics with the traditional surplus being replaced by a deficit. Germany returned to surplus in 2000, but this reflects the depreciation in the euro and the slow growth of the German economy. This depressing performance has done little to endear the euro to the German public, with public support for EMU among the lowest in the euro area and falling rapidly. In November 2003, 60% of the German population were in favour of EMU with a single currency, down 10% from the previous survey (Commission, 2003h).

Table 7.2 Hourly labour costs in manufacturing 2002 (in € per hour)

	Total labour costs	Hourly wages	Non-wage labour costs
Norway	26.52	19.20	9.31
Western Germany	26.36	14.74	11.62
Switzerland	26.24	17.20	9.03
Denmark	25.73	19.64	6.09
Belgium	23.35	12.22	11.12
Finland	23.20	13.05	10.15
Netherlands	22.64	12.63	10.01
USA	22.44	16.18	6.26
Sweden	21.86	11.19	8.97
Austria	21.64	11.16	10.45
Japan	20.18	12.06	8.12
UK	19.89	13.76	6.14
France	19.50	10.20	9.30
Ireland	17.17	12.29	4.88
Italy	16.60	8.53	8.08
Eastern Germany	16.43	9.96	6.47
Spain	15.37	8.42	6.96
Greece	9.47	5.64	3.82
Portugal	6.59	3.74	2.84

Source: IW (2003).

The pivotal question here is whether Germany's participation in EMU is a source of its economic problems or whether it is simply the victim of bad timing, given that the adoption of the euro is only one factor affecting the German economy. Mediocre German economic performance is not, however, new. For the last three decades, the growth of output and productivity has been low and falling. This has been the case for the euro area countries as a whole, but Germany has been consistently amongst the slowest growing economies (Table 7.3). There has been a generalised slowdown in growth of GDP across developed economies and a particular slowdown for euro area countries (Table 7.4). Part of this is due to slow population growth, but even per capita and per worker GDP growth has been slowing (OECD, 2000d). Germany, with only a brief spurt associated with unification, has had growth rates of output per worker below the EMU average and that of France and Italy (Figure 7.1).

An important contributory factor has been declining participation, but even more important for Germany has been the reduction in hours of work (IMF, 2003a: 18). This relatively slow growth was despite a comparatively rapid growth of capital and of the capital output ratio. In Germany's case this stuttering performance was confronted by the shock of unification and of EMU entry; it is little wonder then that economic

Table 7.3 Germany and euro area economic performance 1991–2005

	1991–1995	1996–2000	1999	2000	2001	2002	2003	2004	2005
GDP volume (% change on previous year)									
Germany	2.0	1.8	2.0	2.9	0.8	0.1	–0.1	*1.6*	*0.8*
Euro area	1.5	2.6	2.8	3.5	1.6	0.9	0.6	*2.0*	*1.6*
Unemployment (% civilian labour force)									
Germany	7.2	8.3	7.9	7.2	7.4	8.2	9.0	*9.5*	*9.7*
Euro area	9.5	9.7	8.7	8.2	7.8	8.2	8.7	*8.8*	*8.8*
Harmonised Index of Consumer Prices (% change on previous year)									
Germany	3.1	1.1	0.6	1.4	1.9	1.3	1.0	*1.8*	*1.3*
Euro area		1.7	1.1	2.1	2.4	2.3	2.1	*2.1*	*1.9*
Balance of current transactions with rest of the world (% of GDP)									
Germany	–0.9	–0.5	–0.8	–1.1	0.6	2.4	2.4	*3.8*	*4.1*
Euro area	–0.2	0.8	0.6	–0.1	0.5	1.2	0.6	*0.6*	*0.6*

2004–2005 estimates/forecasts
Source: Commission (2005a).

Table 7.4 Annual GDP growth, 1962–2006 (average annual growth of GDP (%)

	1962–1971	1972–1981	1982–1991	1992–2001	2002–2006
Belgium	4.8	3.0	2.2	2.1	1.9
Germany	4.4	2.7	2.5	1.5	0.8
Greece	8.0	3.6	1.2	2.4	3.7
Spain	6.6	3.0	3.2	2.7	2.5
France	5.5	3.0	2.4	2.0	1.7
Ireland	4.0	4.7	3.4	7.6	5.0
Italy	5.1	3.5	2.3	1.6	0.9
Luxembourg	3.4	2.3	5.9	4.8	3.5
Netherlands	5.2	2.4	2.5	2.8	0.8
Austria	4.7	3.1	2.9	2.3	1.6
Portugal	6.6	4.2	3.5	2.5	0.6
Finland	4.3	3.8	2.2	2.7	2.9
Euro area	5.1	2.9	2.6	2.0	1.4
Denmark	4.3	1.5	1.9	2.4	1.6
Sweden	4.2	1.8	2.1	2.2	2.6
United Kingdom	2.9	1.6	2.6	2.8	2.5
EU-15	4.6	2.6	2.6	2.1	1.7

Source: Commission AMECO database, accessed April 2005.

performance has been poor over the initial years of membership. Like all the other Member States, Germany was faced by the global slowdown over the same period, so that it is relative performance that is perhaps the more illuminating.

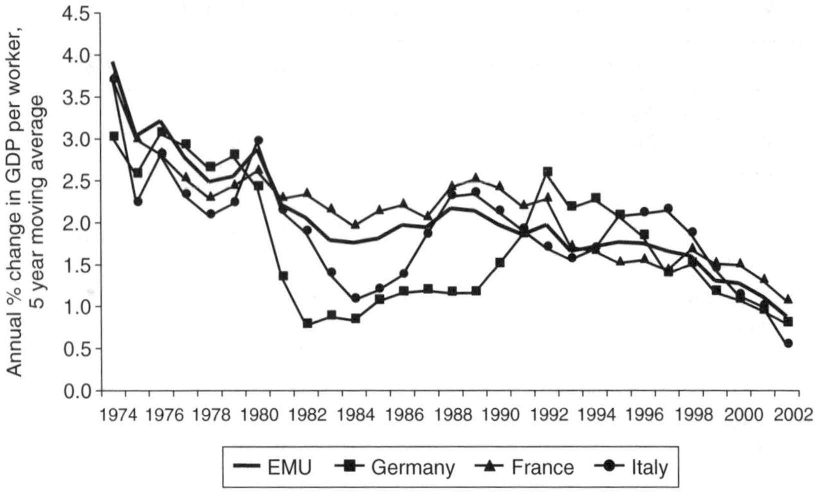

Figure 7.1 Growth in GDP per worker 1974–2002. *Source*: Commission (2000a)

7.4 German economic adjustment under EMU

7.4.1 Acclimatisation

The problematic performance of the German economy under EMU raises the issue of the extent to which this is the result of an economic policy determined by the needs of the euro area rather than by Germany. A country's situation in the early years of EMU is determined partly by its acclimatisation to the new situation and partly by the effects of the EMU policy arrangements. Acclimatisation is the result of *ex-post* convergence to the euro area. There are three acclimatisation processes that are particularly important:

1. An over- or under-valued exchange rate: any German overvaluation against other euro area currencies can be corrected by German inflation being below the area average.
2. The SGP's medium-term requirement for government finances to be close to balance or in surplus, which requires fiscal consolidation from countries, such as Germany, that entered EMU with government deficits even after cyclical correction.
3. The move from national to EMU monetary policy could lead to a significant reduction in interest rates for countries where exchange rate risk led to an interest rate premium. Germany was not such a country.

These acclimatisation factors clearly imply that Germany's initial situation in EMU would not be favourable. The relatively high entry exchange rate required a low rate of inflation. Germany also needed fiscal consolidation to comply with the SGP (Table 7.5). Despite the continuing transfers to East Germany and slow growth, Germany was committed to a significant reduction in its public sector deficit. In addition, Germany did not benefit from interest rate convergence. In the mid-1990s, interest rates among the euro area countries still differed by as much as 5–6%, but by 1998 these rates had almost completely converged on German rates. All euro area countries except Germany and the Netherlands benefited from reductions in interest rates associated with this convergence, which implies that these other countries now have access to more favourable financing conditions (Figure 7.2). This represents a loss of competitive advantage to Germany and there is the potential for the diversion of savings from Germany (Sinn, 2003: 11). Although nominal interest rates have converged, inflation rates have not. With low inflation and common interest rates, German real long-term interest rates have moved from being among the lowest in the euro area to being among the highest (Figure 7.3). Thus, German business finds itself paying the same interest rates as companies in other euro area countries, without the ability to pass on this cost in higher prices.

It is clear that Germany has struggled to acclimatise to EMU and, in such circumstances, will suffer further if the monetary policy set by the ECB is ill-suited to German conditions. However, because the ECB interest rate decisions respond to economic conditions (inflation, GDP growth and so on) in the euro area as a whole (Begg *et al.*, 2002), there is no guarantee that the one-size-fits-all policy will be suitable. Indeed, in the period since 1999 Germany has had inflation and GDP growth below the euro area average, and it follows that the interest rates were above those that would have been warranted by applying the same decision-rule to Germany alone. This placed a greater burden on other adjustment processes to ensure economic performance improved in the future. These adjustment processes include wage and price flexibility in labour and product markets and labour mobility, and it is to these that the analysis now turns.

Table 7.5 German public-sector financing (% GDP)

	1991–1995	1996–2000	1998	1999	2000	2001	2002	2003	*2004*	*2005*
Net borrowing (–) or lending (+)	–3.1	–1.7	–2.2	–1.5	1.3	–2.8	–3.7	–3.8	*–3.7*	*–3.3*
Net borrowing cyclically adjusted	–3.9	–2.2	–2.0	–1.5	–1.7	–3.2	–3.6	–3.2	*–3.3*	*–2.8*
Debt	47.3	60.6	60.9	61.2	60.2	59.4	60.9	64.2	*66.0*	*68.0*

2004 and 2005 are estimates
Source: Commission (2003*f*, *g*).

COUNTRY	TITLE	1990	1991	1992	1993	1994	1995	1996	1997	1998	1999	2000	2001	2002	2003	2004
Belgium	Nominal long-term interest rates	10	9.3	8.7	7.2	7.8	7.5	6.5	5.8	4.8	4.8	5.6	5.1	5	4.2	4.2
Germany	Nominal long-term interest rates	8.7	8.5	7.9	6.5	6.9	6.9	6.2	5.6	4.6	4.5	5.3	4.8	4.8	4.1	4
Greece	Nominal long-term interest rates				23.3	20.7	17	14.5	9.9	8.5	6.3	6.1	5.3	5.1	4.3	4.3
Spain	Nominal long-term interest rates	14.7	12.4	11.7	10.2	10	11.3	8.7	6.4	4.8	4.7	5.5	5.1	5	4.1	4.1
France	Nominal long-term interest rates	9.9	9	8.6	6.8	7.2	7.5	6.3	5.6	4.6	4.6	5.4	4.9	4.9	4.1	4.1
Ireland	Nominal long-term interest rates	10.1	9.2	9.1	7.7	7.9	8.3	7.3	6.3	4.8	4.7	5.5	5	5	4.1	4.1
Italy	Nominal long-term interest rates	13.5	13.3	13.3	11.2	10.5	12.2	9.4	6.9	4.9	4.7	5.6	5.2	5	4.3	4.3
Luxembourg	Nominal long-term interest rates	8.5	8.2	7.9	6.8	7.2	7.2	6.3	5.6	4.7	4.7	5.5	4.9	4.7	4	4.2
Netherlands	Nominal long-term interest rates	8.9	8.7	8.1	6.4	6.9	6.9	6.2	5.6	4.6	4.6	5.4	5	4.9	4.1	4.1
Austria	Nominal long-term interest rates	8.8	8.6	8.2	6.7	7	7.1	6.3	5.7	4.7	4.7	5.6	5.1	5	4.2	4.2
Portugal	Nominal long-term interest rates	15.4	14.5	13.8	11.2	10.5	11.5	8.6	6.4	4.9	4.8	5.6	5.2	5	4.2	4.1
Finland	Nominal long-term interest rates	13.3	11.7	12	8.8	9	8.8	7.1	6	4.8	4.7	5.5	5	5	4.1	4.1

Figure 7.2 Nominal interest rates euro area 1990–2002. *Source*: Commission (2004a)

COUNTRY	TITLE	1990	1991	1992	1993	1994	1995	1996	1997	1998	1999	2000	2001	2002	2003	2004
Belgium	Real long-term interest rates, deflator GDP	7	3.2	5.1	3.1	5.5	6.2	5.2	4.3	3	3.3	4.3	3.3	3.1	2.2	1.8
FR. Germany	Real long-term interest rates, deflator GDP	5.3	4.8	2.7	2.7	4.3	4.7	5.1	4.9	3.4	4	5.5	3.4	3.2	2.9	3.3
Greece	Real long-term interest rates, deflator GDP				7.7	8.6	6.6	6.6	2.9	3.1	3.2	2.6	1.7	1.1	0.7	0.8
Spain	Real long-term interest rates, deflator GDP	6.9	5.1	4.7	5.4	5.9	6	5	4	2.4	1.9	2	0.9	0.4	0.1	–0.3
France	Real long-term interest rates, deflator GDP	6.8	5.9	6.5	4.4	5.4	5.8	4.8	4.2	3.7	4	4.4	3.1	2.5	2.6	2.3
Ireland	Real long-term interest rates, deflator GDP	10.5	7.3	6.[illegible]	2.4	6.1	5.2	5.2	1.8	–1.5	0.9	0.7	–0.6	0.5	2.5	1.1
Italy	Real long-term interest rates, deflator GDP	4.9	5.3	8.3	7	6.8	6.8	3.9	4.4	2.1	3.1	3.3	2.5	1.9	1.3	1.6
Luxembourg	Real long-term interest rates, deflator GDP	5.9	6.2	4	0.8	3.5	4.8	4.2	2.8	2	2.4	1.3	2.9	3.6	1.9	1.4
Netherlands	Real long-term interest rates, deflator GDP	6.6	5.7	5.6	4.4	4.5	4.8	4.9	3.5	2.9	3	1.4	–0.3	1.7	1.1	3
Austria	Real long-term interest rates, deflator GDP	5.6	4.6	4.4	3.8	4.2	5.1	5.3	5.7	4.4	4	3.7	3.3	3.6	2.6	2.2
Portugal	Real long-term interest rates, deflator GDP	2	4	2.1	3.5	3	7.8	5.4	2.5	1	1.6	2.1	0.9	0.6	1.4	1.7
Finland	Real long-term interest rates, deflator GDP	6.5	9.6	10.4	6.1	7.1	3.8	7.4	3.8	1.2	4.9	2.2	2	3.6	4.4	3.3

Figure 7.3 Real interest rates euro area 1990–2002. *Scurce*: Commission (2004a)

7.4.2 Labour market adjustment

The high level of German wage costs places particular emphasis on labour market adjustment. The ease with which improvements in relative wage costs can be adjusted will be reflected in the non-accelerating inflation rate of unemployment (NAIRU), sometimes called structural unemployment. This derives from the expectations-augmented Phillips curve in monopolistic product and labour markets (Layard *et al.*, 1991; Westaway, 1997). According to this view structural unemployment is an equilibrium in the sense that workers and employers have no incentive to change the path of real wages. The NAIRU equilibrium occurs when expectations are met, with wages rising in line with prices, after taking into account the growth of productivity. The higher the level of structural unemployment the more expensive in terms of output, employment and public expenditure it is to control inflation. Hence the NAIRU is a crucial measure of the adjustment efficiency of the labour market.

Structural unemployment will not necessarily be constant over time, since if structural factors in the economy change then it will change (McMorrow and Roeger, 2000). The labour market's adjustment capacity can, therefore, improve or deteriorate. It can also be argued that the NAIRU will follow the actual unemployment rate because of persistence (Gordon, 1998), or that there might be a multiplicity of NAIRUs (Akerlof *et al.*, 2000; De Vincenti, 2001), so that care is needed in interpreting the concept and in its estimation (Staiger *et al.*, 1997).

Estimates of the NAIRU (Figure 7.4) suggest that the efficiency of the EU-15 labour market[7] declined from 1980 until the early 1990s, with higher levels of

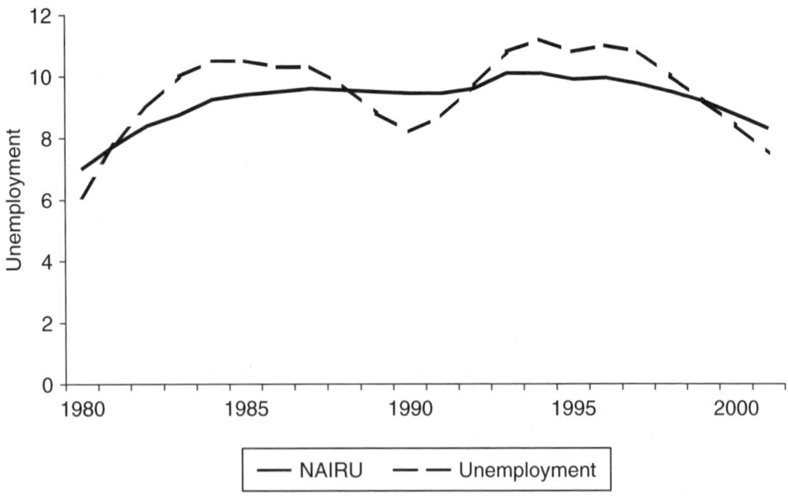

Figure 7.4 EU 15 NAIRU and unemployment. *Source*: European Commission (2002a); OECD (2004)

unemployment required to constrain inflation. In the second half of the 1990s, the EU-15 NAIRU fell, signalling an improvement in labour market efficiency, with the NAIRU appearing to follow the trend in unemployment (Figure 7.4). This improvement in the NAIRU occurred for all EU countries except Germany, Greece, Luxembourg and Austria (Commission, 2002h).

In Germany the Commission estimates suggest that there has been no improvement in the NAIRU (Figure 7.5). These estimates of the NAIRU are for the whole of Germany, though it tends to be the employment situation in West Germany that determines wages and salaries, and with this in mind, further analysis is confined to the West German Phillips curve. When consumer price inflation is plotted against the ILO unemployment rate this confirms that there has been no observable shift of the West German Phillips curve, implying that the NAIRU has been stable (Figure 7.6). Care has to be taken over unemployment as a measure of labour market imbalance as it is the ratio of the unemployed to the labour force, which is the employed plus the unemployed. There is evidence that with the persistence of high unemployment considerable numbers of workers have become hidden unemployed. These workers, who in more favourable circumstances would have been employed, are receiving other government benefits, have retired early, are employed in the informal economy or are inactive (Beatty *et al.*, 2002, Sachverständigenrat, 2002: 99). In Germany, hidden unemployment has been

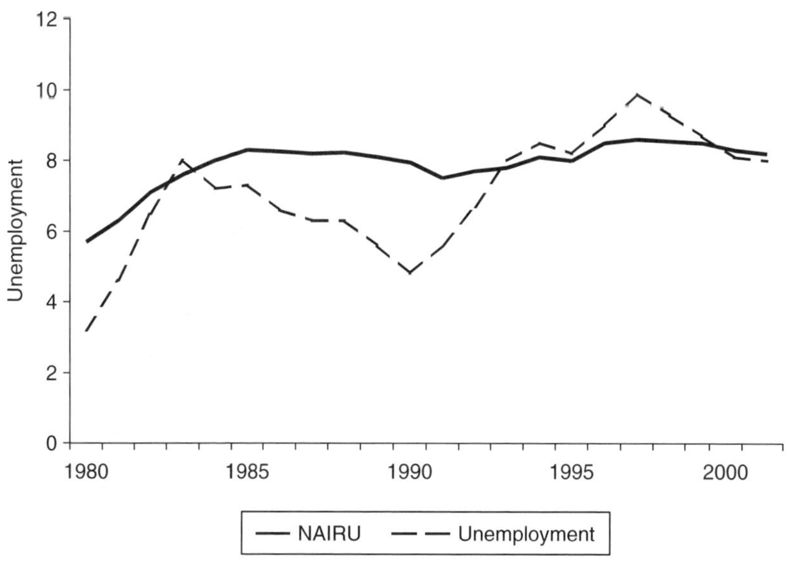

Figure 7.5 Germany NAIRU and unemployment. *Source*: European Commission (2002a); OECD (2004)

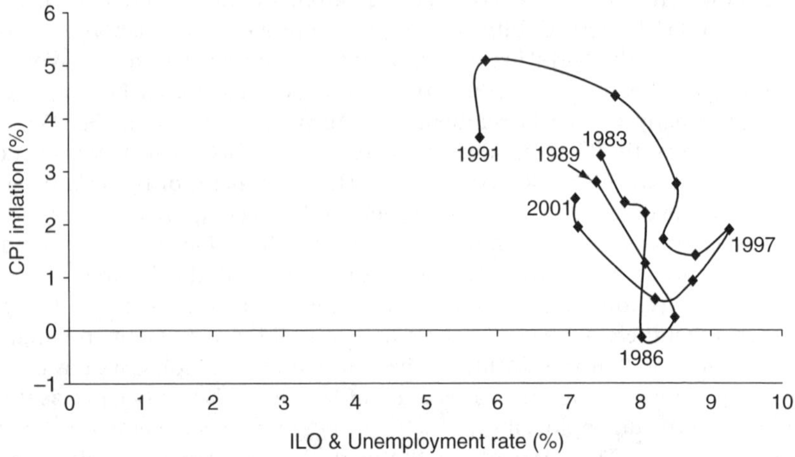

Figure 7.6 West Germany: Phillips Curve (ILO + hidden unemployment). *Source*: Eurostat (2002); OECD (2004)

associated particularly with the adjustment of East Germany to unification. Since West German hidden unemployment is fairly stable (Ardy, 2004), adding hidden unemployment to the ILO definition of unemployment (ILOH) results in a similarly shaped Phillips curve, although it is further to the right (Figure 7.7), as measured unemployment is now higher. Thus there

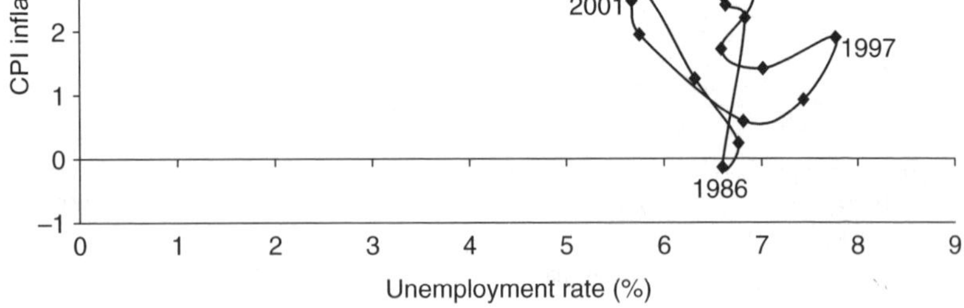

Figure 7.7 West Germany: Phillips Curve (ILO unemployment). *Source*: Eurostat (2002); OECD (2004)

has been no recent improvement in West German labour market performance on this measure.

The inability of Germany to reduce structural unemployment implies that improvements in German competitiveness in relation to the euro area will have to be acquired gradually at a high cost in terms of slow growth and high unemployment. Since structural unemployment is related to the institutional features of the labour market, it is these features and their reform which will determine whether German adjustment can become more efficient. The institutional factors identified as influencing employment and unemployment, are as follows:

1. Social Security Benefits
2. Taxation particularly of labour
3. Employment protection
4. Wage bargaining/trade union strength
5. Mobility: occupational and geographical
6. Labour force education, training and skills/active labour market policies
7. Job matching.

These features of the German labour market and the extent to which they have been reformed are considered below.

Generally, social security systems are being made more employment friendly by gradually reducing the overall tax burden, particularly taxes on labour and other non-wage costs, and by redesigning the system to eliminate poverty and unemployment traps. The complexity of social security systems makes comparison difficult, but the OECD provides regular comprehensive comparative data (OECD, 2002a). A number of factors combine to make up the overall system: the taxation of earnings, unemployment insurance (UI), unemployment assistance (UA) paid once insurance entitlements expire, selective assistance for those not qualified for UI or UA and other benefits. A general measure of the generosity of benefits is supplied by the net replacement rate (NRR), which expresses the income of the jobless as a percentage of their previous income in work. Germany's UI is not especially generous by EU standards at a payment rate of 60% of previous gross earnings available for 12 months. Once UI is exhausted the unemployed usually become dependent upon means-tested UA, if this is available. Where Germany is unusual is in offering UA at a rate related to previous net income, which is also available without a limit on its duration. This open-ended earnings related assistance can, for older workers, finance early retirement. NRRs had fallen only marginally in Germany in the early years of EMU (Commission, 2002e: 11–12), though they are at the heart of the Agenda 2010 reforms currently being implemented.

Measures of the generosity of benefits give no indication of the stringency of the requirements for the receipt of benefit. Such stringency is, however, difficult to measure, which is unfortunate because this is probably crucial in determining the effect of benefits on work incentives (Chapter 2; Danish Ministry of Finance, 1999; Grubb, 1999). Changes in the stringency of regulating access to UI/UA in Germany have been marginal, until recently.

The other side of the equation is the real incomes of people in work. These are affected by benefits to those in work and taxation of labour. Until 2003, again, there had been only limited changes in Germany (Commission, 2002i: 12). Despite the identification as a problem for the labour market of the high level of taxation on labour in the form of heavy social security contributions, the reductions in labour taxation in Germany have been marginal so that German labour remains heavily taxed. This is an important contributor to the high level of German wage costs (Table 7.6).

The legal protection of workers, Employment Protection Legislation (EPL), will tend to make employers more reluctant to hire workers, because it is more difficult to reduce the workforce subsequently (Table 7.7). EPL, however, also discourages employers from making workers redundant

Table 7.6 Structure of the tax wedge in 2001 and change 1997–2001[a] (in %)

	Income tax		Social security contributions				Total	
	2001	1997–2001	Employee		Employer		2001	1997–2001
			2001	1997–2001	2001	1997–2001		
Germany	16.6	–1.4	16.5	–0.5	16.5	–0.5	49.6	–2.4
EU-15	13.2	–0.7	11.2	–1.1	19.2	–1.2	43.5	–3.1
US	15.5	–1.5	7.0	0.0	7.0	0.0	29.5	–1.5

[a] Single person at APW wage level, no children.
Source: Commission (2002j).

Table 7.7 Employment protection legislation

	Late 1980s		Late 1990s	
	Regular employment	Overall	Regular employment	Overall
France	2.3	2.7	2.3	3.0
Italy	2.8	4.1	2.8	3.3
Netherlands	3.1	2.7	3.1	2.1
Germany	2.7	3.2	2.8	2.5
UK	0.8	0.5	0.8	0.5
USA	0.2	0.2	0.2	0.2

Scale 0–6 from least to most restrictive.
Source: IMF (2002b: 44).

during a recession, so that its effects on unemployment are ambiguous, at least in the short term. The evidence on the effects of employment protection legislation on unemployment is inconclusive (Bentolila and Bertola, 1990; Lazear, 1990; Addison and Grosso, 1996; Elmeskov *et al.*, 1998; Nickell and Layard, 1999; Nickell *et al.*, 2002). Part of the problem here may lie in the difficulty of measuring changes in the severity of EPL accurately, because the devil is in the detail of the legislation and its implementation (Bover *et al.*, 2000). Germany's traditionally high level of employment protection has remained largely intact. Flexibility has been introduced within, rather than between, jobs, so that employers adjust to changed economic circumstances by varying the hours of the workforce, rather than the size of the workforce. Such an approach undoubtedly has merit in response to temporary shocks but it may slow adjustment to permanent economic change (IMF, 2002b: 44).

Wage levels will also be affected by trade union strength – their ability to bargain for higher wages. This strength cannot be measured directly so that proxies have to be used. *Density* measures the proportion of workers in trade unions. *Coverage* is the proportion of workers whose wages are determined as a result of collective bargaining agreements between trade unions and employers. There is evidence that trade union power in wage determination is associated with higher wages and unemployment, but that this effect can be offset by co-ordination[8] of wage bargaining (Nickell and Layard, 1999; Booth *et al.*, 2000). German trade union density, at 29.7%, lies close to the EU average of 30.4%, but this is within a wide EU distribution. Membership levels vary from around 70+% in Denmark, Finland, Sweden and Belgium to 15% or less in Spain and France. Union membership has fallen over recent decades, but in Germany the decline has recently slowed (EIRO, 2002a).

Despite relatively low levels of union membership the number of workers covered by collective agreements is high in Germany at 67% (EIRO, 2002a), because of the process of agreement extension (Commission, 2002j: 39–47). Sectoral bargaining allows for some flexibility because deals can vary between sectors and the wage levels agreed are minima. However, these contractually specified minimum wage levels can represent problematic binding floors for the less skilled. Sectoral bargaining between large unions and employers' organisations means that although Germany's wage bargaining is not centralised, there is, in practice, a high level of co-ordination. This is the result of pattern bargaining, with influential agreements becoming benchmarks, and (since 1998) of tripartite discussions between trade unions, employers' associations and the Federal Government in the 'Bündnis für Arbeit'.[9] While this system has achieved wage moderation, there does seem to be some compression in German wage structures, particularly at the lower end of the scale (Commission, 2002h: 86–7).

Labour market adjustment can take place via the physical movement of workers in the shape of geographical migration. This is an important method of adjustment in the USA, but is less so in Europe. Interregional migration is much more sensitive to changes in wage differentials in the USA than in Europe (Eichengreen, 1993). Similarly, estimates of regional labour demand responses to shocks suggest that the migration response is limited in Europe (Obstfeld and Peri, 1998). The low and falling level of migration within Europe indicates the difficulties faced in trying to raise migration (Braunerhjelm *et al.*, 2000: 47). Falling international migration in Europe is familiar, but countries within the EU have also experienced declining interregional migration. In Germany, before unification, gross migration flows between the Länder fell from 13.0 per thousand people in the period 1975–1980, to 10.5 between 1984 and 1988 (Livi Bacci *et al.*, 1996). After large net outflows of migrants in the period when the DDR ceased to exist (1989–1990), migration from the new Länder to West Germany has been very small, amounting to only 0.35% of the population in 2000 (Commission, 2002h: 21). On this basis, the potential for migration as an adjustment mechanism in Germany is extremely limited.

Job matching seeks to ensure that the unemployed are paired with vacancies as rapidly as possible and the faster this takes place, the lower the overall level of unemployment. This requires that the labour force has the appropriate education, training and skills. The matching function is concerned with the provision of information and the process of pairing workers with jobs, but the process has long been hampered in Germany by the ineffectiveness of the Federal Employment Service. After this became a public scandal, rather belated action was taken (EIRO, 2002b), which led to the government to endorse the Hartz Commission proposals for reform.

The Beveridge curve, which shows the relationship between vacancies and unemployment, provides another general measure of the efficiency of the labour market in filling the available jobs (ECB, 2002b). Unemployment should be inversely related to vacancies because, as unemployment rises, it will become easier to fill vacancies and their number will fall. Over the economic cycle, there should be movements along the curve, but shifts of the curve indicate changes in the effectiveness of the labour market. An outward shift, where the unemployment associated with a given level of vacancies increases, indicates a deterioration in the matching efficiency of the labour market. Such an outward shift seems to have occurred for all EU countries[10] between 1960 and the mid-1980s (Nickell *et al.*, 2002). An inward shift indicates a reduced level of unemployment associated with a given level of vacancies, an improvement in the matching efficiency of the labour market. The euro area Beveridge curve seems to have shifted outwards in the 1990s (Figure 7.8).[11] The shifts are most pronounced in Belgium, Germany, Italy, Sweden and to a lesser extent France, Austria and Finland. Although the poor labour market performance of Germany looms large, this is a more general phenomenon across the EU. The

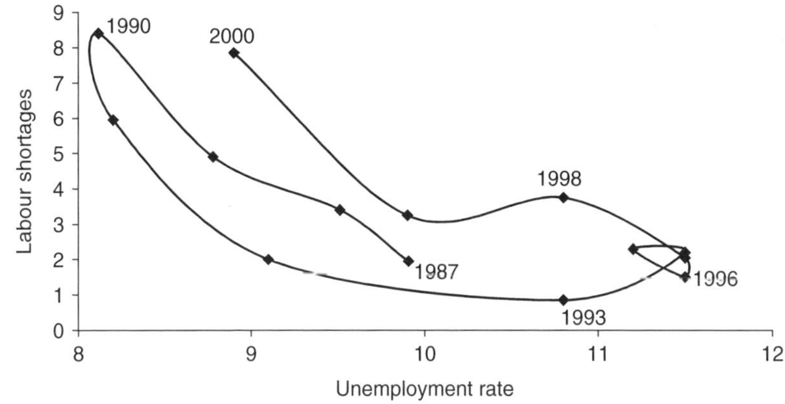

Figure 7.8 Beveridge curve for the euro area (*using business survey data*). *Source*: ECB (2002b)

Beveridge curves for the Netherlands, Denmark and the UK are, however, exceptions, having shifted inwards over the same period (Nickell *et al.*, 2002; ECB, 2002b).

A deterioration in Germany's Beveridge curve in the 1990s is not surprising, given the increase in the regional inequalities in unemployment associated with unification. The observations from 1983 to 1993 are noticeably below those from 1994 to 2001, indicating a reduction in labour market matching efficiency (Figure 7.9). Allowing for hidden

Figure 7.9 West Germany: Beveridge curve (ILO + hidden unemployment). *Source*: Eurostat (2002); IAB (2003)

unemployment by using ILO plus hidden (ILOH) unemployment leaves the shape of the Beveridge curve unchanged, although again its position has moved (Figure 7.9).

7.4.3 German economic reform 2003

Germany has now begun to tackle some of the rigidities of its labour market with the Hartz and Agenda 2010 reforms. There are seven key areas of reform:

1. Restructuring the Federal Employment Service
2. Tightening up of social security for the unemployed
3. Encouraging additional employment by lower tax and social contributions
4. Improvements in education and training
5. The establishment of new businesses and the expansion of new businesses is to be encouraged by tax breaks, reduced protection against dismissal in small firms, liberalisation reducing administrative burdens on business, and relaxing restrictions on shop opening hours
6. Control of expenditure on health and pensions, to reduce the current and future level of contributions necessary to fund the system
7. A reduction of income tax.

The first two of the Hartz I to IV 'Laws for modern services in the labour market' came into effect on 1 January 2003 and April 2003, and the remaining Hartz proposals along with the bulk of Agenda 2010 were agreed on 14 December 2003 (Commission, 2004j: 16).

The Federal Employment Service in Germany has traditionally been concerned with the administration of benefits, but is being reformed, with the emphasis switching to helping and encouraging the unemployed to find jobs. New public-sector agencies have been formed to employ the jobless and hire them out to private firms. The initial numbers involved were small, but the scheme has since expanded. One factor in their favour, from the perspective of stimulating hiring of labour, is that they are able to pay considerably below trade union agreed rates, though there has inevitably been unease about this from the unions.

The reforms of the unemployment insurance/assistance system complement the changes to the employment service, making the eligibility requirements stricter and reducing the length and generosity of benefits. The threshold for jobs that are deemed acceptable has been lowered. These revised eligibility criteria seem to have had an impact, with the number of unemployed stabilising in 2003 despite falling employment (Commission, 2004j: Graph 3.1, p. 16).[12] Other changes that come into effect in 2006 include restriction of unemployment benefit (Arbeitlosengeld) to 12 months,[13] and once entitlement to unemployment benefit is exhausted, a new benefit will replace unemployment assistance (Arbeitslosenhilfe). This new benefit will be flat rate and means tested. Part of this benefit will continue for a period if the individual enters employment. In addition workers can earn up to €400 a month without having to pay welfare contributions or tax. This has resulted in legalisation of informal economy jobs and some new jobs being created, though the impact on measured unemployment has been uncertain.

Little change has been made to the wage bargaining system. The Günstigkeitsprinzip – a legal restriction that only allows enterprise level deviations from industry wide wage agreements if these deviations are not in any aspect less favourable than the collective agreement – remains in place. In practice some employers (particularly in East Germany) are paying below the industry norm. Private sector agencies have reached agreement with the unions to pay 10–15% below collective agreement norms. The upshot is that *de facto*, some wage flexibility is emerging.

The quality of schooling is to be addressed by a boost to all-day schools in federal programmes from 2004 to 2007. An independent agency for standards and evaluation is to develop national educational standards, and a committee of experts is to report on education. Steps are to be taken to improve the quality of teaching. Some initiatives are to be introduced to raise the quality of vocational education. Improvements in education are dependent upon the Länder for the implementation of reform measures, since education remains primarily a Land competence.

Health care reforms aim to shift costs from the state to patients rather than to reduce costs. For example, patients will pay more for dental care and receive less sickness benefit. It is estimated that these changes will reduce the joint employee/employer health contributions by 0.7% in 2004, rising to 1.3% in 2007.

Short-term provisions to reduce the burden on the state of the pension system were the result of a postponement of more extensive reform presaged in 2004 to the pensions system that will mean higher pension contributions. Further steps have been taken to reduce the future burden of pensions. An increase in the mandatory pension age is to be phased-in progressively at a rate of one month a year from 2010, so that by 2034 the pension age will have risen from 65 to 67. A 'sustainability factor' is to be introduced into the calculation of pensions and this will lower future increases in pensions. This change together with simplified supervision should provide some encouragement to the development of private pensions. As with most other pension reforms in Europe, this is only a partial solution that does not resolve the long-term pension sustainability problem.

Tax cuts will interact with reductions in social security contributions[14] and changes in the benefit system to improve incentives for workers at all income levels. Tax reform has not, however, begun to unravel the complexity of the system. In addition to €6.5 billion tax cuts already approved for 2004, another €16.5 billion was approved in December 2004, but to accommodate political opposition, they will be phased in over two years 2004–2005. Given the high level of German taxation, it is plausible that these should be at least partially self-funding through supply-side effects. Other funding comes from increased debt and the privatisation of Deutsche Telekom and Deutsche Post, which should raise €5.3 billion. However, reconciling all these measures with Germany's SGP commitments will be difficult.

The heavy regulation of German business is one factor limiting the establishment of new businesses and the further development of the service sector. Various measures aim to improve this situation by: easing of employment regulations for small firms; introducing special arrangements for one person businesses; liberalising the regulations of craft businesses; and extending shop opening hours. Protection of workers against dismissal has been reduced, but only for small firms employing up to 10 workers. Self-employment has been encouraged by a scheme that cuts tax and administrative requirements for one-person businesses, earning less than €25,000. Under previous legislation in 94 crafts, only those with a master craftsman certificate (Meisterbrief) could establish a business. Since these certificates are time consuming and expensive[15] to obtain, this regulation represented a considerable restriction on enterprise. The certificate will no longer be required in 53 of the 94 recognised crafts, however, 90% of craft-based companies are in the remaining 41 trades (Williamson, 2004). Trained staff without the Meisterbrief can, however, establish a business if they have six years experience including four in a senior capacity.[16] Restrictions on shop opening were one of the regulatory factors limiting the creation of employment in the service sector. Previously, shops had to shut at 4 pm on Saturdays but now they can stay open until 8 pm. Petrol stations, with even longer opening hours, have stretched the definition of 'travel provision' to justify remaining open. While these are all steps towards a less regulated economy, their impact on the restrictive regulatory environment of German business is expected to be only marginal.

Views on these reforms vary. All are agreed that further reforms are needed but some see these reforms as good beginning (Posen, 2003a), others as limited and inadequate (*Economist*, 2003b; Schröder and Walter, 2003). Structural reform has to take place if the adjustment costs of German economy are to be lower. However, effecting them is politically difficult in the face of strong vested interests and a further, more profound criticism is that the reforms are aimed at the wrong target. It is argued that the fundamental problem of the Germany economy has been insufficient investment, with the implication that reform of public-sector banking, regulation and promotion of venture capital markets and the general underdevelopment of the capital market should be tackled first (Munchau, 2003).

Many of the reforms implemented or under discussion in Germany aim to adjust the welfare state to make it affordable, rather than raising growth to provide the resources to finance the society Germans want. This is a dilemma faced by all participants in EMU. The preferred strategy is to use the EMU framework to facilitate faster growth and, by so doing, to create room for manoeuvre in economic adjustment. Yet Germany exemplifies the problem that it is incurring the costs of structural improvement simply to lower the burden of macroeconomic adjustment without, so far, obtaining the anticipated pay-off.

7.5 German unification and EMU

German unification was an enormous asymmetric shock for the German economy, and it can be argued that the adjustment to the shock continued as Germany entered Stage 3. The process of unification made East German industry uncompetitive because wage levels rose quickly, while the extension to the new Länder of the west German social security regime set a floor to wage levels, and in parallel, wage bargainers sought to achieve parity for workers in the east with West German rates. In 2003, wage levels in the East were 65–75% of those in West Germany, but productivity is below 60% (Sinn, 2003: 22). This has meant that East Germany has come to account for a disproportionate share of bankruptcies, non-performing loans and unemployment in the German economy.

The size of these effects is such that they have affected the performance of the German economy as a whole. 'Long-lasting effects of unification seem to play a pivotal role in the twin phenomenon of sluggish domestic demand and anaemic job growth' (Commission, 2002i). These effects were related to the slow growth of domestic demand, especially private consumption and construction investment, which led to weak German GDP growth. The construction boom which unification triggered in the new Länder contributed disproportionately to the growth of East Germany, but the tailing-off of this infrastructure investment since the mid-1990s depressed the East German growth rate. Trends in West Germany meant its construction sector was contracting at the same time. There was a general reduction of construction demand for residential housing[17] from the public sector, and from business. The contraction of construction across the whole of Germany dragged down the growth rate.

Unification has meant continuing transfers amounting to 4% of GDP in net terms from West to East Germany (Commission, 2002h: 2). These transfers have been financed by some expansion of the public-sector deficit,[18] but also by increases in tax and social security contributions, which have contributed to high labour costs. Although the initial effects of this fiscal expansion on demand were positive, it had subsequent negative effects on investment and labour demand. Poor growth and higher taxation also depressed consumption.

It could be argued that Germany was always going to face a more acute adjustment problem in EMU specifically because of the impact of unification, and it is interesting to note that the German position in the 2005 negotiations on reform of the SGP sought to include unification as a form of 'exceptional' circumstances allowing deficits to be above 3%. However, as already argued in this chapter, EMU both introduced new problems and made coping with the aftermath of unification more difficult. It meant that a large burden of adjustment was placed upon relatively unreformed product and labour markets which, while able to cope in the stable pre-unification West Germany, were ill-suited to deal with the shocks that stemmed from unification and EMU entry. These problems were, in particular, wages out of line with productivity, inadequate differentiation between East and West wage rates, and unemployment traps, all of which signal a lack of flexibility. The heavy regulation of markets and restrictions on business also limited the growth of employment opportunities in the service sector.

7.6 German deflation and EMU?

Since 2000 the Germany economy has experienced very little expansion of output and very low rates of price increases. There is concern that there is a risk of sinking into deflation, with parallels being drawn between the German and Japanese situations (IMF, 2003b; Posen, 2003b; Sinn, 2003). The danger of deflation arises from the problems of the German financial sector, the revaluation of the euro and associated problems of demand. German banks, like those in Japan, have considerable holdings in stocks of other companies, the value of which has been substantially reduced by the ending of the 'new economy' stock market bubble. Falling bond prices have exacerbated these problems. The reduction in the value of the banks' assets has posed problems for lending because of difficulties in meeting required liquidity and asset ratios. This has led banks to increase risk premia and to cut lines of credit, which has contributed to rising insolvencies (Sinn, 2003: 6). The German financial sector's problems are not, however, as serious as those of Japan because real-estate prices have not collapsed. Membership of EMU does, however, mean that Germany has particular vulnerabilities. The problems of the revaluation of the euro have already been considered. Germany's exchange rate with its largest export markets cannot be adjusted and the exchange rate with other markets will be determined by euro area rather than German conditions. Demand in Germany has been constrained, partly by the low levels of investment associated with the overall economic situation and the problems of the banking sector. Consumers, as in Japan, have raised their savings rate in response to the uncertain economic conditions. Any public-sector boost to the economy is restricted by the SGP and German problems with meeting the Pact's requirements.

The problem for Germany is that although it continues to be the largest euro area economy, any monetary response to a slowdown in Germany, or indeed, possible price deflation will be only partial, since the ECB cannot base its policy on the circumstances of one Member State, while the aggregate euro area inflation remains above the 2% reference value. The underlying question is whether the immediate threat of deflation is no more than a short-term acclimatisation problem or a symptom of a more enduring problem. German adjustment to acclimatisation could be prolonged and could be worsened by Balassa–Samuelson (BS) effects elsewhere. Higher inflation in countries converging towards the levels of income and prices in richer countries (such as Germany) has to be offset by lower inflation in the higher productivity/higher income countries. During the process of convergence, therefore, such countries will have to have inflation rates below 2% for the overall euro area inflation rate 2% or below. It is unlikely, given its size, that Germany can avoid being a member of this lower-inflation group.

The significance of this effect is a matter of contention. Some estimates suggest that it is large, requiring Germany to keep its inflation level at 1% for the euro area to have an inflation rate of 2% (Sinn and Reutter, 2000). This seems an overestimate. Alesina *et al.* (2001: 16–18) demonstrate that, using results from De Gregorio and Wolf (1994), taking the extreme case of Ireland and making harsh assumptions, would lead to Ireland having an inflation rate 1.5% higher than the euro area average.[19] A figure around this level is also supported by Summers and Heston (1991) who tracked the changes in the consumer price levels of Greece, Ireland and Spain relative to the USA from 1950 to 1980. There is no visible trend in the Greek price level, but Spanish and Irish prices increased relative to the USA by 1.3% per year. Thus 1.3–1.5% seems an upper limit given that productivity and price differences have already unwound to a considerable extent.[20]

A rough measure of current euro area productivity and relative price levels is provided by Table 7.8. GDP per worker is a crude measure of productivity.[21] Productivity is low in Portugal, Greece and Spain, while in Germany it is at

Table 7.8 Relative productivity and price levels in the euro area 2002

	GDP per worker (% euro area average)	**GDP €/GDP PPS (%)**	**Share of EMU total (%)**
Luxembourg	143.4	114.2	0.3
Ireland	134.1	115.9	1.8
Netherlands	124.9	105.8	6.3
France	118.4	104.0	21.5
Austria	117.3	103.7	3.1
Belgium	115.1	100.7	3.7
Finland	109.0	113.1	2.0
FR. Germany	99.9	107.6	29.8
Italy	95.6	91.6	17.8
Spain	80.6	87.5	9.8
Greece	66.5	83.8	2.0
Portugal	47.1	78.2	1.8
Euro area	100.0	100.0	100.0

Source: Commission (2004d).

the EU average. The difference between GDP measured in euros and the Purchasing Power Standard (PPS) provides an indication of the extent of divergence of the internal price level from the euro area average. On this measure the differences are not that great, limiting the extent and persistence of the BS effect. The weight of Portugal, Greece and Spain in the euro area total is small at 13.7%. If, as a result of the Balassa–Samuelson effect, prices in these countries increase by 1% above the euro area average, the euro area inflation rate would increase by 0.14%, this in turn means that the other euro area countries inflation rate would have to be 0.16% below the 2% target.[22] Thus the BS effect would seem to add only marginally to the deflationary impact of ECB monetary policy for countries such as Germany.

7.7 Conclusion

German entry to EMU was always likely to be problematic in the short term, as there were no great macroeconomic benefits for the economy from EMU. A stable macroeconomic environment was present, exchange rates with EMS partners were stable and interest rates were low. At the start of Stage 3, ECB monetary policy had to be attuned to the risk of a rise in inflation for the whole euro area boost to demand in countries other than Germany as they adjusted to lower nominal and real interest rates. The result was that Germany had to face higher real interest rates than it might have done under an independent monetary policy, and this may have exacerbated the slowness of the recovery after the 2001 downturn.

The adjustment was made more difficult by the related problems of German unification and the nature of the economic system. The initial adjustment to unification contributed to an appreciation of the exchange rate, while at the same time undermining the competitiveness of Germany. Entry to EMU prevented further exchange rate adjustment and placed the whole of the burden effectively on labour and product markets. These markets, shaped in a very stable macroeconomic environment, were ill-equipped to deal with the shock of unification, the need to adjust to EMU and the difficulties associated with the recession that struck in 2001.

Given this limited adjustment response coming from labour and product markets, the problematic macroeconomic environment and difficulties with the financial sector, Germany is close to deflation. The responses of the German government, constrained by the consensual political system, have been delayed. There has, with the agreement on the Agenda 2010 reforms, been a first step to significant change. The newness of these changes makes assessment of their impact difficult, but Germany is likely to face a longer period of slow growth before reform and the fading of acclimatisation problems can lead to significantly improved performance.

8
Ireland: Adjusting to Life in the Euro Area Without the United Kingdom

Ireland is no stranger to monetary union, having maintained parity with sterling between 1826 and 1979. When Ireland irrevocably fixed the external value of its currency, the punt, with those of ten other EU Member States on 1 January 1999, however, sterling continued to float. The continued absence of the United Kingdom (UK) from EMU creates an adjustment dilemma for the Irish economy. On the one hand, Ireland's trade dependence on the UK leaves it more exposed than the euro area to economic disturbances of British origin and to fluctuations in the euro–sterling exchange rate. On the other hand, the fact that Ireland accounts for little more than 1% of euro area GDP makes it highly unlikely that euro area monetary and exchange rate policy will adjust to disequilibria in the Irish economy alone. When this dilemma is viewed through the lens of optimum currency area theory (see Chapter 1 and Section 8.1), the ability of Ireland to adjust to life in the euro area without the UK will depend on the extent to which alternative adjustment mechanisms can compensate for the loss of nominal exchange rate adjustment in the face of asymmetric shocks. In the light of these concerns, this chapter examines the significance of nominal exchange rate adjustment in Ireland prior to EMU, before assessing the extent to which fiscal policy and the labour market represent realistic adjustment options for the Irish economy.

Three key empirical findings emerge from this analysis. First, in the two decades before EMU the punt–sterling exchange rate responded to the same variety of shock that drove macroeconomic imbalances between the Irish and UK economies. Thus, even if nominal exchange rate adjustment was an imperfect tool in a small open economy such as Ireland, it was not necessarily an insignificant one. Second, although the Irish labour market traditionally ranks among the more flexible in the EU, its effectiveness as an adjustment mechanism against asymmetric shocks will depend on the ability of the social partnership to deliver continued wage moderation. Third, although the rapid rate of economic growth in the 1990s allowed the government to amass sizeable budget surpluses, Ireland has nonetheless encountered difficulties in sticking to EMU's fiscal rules.

The balance of this chapter is divided into four parts. The first section reviews the literature on nominal exchange rate adjustment in Ireland, before assessing empirical evidence on the shock absorbency of the punt–sterling exchange rate over the period 1982–1998. The second section explores the contribution of labour market mobility and social partnership to labour market flexibility in Ireland under EMU. The third section examines recent trends in Irish fiscal policy, before recounting the impact of the Stability and Growth Pact on Ireland's budgetary stabilisers. The final section concludes.

8.1 Nominal exchange rate adjustment prior to EMU

The central tenet of Robert Mundell's seminal article on optimum currency areas is that the loss of nominal exchange rate adjustment in the face of asymmetric shocks is the principal macroeconomic cost of joining a monetary union (Mundell, 1961). For a small open economy, such as Ireland, however, it is doubtful whether the nominal exchange rate counts as a help or a hindrance in the face of such shocks. As Honohan and Flynn (1986) and Kenny and McGettigan (1996) observe, the high level of import penetration in the Irish economy means that a depreciation of the nominal exchange rate will act as a spur for domestic inflation. A well-known study by O'Connell and Frain (1989) estimates that this 'pass-through' effect is as high as 44% for Ireland, meaning that just under half of the competitive stimulus associated with a depreciation is undone by inflationary pressures. Of course, the fact that a depreciation generates domestic inflation does not preclude the fact that the nominal exchange rate played a role in the adjustment process prior to EMU. It remains an open question as to whether the punt–sterling exchange rate has historically moved to redress macroeconomic imbalances between the Irish and UK economies.

Structural Vector Autoregression (SVAR) analysis, which was pioneered by Bernanke (1986), Blanchard and Quah (1989) and Blanchard and Watson (1986), allows us to examine the response of endogenously determined macroeconomic variables to exogenously determined shocks. Although SVAR analysis cannot establish a direct causal link between exchange rates and macroeconomic imbalances, it can ascertain whether the two were driven by the same variety of macroeconomic disturbances. If there is a high degree of coincidence in this regard, then this supports the hypothesis that the exchange rate acted as a shock absorber. If the degree of coincidence is low, however, it is unlikely that the exchange rate played a significant role in the adjustment process.

A pioneering study of the EU by Canzoneri *et al.* (1996) concludes that macroeconomic imbalances between selected Member States and the EU core were primarily driven by supply shocks, while fluctuations in the nominal exchange rate were driven, on the whole, by demand and monetary shocks. Astley and Garratt (1998) find that roughly one-fifth of the fluctuations in the sterling–euro real exchange rate over the period 1970–1994 can be explained by supply shocks, with demand shocks accounting for most of the rest. A study of macroeconomic adjustment in Sweden over the period 1979–1995 by Thomas (1997) finds that demand shocks account for up to 62% of the fluctuation in the real effective exchange rates, with supply shocks accounting for just 10%. Artis and Ehrmann (2000) conclude that supply shocks can explain most of the fluctuations in output but few of the fluctuations in the ECU exchange rate in Denmark and the UK over the period 1974–1998.

Hodson (2003) applies the SVAR methodology to the study of the Irish economy over the period 1982–1998. His results indicate that supply shocks played a significant role in the determination of relative output between the UK and Ireland and the punt–sterling exchange rate. The results of the forecast error variance decomposition from this analysis are reproduced in Table 8.1.

It is clear that supply shocks predominate when it comes to fluctuations in relative output, accounting for around 84.0% of the fluctuation in relative output during the first quarter of the forecast horizon, as compared with 6.7% for money shocks and 9.3% for demand shocks. After four quarters, supply shocks account for 93.4% of fluctuations in real output. A similar pattern emerges with respect to the nominal exchange. In the first quarter

Table 8.1 Forecast error variance decomposition for Ireland

Variable	Forecast step	Standard error	Disturbances (% share)		
			Nominal shock	Demand shock	Supply shock
Exchange rate	1	0.04	40.8	0.1	59.1
	2	0.04	38.1	3.0	58.9
	4	0.04	37.5	4.4	58.1
	6	0.04	37.6	4.4	58.0
	8	0.04	37.6	4.4	58.0
	20	0.04	37.6	4.4	58.0
Relative output	1	0.05	6.7	9.3	84.0
	2	0.07	3.2	4.3	92.5
	4	0.09	3.3	3.3	93.4
	6	0.09	3.3	3.4	93.3
	8	0.09	3.3	3.4	93.3
	20	0.09	3.3	3.4	93.3

Source: Hodson (2003: 159).

of the forecast horizon, supply shocks account for approximately 59.1% of fluctuations in the exchange rate, with money shocks accounting for 40.8% and demand shocks for 0.1%. After four quarters, demand shocks account for 4.4% of fluctuations in the nominal exchange rate but supply shocks account for 58.1%.

To understand the full import of these findings Hodson (2003) compares them with the results of Canzoneri *et al.* (1996). While the latter is based on a different sample period (and hence on a different exchange rate regime), it nonetheless provide a rough benchmark against which to judge the significance of the Irish result. Figure 8.1 illustrates the ratio of the explanatory power of supply shocks with regard to the nominal exchange rate and relative output respectively. A score of zero suggests that the exchange rate and relative output are driven by entirely different categories of disturbance, while a score of one means that both are driven by identical types of shock. As we can see, the measure of coincidence for the first quarter of the forecast horizon varies from one Member State to another. In the Canzoneri *et al.* (1996) study, Spain and Austria score lowest with 0.06, while Italy scores highest with 0.5. This suggests that macroeconomic imbalances and nominal exchange rates were more closely aligned in Ireland than was the case in other euro area Member States. In the Hodson (2003) study, Ireland scores 0.7.

In summary, empirical studies confirm that exchange rate adjustment in a small open economy such as Ireland is a costly exercise, because of its impact on import prices and hence on domestic inflation. These costs notwithstanding, however, there is also strong circumstantial evidence that the punt–sterling nominal exchange rate moved to redress balances between

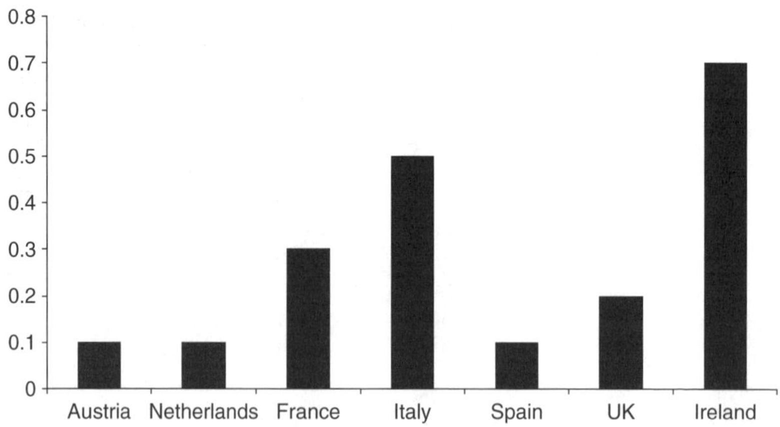

Figure 8.1 A measure of coincidence. *Source*: Hodson (2003: 161)

Note: The measure of coincidence represents the ratio of fluctuations in relative output attributed to supply shocks to fluctuations in the nominal exchange rate attributed to the same variety of disturbance.

the Irish and UK economies over the period 1982–1998. Moreover, when this result is viewed in a comparative context, it suggests that the Irish economy was more heavily dependent on exchange rate adjustment than many of its EU peers. This suggests that the loss of nominal exchange rate adjustment in the face of asymmetric shocks is non-negligible for the Irish economy, thus increasing the importance of alternative adjustment mechanisms.

8.2 Labour market adjustment under EMU

8.2.1 Labour mobility and the Irish economy

One of the stylised facts about EMU is that the EU labour force lacks sufficient geographical mobility to absorb the impact of asymmetric shocks. In one of the more rigorous studies of this proposition, Decressin and Fatàs (1995) compare labour market responses to demand shocks at the regional level in the EU and at the state level in the United States. Their findings for the United States indicate that migration accounts for over half the employment adjustment in the same year that the shock took place in. Migration only assumes this magnitude of importance in European regions in the third year after the initial shock. There is reason to believe, however, that Ireland is a special case. As Figure 8.2 shows, Ireland recorded a significantly

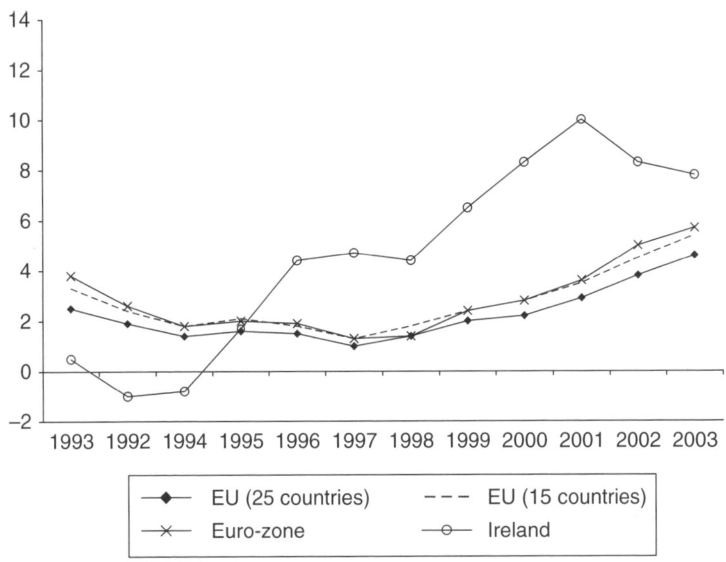

Figure 8.2 Net migration, 1992–2003 (per 1000 inhabitants). *Source*: Eurostat
Note: The crude rate of net migration (including corrections) measures the difference between population change and natural increase during the year.

higher rate of net migration than the EU-15, EU-25 and euro area between the mid-1990s and the beginning of the new millennium. The concentration of highly skilled immigrants in this recent cohort (Barrett and Trace, 1998) and the continuing outward flow of emigrants from the Irish economy (Figure 8.3) suggest that labour mobility could be a more realistic adjustment mechanism for Ireland than for the rest of the euro area (Fitz Gerald, 2001).

The question remains as to whether labour mobility represents a viable adjustment option between Ireland and the UK. Figures 8.4 and 8.5 decompose Ireland's migratory flows into places of origin and destination over the period 1987–2004. The importance of the UK for Irish migration at the beginning of the period is evident, with nearly 47% of Ireland's immigrants coming from Ireland's nearest neighbour and nearly 55% of all emigrants ending up there. This migratory pattern was even more pronounced at the start of the 1990s, with the UK counting for over 56% of inward migration and 65% of outward migration. By the start of the next decade, this picture had changed radically. In 2004, the UK accounted for just 26% of all immigrants, as compared with 39% from countries outside the EU and USA. Similarly, just 27% of Irish emigrants ended up in the UK, as compared with a figure of 40% for countries outside the EU and USA.

Even though the relative importance of the UK for Irish migratory flows is falling, the fact that overall levels of migration and emigration remain substantial, however, would seem to confirm Krugman's observation that the Irish economy is more akin to a small regional economy within the euro area than an autonomous national one (Krugman, 1997).

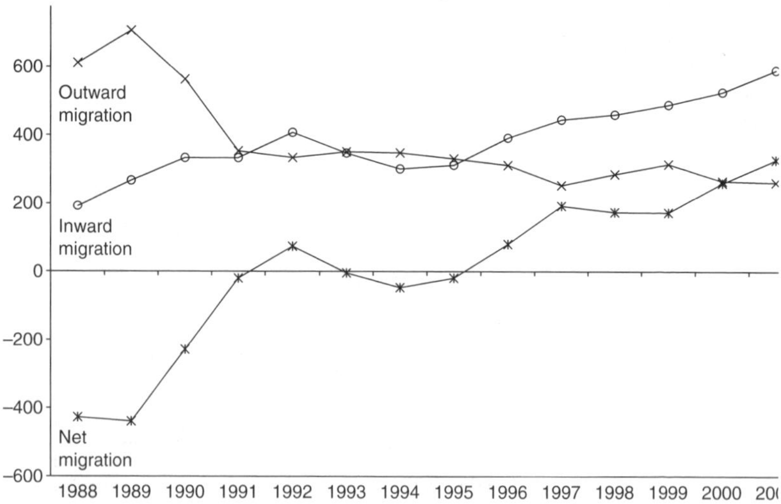

Figure 8.3 Inward, outward and net migration in Ireland, 1988–2001 (persons, 000s).
Source: Central Statistics Office, Ireland

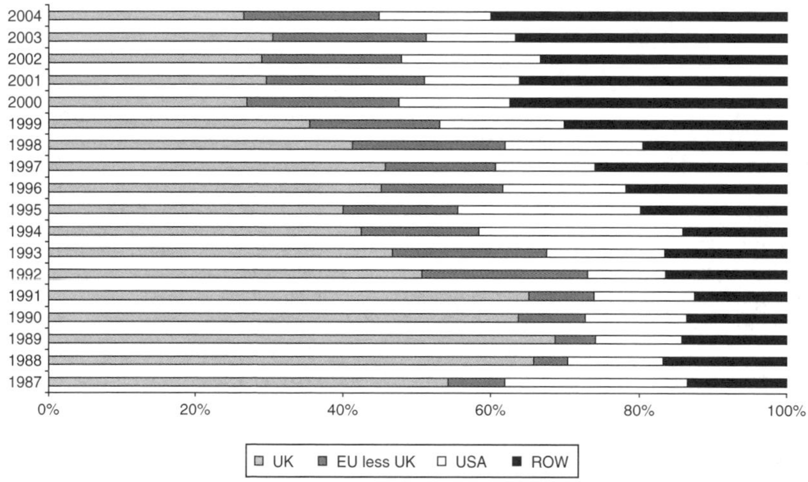

Figure 8.4 Net outward migration by destination, 1987–2004 (percentage of total). *Source*: Central Statistics Office, Ireland

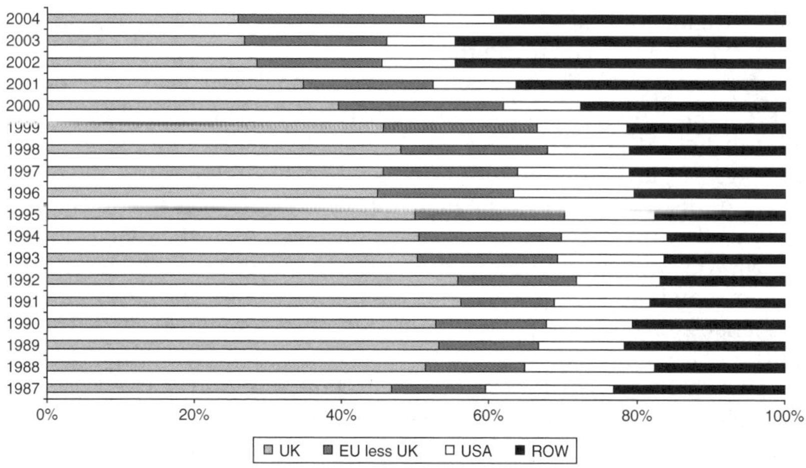

Figure 8.5 Net inward migration by origin, 1987–2004 (percentage of total). *Source*: Central Statistics Office, Ireland

8.2.2 Wage flexibility and the importance of social partnership

If labour mobility represents one plank of labour market adjustment, then wage flexibility represents the other. Comparative measures indicate that the Irish labour is among the more flexible in the EU. Table 8.2 presents Nickell's index of wage flexibility, which is based on the estimated elasticity

Table 8.2 Wage flexibility in the OECD

Aggregate time series measure			
Country	**Short run**	**Country**	**Long run**
France	2.22	Italy	12.94
Italy	2.07	Belgium	4.06
Austria	1.43	France	4.35
Ireland	**0.80**	Austria	3.11
Netherlands	0.66	Netherlands	2.28
Belgium	0.65	**Ireland**	**1.82**
Germany (W)	0.55	Finland	1.55
Finland	0.48	Spain	1.21
Spain	0.17	Germany (W)	1.01

Note: The percentage increase in wages in response to a one-percentage point fall in the unemployment rate.
Source: Nickell (1997: 60).

of wages to unemployment for selected OECD countries. The results indicate that Ireland ranks above Denmark, Finland, Germany, the Netherlands, Belgium and Spain in the short run and above Denmark, Finland, Spain, the UK and Germany in the long run.

In advance of EMU, the Irish Economic and Social Research Council (Baker *et al.*, 1996) conducted a more in depth study of price and wage flexibility in Ireland relative to the UK. The results of this study support the existence of purchasing power parity between Ireland and the UK in the long run. Irish consumer prices are cointegrated with their British counterparts, while Irish producer prices are cointegrated with their German and UK equivalents. In the short run, price adjustment is sluggish with consumer and producer prices taking almost three years to adjust in the UK and Ireland to a 20% depreciation of sterling. Approximately half of the adjustment is achieved by a slow down in the rate of Irish inflation with the other half associated with a more rapid inflation in the UK. Wages on the other hand take nearly four years to adjust to the depreciation, with more than half the gap in competitiveness being eliminated through higher wage inflation in the UK. In short, prices and wages in Ireland are capable of adjusting to a depreciation of sterling, although a significant proportion of adjustment will come from the UK itself.

Although these findings confirm the flexibility of wages in Ireland, the effectiveness of labour market adjustment under EMU is likely to depend, in no small measure, on the contribution of social partnership to wage formation. Since 1987, representatives of employers, workers and the farming community have met with the Irish government in an attempt to 'escape the vicious circle of real stagnation, rising taxes and exploding debt' that had built up over the 1980s (O'Donnell, 1998: 10). The first national agreement set guidelines for public- and private-sector wage increases over a three-year horizon in exchange for a programme for tax reform and health and welfare expenditure. The Programme for National Recovery, as it was called, heralded a new approach to social partnership in Ireland which, to date, has inspired five successor agreements; the Programme for Economic and Social Progress (1991–1993), the Programme for Competitiveness and Work (1994–1996), Partnership 2000 (1997–1999), the Programme for Prosperity and Fairness (2000–2002) and Sustaining Progress (2003–2005).

Collectively, as O'Donnell (1998) notes, these agreements have surpassed the traditional neo-corporatist approach to wage bargaining in two respects. First, with their wage setting, macroeconomic and social policy pillars, the national agreements encourage a shared understanding of economic and social issues. This understanding was particularly evident in Ireland's commitment to European Monetary Union (EMU). Membership of EMU was identified in the national agreements as being of vital strategic importance to the Irish economy and the social partners gave their full support to the process of convergence. That this commitment held firm in the face of high unemployment, currency speculation and British abstinence from EMU is testament to the depth of the consensus on economic and social matters that has been generated between the government and social partners. In the context of a narrower corporatist agreement, the social partners would have found it more difficult to maintain wage restraint in the presence of these exogenous shocks. Second, the national agreements differ from the traditional neo-corporatist model of wage bargaining in their emphasis on inclusiveness. Since the PNR these agreements have transcended the traditional tripartite framework to include representatives of minority groups and the voluntary and community sectors.

At first blush, the prospects for continued social partnership under EMU appear to be unfavourable. As Danthine and Hunt (1992) note, national wage bargains will take on a more regional flavour under monetary union as monetary policy is centralised and the room for decentralised fiscal manoeuvre is restricted under terms of the Stability and Growth Pact. This will weaken the Irish government's position at the bargaining table and could jeopardise the likelihood of striking a wage level that is well suited to prevailing economic circumstances. Nonetheless, monetary integration will also strengthen the degree of economic interdependence between the Member States both through the common interest rate channel and further competition in produce and factor markets (Danthine and Hunt, 1992). In the case of a centralised wage bargaining regime such as in Ireland, this interdependence may force the social partners to give greater recognition to the external consequences of national agreements. An excessive bargained real wage level could damage the competitiveness of the economy and leave all those concerned in a worse-off position. Indeed, concerns about international competitiveness have been at the forefront of national agreements since 1987 when the partners identified membership of the ERM as a strategic objective. Their commitment to both ERM and (in time) EMU held firm amidst the currency crises of 1992/93, even in the light of the UK's exit from ERM. Baccaro and Simoni (2004) confirm the positive impact of social partnership on the competitiveness of the Irish economy, which they attribute to the fact that the national agreements linked wage increases to productivity trends in traditional, labour intensive, manufacturing sectors rather than industries dominated by foreign multinational corporations, where productivity increased rapidly. The initial post-EMU national agreements, the Programme for National Prosperity, and Sustaining Progress showed little tendency towards insularity with the external competitiveness of the economy remaining a strategic objective. It seems unlikely, therefore, that EMU *per se* will blunt social partnership as an instrument of relative wage and price adjustment to any significant degree.

8.3 Fiscal adjustment under the Stability and Growth Pact

The third alternative adjustment mechanism is fiscal policy which, according to the theory of optimum currency areas, is a key policy instrument to turn to in the absence of exchange rate adjustment at the national level. When such developments are considered from a Mundell–Fleming perspective, EMU restores the effectiveness of national fiscal policy by fixing exchange rates and introducing a single and uniform interest rate for the euro area as a whole. For individual Member States, therefore, both domestic and international crowding-out effects under EMU are diminished. Should all Member States take advantage of this fact, however, by pursuing more expansionary fiscal policies, the net result will be a higher interest rate for all concerned and an appreciation in the nominal exchange rate. Fears regarding the potential spill over effects that might arise from eleven national fiscal policies operating within one currency-zone prompted the Member States to sign the Stability and Growth Pact (Eichengreen and Wyplosz, 1998). Under the terms of this agreement, the signatories agree to keep their budget deficits within a reference value of 3% of GDP, except under 'exceptional' economic circumstances. Although this measure guards against the threat of fiscal profligacy it also threatens to constrain the effectiveness of automatic budgetary stabilisers. To avoid such an eventuality, the pact includes the additional clause that Member States must aim for a medium-term budgetary position of 'close to balance or in surplus'. The assumption here is that automatic stabilisers can work within the bounds of the deficit ceiling if such a budgetary position is achieved.

Figure 8.6 shows developments in government borrowing in Ireland from 1990 to 2006. Net government lending increased from a deficit of 2.8% in 1990 to a surplus of 4.4% in 2000, thus leaving Ireland comfortably within the Stability and Growth Pact's deficit ceiling. Since then, the surplus has been eroded, with a budget deficit of 0.6% being forecast for 2005 and 2006. The evolution of cyclically adjusted balances in Ireland gives greater cause for concern. As Figure 8.6 shows, cyclically adjusted net lending fell sharply from a surplus of 2.5% in 2000 to a deficit of 1.8% in 2002. Although the deficit has gradually subsided since then, it is set to remain at around 0.6% in 2005 and 2006. There are two ways to interpret this situation. First, the measurement of cyclically adjusted fiscal positions is a controversial exercise, not least in times of rapid economic growth, when uncertainty about the true rate of economic growth and the magnitude of government revenue is more than usually problematic. Second, leaving measurement problems aside for one moment, the fact that Ireland has run up a considerable budget surplus is no guarantee that fiscal policy will serve as effective adjustment mechanism against asymmetric economic disturbances. In Ireland's

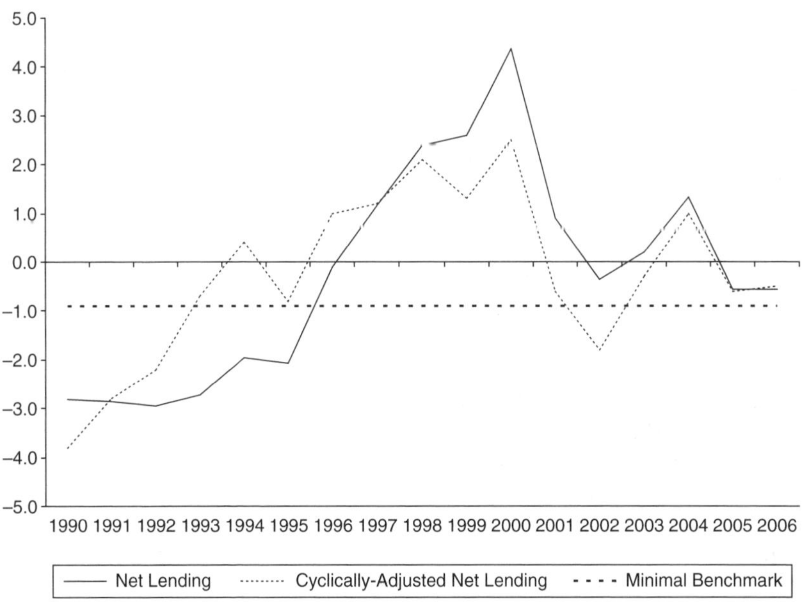

Figure 8.6 Net lending in Ireland, 1990–2006. *Source*: AMECO Database. Commission (1999b: 4)

Note: Data for 2005 and 2006 based on European commission forecasts. Cyclical adjustment of public finance variables based on potential GDP. Minimal benchmarks are indicative of cyclically adjusted budgetary positions that would be consistent with the SGP.

case the more pertinent issue is whether the budget surplus is sufficiently large given the prevailing rate of rapid economic growth. In terms of EMU's fiscal rules, the height of the economic boom witnessed a strong pro-cyclical feel to Irish budgetary policy. This reduces the policy's effectiveness as a replacement for exchange rate adjustment and suggests that a stronger counter cyclical fiscal stance is required to enable shock absorbers.

Concerns over Ireland's adjustment capabilities came to the fore in February 2001 in an early test of life in the euro area. At this time, Ecofin issued a formal recommendation for countervailing budgetary measures under Article 99(4) of the Treaty in response to the Irish government's budget for 2001. Ecofin singled out a number of measures in the budget which it deemed to be procyclical, including the decision to cut direct income tax is in a labour market that was already close to full capacity (Hodson and Maher, 2001: 736).

Ireland's recent growth experience can be likened to the effects of a positive and asymmetric demand shock, which produced a rate of economic growth well in excess of the euro area average and brought with it strong inflationary pressures. By way of adjustment to this shock, Ireland can respond through an appreciation in the relative exchange rate or a tightening of the budgetary stance. The former – which can be induced through a rise in the domestic price level relative to the rest of the euro area – will provide a check on the economy's external competitiveness, thus attenuating external demand. The latter – which can be achieved through a cut in government expenditure, an increase in taxes or by means of the automatic budgetary stabilisers – will reduce domestic demand.

The optimal choice of policy instrument, as Blanchard (2001) explains, depends on the source of the asymmetric shock. The growth of the Irish economy over the last decade has been driven by both internal and external components. This fact necessitates both an appreciation in the real exchange rate and a tighter budgetary policy to restore internal and external balance respectively. From this perspective, Ecofin's criticism of Irish economic policy conflates two lines of adjustment. On one hand, the loosening of Irish policy was likely to perpetuate the problem of overheating by adding oil to the fire of domestic demand. The Council was thus correct in its call for a tighter budgetary stance. On the other hand, an appreciation in the real exchange rate will necessitate a rise in prices in Ireland relative to the euro area. The inflation rate in Ireland will rise unavoidably over the course of this adjustment. The Council's criticism of Irish government's 2001 budget on the grounds that it will 'aggravate' inflationary pressures thus fails to recognise the fact that inflation, as Blanchard (2001: 20) puts it, 'is likely to be part of the optimal policy package'.

Ireland's match with Ecofin thus resulted in a score draw. Ecofin was correct to call for greater fiscal stabilisation in the wake of a sustained and positive demand shock to the Irish economy. Ireland's defence against such measures was porous at best, since the deterioration in structurally adjusted budget balances was evident. To be sure, the measurement of government revenues in times of rapid economic growth poses considerable challenges but, even taking this statistical error into account, efforts on the part of the Irish government were clearly necessary to restore the health of public finances. Ecofin scored an own-goal, however, by insisting on a reduction in the rate of inflation. This effectively ruled out the appreciation in the real exchange rate that was necessary to restrain the external dimension to Ireland's positive demand shock to within comfortable limits.

8.4 Conclusion

Ireland's trade exposure to the UK leaves the former vulnerable to the effects of asymmetric economic disturbances arising in the latter. Participation in EMU without the UK rules out the option of exchange rate adjustment in response to these shocks. Nonetheless, the question of whether the UK will continue its self-imposed exile from EMU or eventually join the euro area makes little difference to Ireland's adjustment capabilities. As a small and peripheral member of EMU, it is unlikely that the euro area exchange rate will respond to asymmetric shocks to the Irish economy, whether the UK is a participant or not. The question of UK membership has greater impact in this regard on Ireland's vulnerability to these asymmetric shocks in the first place. Monetary union is expected to act as a catalyst for deeper trade integration between the members of the euro area and hence for a convergence in national business cycle. If the UK were a participant in this process, Ireland might expect a gradual synchronisation in the business cycles of its trading partners and hence a reduction in the incidence of asymmetric shocks. Hence, over the long term, the UK's absence from the euro area leaves Ireland more vulnerable to the effects of asymmetric shocks and hence in greater need of alternative adjustment mechanisms.

The challenge for Ireland is an acute one since the punt–sterling exchange rate made an important – although imperfect – contribution to the adjustment effort against macroeconomic imbalance over the last twenty years. If the stakes under EMU are high for Ireland, however, then the government's hand is stronger than most. The Irish labour force is among the more mobile in the euro area and there is thus a greater prospect of labour migration in response to an asymmetric shock. Relative wage and price adjustment also represent realistic possibilities, providing that the process of social partnership survives the transition to monetary union and (more importantly) the effects of the economic slowdown. The scope for fiscal adjustment in Ireland is perhaps less promising than it should be, given the pace of economic growth in recent years. Although budget surpluses reached record levels, the structural balance remain in deficit, thus limiting the government's room for manoeuvre within the confines of the Stability and

Growth Pact. A strict adherence to the pact's medium-term budgetary requirement will be essential to ensue that budgetary stabilisers contribute towards the adjustment effort when the need arises.

From the Irish perspective, UK participation in EMU undoubtedly remains preferable to non-participation. This conclusion notwithstanding, however, EMU will continually raise challenges for a small open economy on the periphery of the euro area, whether the UK adopts the euro or not. Concentrated effort is needed on the part of the Irish government to maintain existing adjustment mechanisms and bolster alternative ones. By the same token, Ireland's recent experience of the EMU's fiscal rules serves as a reminder of the importance of the euro area's emerging macroeconomic policy. Due caution must be exercised in this respect to ensure that EU policies bolster rather than hinder adjustment at the national level, while ensuring that such adjustment is not detrimental to economic conditions in the rest of the euro area.

9

Finland: Membership to Encourage Change

Of the five Nordic countries only Finland has chosen to go into Stage 3 of Economic and Monetary Union from the outset. Sweden and Denmark, as members of the EU, could have joined if they had chosen, as they had no problem meeting the convergence criteria in 1998. Norway and Iceland of course were not eligible, as they were not members of the EU but just the EEA. It is easy to put forward a list of economic and political factors that have contributed to these differences in choice. With its large asset base from North Sea oil and gas, Norway cannot merely afford to take an independent line but finds that it is subject to different exchange rate pressures. With extensive fishing industries, Iceland and Norway have something to lose from entry into the Common Fisheries Policy of the EU that the others do not. Finland with its long common border with Russia has stronger incentives to embed itself very firmly in an alternative grouping. One can go on.

What is interesting, however, is that despite these differences, the 'official' assessments of the likely consequences of membership of Stage 3 of Economic and Monetary Union for both Finland (Pekkarinen *et al.*, 1997) and Sweden (Calmfors *et al.*, 1997) were very similar in content. They both came to the conclusion that there was relatively little to choose on purely economic grounds between membership and non-membership, as there were both positive and negative factors and many imponderables about how behaviour might change after membership. There was general agreement that the efficiency gains would be positive but fairly small and that the problem area is the extent to which membership of Stage 3 affects the costs of adjusting to existing economic imbalances and future shocks. However, when it comes to drawing conclusions the two reports part company. The Finnish report is more equivocal, although it sounded a clear note of optimism about the balance of risks from membership. The Swedish report, on the other hand, came down clearly against joining in the first wave. It judged the political considerations to be favourable and the economic considerations to be sufficiently unfavourable to outweigh them at least in the short run. While one might speculate what the conclusions could have been had the balance of public opinion in the two countries been clearly the other way round, it is the detailed reasoning in the two reports that merits attention.

The Swedish Report cites four main reasons for arguing on balance against participation in the first wave of membership:

1. The high level of current unemployment could rise even further if there are macroeconomic disturbances that cannot be countered by monetary and exchange rate policies.
2. The fiscal situation could easily deteriorate sufficiently to require drastic measures with adverse effects on social efficiency.
3. Time is needed for 'a broad and encompassing public debate' on the issue otherwise the decision will not be viewed as *legitimate* by the electorate.
4. Other countries, particularly the UK and Denmark will also stay out so the political costs of postponement will be acceptable.[1]

A list of ten critical factors influencing this decision followed. The key is that the Swedish experts saw continuing risks to macroeconomic stability and thought that there would be much greater costs to the economy, particularly in the form of unemployment, in trying to adjust to them without the benefit of an independent monetary and exchange rate policy. They did not expect the ability of the labour market to adjust to shocks would change dramatically and assumed that Sweden would not be participating in some tight ERM II arrangement.

The Finnish Report too singles out the worries about economic stability as being the key to the appropriate decision but their assessment is noticeably different. They take it for granted that the labour market will have to be more flexible and suggest ways in which this might be achieved, by varying indirect costs over the cycle, for example. They also felt that fiscal policy would be able to cope, as the strong growth would enable debt to be run down and adequate stabilisation to be achieved (largely through the automatic stabilisers). They expected that some of the asymmetries of the past would diminish with most of their trading partners being on the inside. Perhaps the major difference from Sweden, however, was what they saw as the alternative. They assumed that this would involve participating in ERM II, in order to maximise the chances of stability, and that the sorts of changes that would be required inside EMU would be required anyway, as they would not be able to run particularly different economic policies from the participating countries. This would imply that they saw the alternative as behaving like Denmark, rather than being able to behave like a larger country, such as the UK.

There is thus a major difference in approach underlying the two reports' conclusions. In the Swedish case the line of argument is that it is better to reduce unemployment problems first and let the Swedish and euro economies become more structurally convergent before entering Stage 3. In the Finnish case, however, the implication is that it is membership itself that will force the changes in public policy and private-sector behaviour that are necessary both to solve the current unemployment problem and be able to react without unnecessary cost to future shocks. Thus what we see is part of a long-standing and much wider European debate about whether one should only proceed with each step in closer integration at a legislative and institutional level *after* fairly considerable prior convergence or whether the legislative and institutional change should occur early on in the process and act as the driving force for change. In part this may reflect different attitudes towards incentives.

The dichotomy is more complex because overlaid on this debate about whether one should converge first and institutionalise second is the uncertainty about what is the optimal long-run structure. There are conditions for optimal currency areas, some of which relate to homogeneity of climate and natural resources. Even if there is complete convergence of institutions, policies and preferences, diverse areas will be subject to asymmetric shocks and at some point it may be less costly to allow some of the adjustment through the exchange rate, whatever the gains from integration. Finland has a more diversified trade pattern than most of its euro area partners with more of its trade outside the area. Finland also has a more concentrated trade pattern in terms of dependence on the forest industries and on the IT sector (and one company within it) than any of its partners. It is therefore more towards any limits of optimality in the existing area than most of its partners, with the obvious exception of Ireland. This without taking any note of the obvious fact that it is geographically on the edge (it is equally the most northerly and was the most easterly Member State in the EU until Cyprus joined) and at one climatic extreme. While the geographic differences from Sweden and Norway may be small, the differences in economic structure are considerable. Since Sweden is nearly twice as big in economic terms it can diversify more readily.

In what follows we evaluate two features of the Finnish experience. The first is looking backwards over the years before membership to see whether indeed there were facets of behaviour that made membership particularly attractive to Finland compared to the other Nordic countries. The second is looking at the experience after membership to see whether any of the expected changes in behaviour do appear to be occurring. Taking these together we argue that a large part of the point of Finnish membership was to achieve and consolidate a clear regime change, to break away from the unsustainable policies of the past. What EMU offered was a route to credibility that it would have been much more difficult for a small country to achieve on its own.

9.1 An unpleasant experience

9.1.1 The financial crisis

As is clear from Figures 9.1–9.3, Finland's experience of the last 15 years has been unusual. Growth, even before the 1980s, had tended to be above the

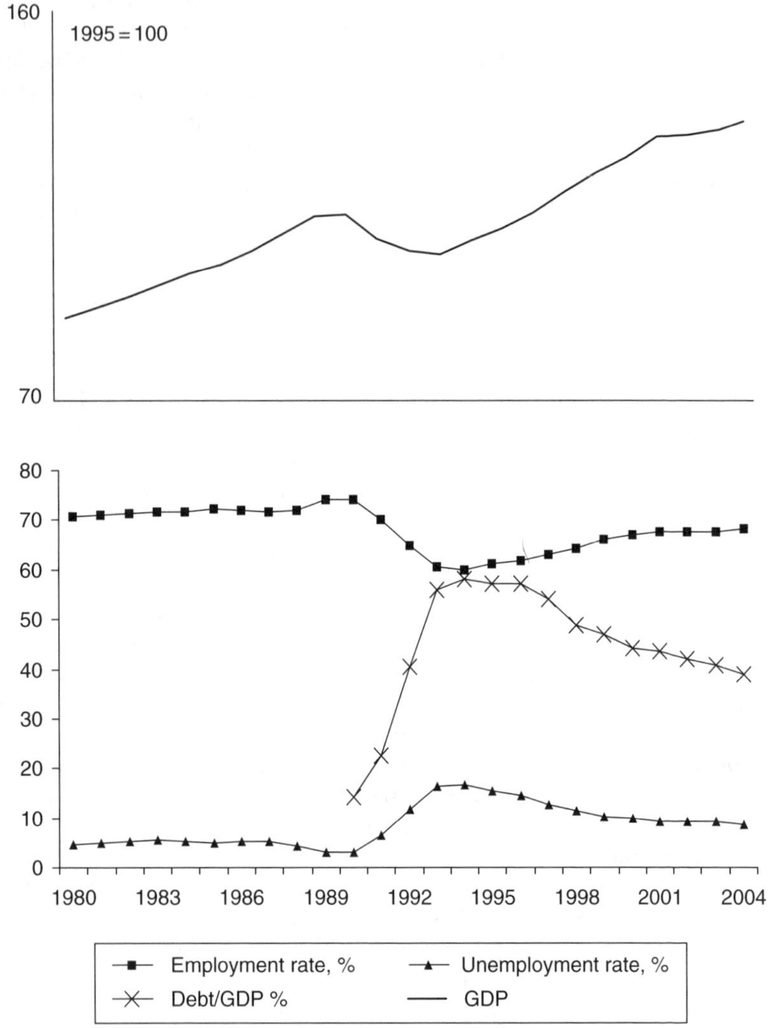

Figure 9.1 Macroeconomic developments in Finland 1980–2004: GDP, employment, unemployment and the debt ratio. *Source*: Bank of Finland

European average and Finland had worked itself upward through the ranks of the OECD members. Unlike many other countries it had not been badly affected by the oil crises, in part because of its special trade relationship with the Soviet Union (Table 9.1). Under the barter trade elements of that agreement as oil prices rose so Finland could sell more goods in return for the oil. Typically the sorts of goods that were exchanged were either less processed

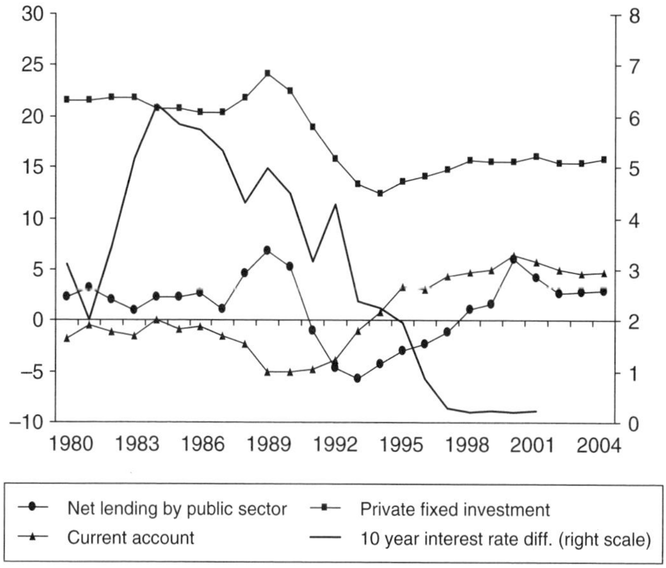

Figure 9.2 Macroeconomic developments in Finland 1980–2004: Public deficit, current account, interest rate differential, investment. *Source*: Bank of Finland

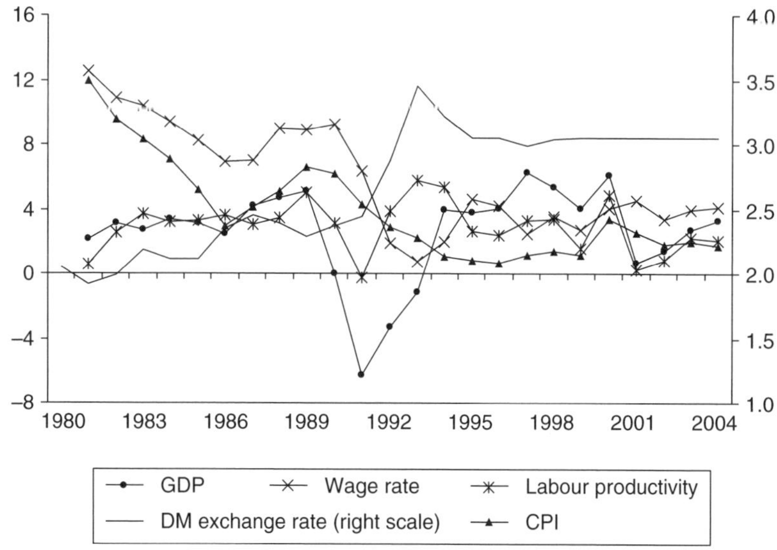

Figure 9.3 Macroeconomic developments in Finland 1980–2004: Inflation, wage rate, productivity, exchange rate, growth of GDP. *Source*: Bank of Finland

Table 9.1 The change in structure of Finnish trade 1985–2001

The shares of Finnish exports

(a) Areas

	EU12	Rest of EEA	North America	Asia	Russia	Baltics	Others
1985	22.8	32.2	7.5	2.5	21.5		13.4
1989	29.8	32.5	7.8	5.3	14.5		10.1
1993	33.6	28.1	8.6	8.7	4.5	1.7	14.8
1997	29.7	25.8	7.9	14.1	7.3	4.3	10.9
2001	32.7	23.0	10.5	12.8	5.9	3.3	11.7

(b) Industry groups

	Electrical and optical equipment	Forest industries	Metal and engineering industries	Other industries
1986	6.8	37.4	31.7	24.1
1989	8.0	39.3	33.8	18.9
1993	12.0	35.3	32.6	20.1
1997	22.5	30.1	28.2	19.2
2001	27.5	26.6	27.9	17.9

Source: Statistics Finland and Bank of Finland.

or more basic than those demanded by the leading edge of competition in Western markets. This enabled Finland to operate less-efficient technologies and prolong the production run of products in a way that kept employment at higher levels than was common elsewhere. Although Finland moved increasingly away from barter trade in the 1980s, the share of trade with the Soviet Union was still 15% in 1986–1989.

In the second half of the 1980s this faster growth continued but to the point where it was clearly above sustainable levels. The abnormal growth was occasioned both by external demand and by changes inside the Finnish economy. In the mid-1980s, in common with many OECD countries, Finland deregulated its financial markets rapidly (Nyberg and Vihriälä, 1994). The resulting boom was allowed to continue until it was drastically reversed by the collapse of the Soviet Union, the problems of German unification and the general world slowdown. A classic financial crisis ensued (Mayes *et al.*, 2001). What distinguishes Finland from Norway and Sweden, who also had financial crises, is the extent of the problem. GDP fell by 12% in real terms in three years, unemployment rose by 13 percentage points and support for the banks from public funds to the tune of 17.2% of GDP was required. (The majority of the public injection was eventually repaid leaving a net cost of 7%.)

One of the major reasons for allowing the boom to continue even when it was clearly too rapid was the government's desire to hold the exchange rate within implicit ERM bands to complement their application for entry into the EU. The Bank of Finland wanted to raise interest rates, which was expected to raise the exchange rate as well, for over a year before circumstances forced it.

What we see therefore is a classic financial crisis of the form studied by Kaminsky and Reinhart (1999) *inter alia*. Of 16 indicators, Finland showed 13 (Norway 14 and Sweden 15). Seven major features led to the crisis (Mayes *et al.*, 2001).

1. A major regulatory change in the financial sector that opens both buyers and sellers to new opportunities and risks in which they have little experience
2. A period of rapid economic growth
3. A rapid rise in asset prices
4. A weak framework for supervision of the financial sector
5. A tax regime that encourages borrowing
6. Unsustainable macroeconomic policies
7. A substantial adverse shock.

9.1.2 Responses to the crisis

Much of the detail of the crisis is not germane to the present analysis. What is more important is that Finland was efficient and effective in handling the crisis once it broke. While the immediate hit was severe, the problem was clearly resolved and within three years the economy was firmly on the road to recovery. Many of the characteristics that led to the crisis have been addressed in a manner that would make them very difficult to repeat. The framework for supervision has been substantially tightened. Supervision, which was the responsibility of the Ministry of Finance in the run up to the crisis, has been transferred to a Financial Supervision Authority (Rahoitustarkastus) that reports to a member of the Bank of Finland Board and works closely with the Bank. Not only have all the criteria of the Basel Accord (on Banking Supervision that is the agreed international standard for good practice) been applied but each of the banks has been subject to close supervision to bring them back to satisfactory capitalisation, corporate governance and prudent management. While all the government loans have been repaid not all of the impaired assets under public management have yet been fully resolved. Thus while the individual banks should be more secure the macroprudential supervision by the Bank of Finland should also help alert the authorities to risks applying to the system as a whole.

Risks will always remain but the memory of the previous crisis will help maintain alertness to future shocks in a way that some countries, more fortunate in avoiding crises in the past, cannot easily emulate. Even with continuing development of the euro and the 'internal market' in financial services there is unlikely to be such a shock from financial regulation again. Both banks and individuals will have learnt of the folly of substantial unhedged borrowing in foreign currency in search of lower interest rates. Such borrowing was one of the factors that made the Finnish crisis so severe when the exchange rate fell by around 30%. Indeed with the advent of the euro area and effective price stability there is much less incentive to consider such external sources of finance. Similarly Finland is no longer exposed to the former Soviet Union nor indeed to any other significant market in an unusual manner compared to its partners (Table 9.1). It is, however, rather more exposed in the forest and telecommunications sectors. EMU is of course of itself intended to prevent unsustainable macroeconomic policies. However monetary policy moved to a sustainable basis quickly in 1993 with the adoption of inflation targeting.

Changing the way the economy behaves is a complex interaction between changing the rules and changing behavioural responses to the rules. As in all regime shifts the intention is to alter the responses made by the system and not just to change the forces bearing upon it. Hence in the Finnish case there was a deliberate attempt to try to move away from previous behaviour.

Some of the changes that took place in the 1990s after the crisis were the result of longer-run changes in policy direction that were already under way. Finland applied to join the EU in March 1992, after Austria (July 1989) and Sweden (June 1991) but ahead of Norway in November 1992. It was already clear by the time of the Finnish application that the EU was going to conduct a round of negotiations with whoever the applicants then were in 1993. Therefore an application had to be made well before 1993 if the Commission's Opinion on the readiness of the applicant for membership was to be ready in time. (Norway's application was actually a little late and negotiations had to start unofficially before the opinion came through.) The Finnish application was not an opportunistic response to the crisis but the outturn of a more fundamental rethink of foreign (and economic) policy in the light of the collapse of the Soviet Union.

Finland joined EFTA, with a special agreement, as early as 1964 but had had to tread a careful neutral path to maintain stable relations with its large eastern neighbour. It was only in 1956 that it had proved possible to get the Soviet Union to withdraw from a large naval base that adjoined the outskirts of Helsinki and give up its military transit rights. Finland negotiated a Free Trade Agreement with the EC along with the other EFTA members when the UK and Denmark joined the Community in 1973 and was in the European Economic Area from the beginning in 1993. Outright membership of the EU required not just a careful assessment of the reactions of Russia but a strong domestic debate, because of the expected impact on regional development as the result of a substantial reduction in agricultural subsidies entailed by adopting the Common Agricultural Policy. The moves towards greater integration with western Europe were thus progressive and involved a cumulative effect on opening up Finnish industry and Finnish public sector practices to the experience of its neighbours. Membership of the EEA and the EU involved substantial changes to domestic behaviour and attitudes.

The evidence on the nature of many of the changes in behaviour in Finland is largely anecdotal (Novack, 2002) but they have the appearance of a more positive wish to join the EU and participate fully rather than a reluctant acceptance of the necessity for membership – by comparison with Sweden at any rate. As pointed out by Brewin (1997), the applicant countries had found the unwillingness of the EU to make concessions in the EEA negotiations a rather unpleasant experience and could see the advantages of being on the inside and at least having a vote, even in a Qualified Majority Voting environment. The smaller size of Finland and the greater differences in economic structure and hence need to change may have contributed to state ownership of industry and services, which was very extensive.

Finland's history since the war had been characterised by a devaluation cycle and concommitant balance of payments crises every time the economy attempted to grow rapidly, as a result of the ensuing inflation. This is an experience very similar to that of the UK. However, this pattern seems to have been broken in the last few years. Finland now not only has high growth but a major balance of trade and payments surplus.

As we were able to show in Mayes and Vilmunen (1999), in the case of the Finnish economy, the exchange rate (terms of trade) acted as an adjustment mechanism to shocks to the system. In Mayes and Vilmunen (1999) we fitted a small vector error correction model to semi-annual Finnish data for the period 1960–1996 to explore how the economy responded to a range of shocks. The reduced form of this model contained unemployment, real wages, the terms of trade and the capital stock (all in difference form). Thus real wages did not directly adjust to shocks, which resulted in higher unemployment. Unemployment was reduced because of the terms of trade improvement that led to higher demand. Real wages were thus rigid in terms of domestic bargaining. (This is in sharp contrast to the New Zealand economy, where the labour market was flexible over the same period, with real wages adjusting rapidly to external shocks.)

If this form of response were to be continued inside EMU then Finland would potentially face severe problems. On the one hand under Stage 3 of EMU the exchange rate is not available to Finland independently as a means of weathering shocks – whether the shocks are external or generated internally, say by increases in labour costs. On the other Finland is more open to external shocks (in the sense of trade external to the euro area forming a greater percentage of trade) than most fellow euro area members. Thus on the one hand the main response mechanism to shocks is removed while on the other the chance of shocks is greater than the average for the euro area as a whole. In these circumstances a change would be essential for Finland to adjust to adverse shocks without major unemployment in future.

The position is somewhat harsher than Mayes and Vilmunen (1999) suggest, as they did not include the role of the public sector as a safety valve. As Mayes and Virén (2002b) show, the public sector has increased steadily as a source of employment up to the late 1980s, effectively absorbing what might otherwise have been unemployment in the private sector. This process clearly has limits. At low levels of public sector activity such a transfer may prove highly beneficial in providing infrastructure and improving the health, skills and mobility of the labour force. However, beyond a certain point (estimated using threshold regressions) it tends to reduce the overall rate of growth of the economy. Those limits were reached in the 1980s, forcing a shift in the way in which shocks were absorbed. The scale of the crisis at the beginning of the 1990s was so large that the proportionate involvement of the public sector had to be reduced if the levels were to be sustainable. (The share peaked at 60% in 1993.) Even so central government debt rose from a little over 10% in 1991 to peak at 70% of GDP by 1997 (Figures 9.1 and 9.2). (On the Maastricht convergence criteria definition the peak was just less than the 60% limit, which might lead to the speculation that this also acted as a hard limit to what the government was prepared to tolerate.)

One obviously important factor is the nature of the wage bargaining system in Finland (Kilponen *et al.*, 2000). Since the bargaining system is centralised in Finland it is possible for government and unions to come to bargains about how the losses and gains at the macroeconomic level will be apportioned, both between the employed and the unemployed and between current and future generations. Put a little differently it was possible for Finland to be at one of the corners of the famous Calmfors-Driffill 'smile' (1988). In earlier periods the bargaining system had tended to result in considerable wage drift as industries and then firms, in two subsequent rounds of negotiations, tended to take the prior national agreement as a minimum from which they could diverge upwards if circumstances justified. Since the crisis the drift has been much more limited.

The change in the structure of production in Finland has been remarkable. The telecommunications industry expanded by a factor of 5 between 1994 and 2000. Although growth rates have slowed, telecommunications are as important as the forest industry. It is not that other sectors have declined since the recovery started in 1993 (only clothing, textiles and leather have not participated in the general growth). Even shipbuilding, which is focused on the repair and manufacture of passenger ships (cruise liners more than ferries) – at the high value-added end of the market – has continued. This growth of industrial output is magnified when it comes to exports. Exports of electronics increased by an average of 25% a year in 1994–1998 and growth has continued despite the turndown in the economy as a whole at the beginning of this decade. This has contributed to a current account surplus that has been running at around 8% of GDP (Figure 9.2 and Table 9.1). The sheer scale of the growth of just one company, Nokia, stands out. It is responsible for around 6% of GDP, double that if its suppliers are taken into account and around 25% of the exports of manufactures (Forsman, 2000). Nokia is the world's largest supplier of mobile telephone handsets, for example.

However, this should not be viewed as a one horse race. The forest industry still contributes 30% to exports, although this is down from the 40% it had at the beginning of the 1990s. The rise in the share of metal and engineering from 40 to 55% has also been at the expense of the remaining sectors.

The fast growth has assisted the government in returning to fiscal prudence and indeed bringing the debt ratio down again towards 40%. Government revenues have blossomed, particularly for local authorities, which receive a large proportion of their revenues from companies. Local government provides about two-thirds of government services. It has proved possible to cut taxes and austerity measures have reduced government spending by 6% of GDP. The crisis raised social security spending by 10% of GDP despite controversial cuts in rates and eligibility.

It seems likely therefore that the fiscal and related moves will have had some impact on behaviour. Increasing the gap between benefits and incomes in employment will have increased incentives to seek employment, assisted by active labour market measures. However the largest impact is likely to have come from the rise in unemployment and fall in participation rates (Figure 9.1). The problem, highlighted by Honkaphja and Koskela (1999), is that, as unemployment rises, so too does its equilibrium rate. While the economy was clearly running unsustainably fast in the period before the crisis, the appropriate unemployment gap estimated for more recent years cannot be contrasted directly with what appeared to be the equilibrium unemployment rate in that pre-crisis period to try to compute the extent of downward pressure on inflation. According to Honkaphja and Koskela equilibrium unemployment in the period 1986–1989 was 6.8% while actual unemployment was 4.6%. However by 1994–1996 the equilibrium rate had nearly doubled to 11.9%. By their methodology both equilibrium and actual unemployment have fallen since that date but, at around 9%, current unemployment is probably not far different from its equilibrium value. The Bank of Finland does not publish an output gap estimate or any equivalent statistic for the labour market but the statement in the June 2001 *Bulletin*, that 'capacity constraints and lack of skilled labour in some sectors of the economy are likely to be growth limiting factors during the forecast period [2001–3]', implies that the system was above equilibrium even at such high levels of unemployment. As discussed in Mayes and Virén (2002a) it is the tightest labour markets that tend to drive inflationary pressure in the economy as a whole, not simply the average.

On its own therefore we could expect Finland to have completed its adjustment period and be at the point where more typical cyclical inflationary pressure cuts in. The fact that inflation went only slightly above 3% in 2000, assisted by the oil price shock to which Finland is rather more exposed than the average of its partners, and that it is now back to the euro area average suggests that there has been some behavioural change (Figure 9.3).

The change in the monetary policy regime, first to inflation targeting in 1993 and then to monetary union (effectively in 1997) will itself have altered behaviour. Inflation targeting is designed to increase the credibility of policy. As Razzak (2001) shows, this has resulted in a clear structural break in New Zealand and Canada. Inflationary demand shocks no longer have such a large effect on price expectations, as the central bank has become more predictable and is expected to counter the pressures successfully. Wage bargainers and price setters are therefore less aggressive in their response, which makes the expectations somewhat self-fulfilling. This in turn means that the authorities do not need to be so aggressive in setting policy.

In the Finnish case it is much more difficult to decide how much the increase in credibility was due to the adoption of inflation targeting in 1993 or the clear intention to go into Stage 3 of EMU that was expressed in 1997. On any account, nominal and real interest rates had converged to German levels by 1997. (As it turned out, Finland was one of the three low inflation Member States that set the convergence criterion for the others.) All that is required for present purposes is that this change had occurred. Clearly a similar credibility applied to fiscal policy, otherwise Finland would have had to pay an interest rate premium. After EMU there is, of course, a clear regime shift, as monetary policy then responds to the requirements of the euro area as a whole and not to expected inflation in Finland. However the structural break we are describing here is not so much that there was a change in the response to disequilibrium, but that lower equilibrium interest rates would have an impact on investment and saving.

9.2 Structural change in the Finnish economy

With only a few years' experience of Stage 3, without any serious adverse asymmetric shocks, it is difficult to judge from the evidence, whether membership of EMU has made any difference to Finnish macroeconomic performance. There are clearly short-run differences, but without seeing through at least one economic cycle it would not be possible to draw any meaningful conclusions. Finland experienced more inflation from late 1999 through to early 2002 than would have been acceptable under the terms of its own previous monetary policy. Since this was predictable, given the very rapid rate of growth of the economy, there is no doubt that the Bank of Finland would have tightened monetary policy to head this off, had it been maintaining its own monetary policy (with no separate objective for the exchange rate). However, Finland's determination to join Stage 3 was already well known before qualification in 1998, so part of this growth may have been in anticipation of membership. Without that prospect, net investment might have been directed elsewhere. We therefore have to be very circumspect in interpreting recent experience. It is easy to recall (Mayes and Burridge, 1993) how the good performance of the early years after the formation of the Single Market in 1987 was initially attributed to the formation of the Market. Yet this form of analysis was rapidly abandoned as economic difficulties appeared in the early 1990s.

Even if the regulatory mistakes that contributed to the crisis had been corrected, a Finnish economy of the 1970s and 1980s would face very real difficulties in the EMU of the 2000s. It would be an extreme example of hoping that a regulatory change would lead to a change in behaviour. However, as we have noted above, the Finnish economy was already different by the end of the 1990s, but that was more related to the crisis than the advent of EMU. Although the two causes cannot be entirely separated, the particular limit to public debt observed is surely too close to 60% of GDP to be entirely fortuitous.

The principal relevant changes are

- Industrial structure
- Level of unemployment/participation
- Macroeconomic policy regime
- Labour market policies and operation.

Although we might wish to add membership of the EU in 1995 as a separate issue. All of these four factors clearly help to add to the ability of the Finnish economy to adapt under EMU much more readily than would have been the case previously.

The move towards the electronics sector and the new economy more generally puts the emphasis on industries where product lifetimes are short and where the industry is frequently changing, not just in terms of products but in terms of participating firms as well (although this latter may change as the industry matures). The more highly skilled nature of the jobs and the involvement of the people concerned with the information industry will make it both more necessary and easier to change jobs rapidly in response to shocks. The need to have people working either fixed numbers of hours during the week or at fixed times of day is also much lower. However, one thing that has not changed is the openness of the Finnish economy, particularly outside the euro area. Much of the electronics sector is global in character and hence is affected by shocks in the United States and Asia very directly.

Second, Finland has not moved towards a service economy to anything like the extent of the US or indeed many other EU countries. Industry is still over 30% of GDP and manufacturing is 90% of industrial output (1998 figures). The recovery has been primarily in export-oriented manufacturing. Trade union coverage is still high and the regulation of employment has not changed Finland away from being primarily an economy where people work full-time normal hours. In 1997 only 7% of men and 15% of women worked part time.

One way to look at this is observe that it means that Finland still has considerable scope to deregulate labour markets and increase employment substantially at the margin. Given that unemployment appears to be bottoming out at around 8% this could have substantial attractions. The problem with any such change however is that it can rarely be at the margin and will affect those already in employment, probably worsening their terms and conditions. The industries that would be affected in other countries, retail trades, unskilled public sector, low skill office and factory workers are unionised and such changes would be difficult to implement even if it were largely through self or small-scale employment. Something more will have to be done to tackle the persistent unemployment, which in Eastern Finland is one of the worst blackspots in the EU. As in other countries, voluntary labour mobility appears to be rather limited. Even the Bank of Finland (2000) has concluded that the government's aim of creating 50,000 new jobs a year until 2003 is 'a very ambitious target, which will not be possible to achieve through growth alone. Rather, structural measures affecting both the supply of and demand for labour are needed.'

One of the most interesting developments in trying to establish a flexible basis on which to respond to shocks under EMU has been the establishment of the buffer funds. The unemployment funds are in the main not administered by the government but by the industries concerned, primarily by the trade unions. They previously had a requirement to be self-financing. But now they can run a surplus or deficit up to the cost of 3% unemployment. This means that contribution rates can be counter-cyclical. Thus in a downturn the cost of labour can be made lower to employers because employees can increase their real incomes by paying somewhat lower insurance contributions. The contribution rates are fixed annually as part of the centralised wage bargain. At present the funds have been built up to their 3% maximum surplus. This can be viewed as an aspect of how co-operative bargains by the social partners in a centralised system can actually improve the ability of the economy to react flexibly. It is also helpful as a precommitment.

This system will only be exportable to other Member States where the insurance funds lie outside the public sector and hence such variations do not feature in the 3% limit on annual deficits. Since it protects those currently in employment it is not quite clear what overall effects it has on the flexibility of the economy. It may inhibit the role of downturns in shaking out excess labour in one firm that can then be re-employed in another during the upturn. However, it will reduce the deadweight cost of unnecessary hiring and firing by the same firm over the course of the downturn and subsequent recovery. The stabilising effect of the funds will obviously depend upon the ability to predict the length or extent of the downturn.

When the deficit reaches its maximum in a continuing recession, contribution rates will not merely have to come up to their equilibrium level but will have to cope with the rising unemployment. This will give a pro-cyclical kick to the process, making the recovery more difficult. This system also does nothing for reducing the marginal cost of re-employment in the recovery or for improving the incentives to the unemployed to gain employment.

The data period for assessing how the Finnish economy has changed is somewhat longer than might be thought at first blush, as Monetary Union effectively started in Finland in 1997, with the two-year transition period for qualification for membership of Stage 3. Inflation, interest rates, debt, deficit and the exchange rate all fall within the criteria from then onwards (Figures 9.1–9.3). There is some clear evidence of a structural break in the economy round about that period, which we can see both econometrically and in the stylised facts. It is of course almost impossible to determine the exact cause. All the changes implemented as a result of the crisis should have been coming to fruition by that stage, particularly the change in structure of the economy. Membership of the EU (as opposed to the free trade area) had begun in 1995 and the European Single Market would have been having a substantial effect (Mayes and Burridge, 1993). However the coincidence with the start of effective EMU is striking.

The work of Ripatti and Vilmunen (2001), using CES production functions, shows clearly that the nature of productive side of the Finnish economy shows a break around that time. Interestingly enough the break appears to be on the capital side of the economy. Rates of investment fell sharply compared to GDP during the crisis and have not recovered to previous levels (which at 30% were high by European standards). Thus we have the contrast of a more rapidly growing economy and lower investment levels. Given that the share of public investment in GDP stabilised rather than fell, the reduction in private sector investment is all the more striking (Figure 9.2). Capital is clearly more productive after the crisis than before.

In part this will simply be a reflection of the change in industrial structure towards electronics and other high-tech industries. These are not as capital-intensive as some traditional manufacturing industries that were run down. They require a far larger input from highly skilled labour in producing new products and services and it is not surprising to see a matching leap in R&D at the same time from 2.5% of GDP in 1995 to 3.5% in 1999 (Figure 9.4). It also seems to be in part simply an increase in the efficiency with which capital is used. Traditionally capital for industry had been somewhat subsidised with compulsory pension funds being prepared to finance industry at low rates of return.

What is particularly interesting is the way the economy seems to be responding in the current growth cycle. Although the surplus is large by anybody's standards, it has been maintained in part because the exchange rate

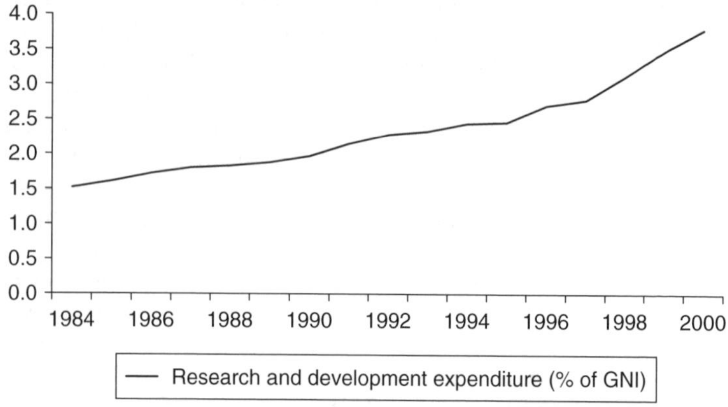

Figure 9.4 R&D expenditures in Finland. *Source*: World Bank

cannot respond by making Finnish prices higher (Figure 9.3). Its counterpart is substantial investment abroad by the private sector and repayment of external debt by the public sector. The private sector investment abroad is coming from firms, not the household sector, which is in approximate balance. In part this overseas investment may be simply that entailed by the increased exporting, needed to set up distribution and service networks, for example. It may also reflect the fact that many Finnish firms are large by domestic standards and have reached the limits of what they can invest in at home. It is not clear how long this process can go on, although if Finnish inflation were to be consistently above that of its competitors, after adjusting for the difference in productivity trends, the surplus and profits would be eroded. Thus far that erosion has only been marginal. The wage agreement for 2002 was 2.3%. With drift and other factors such as changes in hours worked, the overall figure was around 2% higher than that. However with productivity rising at around 2.5% this still gives unit labour cost increases less than 1%. The outcomes for 2003–2005 are expected to be somewhat less favourable, with unit labour costs rising by 2% or so a year.

It therefore appears that, in the absence of a substantial adverse shock, the Finnish economy can continue to prosper, although the downturn in the US may yet turn out to have more adverse consequences than first thought. The problem remains, however, the issue identified by the Swedish (Calmfors) Commission in the introductory remarks, namely, unemployment. Although the growth record may have been good and transmitted throughout the economy, as most benefit rates are proportionate to earnings, the feed through into jobs is becoming progressively more limited. It is not clear that being outside the euro area would offer any obvious advantage in these circumstances. Indeed, outside, the exchange rate and interest rates might be higher and growth lower. There are some ways forward, which are not inhibited by EMU. The Bank of Finland (2001) points to two examples. First, that the tax rate is 'strikingly high'. They conclude: 'A further reduction in the tax wedge is essential if there is to be a substantial improvement in structural unemployment and a rise in the employment rate.' Second, they point out: 'Elsewhere in the euro area the use of "atypical" individual employment contracts (including part-time work) has led to a substantial increase in employment.'

What we see here, therefore, is not a challenge posed by EMU as such but a challenge posed by the traditional 'Nordic model' of social protection (Mayes *et al.*, 2001; Muffels *et al.*, 2002). If the tax burden were lower then both growth and employment could be higher. This of course has implications for expenditure as the Bank of Finland (2003) delicately puts it: 'One of the key challenges in central government finances in the near term will be how to set expenditure at a level that will enable debt reduction [to prepare for the budgetary consequences of an ageing population] in conditions where there is a significantly lower tax burden than at present.' Making further inroads into unemployment/non-participation implies more atypical work. These are not easy decisions but Finland and Sweden both face them. They are not unique to EMU membership. What of course both countries would like to do is to be in the Danish position, where, with a higher income per head, participation is noticeably higher and unemployment noticeably lower, taking away much of the fiscal pressure and permitting greater effort on active labour market policies to tackle the remaining longer-term unemployment and social exclusion. There the Nordic model is not under challenge. But it is not possible to rewrite history and avoid the problems of the crisis and achieve the fundamental improvements earlier in the 1980s as Denmark did. The crisis generated a step up in both unemployment and public sector debt and a step down in participation, thus combining the need to correct a structural problem and to confront the problem of flexibility under EMU at the same time. While 10 years may be enough to bring real incomes back to their previous track, restoring wealth and employment takes a great deal longer.

As the cycle has developed, successive forecasts have postponed the stronger recovery and there is always the danger that, at the time of publication, remarks made earlier will be obviously outdated. Nevertheless, it still appears, on an annual basis at any rate, that during the cycle employment did not fall in absolute numbers, and has only declined marginally as a share of the population of working age (Bank of Finland, 2003) (the forecast summary is reproduced as Table 9.2). The system appears to be stabilising out with growth around 3%, inflation around 2%, current account/GDP 6%, productivity 2%, wage growth 4%, government surplus 3% and net household savings ratio a little over 3%. While looking backwards this is remarkable in the face of the size of the world downturn and the reduction in stock

Table 9.2 Bank of Finland forecast, September 2003 (2000 prices)

	2000[a]	2001	2002	f 2003	f 2004	f 2005
%-change on a year earlier						
Gross domestic product	6.1	1.2	2.2	1.3	2.9	2.8
Imports	16.0	0.2	1.3	0.9	6.1	6.4
Exports	20.1	–0.8	4.9	1.4	6.3	5.8
Private consumption	2.6	2.0	1.5	3.4	2.1	2.4
Public consumption	–0.2	2.2	4.0	1.4	1.6	1.6
Private fixed investment	5.5	3.7	–5.9	–2.9	5.9	5.7
Public investment	–5.4	8.1	8.0	–3.9	–5.5	–2.3
Inventory change and statistical discrepancy, % of year-earlier total demand	0.5	–0.5	–0.2	–0.3	0.0	0.0
Total demand	8.5	1.0	2.0	1.2	3.7	3.7
Final domestic demand	2.9	1.8	0.6	1.1	2.4	2.7
Key economic indicators						
%-change on a year earlier						
Harmonised index of consumer prices	3.0	2.7	2.0	1.4	1.0	1.8
Consumer prices	3.4	2.6	1.6	1.1	1.0	1.9
Earnings	4.0	4.5	3.5	3.9	3.7	4.1
Labour productivity	4.8	0.7	2.3	1.2	2.3	2.6
Unit labour costs	–0.6	5.2	0.7	2.3	2.0	2.0
Number of employed	1.7	1.4	0.2	–0.3	0.2	0.6
Employment rate, 15–64 year-olds, %	66.9	67.7	67.7	67.3	67.4	67.7
Unemployment rate, %	9.8	9.1	9.1	9.3	9.2	9.0
Exports prices of goods and services	2.9	–4.7	–4.7	–2.8	–0.5	0.7
Terms of trade	–3.6	–2.5	–2.5	–4.9	–1.1	–0.6
% of GDP, national accounts						
Ratio of taxes to GDP	47.1	45.8	45.8	44.9	44.4	44.5
General government net lending	7.0	4.2	4.2	2.4	2.1	2.4
General government debt (Maastricht definition)	44.0	42.7	42.7	45.2	45.0	44.3
Goods account, BOP	11.4	9.9	9.9	8.6	8.4	8.2
Current account, BOP	7.6	7.6	7.6	5.8	5.9	6.1
Average interest rate on deposit banks' new loans, %	5.2	4.2	4.2	3.5	4.0	4.7

f = forecast;
[a] = September 2002 estimates.
Sources: Statistics Finland and *Bank of Finland Bulletin* (2003), vol. 77(3), p. 2.

market prices by two-thirds, looking forward it suggests that trend improvements are limited. Perhaps this tells us more about the forecasters than the economy but it could mean that Swedish fears of stabilising with a continuing imbalance in the labour market are being realised in Finland.

10
Sweden: Not Now or Not Ever?

Sweden has chosen a unique approach to joining Stage 3 of EMU, which is to agree to the principle of membership but to postpone actual entry until economic circumstances are appropriate. The other two countries among the EU members that have not joined Stage 3, Denmark and the UK, both have an opt out. They can stay out permanently if they wish. Sweden cannot. Furthermore, many of the countries that joined the EU in 2004 have expressed a wish to proceed to EMU membership rapidly thereafter. This chapter explores whether there are some unique reasons for Sweden's choice, particularly in the light of the referendum in September 2003 rejecting membership.

The Nordic countries, Denmark, Finland, Iceland, Norway and Sweden, provide an interesting set of contrasts in the choice of exchange rate regime. Not only have the countries chosen a variety of different regimes but their circumstances are crucially different, despite the existence of strong common social and political frameworks. Perhaps the most important distinction is simply size. Iceland with less than 300,000 inhabitants is in a class of its own, but Norway, Finland and Denmark are very similar with populations ranging from a little under 4½ million to just over 5¼ million. Sweden stands out with a population of around 9 million. Sweden can be regarded as one of the main group of medium-sized countries in Europe, whereas the others are essentially 'small'. In the context of countries such as Germany, France, Italy and the UK, such a difference might appear trivial but at some point in the spectrum of choice size begins to matter, as Schembri (2002) explains for the case of Canada.

Sweden is not distinct by some other measures. Norway and Denmark have noticeably higher incomes per head and Sweden falls between Finland and Iceland. Indeed in Purchasing Power Parity terms the last three countries are very much on a par. Sweden is also somewhat distinct in terms of its decidedly 'imperial' history and an industrial structure reflecting a network of strong international investment relatively uninterrupted by the war. With a central bank whose history goes back at least 400 years to 1590 it is perhaps understandable that there should be some pressure for an independent monetary policy. A substantial 'trust' in the activity of such an institution has been achieved (Jonung, 2002). The political history of independence and indeed neutrality was only altered very rapidly in the beginning of the 1990s after the collapse of the former Soviet Union. Unlike Denmark, which has been a member of the EU since 1973, Sweden did not even apply to join until the summer of 1991 and has only been a member since 1995.

It is therefore possible to build up a framework for decision-making, which puts Sweden in a slightly different position from its Nordic neighbours, both in terms of economics and wider socio-political factors. Unlike Iceland and Norway, which are subject to important asymmetries, through fishing and oil respectively, Sweden is not so economically distinct from its European partners to the South; even though it shares with Finland some historical exposure to the forest and paper industries. It therefore becomes more difficult to explain Swedish policy and experience on the basis of the standard Optimal Currency Area literature. Small countries pay an interest premium for their monetary independence and the risk of asymmetric shocks. They can only avoid this by having assets to fall back on, as in the case of Switzerland, in particular, and to a lesser extent Norway, with oil. Denmark on the other hand has avoided paying any premium by its close and successful pegging to the euro and earlier close adherence to the ERM. Finland, of course, has gone the whole way and joined the euro area from its inception. It is important not to underrate the extent of development of the Swedish economy as an explanation of its different position. Sweden has been second among the EU countries after the UK in terms of equity market capitalisation compared to GDP, with levels similar to the US. Its spending on IT as a share of GDP has been highest in the EU (Kinnwall, 2000) again on a par with the US. Crucially perhaps, as Rollo (2002) explains for the case of the UK, it is difficult to show convincingly to voters that Sweden is somehow suffering economically by being outside EMU. Swedes are used to changing exchange rates. As a result, when the issue of joining EMU was put in a referendum in September 2003, it was decisively rejected. Membership is likely to be off the agenda for some time to come.

10.1 The Swedish context

Sweden is one of the three new members of the EU who joined in 1995. Although it was a founder member of EFTA and a major participant in economic integration in Europe from an early stage through trade and investment, political concerns relating to neutrality precluded any consideration of membership of the EU until the 1990s (Miles, 2000). Public enthusiasm for EU issues has been moderate (Lindahl, 2000). Only 52.2% were in favour of joining in the November 1994 referendum. Eurobarometer polls after joining indicated that far more people in Sweden thought that the country had not benefited from membership than those who thought it had benefited. Indeed at the time of the setting up of the ECB and agreement on the membership of Stage 3 of EMU in 1998, twice as many people thought that it had not benefited as those that thought it had (53 vs 26%). Sweden's history of full participation in co-operation among the Nordic countries has meant that its participation in EU activities has been more enthusiastic in some areas than others. For example, the experience of the free flow of Nordic citizens across borders helped in Sweden's decision to join the Schengen agreement at an early date. While political leaders may have been more in favour of greater participation in the EU, the lack of public popularity, as in Denmark, has meant that the holding of referenda on these issues has always risked rejection. Despite very careful preparation over timing, the referendum on joining Stage 3 of EMU held in September 2003 fulfilled the government's worst fears. While sentiment was positive at the outset, it was firmly negative by the decision day.

Of all the European countries, Sweden has had one of the most extensive debates about the appropriate macroeconomic policies in the face of closer European integration. This perhaps reflects the long tradition of involvement of economists in the public debate (see Findlay *et al.* (2002) as an example).[1] This in itself may help explain why, unlike some other countries that might seem less convergent to the general European economy, Sweden has thus far opted to remain outside Stage 3 of EMU. While political reasons for membership may be fairly straightforward to justify, making an economic case whether positive or negative is much more difficult. There has thus been considerable reasoning in the debate and fundamental issues are still live rather than being 'irrevocably' decided many years ago. It is inevitable with such a short period of membership and a long history of successful independent economic development that EU involvement is less ingrained than in countries that have been members since the beginning or even for 30 years like Denmark and the UK.

The economic position regarding membership of EMU is straightforward. Sweden has clearly converged to the criteria for membership of Stage 3 of EMU as explained in the ECB's Convergence Report for 2002. Indeed only two things prevent the triggering of Swedish membership. The first is that Sweden is not participating in ERMII and therefore cannot meet the exchange rate criterion. The second is that the Riksbank Act is not quite in conformity with the independence required for membership. Both of these 'failures' could be put right almost at the stroke of a pen. The reality of the behaviour of the exchange rate does however still show relatively high volatility compared to the euro. The krona depreciated by 18% between the beginning of the second quarter of 2000 and the beginning of the fourth quarter of 2001 (Figure 10.2). Since then it has appreciated somewhat (by 8% at its maximum in the first quarter of the year). The krona has thus been following the same sort of pattern as the euro itself but with an even wider amplitude in terms of the effective exchange rate. Thus in practical terms Sweden has actually been making use of its independence in monetary and exchange rate policy since the inception of the ECB, unlike

Denmark. The Riksbank has varied interest rates more than the ECB, in general reacting somewhat earlier. However, rates have tracked their Eurosystem counterpart fairly closely.

Sweden appears to have a lot in common with Finland regarding convergence (compare Figures 10.1–10.3 and Figures 9.1–9.3). We noted in

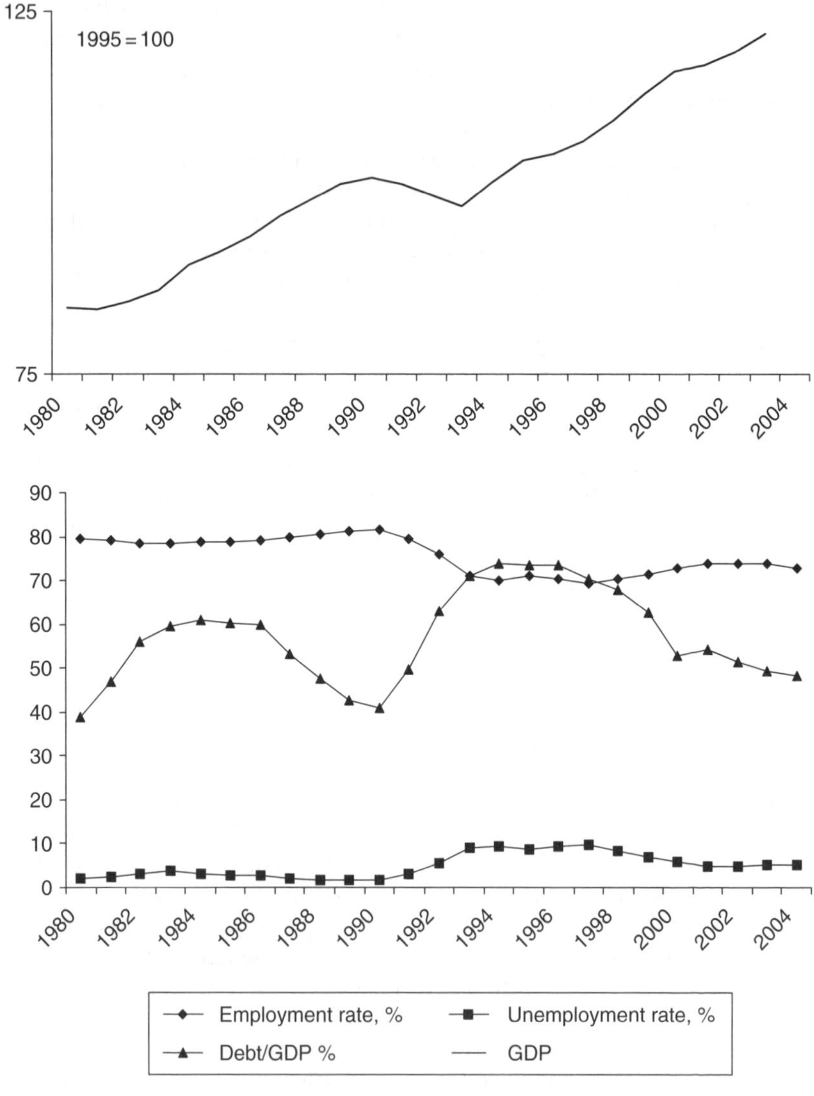

Figure 10.1 Real GDP, debt, employment and unemployment in Sweden 1980–2004 (OECD forecast)

Chapter 9 that by some counts Finland had achieved credibility before the decision to join the euro area. The period concerned was short, reflected considerable strength in the period of adjustment after the economic crisis at the beginning of the 1990s and was not disturbed by any serious adverse shocks. The experience was similar for Sweden. The exchange rate depreciated rapidly in 1992 (Figure 10.2). The collapse of shadowing the ERM was replaced by inflation targeting.[2] Fiscal consolidation and a rapid economic turnround meant that confidence was quickly re-established (Figures 10.1 and 10.2). Like their Finnish counterpart, Swedish interest rates have also to a large extent converged. There is a premium in long rates of around 0.5% over Germany but this could be simply explicable in terms of inflation expectations. Sweden's target is for inflation in the range of 1 to 3% whereas the Eurosystem is aiming for inflation in the medium term of less than but 'close to' 2% (ECB, 2003a). That would explain the differential if both were credible. Sweden has now regained its triple A rating. In any case financial markets may have been assuming that Sweden would join the euro area in the reasonably near future. The alternative view (Kinnwall, 2000) is that

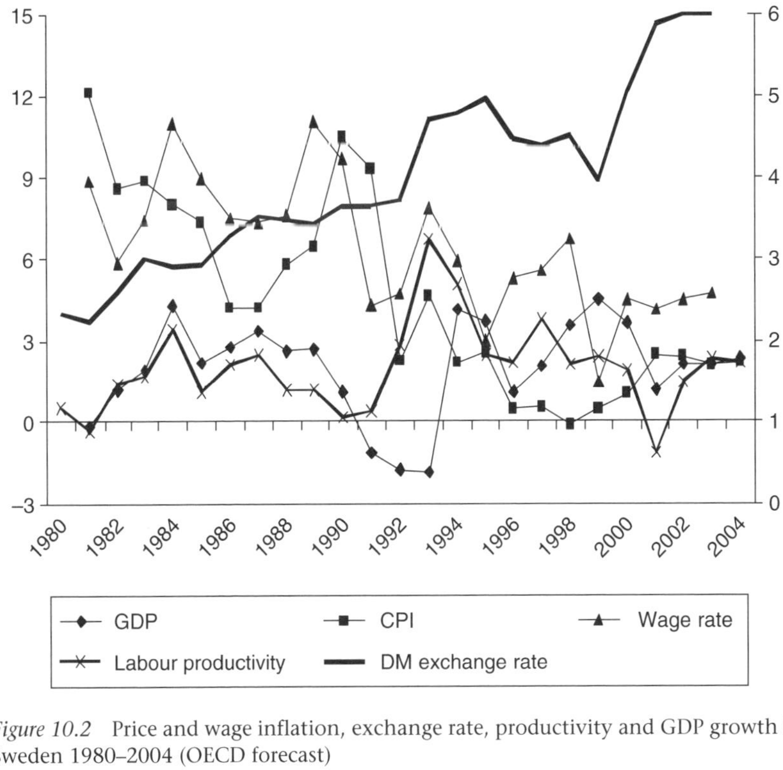

Figure 10.2 Price and wage inflation, exchange rate, productivity and GDP growth in Sweden 1980–2004 (OECD forecast)

Sweden, like Finland, achieved credibility on its own, without the need for prospective EMU membership to force the adjustment.

The Swedish turnround and convergence process did not follow such a dramatic shock as in Finland (Figures 10.1 and 9.1). The impact on real incomes from the crisis in Sweden was about half that in Finland according to Jonung and Hagberg (2002). The recovery, however, was relatively slow compared to other crises over the last century and took about as long as the recovery from the 1929 Crash and was only exceeded in slowness by the recovery after the Second World War.[3] Fiscal recovery was a little slower than in Finland but the recovery of the labour market was much more rapid. In most respects Sweden can be judged to have returned to balance, whereas the labour market disequilibrium persists in Finland.

Taken together, therefore, it appears that Sweden has been able to respond relatively well without EMU membership. Indeed, since the labour market developments have been relatively favourable, compared to the EU as a whole, and Finland in particular, it is interesting that Sweden should have placed so much emphasis on labour market difficulties as a reason for staying out of Stage 3. The next two sections therefore deal first with the Swedish concerns and then with a broader consideration of the extent to which the Swedish economy has indeed returned to a sustainable path without membership of EMU.

10.2 The Swedish concern

The nature of the Swedish debate has been well documented. Much of the discussion in the Swedish Commission on EMU (Calmfors *et al.*, 1997) and subsequently (Johansson *et al.*, 2002) has focused on the problems of stabilising employment in the face of asymmetric shocks.[4] Indeed the full title of the second Commission is 'The Committee on Stabilisation Policy for full Employment if Sweden joins the Monetary Union'. The Committee concludes 'Our view is that changes in the degree of nominal wage flexibility are likely to compensate only to a minor extent for the loss of national monetary policy as an instrument of stabilisation policy' (p. 3). Indeed they see that wages in Sweden might themselves be a source of shocks. This reaction reflects a general expectation that flexibility will not work. The same argument is applied to fluctuations in working hours. Because so much of working hours are statutorily controlled the Committee (pp. 5–6) did not see them as being able to act as a shock absorber. If rules were changed they would apply to all sectors. The rigidities imposed on the labour market mean that it is necessary to look elsewhere for offsetting fluctuations in the system. This implies that much of the successful readjustment of the Swedish economy to the crisis at the beginning of the 1990s can be attributed to the operation of monetary policy and to the movement in the exchange rate.

The Committee rejects one of the major ingredients of the Finnish arrangements as being unlikely to survive, namely cooperative bargaining between employers and trade unions with the government as a third party. They do not discuss the wider cooperation arrangements that have been operating very successfully in Ireland (Chapter 8) and contributing substantially to the economic success. In the Irish case it has only been possible to get a balanced outcome by having a wide range of parties involved. Governments tend to behave asymmetrically (IMF, 2002a; Mayes and Virén, 2002b) while Halko (2002) points out that leaving negotiations just to the social partners also tends to discriminate against those that are not currently employed. The idea that Sweden might not be able to operate at one end of the Calmfors-Driffill 'smile' must obviously cause considerable concern as a move right through the spectrum to the other corner of the smile is unlikely in Sweden's heavily social democratic environment.

The response by the Committee has been to suggest setting up a substantial buffer fund plus a much greater role for automatic and discretionary stabilisation in the tax system. This fund is crucially different from those already in place in Finland (Chapter 9). Not only is the Swedish fund much larger but the Finnish funds are intended to offset what would be regarded as an anomaly in many countries in that balancing the unemployment fund, in particular, each year requires contributions to rise when payouts rise. Thus if the number of unemployed rises then the contribution by employers and the remaining employees has to rise. The net result of this arrangement was pro-cyclical non-wage labour costs, which rose just at the time that there was downward pressure on labour demand. Employees would need a pay rise to prevent their takehome pay from falling. The incentives were thus perverse. It is not surprising that Finland wanted to move to a position where the contribution rates could remain flat during a downturn. The Swedish proposals are an order of magnitude more ambitious.

There are two parts to the Johansson *et al.* proposals.[5] Under normal circumstances, the 'automatic' stabilisation that takes place over the cycle should be enhanced by between 0.5 and 1% of GDP, with little discretionary addition except in labour market programmes.[6] Normality is defined as an output gap less than plus or minus 2%. Thus in the first part it is intended that the Swedish fiscal system be more than normally reactive compared to the other Member States. In order to achieve this without being in danger of breaching the 3% Stability and Growth Pact deficit ratio limit, the Swedish government will have to aim slightly more towards surplus in equilibrium. The second part, the buffer fund, would only cut in outside this normality – although of course it would need to be built up and then topped up. In practice, despite the enormous difficulty in defining an unobservable variable like the output gap, this would mean that the only time the buffer fund would have been triggered over the last 20 years would have been during the Swedish financial crisis. IMF (2002a) conducts a range of simulations to illustrate how frequently the limits might be reached and what surplus would need to be aimed for through the cycle. The report does not apparently place much emphasis on the role of the single monetary policy as a stabilisation mechanism for the considerable proportion of fluctuations in Sweden that will be 'coordinated' (in the sense of symmetric i.e. correlated) across the euro area. Symmetric rather than asymmetric shocks are likely to be the norm. As Mayes and Virén (2002b) point out, EMU heightens the response to symmetric shocks as both fiscal and monetary policy respond more effectively in this more closed economy environment.

What is particularly interesting about the Swedish proposals is that the Committee feels it necessary for the assessment of what is needed for fiscal policy in stabilisation to be independent of the usual government processes. Given the heavy politicisation of fiscal policy in most countries this wish is understandable. As is shown in Mayes and Virén (2002b), there are considerable asymmetries in the way the euro area countries undertake not just stabilisation policy but any changes in the structure of fiscal policy. The asymmetry that has been observed tends to ratchet up problems as governments are keener to lower taxes or allow expenditure to expand when the economy is doing well than they are to raise taxes or cut expenditures in a downturn. The implication therefore is that the independent assessment will be necessary to prevent the fund being activated too readily or replenished too slowly.

The Swedish buffer funds would be a voluntary arrangement between employers and unions (voluntary in the sense that government would permit rather than require them). The labour market partners would administer them without government involvement and without subsidy from public funds. They should be neutral across sectors and only triggered by 'strong negative shocks'. There is clearly a problem if such funds are to be industry-based, rather than national. Given the size of the public sector in Sweden, however, the government will inevitably be involved as an employer.

These proposals clearly raise a number of central issues about how an economy can maintain flexibility, not just under the terms of the Stability and Growth Pact but more generally. The primary aim of the SGP is to ensure that the Member States run fiscal policies that are prudent and sustainable. This requires not merely that the longer-term path of likely expenditure and revenues should be credible but that short-run movements in response to shocks should not be destabilising. (At present this entails a combination of aiming for surplus or near balance through the cycle and not exceeding a 3% deficit/GDP ratio at any stage outside a major recession.) Such requirements would apply to any fiscal policy, whether inside or outside the euro zone. Indeed, the need is greater outside the euro zone as individual countries receive a valuation for their debt that reflects the credibility of their policies much more closely. Inside the euro zone, the spreads between the individual countries are much smaller than they would be if there were no expected element of collective action to handle problems. When the Fiscal Responsibility Act in New Zealand was enacted in 1994, the then Minister of Finance, Ruth Richardson, hailed it as a more important step in achieving credibility for macroeconomic policy than the Reserve Bank Act of 1989 that wrote inflation targeting onto the statute book. Not only did the FRA transform the nature of the budgetary debate but it made the inflation targeting strategy more plausible.

The key facets of such systems are that the accounting basis needs to be realistic and comprehensible, policy needs to show a long-term sustainable path and, in instituting any short-run deviations from that path, the government needs to provide a credible explanation of how the fiscal balance is going to return to sustainability.[7] The Swedish proposals not only help achieve this but go rather further. They apply some measure of independence to the assessment, although it is not clear that this is particularly different from the assessments made by the Commission of Member States' cyclically adjusted positions. That assessment is also independent and since it is made public any deviation from the highest standards of estimation will be vigorously disputed. The primacy of parliament over fiscal policy is maintained in that it is the government that decides the overall framework and the independent fiscal commission merely produces the technical calculations that then generate the actions under the previously agreed rules.

The problem with any such system is of course that the government cannot conclusively bind its successors. Wage bargainers and indeed all those involved will base their actions on what they think will apply in the future and not just on what the legal arrangement at the time happens to say. (This could be more or less optimistic than the proposed arrangement.)

Furthermore, by funding the provisions, the problems of sustainability only surface when it looks as if the funding will be inadequate and fiscal policy will have to be used to continue the net payments until the downturn is over or the destabilising effect on the real economy will have to be realised because the funds have run out. Given that downturns have been relatively short-lived in Sweden (Jonung and Hagberg, 2002), such arrangements could work. However, the profile of stabilisation will be different if they run out, particularly if the assessment of what is cycle and what is change in trend turns out to be mistaken. The 3% deficit limit in the SGP, while arbitrary, places a cap on the degree to which there can be a misestimation of the trend/cycle mix. However, it also places an equally arbitrary cap on the degree to which Member States can limit the real consequences of shocks, which the Swedish proposals could circumvent.

Sweden's debt position has improved dramatically in recent years, falling by 20 percentage points between 1998 and 2001 (from 72 to 52% of GDP) as a result of running clear surpluses and having satisfactory economic growth. It is thus beginning to get far enough inside the limits for the debt ratio under the SGP that it could benefit from recent proposals to alter the balance of the SGP for countries with low debt ratios. Under those proposals agreed at the March 2005 European Council, a Member State that would not be near breaching the 60% debt ratio limit could be permitted more licence with respect to the 3% deficit ratio limit provided long-run sustainability was not threatened.

For countries, like Sweden, that are particularly concerned to stabilise their economies in the face of shocks, these new proposals offer an encouragement to continue fiscal 'consolidation', that is debt reduction, to the point that they have leeway both to meet short-run fluctuations and longer-term structural pressures such as the ageing of the population. However, it remains a different issue as to whether buffer funds administered by the social partners or more sweeping 'automatic stabilisation' administered by the government is the better route to achieve the flexibility. An argument for government involvement is that not everyone affected is represented by the social partners, particularly those already unemployed or outside the labour market. It would however be open to government to develop matching funds for those groups.

It is of course also a different concern whether the impact of net change in the balance of revenues and expenditure is different if the funds have been assigned to the social partners or left in a government balance. If they are to be replenished by a similar means of charges on employers and employees it is rather difficult to see how the impact differs and the difference becomes one of accounting convention rather than economic content. There is however some merit in hypothecated funding rather than the use of generalised funds. A more direct relationship between contribution and benefit tends to make the use of funds more efficient.

The sorts of independent fiscal council suggested by the Johansson commission have been extensively considered before (Von Hagen and Harden, 1994; Blinder, 1997; Gruen, 1997, 2000, for example). Technocratic bodies may be able to operate rather faster than governments and hence reduce the risk of discretionary actions having a pro-cyclical outcome, despite their counter-cyclical intention, because of the lags involved. Von Hagen and Harden (1994) argue that such a body needs to be given asymmetric powers in order to overcome the deficit (or inflation) bias inherent in government policy in practice. Otherwise the temptation is to be trigger happy at the first sign of a downturn but cautious in easing the policy in an upturn.

10.3 Recent experience and prospects

The Sveriges Riksbank remains quite optimistic about the Swedish economy, seeing the country growing by over 2% in the 2004–2006 period, slightly better than the ECB's revised forecast for the euro area. Targeted inflation seems set to remain a little below 2%. Unemployment has come down to an enviable 4% and seems likely to stay around this number (although there is substantial use of active labour market policies that keep the numbers a little lower than in some comparable economies). It is thus difficult to point to economic reasons why Sweden should be better off inside the euro area in the immediate future. Progress outside seems to be quite satisfactory. With a projected surplus of 2% of GDP over the medium-term, Sweden should be in a position to meet the increased pension demands that will appear in coming years as the population ages.

Up until 1970 the Swedish economy was clearly a success story (Lindbeck, 2000). Sweden was fourth in the ranking of OECD countries by GDP per head. Since then the position has slipped and Sweden is now in the bottom third of the OECD group. It is not that Swedish performance has been dramatically worse than that of its competitors. It is merely that with annual growth just 0.5% slower than that of the OECD, this amounts to a major change over a 30-year period. It appears that in the last few years this process of relative decline has been reversed but the period is short and the evidence debated.

The main factor widely blamed for the relative decline is the high marginal tax rates and the shift from being a market-financed economy to the position where now two-thirds of the population is tax-financed. This shift reflects a period of increasing centralisation, regulation (particularly in the labour market) and reduction in incentives for both households and firms (Lindbeck, 2000: 35). Blomström's (2000) conclusion that Swedish multinationals (in contrast to the US) tend to 'expand their more advanced activities abroad and keep the low-wage operations at home' (p. 185) must be a worry for those who think that outlook may be changing markedly for the better. It may be that a long period of accumulation of wealth is being used to finance activities elsewhere rather than the generation of new wealth by activity in Sweden itself.

Sweden has prided itself on the quality and extent of education of its labour force (Storesletten and Zilibotti, 2000). Total public and private resources devoted to education are among the highest in the OECD (OECD, 1998). Given the emphasis on the 'knowledge economy' as the potential source of growth in Europe, this should imply that Sweden is well placed. However, the compression of wage differentials, as a result of the tax and benefit system, has meant that the pay-off to the education and the incentive to opt for the acquisition of the most suitable skills has been low.[8] Achievements, given the education, have been relatively weak and the margin by which Sweden has exceeded the average in the OECD has been relatively constant. Storesletten and Zilibotti therefore join the chorus arguing for further labour market reforms to generate the incentives for greater achievement.

Up until the banking crisis at the beginning of the 1990s there had been considerable debate about the sustainability of Swedish employment and fiscal policy. The share of government in employment and the share of the rates of taxation had been growing to the point where further increases looked implausible. The share of general government has turned round since then, with the expenditure to GDP ratio falling from 70% in 1993 to around 55% currently. Over the same period government revenues have stabilised at a little below 60% of GDP. As a result the deficit of 12% in 1993 was eliminated by 1998 and surpluses have followed since then. The debt ratio has nearly returned to pre-crisis levels. It is thus clear that while Finland may have recovered from the crisis, Sweden has done much better and has not merely largely eliminated any legacy from those difficulties but has reversed the unsustainable trend. (In relative terms, of course, the shock to the Swedish economy from the banking crisis and the collapse of the former Soviet Union was much smaller than in Finland.) GDP declined by only 5% over a period of 3 years (1991–1993) and while unemployment doubled, its maximum of around 8% is still lower than Finnish unemployment has yet reached on the way down. Special employment measures have disguised perhaps another 4 percentage points of unemployment (NIER, 2000).

Sweden also seems to have adjusted its pension system to the strains of the ageing of the population by using the opportunity of running surpluses and running down debt to switch to a substantial element of funding (NIER, 2000). This will keep funds accumulating for a decade, by which time it will be possible to make a further judgement about longer-term sustainability (IMF, 2002a).

It does therefore appear that it has been possible to adjust without the added compulsion of EMU membership in a manner that is rather more satisfactory than for some of the existing members such as Italy and Spain. In one way this could be taken as a vindication of Sweden's decision to stay out until the adjustment had taken place. Even if the exchange rate adjustment was not crucial and action would not have been inhibited by the SGP, it is still possible to argue that having the option was a sensible precaution. While membership may not offer much in the way of additional benefits, it would act as a deterrent to any reversal and as a dampener on wage demands. Having been on the unsustainable path of increasing involvement of the public sector it would not be impossible to envisage a similar sequence of developments arising again as 'temporary' attempts to offset short-run shocks get locked in.

We could therefore argue, along with a recent Article IV consultation by the IMF (2002a), that the Swedish crisis was followed by a successful fiscal contraction. However, earlier history suggests that Sweden was somewhat prone to pro-cyclical discretionary fiscal policy contrary to this counter-cyclical experience. Hence while the crisis may have provided the stimulus for a one-off improvement, the prospects for repeated performance in the same vein may be weaker. (We saw in Chapter 9 that one feature that propelled Finland towards membership of Stage 3 was the hope that the discipline of membership would make the changes in behaviour achieved after the crisis more enduring.) One of the ironies about Sweden's preoccupation with the ability to use discretionary fiscal policy to offset the impact of asymmetric shocks is the finding by Hemming *et al.* (2002) and Mayes and Virén (2002b) that while such policies may have some effect in relatively closed economies they have less in relatively open ones. According to IMF (2002a) Sweden is not particularly different in this regard to other advanced economies. Membership of EMU might actually make some of the measures more effective.

The extent of the Swedish concern with the impact of EMU can be seen from the fact that not only did Calmfors and his colleagues produce a comprehensive 365-page report, but the published background papers take up 594 pages of two issues of the *Swedish Economic Review*. Many of these submissions came from outside Sweden. The Calmfors Report reflects the rather ambivalent nature of many of these contributions. They did not argue that there would be strong gains from membership or clear losses from staying outside. They did however emphasise the difficulty of making reliable measurements. Friberg and Vredin (1997), for example, in considering the costs imposed on businesses from uncertain exchange rates, repeated the difficulty in assessment. But rather than concluding, as in Mayes and Webb (1993), that with hedging the cost could be small, they argued that many firms do not hedge because of the inability to estimate the net benefits and hence face considerable exposures. Membership of EMU or a monetary policy of exchange rate targeting, as practised by Denmark, would remove much of that risk.

Per Jansson (1997) in his assessment of the risks of asymmetric shocks (based on behaviour over the period 1960–1994) shows that Sweden is very clearly a member of the group of less well-synchronised countries with respect to GDP. In his study of 11 EU countries (not Greece, Italy, Spain or Portugal) he shows that there are two very distinct groups. Germany, Belgium, the Netherlands, France, Austria and Luxembourg clearly form a very symmetric group, while the others – Sweden, Finland, Ireland, the UK and Denmark – do not show the same characteristics. Interestingly enough there is no such common experience for inflation. For Sweden not to be subject to such asymmetric shocks in the future there would need to be a dramatic change in behaviour. But Stage 3 of EMU is anticipated to have a significant effect. Jansson (1997) therefore has somewhat cautious conclusions. Frankel and Rose (1997) in the preceding article show evidence of the possibility of just that change from a survey of 30 countries. They show that increasing economic integration tends to be associated with more synchronised cycles. Hence they argue that if Stage 3 of EMU leads to closer integration then more symmetric behaviour could also be expected. Even if the past behaviour were to be continued IMF (2002a) argues that Sweden would only breach the SGP guidelines in exceptional circumstances. Since the SGP itself allows for exceptional measures under significant recessions it is not quite clear, in their view, what the constraints on Swedish fiscal policy might be under membership of Stage 3.

We thus see two things: first, a rather tentative approach to estimating Sweden's likely net benefits/costs from membership of Stage 3; but second, no clear means of distinguishing Sweden from the other countries that have decided to stay out (the UK and Denmark) and Finland and Ireland that went in. In both of the latter two cases there were clear special factors that contributed to the decision.

10.4 Concluding remark

Sweden like other countries outside the euro area faces a difficult choice. It can control domestic inflation successfully by inflation targeting but at the expense of a floating exchange rate, which it cannot control or it can eliminate exchange rate fluctuations with other euro zone members but have much more limited control over its own price level. As Jonung (2002) and Mayes and Suvanto (2002) have pointed out, membership of the euro area has resulted in less not more price stability for many countries. A glance at Figure 10.3, drawn from Jonung (2002), shows that five of the current euro area members would not have qualified for membership in 2001, according to the inflation criterion. Sweden did, as the convergence report indicates (ECB, 2002a). Moreover, Denmark and the UK form two of the three countries that set the standard against which Sweden needed to qualify.

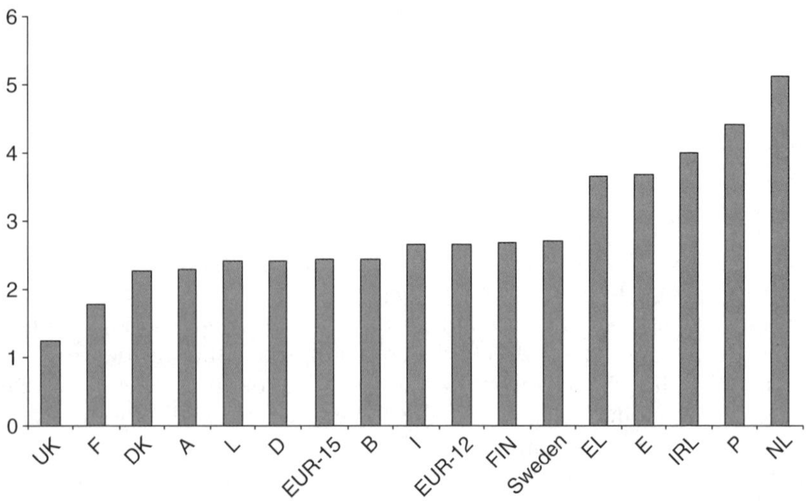

Figure 10.3 Inflation rates in the EU 2001 (Jonung, 2002)

If we add to the successful inflation experience the satisfactory growth, the good performance of unemployment, the fiscal consolidation and the prospects for the future it seems relatively difficult to produce a strong economic case for Swedish membership of Stage 3. The arguments on the other side of the coin would relate to whether the change in behaviour stimulated by the crisis of the early 1990s can be sustained and whether markets' assessment of Swedish success would change if membership of the euro area no longer seemed likely in the reasonably near future.

The 2003 referendum may have ended this speculation. Opposition to EMU membership now appears rather more deep-seated and the idea of only entering when the economy has adjusted sufficiently is now looking a rather tenuous description of the actual position. Something more permanent along the lines of Denmark might be more plausible. In any case, in most countries, the decision has been dominated by political rather than economic considerations. What we can see from the case of Sweden, as from the case of Finland, is that the necessary impetus for fiscal and structural reform can be obtained without EMU membership or the drive to achieve it. However, none of the other EU Member States would have been keen to endure the economic crisis that stimulated the action.

11
The United Kingdom: Prospering Outside the Euro Area?

The most distinctive feature of the UK's approach to EMU is its reluctance to participate. This ambivalence about the political and economic benefits lies behind the concession of an opt-out[1] giving the UK the option not to join until it is ready to do so, negotiated as part of the December 1991 Maastricht agreement that paved the way for EMU. By contrast, the two other EU-15 Member States which are not part of the euro area, Denmark and Sweden, have had governments committed to membership, but have been prevented from going ahead by the results of referenda. The current UK government has expressed its political agreement to membership (HM Treasury, 1997a) provided that the economic conditions are right, and put forward five economic tests by which that stipulation was to be judged. While these tests have been portrayed as being purely about the economic case for UK accession to the euro area, in practice they are also political, not least in requiring that the case for membership be 'clear and unambiguous'. All major parties have also pledged to call a referendum on membership, which will be a tough test given that support in the UK for European integration in general, and monetary union in particular, is consistently the lowest in the EU.

Ironically, with the publication of a series of studies and an assessment of the five tests (HM Treasury, 2003a), the economic case for membership has now been examined more thoroughly in the UK than in any of the euro area Member States. The verdict reached in 2003 was that the five tests had not been met, and a commitment was made to review the position annually. The first such annual review in 2004 was desultory, suggesting that full participation in EMU is off the agenda for the next few years, and in 2005, the examination barely registered on the political seismographs.

11.1 The UK and European monetary integration

Despite being a member of the EU since 1973 the UK has participated directly in European exchange rate systems for only two brief periods. Even before formally acceding to the EU, the UK participated in the EC's first monetary system – the Snake – from its inception in April 1972. Five weeks later the pound fell out of the system, when its exchange rate parity became unsustainable. The UK did not participate in the Exchange Rate Mechanism (ERM) of the European Monetary System[2] (EMS) when it was launched in 1979 and repeatedly refused to do so on the grounds that 'the time is not ripe'. A reluctant Margaret Thatcher eventually took Sterling into the ERM in October 1990 as the UK economy slid into recession after the excesses of the late 1980s, but, after two years of economic stagnation and rising unemployment, a wave of selling on the foreign exchange market forced the government to devalue the pound and leave the system.

Since its exit from the system the UK has enjoyed a period of steady growth, low inflation and rising employment. In fact, compared to the volatility of the previous decade and relative to most of its EU partners, the performance since then has been impressive. This history compounds the difficulty of convincing the UK public that the adoption of the euro would be good for Britain. Despite a new Labour government which was pro-European and in favour of the adoption of the euro in principle, the UK opted out of the third stage of EMU when decisions on entry were made in 1998.

The approach adopted by the UK government since 1997 has, effectively, been to insist on prior adjustment of the economy to allow it to cope with full EMU. The UK approach to euro membership was explained in the 2003 assessment, the four dimensions of which are set out in an excerpt from the assessment presented in Box 11.1.

Box 11.1 The UK approach to full participation in EMU

According to HM Treasury (2003a), the four principles governing the UK approach to EMU are:

- First, a successful single currency within a single European market would in principle be of *benefit* to Europe and to the UK: in terms of trade, transparency of costs and currency stability
- Second, the *constitutional* issue is a factor in the UK's decision but it is not an overriding one, so long as membership is in the national interest, the case is clear and unambiguous and there is popular consent
- Third, the basis for the decision as to whether there is a *clear and unambiguous* economic case for membership is the Treasury's comprehensive and rigorous assessment of the five economic tests
- Fourth, whenever the decision to enter is taken by the Government, it should be put to a *referendum* of the British people.

Source: Treasury (2003a: 1).

The five economic tests – see Box 11.2 – have, therefore, been established as pivotal to the UK decision and have to be satisfied before the political process culminating in a referendum will be engaged.

Two assessments of these tests have been carried out in 1997 (HM Treasury, 1997b) and in 2003. The second assessment concluded that although real progress on convergence had been made, 'A clear and unambiguous case for UK membership of EMU has not at the present time been made and a decision to join now would not be in the national economic interest' (HM Treasury, 2003a: 6). Whether such a clear and unambiguous case is possible is contentious, with the decision ultimately being one of political will.

Box 11.2 The five economic tests

As explained by the Treasury (2003a) the five economic tests are:

- Are business cycles and economic structures compatible so that we and others could live comfortably with euro interest rates on a permanent basis?
- If problems emerge is there sufficient flexibility to deal with them?
- Would joining EMU create better conditions for firms making long-term decisions to invest in Britain?
- What impact would entry into EMU have on the competitive position of the UK's financial services industry, particularly the City's wholesale markets?
- In summary, will joining EMU promote higher growth, stability and a lasting increase in jobs?

Source: Treasury (2003a: 1).

11.2 Recent UK economic performance

Since the UK is not part of the euro area, the convergence criteria continue to be relevant to its potential entry to the euro area. The 2003 Treasury assessment states that the UK fulfils four of these criteria (inflation rate, long-term interest rate, public deficit and public debt), but avoids mentioning the fifth criterion, namely the exchange rate. Since 1999, the pound has fluctuated quite a bit over any recent two-year period and the UK has refused to become part of the ERM, so that it is clear that the UK would not easily meet the exchange rate stability test. That said, the pound has traded in a much narrower range of 1.38 to 1.54 against the euro since 2003, suggesting that a rate around 1.45 is a sustainable one. Although the UK fiscal deficit increased in 2003 as a result of a surge in public spending to just over the 3% threshold, drawing criticism from the European Commission, the more robust growth in 2004 and expected in 2005 will allow the UK again to meet the deficit test. In any case, the UK's record on all four variables since the mid-1990s signals that there would not be any significant adjustment problems in meeting the four nominal criteria.

1. Since 2000, UK inflation has been among the lowest in the euro area (Figure 11.1), as measured by the Harmonised Index of Consumer Prices, easily satisfying the convergence requirement.
2. Similarly, the UK's long-term interest rate has consistently been well within the limit of two percentage points of the average of the three best.
3. Public deficits have been reined in since the first half of the 1990s, and from 1996 to 2002, were below the 3% limit, so that again the test is easily met, despite creeping just above 3% in 2003, partly as a result of a policy decision to boost public spending.
4. Public debt too is far below the limit of 60% and, with the combination of a moderate deficit and reasonably robust growth, will remain at a level that is comfortably below the Maastricht criterion. Table 11.1 shows the trend in these public finance data and the spread among euro area countries.

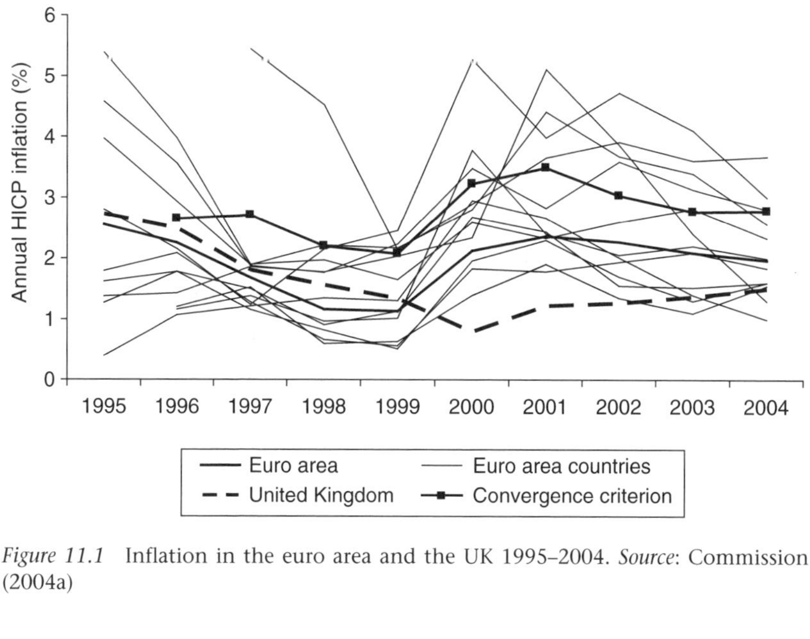

Figure 11.1 Inflation in the euro area and the UK 1995–2004. *Source*: Commission (2004a)

Table 11.1 Public finances in the euro area and the UK 1990–2003 (% GDP)

	1992	1993	1994	1995	1996	1997	1998	1999	2000	2001	2002	2003	2004	2005
Net lending (+) or net borrowing (–) of general government														
Euro area				–5.0	–4.3	–2.6	–2.3	–1.3	0.1	–1.6	–2.3	–2.7	–2.7	–2.6
UK	–6.4	–7.9	–6.7	–5.8	–4.2	–2.2	0.1	1.1	3.9	0.7	–1.6	–3.2	–2.8	–2.6
Cyclically adjusted net lending (+) or net borrowing (–) of general government														
Euro area				–5.2	–4.7	–2.3	–2.3	–1.7	–1.9	–2.4	–2.5	–2.2	–2.2	–2.2
UK	–5.0	–6.6	–6.3	–5.4	–4.2	–2.2	–0.3	0.8	0.8	0.3	–1.5	–2.9	–2.6	–2.3
General government consolidated gross debt														
Euro area	60.4	66.3	68.9	73.5	75.1	74.9	74.2	72.8	70.4	69.4	69.2	70.4	70.9	70.9
UK	39.2	45.4	48.5	51.8	52.2	50.8	47.6	45.0	42.1	38.9	38.5	39.9	40.1	40.6

Source: Commission (2004a).

11.3 Capacity to adjust in future

The UK has radically overhauled its macroeconomic policy framework since the signing of the Maastricht Treaty and inclines to the view that its model is superior to the EMU one, as constituted by the Stability and Growth Pact – even as reformed in 2005 – and the two-pillar monetary policy. While the reformed SGP has manifestly moved in the direction of the UK one by focusing more on debt, medium term flexibility and the importance of structural reforms, it is a moot point whether the UK and SGP II approaches can be reconciled.

This section presents an overview of the macroeconomic model and an analysis of real economic variables: growth, employment/unemployment, trade and the balance of payments. The purpose of this analysis is twofold: first, to examine the likely effects of a possible UK entry to the euro area; and, second, to assess the extent to which it has been advantageous to the UK to remain outside the euro area while following its distinctive macroeconomic approach. The next sub-section briefly describes the macroeconomic framework that has been established in the UK in the last decade. The remaining parts of this section look in more detail at different facets of the economy.

11.3.1 Outline of UK macroeconomic framework

Since the UK was forced out of the ERM in 1992, it has established a new macroeconomic framework that has a number of distinctive features that bear on economic adjustment. Monetary policy was initially made more transparent with the institution of the Inflation Report and more public explanation of the decision-making by the Bank of England and the Treasury – sometimes labelled in the press 'the Ken and Eddie show' in deference to the then Chancellor and Governor. Then, in 1997, the incoming Labour government took the much more radical step of giving full operational autonomy to the Bank of England. However, the mandate for monetary policy was somewhere between that of the ECB and the Federal Reserve. An explicit target for inflation was set, but rather than being an upper limit, it was pitched symmetrically as a range of one percentage point on either side of the 2.5% inflation target. It is an open question whether the symmetry of the target has ultimately led to different decisions, but an interpretation is that it allows the Bank of England to pay more heed to an economic downturn in setting interest rates, a contrast to (or a least, a distinction from) the ECB's mandate.

At the macroeconomic level, the UK fiscal policy framework adopts an approach which, arguably, gives more short-term flexibility and permits some discretionary fiscal policy over and above the automatic stabilisers. This greater flexibility is embodied in two fiscal rules. There is, first, a golden rule which is that over the economic cycle, government is permitted to borrow, but only to fund public investment, not to increase current spending. Though very straightforward, this rule potentially allows a fair degree of discretion insofar as the duration of the cycle is an unknown and the definition of investment might be open to challenge.[3] The second rule is labelled by the Treasury as 'the sustainable investment rule' and can be regarded as a commitment device to maintain the sustainability of the public finances, by keeping public sector net debt as a proportion of GDP within a 'prudent' target level. The benchmark that has, thus far, been adopted is net debt below 40% of GDP, though again there is an element of flexibility by setting the target as being over the economic cycle.

11.3.2 Public finances

In common with many other countries, the UK's public finances were in very poor shape in the early 1990s, as a result of the failure to control public expenditure, the slow growth of output and rising unemployment. The public sector deficit peaked in 1993 at 7.9% of GDP (Table 11.1) and the debt three years later at 52.2%, still comfortably below the Maastricht 60% benchmark, though it had been flattered by privatisation proceeds. With more rapid growth and falling unemployment, tax revenues rose and expenditure was contained, so that the public sector was in surplus by 1998 and the debt fell substantially to a low of 38.5% in 2002. A significant expansion of expenditure and lower tax revenues, associated with slower growth, began to eat into these surpluses, so that, by 2002, the public sector was again in deficit. The rapid turnaround in the government's financial situation has raised doubts about conformity with the golden rule, while the debt level is hovering around the self-imposed sustainable level, though the government claimed in the presentation of its budget for 2005/2006 that the rules had been respected. However, the UK public sector debt is one of the lowest in the EU and long-term pension liabilities are small. This means that the UK public finances can be regarded as sound and will not pose problems of adjustment for the foreseeable future.

Remaining outside the euro area has meant that the UK could be more relaxed over its public finances. But, as the data in Table 11.1 show, even if the UK had been subject to all the stages of the Excessive Deficit Procedure, it would only have courted a warning in 2003 and, in that respect, is in a stronger position than the other three largest Member States. The UK might have been ticked-off for not shifting closer 'to balance or in surplus', but the need for public investment to support growth is acknowledged, so that it is unlikely that the UK would have been called to account by the Commission or Ecofin, as Ireland was, for taking insufficient steps to conform to the BEPGs. Given that the UK has been in line with its own rules, remaining outside the euro has meant that a flexible fiscal policy could be used for micro and macroeconomic purposes, although whether this freedom has been used in an entirely appropriate manner is another issue.

11.3.3 Interest rates

UK nominal long-term interest rates have tracked those in the euro area (Figure 11.2), and with inflation predicted to remain low this is likely to continue to be the case. Despite the similarity of long-term interest rates the UK has used the monetary flexibility it enjoys outside the euro area to manage the economy. *Short*-term interest rates have consistently been higher than in the euro area, and although they appeared to be converging in 2002, have since diverged again. These interest rates, together with the high value of the exchange rate up to 2002, have meant a tighter monetary policy in the UK than in the euro area. Membership of the euro area would, therefore, have implied lower short-term interest rates, potentially boosting consumer and housing demand, and adding to the unbalanced nature of the expansion in the UK. The UK would probably have also been one of those countries where acclimatisation would have led to higher inflation.[4]

11.3.4 Exchange rate

After the traumatic exit from the ERM in October 1992 Sterling weakened until 1996 and then rebounded strongly. Since 1998 the Real Effective Exchange Rate[5] (REER) of the pound has been 26% above its 1993–1995 average and 14% stronger than its long-run average.[6] Unit labour costs have increased even more rapidly because of a higher rate of wage growth in the UK (IMF, 2001: 28) and only marginal relative productivity improvements. There is a very wide range of estimates of the pound's 'equilibrium' value against the euro (OECD, 2002b: 158) ranging from 1.04–1.27 (Wren-Lewis

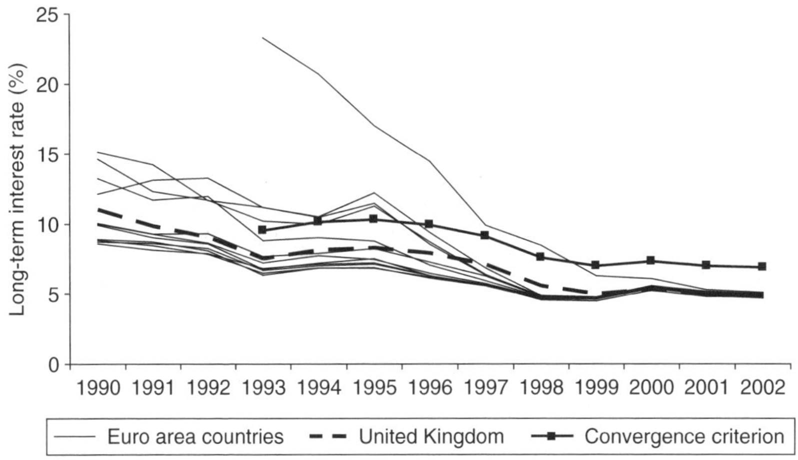

Figure 11.2 Nominal long-term interest rates in the euro area and the UK 1990–2002. *Source*: Commission (2004a)

and Driver, 1998), to 1.37 (Wren-Lewis, 2003) to 1.50–1.55 (Barrell, 2002). The estimates differ with the method employed and with the period of assessment: on the whole, more recent and forward-looking assessments provide higher estimates. The recent estimates give a range of 1.37–1.55 € to the £, quite close to current values. These analyses seem to be at odds with recent work, which ascribe the poor performance of UK manufacturing exports to problems with cost competitiveness (Carlin *et al.*, 2002; Carlin and Glyn, 2003).

Throughout the whole floating exchange rate era, Sterling has been one of the most unstable major European currencies. This is shown clearly by the large swings of the REER leading to periods of over and under valuation (Figure 11.3). It is also demonstrated by the standard deviation of the REER over the whole period and in the sub-periods (Table 11.2). Even though, in the 1990s, the new macroeconomic policy regime successfully stabilised the output of the UK economy, it has manifestly not stabilised the real exchange rate. This experience with a floating exchange rate raises questions of the utility of maintaining an independent currency.

Finding the right entry rate for EMU will not be easy, given the Maastricht convergence requirement for the exchange rate.[7] All current members maintained fixed exchange rates in the ERM before the examination of the convergence criteria and this central rate became the permanently fixed rate against the euro. Finland, Italy and, later, Greece joined the ERM in order to participate in EMU. In the case of Finland and Italy the central rates chosen against the ECU were close to the current exchange (within 2% of the

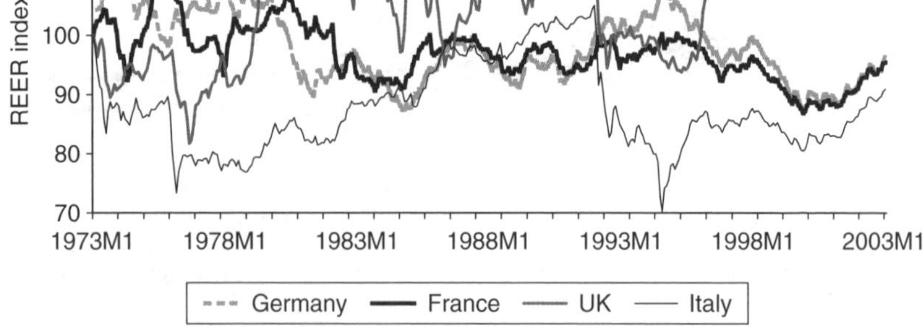

Figure 11.3 Real effective exchange rates. *Source*: OECD (2004)

Table 11.2 Variability of the real effective exchange rates (Standard deviation of the monthly REER)

	1974–2004	1974–1984	1984–1994	1994–2004	1999–2004
UK	5.3	5.2	3.6	5.3	2.7
Germany	4.6	4.5	2.4	3.8	2.5
France	12.5	14.5	6.8	12.3	2.5
Italy	9.5	5.2	7.7	4.6	3.6

Source: OECD (2004).

average for the previous year). Greece's central rate represented a devaluation of 15.4%. The implication is that, with the approval of the Council, it is possible to devalue so as to set an appropriate exchange rate for EMU entry. Once in the ERM, the UK would have to maintain the exchange rate without devaluation or other significant tensions for a period of up to two years,[8] though for political reasons it would be very hard for any UK government to take the country into the mechanism. Thus, negotiating for the entry of Sterling into the euro area presents formidable challenges at the EU level. With this one exception, therefore, the UK currently satisfies, and is likely to continue to satisfy, the TEU requirements for euro area entry in the near future.

11.3.5 Balance of payments and trade

Membership of the ERM was associated with a deterioration in the current account of the UK's balance of payments, but the devaluation which followed the exit from the system was followed by an improvement in trading position (Table 11.3). The current account balance narrowed and the UK's share of world trade in goods rose from 1993 to 1997 (Figure 11.4). But since then, the high value of Sterling and the relatively rapid rate of UK growth has resulted in a deteriorating balance of payments and a shrinking share of world trade. The persistent misalignment of Sterling between 1997

Table 11.3 UK balance of payments current account and share of world trade

	1991	1992	1993	1994	1995	1996	1997	1998	1999	2000	2001	2002	2003	2004
Balance of current transactions with the rest of the world % GDP														
UK	−1.8	−2.1	−1.9	−1.0	−1.3	−0.9	−0.1	−0.5	−2.3	−2.1	−2.3	−1.7	−1.9	−2.0
Share of world exports including intra-EU trade %														
UK	5.3	5.1	4.6	4.8	4.7	4.9	5.0	5.0	4.7	4.3	4.7	4.6	4.4	

Source: Commission (2003a, 2004a).

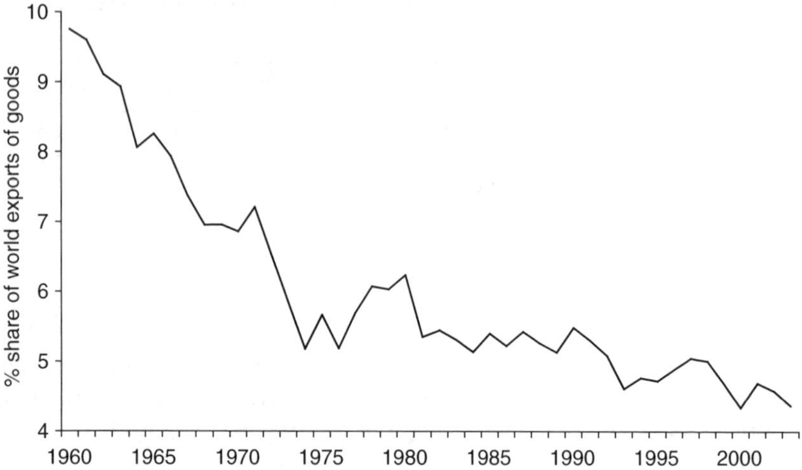

Figure 11.4 UK share of world exports of goods. *Source*: Commission (2004a)

and the middle of 2002 has caused costly imbalances in the real economy (Buiter and Grafe, 2003b: 27).

Permanently fixing the exchange rate of the pound against the euro would not of course eliminate all exchange rate variability because real effective exchange rates can still change as a result of differences in inflation rates. The external value of the euro can also fluctuate. Whether fixing the exchange rate of Sterling against the euro will stabilise the exchange rate, will depend upon four factors:

1. The proportion of total trade, that is with the euro area
2. The difference in the variability between the euro and Sterling and between Sterling and non-euro area currencies
3. The nature of the exchange rate variability, in terms of volatility and misalignments. Volatility is shown by random fluctuations around the long-run trend. Misalignments, by contrast, are large movements away from long-run trends with real exchange rates becoming over- or under-valued for extended periods. Volatility can largely be dealt with (at some cost) but misalignments, if they are sustained, can have more profound effects.[9]
4. The sensitivity of non-trade transactions to variations in exchange rates.

Fixing Sterling against the euro should stabilise the UK exchange rate for two reasons. First, in 2002, just over half of UK trade in goods and services was with the euro area (ONS, 2004). Second, there is no clear correlation of movements of the pound vis-à-vis other currencies (Figure 11.5). The variability of the euro exchange does seem to have been higher since the launch

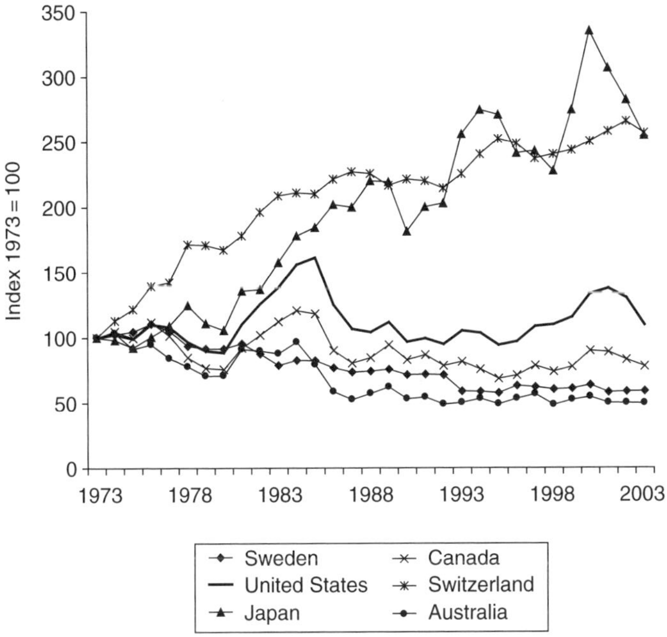

Figure 11.5 Euro exchange rates 1973–2003. *Source*: Commission (2004e)

of the system, but while there is an increase in variability compared with the 1990s, the experience is not out of line with that which occurred during the 1980s.

That membership of the euro area will increase UK exchange rate stability is contested by Bootle (2001), who argues that the rest of the world is more important for UK international transactions than the euro area and that joining the euro would not increase stability for our foreign trade. This, it is argued, is because the euro area's share of UK trade in services, investment income and transfers is much less than 50%. Trade in goods is obviously sensitive to the exchange rate and the euro area accounted for 58.5% of UK trade in goods in the 1996–2003 period. Some services, such as transport and travel, are also sensitive to exchange rate movements, while others (such as financial and business services) are perhaps less so. The euro area is a less significant partner for services than for goods, accounting for 37.3% of the value of transactions. Nevertheless, the euro area accounted for 52.2% of transactions in goods and services and probably a higher share of the more exchange rate-sensitive transactions. Nearly two-thirds of investment income is outside the euro area but the effect of fluctuations in exchange rates is not clear. Obviously, the Sterling value of investment income is affected but the market response to exchange rate volatility is ambiguous.

There can be no demand response and the supply response would be on the volume and direction of portfolio and foreign direct investment (FDI). Exchange rate volatility, because of its effect on risk, may discourage foreign investment, but the diversification of portfolios and FDI may, in contrast, be encouraged. Consequently, the inclusion of investment income in an assessment of exchange rate-sensitive transactions is questionable.

Two other issues are raised by Bootle (2001): the UK trade balance in the long run and dollar invoicing/pricing. While population and growth projections might suggest an increasing importance of non-euro area trade in the future, the expansion of the euro area membership and the consequent relative growth of intra-EU trade will increase UK trade with the euro area. The currency of invoicing seems a red herring because of the weak linkage between invoicing and pricing and, in any case, 63% of UK imports and 72% of UK exports were invoiced in EMU currencies or Sterling in 1999 (Bootle, 2001: 17). It is also true that a number of goods have their international prices set in US dollars. Allowing for this effect may marginally reduce the significance of the euro in UK current account transactions. The crucial point is that the current situation does not allow the UK to stabilise the value of Sterling. Fixing the exchange rate against the euro would eliminate a significant amount of existing exchange rate instability. Unless the euro were to be very much more unstable than Sterling, then, overall, joining the euro area will represent an increase in exchange rate stability (HM Treasury, 2003c).

11.3.6 Economic growth

Up to 1993 the UK had been one of the slower growing economies in Europe. Between 1974 and 1993 the UK grew at 0.4 percentage points below the EU-15 average.[10] From 1994 to 2003 the UK has, by contrast, enjoyed substantially higher growth, 0.7 percentage points above the EU-15 average and 0.8 points above that of the euro area. Growth in the UK has slowed only slightly since 2000, in contrast to the euro area where it has fallen substantially. The UK has also enjoyed more stable growth, after the adjustment to ERM exit (Figure 11.6). Macroeconomic stability in the UK since the mid-1990s contrasts with the previous instability (Kontolemis and Samiei, 2000; Barrell, 2002). The UK has gone from having one of the lowest rates and highest variability of GDP growth in the EU,[11] in 1974–1993, to having one of the highest rates and lowest variability of growth in 1994–2003 (Table 11.4). This testifies to the success of the current macroeconomic regime in the UK.

11.3.7 Employment and unemployment

The performance of the UK labour market since 1992 has been robust, with falling unemployment and rising employment. Between 1993 and 2003, the UK created nearly 3 million jobs, an increase of 10.9%, raising the UK employment rate by 4.8 percentage points, from 71.7 to 76.6% (Commission, 2004a). The overall increase in employment in the euro area was below the UK's at

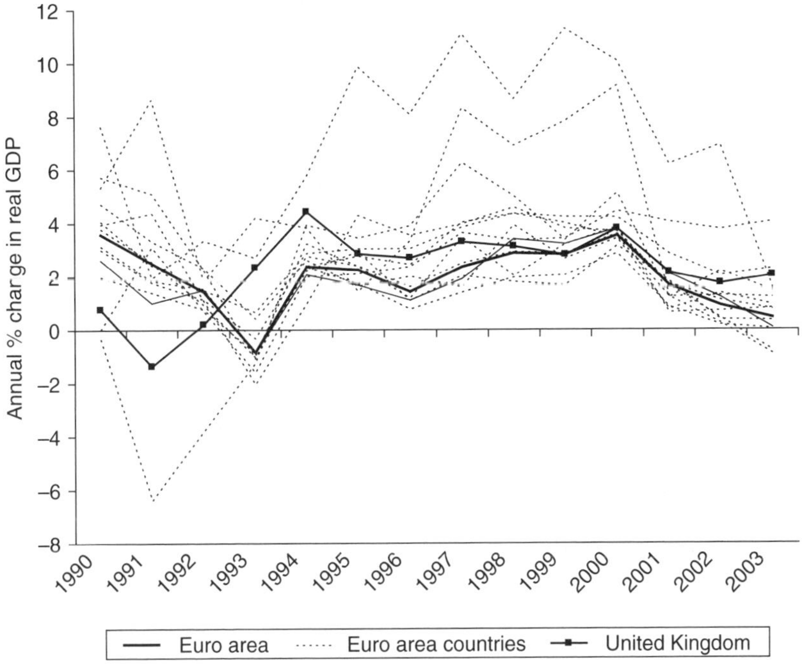

Figure 11.6 GDP growth euro area and UK 1990–2003. *Source*: Commission (2004a)

9.5%, held down by an especially poor performance in Germany, where employment only increased by 1.8%. Even so, several other euro area members[12] created proportionately more employment than the UK. Overall, the employment rate in the euro area rose 4.2 percentage points, from 60.4 to 64.6%.

Table 11.4 Stability of GDP growth 1974–2001 (% annual change)

	1974–1993		1994–2003	
	Average	**Coefficient of variation**	**Average**	**Coefficient of variation**
UK	1.7	1.2	2.9	0.3
Germany	2.3	0.9	1.4	0.7
France	2.2	0.6	2.1	0.6
Italy	2.4	0.9	1.7	0.5
EMU 12 average	2.2	0.6	2.1	0.5
EMU 12 range	1.3–3.8	0.6–2.3	1.4–7.9	0.3–0.7

Source: Commission (2004a).

Given the already high level of employment in the UK, however, it is clear that higher GDP growth has facilitated a strong employment performance.

Whether the overall efficiency of the labour market has improved is perhaps best examined by two summary measures: the non-accelerating inflation rate of unemployment (NAIRU) and the Beveridge curve. The NAIRU measures the level of unemployment necessary to stabilise inflation, while the Beveridge curve depicts the relationship between unemployment and vacancies, reflecting the extent to which the unemployed are able to fill the available jobs.

11.3.8 The non-accelerating inflation rate of unemployment (NAIRU)

Estimates of the NAIRU suggest that the efficiency of the EU-15 labour market[13] declined from 1980 until the early 1990s, with the result that higher levels of unemployment were required to constrain inflation. In the second half of the 1990s, the EU-15 NAIRU fell, signalling an improvement in labour market efficiency. This improvement in the NAIRU is apparent for all EU countries except Germany, Greece, Luxembourg and Austria. The NAIRU does, however, seem to follow the trend in unemployment, casting some doubt on the independence of this measure (Figure 11.7).

There is a clear improvement in the Phillips curve relationship for the UK from the mid-1980s onwards, with increasingly low levels of unemployment being associated with low consumer price inflation (Figure 11.8). Estimates indicate that the UK's NAIRU has improved more than most EU Member States, having fallen continuously since 1984, from over 10% in 1985 to just over 5% in 2002. The Phillips curve estimated on the CPI, however, probably paints a flattering picture for two reasons. First, the rise of Sterling in the 1990s has been an important constraining factor on consumer prices. Second, the official unemployment figures probably understate the true extent of the problem.

The unemployment rate is an unreliable measure of labour market conditions. This is due to the labour market's response to changing employment conditions and the effect of government measures on unemployment. In particular, it appears that in the UK a considerable proportion of unemployment is hidden by government measures, so that to evaluate labour market performance, it is essential that account be taken of this hidden unemployment (Dickens *et al.*, 2001; Beatty *et al.*, 2002). The hidden unemployed in the UK are mainly drawing sickness and invalidity benefits, and there has been a very large increase in the number of the people on these benefits in the 1980s. To estimate the number of workers who have 'disappeared' from the unemployment statistics the following procedure was followed. The age and sex distribution sickness of claimants for 1972, well before the numbers started to swell, was used to calculate the expected proportion of claimants in each age and sex group. These proportions were simply applied to the population in each year between 1983 and 2001 to obtain an expected number of claimants.

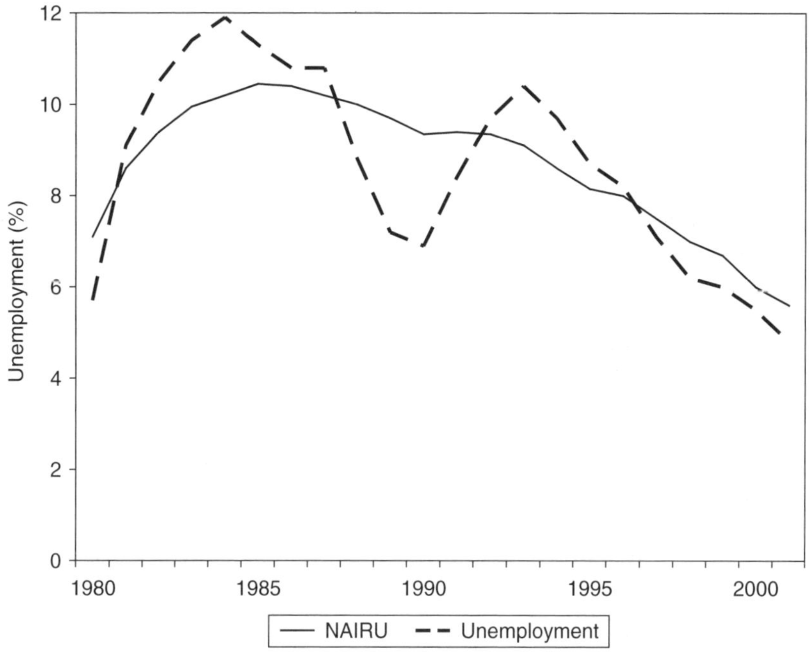

Figure 11.7 UK NAIRU and unemployment. *Source*: Commission (2002a); OECD (2002a)

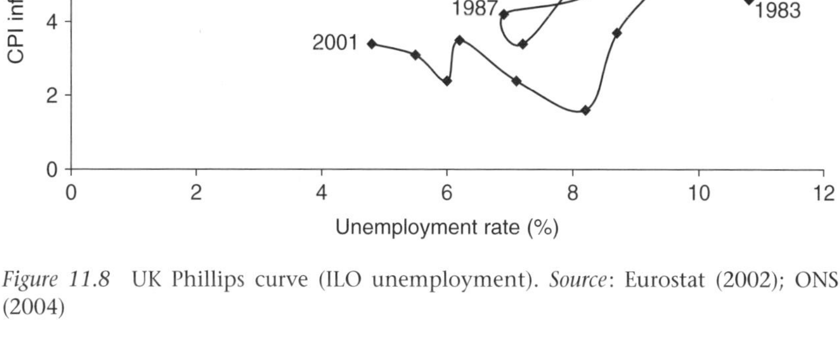

Figure 11.8 UK Phillips curve (ILO unemployment). *Source*: Eurostat (2002); ONS (2004)

The expected number of claimants calculated in this way was subtracted from the actual claimants to obtain a measure of hidden unemployment.

With this adjustment it is possible to compare inflation measured by the percentage change in the Consumer Price Index (CPI), with both ILO unemployment[14] (Figure 11.8) and the sum of ILO and hidden (ILOH) unemployment (Figure 11.9). It can be seen that on these measures, both unemployment and inflation rose at the end of the 1980s, with the end of the Lawson boom. Then, from 1990, inflation fell sharply and there was a marginal reduction in unemployment. From 1993, unemployment fell, while inflation remained at a low level. This indicates an improvement in the NAIRU since, from 1993 onwards, the observations lie below and to the left of the earlier ones, indicating that low inflation is occurring in conjunction with low unemployment. The NAIRU again improves when ILOH unemployment is used but the movement is smaller.

The reduction in the NAIRU in most of the EU-15 and the UK is widely believed to be the result of the effects of more flexible labour market policies on equilibrium unemployment. The UK does seem to have improved the trade-off between inflation and unemployment, even when hidden unemployment is taken into account. Since 2001, unemployment has fallen further and inflation has remained low, but confirmation of this improvement awaits a longer period of observation, particularly as UK inflation is no longer restrained by the exchange rate.

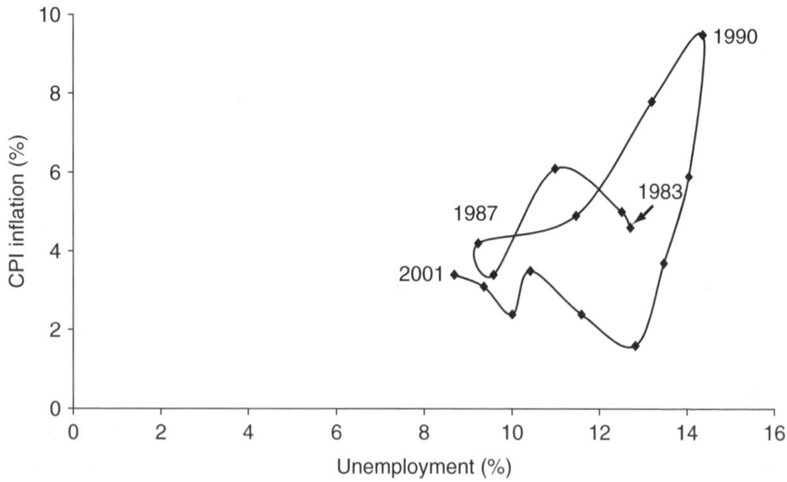

Figure 11.9 UK Phillips curve (ILO + hidden unemployment). *Source*: Eurostat (2002); ONS (2004)

11.3.9 Unemployment and vacancies: The Beveridge curve

The Beveridge curve shows the relationship between vacancies and unemployment, and provides another general measure of the efficiency of the labour market (ECB, 2002b). Unemployment should be inversely related to vacancies because as unemployment rises it will become easier to fill vacancies and their number will fall. Over the economic cycle, there should be movements along the curve, but shifts of the curve would indicate changes in the efficiency of the labour market. An outward shift, where the unemployment associated with a given level of vacancies increases, indicates a deterioration in the matching efficiency of the labour market. Such an outward shift seems to have occurred for all EU countries[15] between 1960 and the mid-1980s (Nickell *et al.*, 2002). An inward shift indicates a reduced level of unemployment associated with a given level of vacancies, an improvement in the matching efficiency of the labour market. The euro area Beveridge curve seems to have shifted outwards in the 1990s.[16] The shifts are most pronounced in Belgium, Germany, Italy, Sweden and (to a lesser extent) France, Austria and Finland. Thus, although the poor labour market performance of Germany looms large, this is a more general phenomenon across the EU. The Beveridge curves for the Netherlands, Denmark and the UK are, however, exceptions, having shifted inwards over the same period (Nickell *et al.*, 2002; ECB, 2002b).

When ILO unemployment is compared with vacancies for the UK, the expected inward shift of the Beveridge curve can be observed. The observations for 1983–1988 are above those for 1989–2001 (Figure 11.10). This indicates that the UK labour market has become more efficient at converting potential

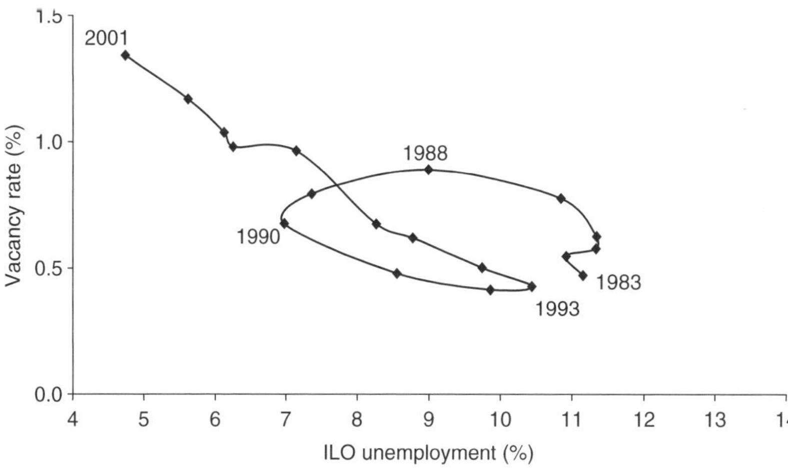

Figure 11.10 UK Beveridge curve (ILO unemployment). *Source*: Eurostat (2002); ONS (2004)

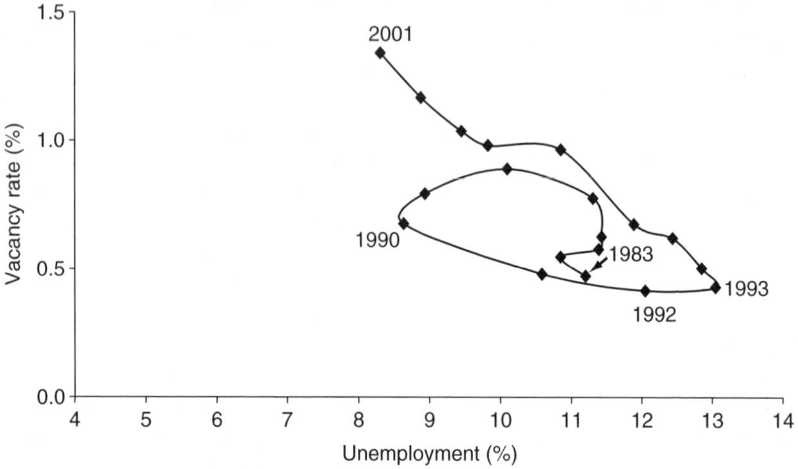

Figure 11.11 UK Beveridge curve (ILO+Hidden Unemployment). *Source*: Eurostat (2002); ONS (2004)

jobs (vacancies) into actual employment. If, however, vacancies are plotted against ILOH unemployment (Figure 11.11), the Beveridge curve now appears to shift outwards. The observations for 1983–1992 lie below those for 1993–2001. The UK labour market on these figures has become less efficient. More vacancies are associated with each level of unemployment. Thus the improvement in UK labour market performance is apparent only when the steep rise in UK hidden unemployment is ignored.

11.3.10 Investment

Investment is a necessary requirement for increasing productivity, acknowledged to be the basis of future growth. One of the factors underlying the UK's relatively low level of productivity is its small capital stock. There are two crucial factors determining the level of investment. First, there is the expected return, taking account of the uncertainty attached to these flows of returns; then, second, there is the cost and availability of finance which also significantly influences the level of investment.

Uncertainty is an important determinant of fixed capital investment (Carruth *et al.*, 2000) but its effect varies across industries and types of capital goods (HM Treasury, 2003d). Two particular forms of uncertainty have affected UK investment in the past, relating to the rate of economic growth and the exchange rate. Exchange rate volatility has been shown to have a negative long-run effect on investment in France, Germany and the US but only temporary effects in the UK and Italy (Darby *et al.*, 1999). Sustained exchange rate misalignment is, however, found to have a negative effect on long-run investment in the UK, France and USA. There may, however, be an aggregation problem, because not all investment is sensitive to the effect of the exchange rate and the assumption of exogeneity of investment is questionable. Thus, in disaggregated studies the real exchange rate is shown to have an important impact on export performance in contrast to the results of aggregate studies (Carlin *et al.*, 2001: 140). Exchange rate misalignment has contributed to the two-speed economy characteristic of recent UK economic performance, with recession in the exchange rate-sensitive manufacturing sector but a booming service sector. Manufacturing investment is thus probably too low and service sector investment too high. While this may have contributed to job creation, it may also have been a limiting factor in productivity growth and led to associated problems for UK trade.

Greater stability of growth has, arguably, contributed to an upturn in business investment (HM Treasury, 2003a: 140), although this investment has been concentrated on the service sector, again reflecting the unbalanced nature of the UK's recent economic performance. The effect of euro area membership on investment will depend crucially upon its effects on uncertainty. It seems probable that greater exchange rate stability will be achieved and this will give a significant boost to manufacturing investment. The effects on macroeconomic variability more generally are a matter of some dispute. It is likely that there will be some short-term instability associated with acclimatisation to euro area membership, but overall it seems unlikely that euro area membership would have a significant impact on the long-term cost of capital (HM Treasury, 2003e). There would be a reduction in short-term interest rates, but this could be at the expense of macroeconomic stability.

11.3.11 Foreign direct investment

The Single Market Programme had clear effects on the level of inward investment into the UK (Arrowsmith *et al.*, 1997; Dunning, 1997; Pain, 1997). The UK has been an attractive location with a welcoming business environment and comparatively low labour cost per unit of output, with guaranteed access to the EU market. In remaining outside the euro area, the UK faces a currency barrier to trade and uncertain costs of production. Thus EMU seems likely both to stimulate further FDI and to encourage its location within the euro area.

Exchange variability adds additional uncertainty to returns from investment overseas and so may discourage it. There are, however, gains from production flexibility and from diversifying risk which may encourage FDI in the presence of exchange rate volatility (Aizenman, 1992; Goldberg and Kolstad, 1995). Operating several plants in different currency zones makes it possible to move production in response to the effect of exchange rates on costs. Producing within a currency zone ensures that the revenue and costs are denominated in the same currency, avoiding a large element of exchange rate uncertainty.

Given the unclear theoretical picture, it is not surprising that empirical studies provide ambiguous results. Exchange rate volatility is found to reduce FDI into the US, according to Campa (1993), but to increase it according to Goldberg and Kolstad (1995) and De Ménil (1999). These contradictory results may be due to the effect of exchange rate volatility varying with the type of investment and the size of the economy. The fact that US and Japanese firms in the UK export a large proportion of their output to Europe may explain why they are particularly keen on UK membership of EMU (Pain, 1997: 105). Interpreting recent FDI flows is difficult, because of the lags in the process and the impact of overall economic conditions. The UK share of EU inward flows has fallen since the start of Stage 3 in 1999, but it has maintained its share of extra EU inward flows (Treasury, 2003a: 155–7). On the basis of this evidence it seems unlikely that joining EMU and reducing currency volatility would have very large effects on inward FDI in the UK.

There is, however, clear evidence that location decisions by foreign companies are significantly influenced by the relative cost of production (Pain, 1997). Thus the rate at which Sterling enters EMU will have an impact on FDI. Since it will take a considerable time for changes in relative prices to correct any misalignment and since the effects could be long-lived, this indicates the importance of achieving entry at realistic rate.

11.4 Recent economic performance overall

Compared with the period after the first oil shock in 1974, the recent performance of the UK economy has improved. A relatively high and stable rate of economic growth has been achieved, leading to a sustained increase in employment and reduction in unemployment. Unlike other periods of growth, this one has been sustained over a period that now stretches back over 13 years without the 'stops' that characterised previous decades. Another difference from the past is that inflation has been restrained despite a tight labour market. The government's financial position has been sound and, despite a moderate increase in the deficit in the last couple of years, borrowing has been low.

This growth has, however, been unbalanced and accompanied by an accumulation of problems that may hinder its continuation. It is founded upon demand primarily from consumers, who became increasingly indebted as a result, and more recently from an expansion of government expenditure. Consumers' increased debt was made possible by reduced nominal servicing costs and the collateral of increasing house prices. This borrowing is now at historically very high levels and a slowing in its growth, or in house price growth, could result in an unpleasant period of adjustment. Concerns over these developments have been one factor increasing short-term interest rates and contributing to a rise in the exchange rate which has had an adverse impact on the manufacturing sector. However, the service sector has remained buoyant and, because it accounts for such a high share of total output, the economy as a whole has prospered, though one consequence of high growth has been an escalating balance of payments deficits. The adjustment of these imbalances could be smooth, but it could also cause a significant shock to the economy. So far so good, but the success of UK economic policy outside the euro area will have to be judged in a longer perspective.

11.5 Suitability of euro area economic policy for the UK

Whether the common euro area monetary policy is suitable for the UK depends upon three factors. First, the common monetary policy might have different effects on the UK. In particular, the UK might be more sensitive to interest rate changes. Second, the UK could be subject to different shocks from other euro area countries. The third is whether the UK economy has enough flexibility to adjust in the absence of an independent monetary policy and exchange rate.

It is possible that the sensitivity of output to interest rate changes differs among countries. Unfortunately studies that have sought to evaluate asymmetries in monetary policy transmission have failed to provide consistent and robust estimates of cross-country differences (Kieler and Saarenheimo, 1998; Guiso *et al.*, 1999; HM Treasury, 2003b). There are undoubtedly differences between EU countries, which could affect the transmission of monetary policy to output, such as the structure of banking, the interest sensitivity of output, household debt, size and composition of household assets, openness to trade, the character of bank finance to business, structure of firms and their gearing. The UK housing market was especially prominent in the assessment of the 'five tests' because of the size of mortgage-related debts, while the preponderance in the British housing finance market of variable interest rates is seen as a particular problem (Meen, 2003; Muellbauer, 2003). The range of these possibilities and the differences between countries suggest that although there are some indications that the UK (and Sweden) may be more sensitive to interest rate changes, this is only a tentative possibility (Suardi, 2001). Moreover, Byrne and Davis (2002) suggest that differences between UK and continental financial systems may have been exaggerated. The UK is found to have much in common with the continental countries, especially France, and there is some evidence of convergence towards a more market-oriented system, even in the most bank-oriented country, Germany.

If the common monetary policy is to be suitable, then the shocks experienced by the UK should be similar to the euro area average in timing and magnitude. Many studies have analysed shocks in the EU (OECD, 1999b: 93–7). One of the chief questions considered by this literature is the extent to which there is a core group of countries with a high degree of commonality in their economic cycles. Structural vector auto regressive models have been used to make this assessment. Bayoumi and Eichengreen (1993), in a notable paper, established that there was a core of European countries with closely related economic cycles and that the UK was not part of this core. These results have largely been confirmed by other studies (Helg *et al.*, 1995; Artis and Zhang, 1999; Kontolemis and Samiei, 2000).

Although the correlation of the UK's with the euro area's business cycle has increased recently (Artis, 2003), this has been with a robust growth of consumer demand and a much tighter monetary policy than the euro area. The UK remains more correlated with the euro area than some members and less so than others. If the UK joined EMU, the lower exchange rate and lower euro area interest rates in the UK would boost economic activity in the UK, increasing demand and output and putting pressure on inflation, although the UK's low rate of inflation means that there is some room for manoeuvre.

That the UK business cycle did not coincide with that of Europe is not surprising. Economic policy was very different because Sterling was only part of the ERM for a comparatively brief period. Artis and Zhang (1999: 130) show that 'a higher degree of synchronisation of business cycles is indeed associated with a lower volatility of exchange rates'. It is not only the exchange rate, but also monetary policy (Kontolemis and Samiei, 2000) that is important in explaining the UK's economic cycle. Even now the UK has not stabilised the value of Sterling against the euro, but two factors may have increased the correlation of UK and euro area economic cycles. The first is the greater stability of UK macroeconomic policy-making, formalised in the independence of monetary policy under the Bank of England, while the second is the increasing integration of the UK economy into the EU.

Adopting the euro could itself lead to further integration of the UK economy into the euro area, further increasing the correspondence of economic cycles. Some changes contingent upon joining a monetary union should increase convergence, such as increasing levels of trade, competition and price transparency. Generally economists suggest that the effect on trade of reducing exchange rate volatility is relatively small (FitzGerald and Honohan, 1997). This result is questioned by Rose (2000), who, in a cross-section study of 186 countries, found that trade between countries that shared a common currency was three times the level expected. This result has been challenged, because of the small number of same currency observations, most involving small underdeveloped countries, often colonial/post-colonial monetary unions associated with many other changes affecting trade (Honohan, 2001). The data used by Rose (2000) also contain very few examples of currency switching, that is adopting or abandoning a common currency. More recent work suggests that the currency effect, although reduced, still remains very substantial (Rose, 2003) and much was made in the Treasury's 'five tests' assessment of this factor. The applicability of these results to monetary unions involving larger well-developed countries is thrown into doubt by a recent study of the ending of the link between the Irish punt and Sterling in 1979 (Thom and Walsh, 2002). This suggests that the ending of the Sterling link had negligible and statistically insignificant impact on the level of Anglo-Irish trade.

11.6 Conclusion

Following the comprehensive assessment conducted in 2003 and the conclusion that the UK was not yet sufficiently convergent, it seems probable that the UK is going to remain outside the euro area for a considerable period. This is, however, less a problem of whether the economy is capable of adjusting to EMU than a political challenge. The UK meets the convergence criteria for entry, except for the exchange rate, and with the pound apparently settling in a much narrower range since it retreated from the peak reached in 2001, even this could be resolved if the 15% fluctuation margin were used. Consequently, the conclusion has to be that the UK can easily achieve Stage 2 adjustment and has moreover been, for some time, in as strong a position to do so as most of the inaugural euro area members. The political challenge arises from, on the one hand, the self-imposed requirement to have a referendum, combined with a lack of public support; and, on the other, from the perception that the UK has 'done better' by staying outside the euro area. This creates a policy bind. Because of the requirement that the economic case be 'clear and unambiguous', a formulation that inevitably demands judgement and for which there are no explicit benchmarks, the economic analysis of the five tests can never provide a definitive answer. Instead, the decision is ultimately an issue of political will.

Compared to the larger EU Member States, the UK's economic situation outside the euro area has been pleasanter than that of France, Italy and Germany within. This raises two issues. First, to what extent is this success the result of remaining outside the euro area? Second, how permanent is the success?

Outside the euro, the UK has developed a successful model of macroeconomic policy that has delivered the sought-after conjunction of stable and sustainable growth, low unemployment and low inflation. Monetary policy since 1999 has been somewhat tighter in the UK than in the euro area, with higher short-term real interest rates and, for some of the period, a high real exchange rate, despite low inflation. Fiscal policy has also been looser than it would be if the UK were strictly respecting the rules of the Stability and Growth Pact.[17] Whether this is the correct policy stance is arguable: a tighter fiscal policy and looser monetary policy, with a lower exchange rate, might have delivered a more balanced expansion as between tradables and non-tradables. But the same conjunction could have aggravated asset market problems, especially in the property market. Nevertheless, results in the short term speak for themselves and UK economic policies in the early period of the euro have assured successful stabilisation policy.

With regard to the long term, some nagging doubts remain. The economic expansion has been very unbalanced, dependent on services and with little growth in manufacturing output. This has been accompanied by an unprecedented expansion of consumer debt, house price inflation and a growing deficit on the balance of payments' current account. The adjustment of these imbalances may be smooth, but there is the chance of a difficult economic period. Membership of the euro area, associated with increasing integration, could provide a more stable long-term economic policy for the UK by offering a means of resolving the problem of exchange rate instability and misalignment. Yet the paradox is that although EMU may offer a more suitable long-term economic policy, short-term adjustment may well be easier outside the euro area. The politics also point to continuing non-membership. It seems as if the UK will continue with its Augustinian policy towards EMU 'O God make me a member but not just yet'.

12
The New Members: Big Bang or Slow Transition to Stage 3?

The ten new members that joined the EU in 2004 face a tantalising dilemma: should they aim to participate fully in Stage 3 of the euro as soon as possible, or retain monetary autonomy until their economies have adjusted more fully to the challenges of full EU membership? Plainly, their circumstances differ and, in many ways, these circumstances reflect the challenges of adjustment analysed in previous chapters. Six of the new members are very small economies which can expect to becoming increasingly open as they integrate, three are medium-sized, while Poland has a population comparable to Spain of 39 million. However, collectively, the GDP of the new members, measured in purchasing power terms, is barely 5% of the EU25 total.

In this chapter, we first explore the case for rapid entry into Stage 3 and consider the challenges of adjustment faced by the new members. We then present a more detailed assessment of one of the new members, Estonia, one of the three Baltic States that became independent from the Soviet Union in 1992, as it has chosen the fast track of membership at the earliest possible date.

12.1 To join or not to join?

The decision for the new Member States that acceded to the EU in 2004 on whether or not to participate fully in monetary union is a crucial one which will necessarily require a balancing of different considerations. On the one hand, as Leszek Balcerowicz (President of the National Bank of Poland) explained in 2001,[1] early 'entry of the candidate countries into EMU would allow them to start reaping the related advantages (more price transparency, reduced transformation costs, stronger macroeconomic framework)' as quickly as possible and would help to consolidate the momentum towards structural reforms. He also argues that setting a firm deadline is advantageous and that his reasoning is applicable to most of the new members. CEPS (2002), similarly, supports early EMU entry for most of the new members on the grounds that a stable macroeconomic framework is an essential precondition for real convergence.

Opponents of early participation in EMU, on the other hand, are concerned that EMU will impose too rigid a macroeconomic policy framework on countries which are bound to face turbulent times as they continue to restructure. The new members will have to cope with the demands of transition not only to a market economy, but also the EU single market (for a summary, see Landesmann and Richter, 2003). The core of this latter position is that a greater degree of flexibility will be required and that the capacity to adapt monetary conditions and alter the nominal exchange rate will be essential tools. There is also a significant risk of greater macroeconomic volatility from early membership of ERM II (Pelkmans and Hobza, 2002), a system that requires a fair degree of nominal convergence to be generally beneficial for its participants, but could prove to be damaging if exchange rates tend to diverge.

Rostowski (2003) also highlights the risk of macroeconomic instability, a possible 'capital inflow stop' and thus a risk of currency depreciation, but he draws the opposite conclusion that the answer is to move rapidly to adopt the euro. He argues, in particular, that the effect may be to damage the prospects for real convergence and that this is the worst possible outcome, especially if pressures for easy monetary policy create unsustainable short-term booms or at least tend to be pro-cyclical. Rowstowski also notes that most central and eastern European countries (CEEC) have trade patterns that are at least as consistent with OCA theory as existing euro area members. Even Poland, the largest, has many of the requisite characteristics.

In a statement of its policy position on enlargement of the euro area, the ECB (2003b: 1) notes that while the new members are obliged 'to treat their exchange rate policy as a matter of common interest and to pursue price stability as the primary objective of monetary policy', they are free initially to adopt their own monetary strategy. However, not following the prescribed path towards full participation in EMU is a derogation rather than a choice, and the new members are expected to join the ERM and to move towards meeting the Maastricht convergence criteria in order to be eligible to adopt the euro. The ECB makes clear that any other route to 'euroisation' (for example unilateral adoption of the single currency) is 'outside the Treaty framework [and] would run counter to the economic reasoning underlying Economic and Monetary Union, which foresees the eventual adoption of the euro as the end-point of a structured convergence process within a multilateral framework'.

The ECB note confronts the option of a currency board arrangement which it finds acceptable, provided that it is within the framework of ERM II, but not as a substitute for ERM II membership. The ECB (2003b: 3) signals that a new member 'may therefore participate in ERM II with a currency board as a unilateral commitment, enhancing the discipline within ERM II.

However, the ECB has stressed that such an arrangement will be assessed on a case-by-case basis and that a common accord on the central parity against the euro will have to be reached.' Part of the challenge of ERM II is to establish a central parity that is close to being an equilibrium exchange rate, and the ECB also recommends prior attention to the fiscal position and price liberalisation.

But the ECB also highlights the importance of taking account of the prospects for catch-up and real convergence and points to the risks associated with premature exchange rate rigidity. The Lisbon Agenda also has to be seen as an essential complement to EMU. For the new members, it can be argued that bringing these supply-side considerations into the equation must be part of the decision on how rapidly to move to full participation in EMU.

A specific challenge for the larger new members will be how to respond – if at all – to the widening of regional disparities. The evidence shows that capital-regions have gained most from the post-communist transition, and the experience of Portugal, Ireland and Greece suggests that market forces have favoured agglomeration in favoured regions at the expense of the most backward regions. To illustrate the point, according to the Commission's Cohesion reports and updates (Commission, 2003l and 2004b,h), the Mazowieckie region (which includes Warsaw) converged from 43% of EU GDP to 62% between 1995 and 2001, whereas the Lubelskie region on the Polish eastern border only advanced from 26% to just over 28% of the EU average.[2] In Slovakia, the contrast is equally pronounced between the Bratislavský region (from 91.5 to 101) and the Východné Slovensko region in the east of the country (which diverges from 36.4 to 34.0), while in Hungary Közép-Magyarország, the region that includes Budapest, moves from 65.7 to 81.3, compared with Észak-Magyarország on the north east border with Poland which converged only from 33.1 to 33.7.

12.1.1 The exchange rate as an adjustment mechanism for the new members

The question of whether the new members would do well to retain the exchange rate as an instrument of adjustment in the early years of EU membership depends on the likely form of shocks. In essence, if shocks are financial or monetary, an independent exchange rate will be damaging, whereas if shocks mainly affect demand, then a relative price movement brought about by an exchange rate movement may be beneficial. A study by Borghijs and Kuijs (2004) surveys the evidence on the experience of the CEECs in this regard and suggests that although the exchange rate may have been useful in dealing with real economy shocks in larger countries, in smaller economies it has not. They explore how useful exchange rates have been in resolving shocks in five CEEC and conclude that exchange rate variability has probably been unhelpful or even counter-productive.

A notable aspect of exchange rate positions of the CEECs, according to Coudert and Couharde (2002: 33), 'was the process of continuous real appreciation seen in the last decade, [implying] that exchange rates were substantially undervalued in the early transition period'. They suggest that early entry into Stage 3 could be potentially damaging not only for the new members, but could also 'affect market confidence in all EU countries, and thus be at the root of a contagion phenomenon spreading over'. They also draw attention to the infrastructure needs of the new members and the difficulties likely to arise in sticking to the SGP limit of 3% deficits if public funds are called upon to fund infrastructure development. However, Coudert and Couharde note that the new members would gain from early entry into Stage 3, because it would greatly diminish nominal exchange rate volatility and avoid excessive real appreciation.

Landesmann and Richter (2003) note, though, that in recent years several of the CEECs suffered 'major exchange rate crises which entailed exchange rate realignments (Czech Republic 1997, Slovak Republic 1999; see also the realignment in Poland 2002, etc.)'. They therefore contend that joining EMU swiftly could necessitate the over-riding of other macroeconomic policies while at the same time slowing structural reforms. Both could result in heavy costs in terms of output foregone. They also point to the fact that one potential adjustment mechanism – migration – will be even weaker than it is at present in EU-15 because of the agreement on a seven-year transitional period during which the restrictions will remain in place on migrants from the new members. A further important element in the macroeconomic assessment of early EMU entry is whether capital flows are likely to have a destabilising impact. In this regard, the free capital movement that characterises all current and new EU members means that there is limited scope for dealing with destabilising capital flows.

However, choice over what to do next depends very much on the choice that has already been made. Those countries with currency boards based on the euro or hard pegs to the euro will have a strong motivation to persevere, as moving to another strategy – even in the interim – would represent a step away from the goal not towards it. As a result it would be easy for this to damage the credibility of the process and for it to impose inflation costs on the economy. It is probably the inflation-targeting countries that have the greatest freedom of choice.

12.1.2 Dealing with differences in the price level

The new members have, in addition, to take account of likely Balarsa–Samuelson effects. The low price level and the under-developed service sectors in the eight CEECs that joined in 2004 imply that there will be some appreciation of the real exchange rate, as has already occurred. Fischer (2002: 26) argues that while this effect has arisen, it is not purely because of standard BS effects, but is more to do with high demand for investment. He argues that the 'upward pressure on the real exchange rates of transition countries should be expected to continue in the future if these countries enjoy further productivity gains', and he notes that an implication is the likelihood of continuing inflation differentials if the new members accede rapidly to EMU. The impact of this effect is limited by two factors: first the share of non-tradeables in consumption is relatively low at around 28% (IMF, 2003c: 30). Second productivity growth has been relatively high in the non-tradeable sector (Halpern and Wyplosz, 1997).

Nevertheless, it is likely that price convergence will continue and empirical estimates (see Halpern and Wyplosz, 2001; Cihak and Holub, 2003) suggest that if there is real convergence of the order of 2 percentage points per annum, it will be associated with a slightly lower real exchange rate appreciation. In addition, as Cihak and Holub point out, price convergence may be accelerated for reasons other than the conventional BS effect. If so, one of two problems for eligibility for Stage 3 will arise, depending on the exchange rate regime in operation. For new members that operate currency boards, the real appreciation will have to be accommodated by higher inflation, which could threaten achievement of the Maastricht inflation criterion during the period when convergence is being assessed. Where there is nominal exchange rate flexibility, on the other hand, it will be the stability of the exchange rate that is threatened. A crucial issue, therefore, will be whether the 15% ERM band or a much narrower band is applied in assessing the Maastricht exchange rate criterion.

12.1.3 Implications for the euro

Quite apart from the impact on the new members, there is the question of whether full participation by them in Stage 3 would create problems for the conduct of monetary policy. Specifically, since there is the expectation that the new members will have faster growth that is likely to be accompanied by higher inflation, especially if BS effects arise, will monetary policy have to be tighter? The arithmetic is crucial: given the small share of the new members in EU-25 GDP, the impact is unlikely to be great until they have grown substantially. Even if they are measured as being 10% of the euro area economy – well above the current level – every percentage point of excess inflation in the new members would only contribute 0.1% to the euro area HICP. Moreover, not all new members can be expected to impart an inflationary bias.

Rostowski (2003) identifies a further issue which is that additional members of the euro area might induce further strains in an already complicated institutional environment. The SGP as well as the structure of decision-making in the ECB are potential flashpoints, although it is worth recalling that the ECB has already anticipated the problem by deciding on a form of rotation in voting, while the reform of the SGP agreed in March 2005 will ease some of the pressures on fiscal policy. In any case, Rostowski argues that while there may indeed be such strains, they cannot reasonably be adduced as a reason to oppose rapid accession.

12.2 Strategy for adjusting to EMU

For the new members of the EU, the issue of full participation in EMU coalesces into two sets of question: can they pass the entry tests and can they live with the obligations and consequences of the EMU macroeconomic regime? The Maastricht convergence criteria remain the benchmark for entry and, on the whole, are positive. But living with the euro may be more problematic. A further question is, therefore, how quickly should the new members seek to embrace full monetary union? Three options can be delineated:

1. Entry into Stage 3 of EMU as rapidly as possible, that is a form of big bang. This would entail rapid entry into ERM II as some have done, the adoption of macroeconomic policies aimed at fulfilling the Maastricht convergence criteria within two years and thus an expectation of spending not much more than the minimum period of two years in ERM II.
2. An extended period in ERM II to assist acclimatisation, but with the corollary that monetary policy would remain with the Member State. This might be similar in duration to the Stage 1 and 2 'apprenticeship' followed by the current euro area members following the agreement of the Maastricht Treaty.
3. Retaining flexibility in the exchange rate in order to deal with possible shocks or problems associated with transition both to EU membership and more comprehensive market economy structures. Here the model is more that of Sweden (or, indeed, the UK) where the strategy is to adjust first and only then to go for full participation in Stage 3.

Devereux (2003) models the second and third options and shows that, in most respects, the ERM option is the least attractive for reasons that are well-rehearsed in the literature. Being part of ERM only partly captures the benefits of the fixed exchange rate, notably forgoing the credibility gains that would arise from full participation in EMU, leaving the currency (and the economy) vulnerable. Retaining exchange rate flexibility would, according to Devereux's simulations, make it easier to ensure efficient adjustment to cyclical and structural shocks. A rapid move to full participation in EMU, keeping the transitional ERM II stage to a minimum, may however be better.

12.2.1 Budgetary policy

Large public deficits proved to be the norm during transition, reflecting rising demands for public expenditure (such as compensating for rising unemployment), increasing costs of infrastructure and rising expectations. There were also difficulties with establishing new tax systems and raising tax rates. For most of the countries, the deficits remain high from the perspective of reaching the 3% threshold and there are bound to be new demands for public investment to promote real convergence (Table 12.1). Despite these pressures, all the new members are close to or below the debt

Table 12.1 Maastricht criteria – New members and Mediterranean countries

	Budget deficit	Debt	Inflation	Long-term interest rates
New members 2003				
Cyprus	–5.3	60.3	4.3	**4.6**
Czech Republic	–8.0	**30.7**	**0.0**	**4.1**
Estonia*	+3.1	5.3	1.4	n.a.
Hungary	–5.4	**57.9**	4.6	6.5
Latvia	**–2.7**	**16.7**	**2.5**	**5.1**
Lithuania	**–2.6**	**23.3**	**–0.9**	**5.1**
Malta	–7.6	66.4	**2.7**	**5.8**
Poland	–4.3	**45.1**	**0.7**	**5.9**
Slovakia	–5.1	**45.1**	8.5	**4.9**
Slovenia	**–2.2**	**27.4**	5.9	**5.5**
AC 10 average	–5.0	**42.4**	**2.8**	**5.5**
Criterion 2003	**–3.0**	**60.0**	**2.8**	**6.1**
Mediterranean countries 1995				
Greece	–2.5	108.7	4.5	8.5
Spain	–6.6	63.9	4.6	11.3
Italy	–7.6	123.2	5.4	12.2
Portugal	–5.5	64.3	4.0	8.3
Average	–6.9	102.2	5.0	11.5
Criterion applied	–3.0	60.0	2.7	7.8

Criterion satisfied in bold. * Estonia has no long-dated government debt so it is not clear how this criterion will be assessed.
Source: Commission (2004a).

criterion of 60%, so that to be eligible for Stage 3 of EMU, they do not face the challenge of simultaneous reduction of debt and deficit that, notably, Greece and Italy had to meet. Nevertheless, there has been a trend towards a worsening of the fiscal indicators that has led to more than half the new members attracting censure under the excessive deficit procedure since 2003.

Equally, if the SGP is problematic for growth in EU-15, what about the new members? For Buiter and Grafe (2003a: 2), the answer is clearcut:

> both the Stability and Growth Pact and the Broad Economic Policy Guidelines currently in place are ill-designed to address the economic realities of countries that differ significantly from the current EU average as regards their expected future inflation rates and real GDP growth rates, and their inherited stocks of environmental and public sector capital.

The same authors (Buiter and Grafe, 2002) nevertheless believe that the new members should accede to EMU at the earliest possible opportunity, arguing that the benefits of a correct 'fiscal financial programme' are paramount. But the implication is that the fiscal rules may well water-down the potential benefits. The dilemma here is that EMU is a package deal which includes fiscal rectitude, yet the new members (and indeed countries such as the UK which have neglected public investment) have obvious needs for enhancement of infrastructure and other forms of public capital.

12.2.2 The Maastricht criteria

In assessing the capacity of the new members to fulfil the criteria for Stage 3, it is reasonable to assume that a target for assessing their eligibility will be 2007 or 2008, suggesting that they have three or four years to adjust within ERM II. However, the first three countries – Estonia, Lithuania and Slovenia – joined ERMII on 28 June 2004, so that in theory they could be assessed in mid-2006.

How daunting is the challenge? Here a comparison with the EU-15 Mediterranean countries is instructive. In 2004, the new members were much closer to satisfying the criteria than the Mediterranean Countries were four years before the start of Stage 3 in 1999. Furthermore the debt to GDP ratios of the Mediterranean countries increased by over 20% in the assessments made between the early 1990s and in 1998, whereas debt levels in the new members remain moderate.

The data, therefore, clearly suggest that the new members are much closer to meeting the convergence criteria than the Mediterranean countries were four years before assessment. The inference to draw is that these countries could become euro area members relatively quickly and without enduring excessive trauma, but the question that remains is whether this would be desirable. However, the outlook may be less promising insofar as several of the new members have seen deteriorating fiscal indicators. Indeed, in July 2004, the Council decided that excessive deficits existed in the Czech Republic, Cyprus, Hungary, Malta, Poland and Slovakia, and put forward recommendations for how these deficits should be corrected. These recommendations explicitly recognised the different starting points and different budgetary plans of the Member States concerned and, accordingly, stipulated different adjustment trajectories. Moreover, all bar Cyprus were deemed to have special circumstances in the form of the need for continuing structural adjustment related to their recent accession to the EU. However, in December 2004 all bar Hungary were adjudged to have taken actions that put them on course for dealing with the excessive deficits in line with the earlier recommendations. Hungary was again the subject of recommendations to accelerate its fiscal consolidation, notwithstanding the recognition of special circumstances related to structural reform.

12.3 Living with EMU

If 'Stage 2' adjustment does not look especially problematic, what of the changes that will be needed to function effectively within EMU. There are aspects of the economies of the new members that could enable them to achieve 'Stage 3' adjustment with less difficulty than some existing euro

Table 12.2 Labour costs in the new members and the EU-15 (2000)

	Hourly labour costs in industry and services (€)
EU 15 highest Sweden	28.56
EU 15 average	*22.19*
EU 15 lowest Portugal	8.13
New members	
Cyprus	10.74
Slovenia	8.98
Poland	4.48
Czech Republic	3.90
Hungary	3.83
Slovakia	3.06
Estonia	3.03
Lithuania	2.71
Latvia	2.42

Source: Eurostat (2003).

area members. A crucial one is low nominal labour costs. As can be seen from Table 12.2, the gap is considerable. There are bound to be pressures on wage rates from EU accession itself and from the rapid growth that is anticipated. But there is also plenty of room for manoeuvre. Prospects for productivity growth will also be critical and some new members have an enviable record in this regard. Thus, a factor offsetting wage increases in Estonia, as well as the other Baltic states, is the rapid growth of productivity that has been maintained. Such higher productivity growth may reflect the lower starting point of the Baltic States and also the fact that their transition started later. Even bearing this in mind the productivity growth has been exceptional, as can be seen from the data in Table 12.3.

More generally, because the scope for catch-up in productivity levels is substantial across the CEECs and there is the prospect of increased inward investment, there is a platform for building and sustaining competitiveness. Yet there are also dangers. If pent up consumer demand starts to surface, engendering a surge in imports, the external position could deteriorate, leading to macroeconomic problems. Asset prices might also be a problem if rapid appreciation leads to macroeconomic imbalances that, in turn, fuel wage expectations. The experience of Portugal and Ireland under EMU in this regard is an indicator of what might occur.

The outlook for competitiveness and the capacity to adjust will also be affected by medium-term trends in key supply-side variables central to the Lisbon agenda, such as rates of innovation or the level of investment in R&D. Some new members have tried to make a virtue of making a technological leap forward – for example with the coining of the term 'E'-stonia – and the R&D track record of some CEECs compares relatively favourably

Table 12.3 Growth of GDP per head and per worker 1994–2003 (%)

	GDP per head	GDP per worker
Euro area	*1.7*	*1.2*
Cyprus	2.6	2.1
Czech Republic	2.2	2.4
Estonia	5.4	6.4
Hungary	3.7	3.3
Latvia	5.6	6.5
Lithuania	4.4	5.3
Malta	2.8	2.5
Poland	4.3	4.2
Slovakia	4.1	3.8
Slovenia	3.9	3.5
10 Acceding countries	3.9	3.6

Source: Commission (2004a).

with the 'cohesion' countries in EU 15 (Table 12.4). However, they are well behind compared with the richer Member States, not to mention the Lisbon strategy target of 3% of GDP, and the rates of R&D investment in Cyprus, Latvia, Lithuania, Poland and Slovakia in 2001 were the lowest in the EU 25.

It is, though, important to recognise that despite being the most recent figures for the R&D indicator, they may be misleading in terms of identifying

Table 12.4 R&D spending as a percentage of GDP (average, 1999–2001)

	R&D ratio
Euro area	*1.89*
Greece	0.66
Ireland	1.17
Portugal	0.80
Spain	0.93
Unweighted average for 'cohesion' countries	0.89
Cyprus	0.26
Czech Republic	1.22
Estonia	0.73
Hungary	0.81
Latvia	0.44
Lithuania	0.61
Malta	n.a.
Poland	0.67
Slovakia	0.58
Slovenia	1.49

Source: Commission (2004a).

technological potential. On the one hand, transfers from the EU budget and inward investment can be expected to add substantially to the potential resources for R&D as well as providing scope for technology transfer that is not captured by the R&D indicator. On the other, it may be that the main source of competitive advantage will be more in the diffusion of innovation and the receptiveness to change than in primary investment.

The extent of the balance of payments problems is perhaps better judged by considering the deficit in relation to total exports of goods and services. This is because it is exports (and imports) that will have to change to redress any balancc of payments imbalance. The current account deficits in relation to exports of the new members and the Mediterranean countries are shown in Table 12.5. It can be seen that the deficits of the Baltic countries that operate currency boards are among the largest in the EU. Estonia's very large deficits relate to 2002–2003. Greece's deficit in the period leading up to membership was expanding and became very large in 1999.[3] This was despite a rapid depreciation of the Drachma over this period. The deficits of the other Mediterranean countries were large at times, though with rapid improvements for Spain and Italy but not for Portugal. The Peseta and Lira depreciated substantially in the first half of the 1990s, whereas there was only a more marginal depreciation of the Escudo.

Table 12.5 Current account deficits (% of export of goods and services)

	1994	1995	1996	1997	1998	1999
Greece	7.37	–5.09	–13.55	–10.83	–17.79	–25.57
	1991	**1992**	**1993**	**1994**	**1995**	**1996**
Spain	–22.7	–22.0	–6.6	–7.7	0.0	0.6
Italy	–11.4	–13.1	3.6	5.1	8.3	12.4
Portugal	–6.7	–8.5	–8.0	–13.3	–9.5	–12.8
	1998	**1999**	**2000**	**2001**	**2002**	**2003**
Cyprus	–12.7	–3.1	–6.1	–7.0	–10.4	–9.7
Czech Republic	–3.7	–4.4	–7.6	–8.1	–10.0	–10.1
Estonia	–11.5	–6.1	–6.2	–6.7	–15.3	–19.7
Hungary						–9.5
Latvia	–20.7	–22.2	–15.2	–21.5	–16.8	–18.2
Lithuania	–25.6	–28.2	–13.2	–9.5	–9.9	–10.5
Malta						–7.7
Poland	–14.8	–21.1	–21.5	–10.4	–8.8	–8.6
Slovakia	–15.1	–5.7	–3.6	–10.1	–11.3	–5.1
Slovenia	–1.1	–6.7	–5.0	0.3	2.9	1.0
New members						–8.7

Source: Commission (2004a).

12.4 Case study: Estonia

What distinguishes Estonia from all the other new members is that, since it established the Kroon to replace the Rouble in 1992, it has operated a currency board arrangement to peg the currency, together with full convertibility for current and capital transactions. Fiscal and financial policies have been conservative with the central government borrowing constrained by legislation. Initially, the peg was to the DM, then when the single currency came into being, the euro. Having, de facto, been fixed to the core EU currency, this history implies that Estonia would have to adapt least to fit in with the euro, so that it can be portrayed as a 'best case' for the potential costs of adjustment to the single currency.

The process of transition and disentanglement of Estonia from the USSR could be said to date from May 1989 when the Supreme Soviet of the USSR approved a law on economic autonomy. From this time, economic reforms accelerated, particularly in relation to price and wage determination, fiscal policy and the financial sector. After Estonia was granted political independence in October 1991, it consistently pursued free market economic policies and its stance on macroeconomic policy was complemented by wide-ranging structural reforms. On the EBRD's assessment Estonia is at the forefront of implementing structural reforms (EBRD, 2003). Estonia became a member of the IMF in 1992 and the 135th member of the WTO in October 1999.

In an overview of the period since independence and the role of the IMF therein, Knöbl and Haas (2003: 3–4) commend the three Baltic economies for their success in transforming their economies. They point out that these economies went 'through four distinct phases of transition:

- Economic stabilisation 1992–1993
- Consolidation and economic recovery 1994–mid-1998
- Recession – the effects of the Russian crisis mid-1998–1999
- Recovery and preparation for EU accession 2000–present'.

The starting point for all three countries was not encouraging because of the magnitude of the shock from their 'divorce' from Russia: this arose from the systemic crisis of the break-up of the Soviet Union, which directly affected the Baltic countries, while the rapid move by Russia to charge market prices for energy and raw materials had a pronounced, adverse terms of trade effect. The upshot was that the Baltics were hit by a shock that greatly exceeded those that affected other CEE countries at the start of transition. Nevertheless, the pace of transformation was rapid and the assessment by Knöbl and Haas suggests – on the sort of criteria stressed by the IMF – that Estonia was the star pupil, whereas Lithuania is criticised for having been slower to adopt appropriate stabilisation policies.

Since pegging its currency in 1992, Estonia has managed to maintain the momentum of reform and is now one of the more rapidly growing of the new members. Whether the fixed exchange rate has helped or not is difficult to ascertain. Hinnosaar *et al.* (2003) show that, depending on the estimation technique used, the Kroon may have been slightly over-valued, especially during the Russian crisis in 1998, but over the full period, has been reasonably close to an equilibrium value. The impact of the Russian crisis on Estonia was limited, but measures taken to cool the economy meant that the rate of growth slowed in 1998. The real impact of the deflationary measures was felt in 1999 with the economy contracting by 0.6%. Robust growth resumed quickly, attaining 7.1% in 2000 and 6.0% in 2001 and averaging more than 5% since.

The country, according to the IMF has one of the most liberal labour markets of the new members, with a low replacement rate for unemployment benefit. The generosity of the system has recently been increased a little, but is still limited. By contrast, employment protection remains fairly strong, a characteristic that Estonia shares with other transition countries, and is above the EU and OECD averages.

The IMF judges that Estonia has followed sound macroeconomic policies, though it notes the high deficit on the current account of the balance of payments as a potential problem. But given the favourable outlook for growth and a healthy banking system, the IMF believes that investor confidence in the country will remain strong and that it is not especially vulnerable to external shocks. Clearly, though, the fact that the economy was hit by the 1998 crisis in Russia, its exposure to the latter could still be awkward, even if integration into the EU progressively lessens the threat. However, with Russia now growing considerably faster than the EU, the threat is from asymmetric shocks rather than the pattern of trade.

The EU and Estonia signed a Europe Agreement on 12 June 1995 that became operative from 1 February 1998. Estonia's progress in transition was recognised in December 1997 when the EC decided on the basis of the Commission's opinion that Estonia would be one of the five CEECs that could commence negotiations for EU membership. These accession negotiations were successfully concluded on 13 December 2002, then the Treaty of Accession was signed on 16 April 2003 and endorsed in a referendum held on 14 September 2003. Along with nine other new members, Estonia joined the EU on 1 May 2004.

12.4.1 The Maastricht convergence criteria: A viable euro area member?

Although the Russian crisis of 1998 had severe repercussions for the Estonian economy, it bounced back rapidly and remains well-placed to fulfil the convergence criteria for accession to Stage 3 of EMU. In addition, its central bank is very close to the form of independence required by the Treaty.

The Bank of Estonia is legally independent from all Government Agencies, is not subordinated to the Government of the Republic of the Estonia and reports only to the Estonian Parliament. A board consisting of a chairman and eight board members runs the Bank. The chairman is nominated by the President and appointed by the Parliament for a term of five years. The members of the board are also appointed by the Parliament. It is the board that is responsible for the formulation of monetary policy and the chairman for its implementation. The Bank of Estonia meets EU requirements with respect to the prohibition of direct financing of the public sector and of privileged access of the public sector to financial institutions, but some fine-tuning is needed in relation to independence. 'One final specific amendment to the Central Bank Law should be adopted concerning possible conflicts between managing bodies of the bank and potential interference of the Parliament' (Commission, 2003m: 32).

In contrast to most other transition economies, Estonia has been very restrained with its public finances. The State Budget Law constrains the Estonian government's borrowing, the government cannot borrow from the Central Bank and it is required to follow the 'golden rule', only borrowing to finance investment. The fixed exchange rate and the associated monetary policy is a further restraint. Local government deficits are also kept in check by limited borrowing capacity. Government expenditure has been capped at around 40% of GDP and the level of taxation has kept pace (Table 12.6). These arrangements have ensured that Estonia has consistently had the lowest level of borrowing among the new members and comfortably met the 3% deficit criterion every year.

Because Russia took over the debts of the Soviet Union, including foreign debt, Estonia started the transition process with no debt and, having kept borrowing low, still only has very low government debt of 5.4% of GDP in 2003, comfortably the lowest among the new members. In addition to meeting the two 'Maastricht' fiscal criteria, it has met the medium-term requirement of close to balance or in surplus, with an average deficit of 0.1% of GDP between 1994 and 2003, a feat that has eluded all the other new members[4] (Commission, 2004a). With the aid of foreign investment in

Table 12.6 Estonian government expenditure and revenue (% of GDP)

	1993	1994	1995	1996	1997	1998	1999	2000	2001	2002	2003	2004
Total government expenditure	39.4	40.0	40.8	42.5	40.0	40.4	43.2	38.5	37.3	35.5	35.6	37.0*
Public Sector Deficit–/Surplus+	10.2	4.6	–0.1	–2.3	1.5	–0.9	–2.8	–0.3	0.3	1.4	3.5	0.1
Public sector debt					6.9	6.0	6.5	4.7	4.4	5.3	5.3	4.2

Source: Statistical Office of Estonia * first 3 quarters.

privatised assets, net external debt had fallen to less than 2% of GDP in 2002 Statistikameet (Statistical Office of Estonia).

Price stabilisation in Estonia has been impressive: the annual average rate of increase of consumer prices has fell from 19.8% in 1996 to 2.0% in 2004. The constraints on monetary policy of the currency board and the statutory limits on fiscal policy clearly contributed to this performance. Estonia is close to the average for the new members in relation to price stability and has been close to satisfying the inflation criterion since 1999. Balassa–Samuelson effects are estimated to have contributed an annual inflation differential of 0.2–0.5% between Estonia and the euro area over the period 1997–2001 (IMF, 2003c: 31; see also Commission, 2002a: 235–45). However, if anything is going to trip up Estonia in qualifying for Stage 3 at the first attempt it will be inflation. Like all other applicants it has to converge to within 1.5% of the average of the lowest three inflation rates among the Member States of the EU. With 24 to choose from the chances of one or two having special factors that apply is high. For example, in the year following enlargement, Finnish inflation has been near zero because there was a major reduction in the taxation of alcohol to, ironically reduce the large discrepancy with Estonian rates.[5] Thus although Estonia may be usually within 1.5% of the euro area average inflation this may not be enough and the transparency of government there suggests that one-off attempts to manipulate the price level downwards for a year, simply in order to qualify on a technicality will be avoided.

Tight monetary and fiscal policies, together with the low level of government borrowing, facilitated a rapid reduction in Estonian interest rates (Table 12.7), although the tight monetary policy implied by the currency board and the need to finance the gap between high investment and low savings has meant higher rates than in other new members. The Maastricht convergence requirement for one year of long-term interest rates no more than 2% above the average of the three best performing Member States is currently fulfilled by Estonia, although the basis for assessing this is not clear as Estonia has no long-dated government debt and a limited commercial market.

Table 12.7 Estonian nominal interest rates (%)

	1997	1998	1999	2000	2001	2002	2003	2004
Estonia general government short term	–	17.5	11.0	8.3	6.2	5.1	7.0	6.9
Estonia general government long term	10.2	–	11.3	10.6	7.7	9.2	6.4	5.7
Reference rate for EMU			7.0	7.3	7.0	6.9	6.1	6.4

Source: ECB Statistics Pocket book (2005), Commission (2004a).

The fact that the Kroon is already fixed by the currency board arrangement raises two important issues: first, what are the implications of this arrangement for EMU entry; and, second, is the current parity appropriate for EMU membership? Estonia joined ERM II shortly after its accession to the EU in May 2004, with the currency board as a unilateral commitment. The Commission (2001a) signalled that a currency board is not an acceptable substitute for ERM II membership, but that it *may* be an appropriate unilateral commitment within the ERM. Entry into ERM II required a multilateral agreement with the euro area, other ERM II Member States and the ECB, and essential to this agreement was a decision on the central parity.

Having entered the ERM II at its current parity, the exchange rate criterion should be satisfied relatively quickly, as the Commission (2004i) makes clear in its 2004 convergence report. Estonia is, therefore, already close to satisfying the Maastricht convergence criteria, and would be able to qualify for membership comparatively rapidly. The only obstacle in its path would appear to be the two-year membership of ERM which formally leaves it in the position of 'Member State with a derogation' according to the Commission convergence report. Once the exchange was pegged to the DM in 1992, Estonia became a de facto member of the ERM of the European Monetary System and by pegging the Kroon to the euro has become a de facto member of EMU, albeit without enjoying the advantages of the common monetary policy. Estonia has already achieved a substantial degree of macroeconomic policy integration with the EU, and not just through the currency board. Government borrowing is restricted by legislation, so that adherence to the SGP should not be a major problem. Finally it has an independent central bank charged with 'maintaining the stability of the legal tender of the Republic of Estonia' (Bank of Estonia, 1993; Article 3.1).

12.4.2 Competitiveness

For a country with a currency board, like Estonia, rapid entry can only be achieved at the current parity, so that its desirability depends upon the appropriateness of that parity for permanent fixing. This, in turn, calls for an assessment of the competitiveness of the Estonian economy. The desirability of entry to the euro area also depends upon the suitability of euro area economic policy for Estonia and the ability of Estonia to adjust to conditions in the euro area.[6]

Two factors in particular have given rise to concern: the large current account deficit; and the rapid rise in manufacturing wages, which has been reflected in the escalating real exchange rate of the Kroon. The Estonian current account deficit has been substantial throughout the transition process, averaging 8.8% of GDP 1995–2003, among the highest of the accession countries. There was a substantial deterioration in 2002–2003 with the deficit reaching 13.2% in 2003, and the deficit is also forecast to remain large in the near future (Commission, 2005a). At least some of this deterioration is the result of special factors. Low interest rates in the euro area have meant that monetary conditions in Estonia have been easy and this has contributed to an expansion of demand and of imports. There have also been large one-off investments in the energy and transport sectors. Even allowing for these factors, deficits seem to be above the sustainable level of 7.5% of GDP in the medium term and 5% of GDP in the long term (IMF, 2003b).

Estonia's large current account deficit has been made possible by large capital inflows, a significant proportion of which has been direct investment. Net FDI averaged 6.2% of Estonian GDP from 1993 to 2003, the highest rate among the CEE countries.[7] FDI in the CEECs in general, and in Estonia in particular, has varied substantially over time. If Estonia is to continue to be able to finance large current account deficits it will need to be able to maintain large flows of inward investment. Spain, Greece and Portugal enjoyed lower levels of FDI when they joined the EU,[8] and in the 1990s net inflows have fallen, so that recently these countries have become net outward investors. The income levels in CEE accession countries is much lower and so the potential for FDI much greater. Hungary and Poland's longer experience with transition provides a contrast, though the level of FDI in Hungary has fallen, whereas it has grown in Poland. These differences probably have more to do with the pace of privatisation than underlying incentives. It is also possible that the direction of causation is different. Rather than financing the current account deficit, inward investment may have been determining that deficit. With saving at a relatively low level and government borrowing tightly controlled, an influx of foreign investment can only be accommodated by an expansion in the current account deficit.

This view of events is supported by the observed relationship between changes in investment and changes in the current account for the accession countries (Gros, 2003: 94–5). If the current account is accommodating the inward investment inflow then a reduction in the inflow would lead to a reduction in the current account deficit. Whether this is the case depends upon the competitiveness of Estonian production and it is to this issue that the analysis now turns.

There are some reasons for concern over the competitiveness of the Estonian economy. Average wages and salaries have outstripped prices by a considerable amount, a tendency that has been maintained despite falling inflation (Table 12.6). The measurement of wages in Estonia is complicated by the extent of the informal economy, but rapid wage growth in 2000–2002 appears to be the result of changes to the social insurance system which has encouraged increased declaration of wages. Nominal wage growth may in fact have been 3% below that recorded (IMF, 2003c: 16). This effect should have been tailing off by 2003 but the estimated wage increases have accelerated. Wage levels, however, remain very low, having reached only 13.7% of the EU-15 average in 2000 and just a third of those in Portugal, the lowest in the EU 15.

When exchange rates are first established in transition countries they are typically undervalued (Begg *et al.*, 1999) reflecting the difficult circumstances in the early stages of transition, such as low productivity and poor quality of products. Governments are also likely to be cautious and thus to undervalue the exchange rate, with the result that one characteristic of transition has been appreciation in the real effective exchange rate (REER). Estonia in common with the other two Baltic States, with their various fixed exchange rate ties combined with high rates of inflation, has shown a consistent rise in its real exchange rate. Other things being equal a rise in the real exchange rate represents a reduction in competitiveness making it less profitable to sell abroad. To an extent this may be seen as an unwinding of the under-valuation of the real exchange rate. It also looks like a Balassa–Samuelson effect, with productivity increasing rapidly in the traded goods sector, particularly manufacturing, to attract resources to the sector, but higher wages and other factor costs offset this rising productivity. However, the general description of the process does not seem to fit transition economies (Halpern and Wyplosz, 1997) and Estonia seems to be no exception. The non-traded sector (services) was constrained under the planned economy, and transition offers the prospects for both expansion and rapid productivity growth in this sector. In this situation real exchange rate appreciation acts as a mechanism both to raise real wages in the 'modern' sector and to squeeze the 'traditional' sector to shed labour.

12.4.3 Vulnerability of the Estonian economy to external shocks

For a country with quite low GDP per capita Estonia has an unusually large service sector and an unusually small industrial sector, and is similar in this regard to the euro area. However, the similarity of the Estonian economy at a broad sectoral level hides pronounced differences at a more disaggregated level. The industrial sector of Estonia still has over 40% of production in food and wood processing. In the service sector, travel and transport are predominant industries. The structure of Estonian industry has remained fairly stable since the early 1990s, although the food industry, the largest industrial sector, experienced a very sharp decline in output in the early transition period, though it has since stabilised.

In the early 1990s the forests, the most important natural resource of Estonia, were exploited as an extractive industry, round timber being exported with minimum processing. Output and exports of the wood industry have increased substantially as the level of processing has been raised, so that this is now the second largest industrial sector. It is also an important exporter with two-thirds of its output being sold abroad. This industry has attracted a high level of investment.

Light industry (textiles, clothing, leather and footwear) has grown relatively rapidly during transition. These industries are labour intensive and benefit from the low level of Estonian wages, but with rising real wages this competitive advantage has been eroded, slowing the growth of production. The textile industry (the most important light industry) is showing signs of future potential with an increasing share of exports. Other sectors of Estonian industry such as metalworking and mechanical engineering, electrical, electronic and instrument engineering export around two-thirds of their output. This is because they are heavily involved in sub-contracting and assembly. Further expansion of these industries is however constrained by a lack of suitably trained workers.

Labour market flexibility

As in other areas of the Estonian economy, labour market reform was radical and market-oriented. The near absolute job security of the Soviet era was ended. The Law on Employment Contracts that was introduced in July 1992 gave employers the right to lay off workers with two months notice. Severance pay depends upon length of employment, but is limited to between two and four times previous monthly earnings. Under certain conditions, temporary contracts can be used and these contracts can be renewed up to a maximum of five years. In practice, this allows the widespread use of temporary contracts. In 1998, 8.6% of employment was part-time, with more women (11.2%) than men working part-time. Part-time work is concentrated in the service sector which accounts for 74% of the total. Most part-time work was involuntary and is explained by an inability to find full-time employment (29.4%) or employer-related reasons (27.7%). Part-time work was most common among older workers over 50 who accounted for 35% of part-time workers. Wages have been freed from government controls and, since 1990, the government has decided only the minimum wage, which has been set at a rather low level (Noorkoiv *et al.*, 1997).

Unemployment benefit does not act as a significant impediment to labour market flexibility because, although qualifying for benefit is easy, benefit rates are very low. Qualification for unemployment benefit requires an individual to have worked 180 or more days in the year preceding registration. This requirement does not apply to entrants and re-entrants, but quitters and school leavers have to wait for two months before they can receive benefit. Unemployment benefits are very limited and the period of benefit is six months with a possibility of extension for another 3 months. There is also the safety-net of social assistance when unemployment benefit is no longer available. The level of benefits is extremely low, having originally been set at 60% of the low minimum wage, and subsequent increases have not kept pace with even price inflation. There are also strict conditions applied to the receipt of unemployment benefit. A legal requirement is to report to the employment office three times a month and there are penalties for refusing job offers: a first refusal means the suspension of benefit for ten days, then a second refusal means the permanent suspension of benefit. After six months, job offers may be below the appropriate level of skills. Individuals drawing unemployment benefit must participate in public works programmes if required and earnings allowed before benefit is eliminated are extremely low.

Estonia would seem to have in place conditions to achieve flexible real wages, one of the possible adjustment mechanisms available to a country in a monetary union. The legal and administrative system limits workers' rights and provides only very limited benefits to the unemployed. There is also a strong regional and ethnic dimension to the unemployment problem. Regional unemployment rates vary between 5.6 and 14.3%. The regions with highest unemployment are those with Russian ethnic populations: the unemployment rate of non-Estonians who do not speak Estonian is 14.4%, whereas the employment rate among Estonians is 7.8%. Production of oil shale is concentrated in these Russian areas and the main obstacle to the closure of this uneconomic industry with adverse environmental effects is this ethnic problem.[9]

Employment growth has been concentrated in Tallinn and Western Estonia (Parnu and Tartu). These areas have benefited from the reorientation of trade to the West, FDI, the emergence of entrepreneurship, and the rapid growth of services and tourism. By contrast the east of the country was hit by the closure of large-scale industrial plants, problems with markets in the CIS, the decline of agricultural employment, and language and cultural problems.[10] This regional dimension of unemployment suggests a lack of spatial mobility.

The large numbers of unemployed and economically inactive represent not only a waste of economic resources and a drag on the economy, but also a potentially serious social and political problem. There is a shortage of qualified workers because many of the unemployed do not have the necessary skills for the jobs that are being created. Education has traditionally been highly valued in Estonia, but vocational training is seen as being of low prestige.

12.4.4 Ability of Estonia to adjust under EMU

As in other areas of transition, Estonia has established the legal and administrative conditions for a flexible labour market, necessary to provide adjustment to changing economic circumstances. This includes limited social protection with low replacement ratios, with strong administrative controls to encourage workers to move from benefit to work. Flexible contracts include provision for part-time working. The limitations to labour market flexibility lie in areas less amenable to government policy action in the short to medium term. The qualifications and training of the workforce in general and the unemployed in particular need to improve to enable employment opportunities in services or in the expanding high-tech industries to be filled. The second major weakness is the concentration of unemployment and of problem industries in Russian-speaking areas, where spatial and occupational mobility is likely to be low. Spatial mobility is likely to be reduced by language and cultural problems. These also seem likely to limit the ability to upgrade workers in these areas. At the moment these factors seem to limit Estonian labour market flexibility as measured by real wage change. Estonia has, however, laid the legal foundation for a flexible labour market.

12.5 Conclusion

For all the new Members, the decision on full participation in EMU will be a pivotal one for their medium- and long-term position in the EU, so that the timing and terms are critical. On balance, the signals from the capitals of central and eastern Europe suggest that early accession is the preferred strategy for most (the Czech Republic is likely to be an exception, while others, such as Hungary, have recently become more cautious as they have struggled to contain their nominal indicators), notwithstanding the risks. In any case, they do not have an opt-out that allows them to delay for long and they will be required to produce convergence plans that map out a route to full participation, although Sweden has probably paved the way politically for others to prolong delay. As Rostowski (2003) points out, neither the ECB nor the Commission has displayed great enthusiasm for early accession, which also makes delayed accession politically feasible.

Meeting the convergence criteria will, nevertheless, require hard choices. Several of the new members can expect higher inflationary pressures than the average of the current euro area members and, faced with high unemployment and evident needs for infrastructure, their governments will face demands for increased public spending that could undermine budgetary discipline. This was also the experience of Spain, which faced substantial challenges in convergence, especially given its very high level of unemployment at the outset. The success enjoyed by Spain suggests that provided growth remains reasonably robust the prospects may be quite encouraging. There may, though, be an element of luck in the timing that the accession countries pick for entry to Stage 3. This was demonstrated by the virtually total failure of the existing members to meet the convergence criteria in 1995/1996, at the first attempt, just two years before the actual qualification: circumstances can be quite volatile.

For the smaller countries, there may be little choice but to move rapidly towards Stage 3 and here the experience of Estonia, which has clearly made enormous progress in the process of transition, is auspicious. Macroeconomic stabilisation occurred rapidly and the country should comfortably meet the convergence criteria for EMU. The competitiveness of Estonian industry may have been affected by the exchange rate policy leading to the large current account deficit in which an enormous trade deficit is partly offset by a large surplus on services trade. Estonia does however depend rather heavily on tourism and transport exports and upon markets in Finland and Norway. With the currency board tie of the Kroon to the euro, Estonia is already a *de facto* member of EMU, but early entry to EMU could nevertheless carry some risks.

On balance, the risks from macroeconomic instability for all new CEEC members, with all the consequences that might follow from it and the not insignificant risk of major problems, probably outweigh the costs of clamping down on the economies needed to fulfil the Maastricht convergence criteria. The adjustment may be painful, though probably short-lived, but the real challenges will come with living with EMU. Here the experience of over a decade of rapid structural change will be both an advantage and a potential threat.

The advantage is that the imperative of structural change should have become accepted, though the other side of the coin is that a 'transition fatigue' may have set in that prompts voters to say enough is enough. EU assistance via the Structural and Cohesion Funds can be a help in this regard. A potential problem, emphasised by Weber and Taube (1999), is that the combination of transfers from the EU Structural Funds reaching 4% of GDP and a surge of inward investment, while enabling new members to continue to sustain current account deficits, could put inflationary pressure on the economy. Careful application of these funds and, more generally, astute sequencing of reforms will be needed if living with EMU is to be comfortable.

13
Adjusting to EMU: Conclusions and Policy Implications

The achievement of EMU has been a slow and tortuous process. It has had to overcome significant political and social opposition, changing views on how to effect the shift from national currencies and policy systems to what is now in place, and vacillation over the institutional design. Today, the euro is taken for granted and the debate has moved on to the no less complicated questions of how to manage the economic policy system and whether and/or when reforms of particular instruments are needed. With poor economic performance compared to aspirations, this has been generating some quite severe tensions recently, as people look for something to blame.

Yet it is easy to forget, first, that less than a decade ago many would have bet against a single currency being attained by 1999, if ever; and, second, that it represents a sizeable move in the tectonic plates of international finance. To put it another way, and irrespective of the case for or against monetary integration, it is hard to imagine any other setting in which a major new international currency might emerge in a foreseeable future measured in decades, except possibly in Asia.

That said, it is evident that the process of creating the euro has induced, and will continue to require, extensive changes in economic behaviour as well as constitutional change and institution-building both by those states within EMU and those aspiring to join. EMU represents a substantial regime change that requires countries participating in it to re-learn their approach to policy. They have to rethink the processes of policy formulation and implementation, and economic actors have had to learn to deal with a new policy environment. All sides, plainly, have had to adjust in some cases quite extensively. This book has confronted questions of adjustment from two very different perspectives:

1. The strategies adopted by countries as they sought to prepare themselves for EMU (what might be labelled Stage 2 adjustment)
2. How economies adapt their policy machinery to deal with (and/or anticipate) problems once they participate fully in EMU (Stage 3 adjustment).

In this concluding chapter we summarise some of the key findings presented in earlier chapters, draw out inferences for the evolution of the EMU framework, including how it will be affected by the participation in Stage 3 of further Member States, and explore ramifications for policy reform.

13.1 EMU as a macroeconomic system

The institutional form of EMU and its main characteristics as a macroeconomic system were largely settled in the Maastricht Treaty. But, as the discussion in Chapters 1 and 3 show, while the constitutional blueprint is explicit, how EMU was to be implemented has only gradually become clear and there are reasons to doubt elements of the constitutional settlement. The Sapir report, in particular, noted that 'the picture that emerges is one of confusion and tension–confusion created by the complexity of the system and diversity of the roles performed, tension in the gap between goals and means' (Commission, 2003e: 3). The main traits of the system can be summarised as being:

- A strongly independent and supranational monetary authority
- Priority to price stability in the aims of monetary policy
- Fiscal policy assigned to Member States, but with rule-based constraints on their autonomy and freedom to engage in discretionary fiscal stimulation of the economy
- An expectation that fiscal policy should play a key role in absorbing asymmetric shocks, with the implication that room for manoeuvre has to be created for fiscal adjustment
- Increasing demands on the supply-side of the economy to create conditions in which shocks become less probable and adjustment mechanisms work more efficiently
- Extensive use of forms of policy co-ordination, using novel mechanisms, to provide the means of assuring policy coherence without forgoing national 'ownership' of policy areas
- A mix of hard and soft law to underpin the conduct of policy, but ambivalence about the balance between them and the exercise of sanctions to enforce policy rules and commitments
- It is a system in flux (or, more charitably, that is learning by doing) in which the broad structure may not change much, but where a number of specific features may well change.

An obvious question to pose is whether the system works. That economic policy decision-making shifted from a system based around 12 currencies to the single currency with little visible disruption testifies to the robustness of the policy machinery. In a process sense, therefore, it can be said unequivocally that all the necessary adjustments did occur. A more testing question is whether the system is proving to be effective in delivering a good economic performance, since that, ultimately, is the rationale for monetary integration. In this respect, although Chapter 2 provides a wealth of evidence, the jury is out. Some Member States have seen improvements in their immediate economic performance and, more tellingly, seem to have established a platform for sustainable, non-inflationary growth. The implication is that they have managed to adjust successfully. Others have struggled, suggesting that in either Stage 2 or Stage 3 something has gone awry (see Chapter 6), although it is important to note that where supply-side factors lie behind the problems, EMU may simply have exposed underlying weaknesses that would have had to be dealt with anyway.

13.1.1 Conduct of policy

The euro area as a whole had a lacklustre economic performance for much of the last decade, inviting the conclusion that the shift to EMU has been to blame. While it is undeniable that, for some Member States, EMU has prompted significant macroeconomic adjustment, this would be a disingenuous inference. As Allsopp and Artis (2003) have stressed, the fiscal overhang from the 1980s would, sooner or later, have had to be dealt with, and the differences between the euro area members also have to be taken into account. Slow growth in Germany and Italy has, especially since the start of Stage 3, been at least partly offset by dynamism in Spain, Finland and Ireland. The evidence we adduce in Chapter 2 also shows that adaptation on the supply-side has been very uneven, with some euro area members adjusting well, while others have struggled.

Monetary policy has, probably, been about right: some rate changes could have been a month or two sooner or been 50 rather than 25 basis points, but these are fine technical judgements. The Federal Reserve has, manifestly, been more activist in its approach, but monetary policy is a slow acting instrument and excessive changes can be counter-productive, so that again it is a moot point whether the Fed or the ECB has followed the best route.

Fiscal policy, though, has been more problematic. Several countries have struggled to contain deficits and the most heavily indebted Member States have made little headway in reducing the burden, even though lower interest rates have provided sizeable windfall gains by lowering debt servicing costs. Fiscal consolidation in the upturn of the second half of the 1990s was less than hoped in some Member States. Yet a paradox of the SGP is that despite being breached it has almost certainly succeeded in its primary aim of assuring sustainable public finances by restraining deficits. Moreover – a second paradox – it has done so more by 'soft' measures deriving above all from the domestic and peer group pressures on governments, than the hard sanctions envisaged in Regulation 1466.

The BEPGs also cover fiscal policy and are the context in which the overall stance of policy should be set, notably bringing in the supply-side.

Here, however, the problems seem to be that the scope for enforcement – even by soft means – is just too limited. Hence the challenge for fiscal policy co-ordination is to find the middle-ground between allowing flexibility in the application (and, where appropriate, interpretation) of rules and having enforcement mechanisms sufficiently strong to exert a discipline. Our contention is that the answer is to bring an element of political choice back into policy-setting, but to constrain discretion. How what might be dubbed a third way could be made to work is explored further below in a discussion of economic governance.

It is, however, on the supply-side of the euro area economies that problems have been most evident. Labour market mismatch has been a feature in several countries, productivity growth has slowed and investment in R&D has been disappointing. These shortcomings have been extensively documented (see, for example, the Sapir report – Commission of the European Communities, 2003e – and the Kok report, 2004) and have given rise to the Lisbon agenda. But are they linked to EMU? One sense in which they are is that as fiscal consolidation has proceeded, Member States have – as is so often the case – found it easier to cut public investment than consumption. Yet it also has to be pointed out that as nominal interest rates have declined, there ought to have been greater incentives for the private sector to invest more.

A second sense in which supply-side difficulties may have been affected by the shift to EMU is that the extended period of slow growth associated with the transition to the euro may have inhibited structural reforms. Such reforms are typically easier to push through when the economy is booming and the social and political costs of change can more easily be accommodated, whereas stagnation often entrenches defensive attitudes. At one level, as we explain in Chapter 5, the challenge is political insofar as it calls for leadership and astute mediation between competing interests. But there is also a question of whether the supply-side is sufficiently (or, indeed, excessively) integrated into the EMU policy framework. Here, the Sapir report is trenchant: 'achieving the objective of higher growth requires a higher degree of coherence across the range of economic policies and across the different levels of decision-making powers. This implies improving the content of policies and the governance processes behind their implementation' (Commission, 2003e: 124).

The discussion in Chapter 5 suggests that supply-side co-ordination has, on the surface, worked better than fiscal co-ordination to the extent that it has evolved procedures that appear to do what they say they will do. But are there results and was the decision to re-launch the Lisbon strategy in March 2005 really an admission that despite the plethora of action plans and the like, not much was happening? Even employment policy, the most developed sphere of supply-side co-ordination, as yet has little to commend it in terms of improvements in the labour market. It may, too, be hampered because it only embraces the politically easy elements of labour market policy such as measures to promote employability (who could be against?), but ducks the tougher dossiers such as modernising labour market regulation or, whisper it, wage levels. There is also an open question of whether Member States do any more than pay lip-service to the co-ordination processes (Kok report, 2004: ch. 3), such that when it comes to the crunch it is almost exclusively national discourses which shape policy change. Similarly, despite the general agreement on the goals and emphases in the Lisbon agenda, it is not easy to identify what has actually changed in Member State policies as a result.

13.1.2 Findings from the country case studies

The countries examined in Chapters 6–12 were deliberately chosen to cover a range of circumstances and to capture different strategies for adjusting to EMU. These can be grouped in a number of ways. France, Germany and Ireland were countries that did not have to run especially hard in Stage 2 to be founder members of the euro area. Finland and Italy, by contrast, had to make substantial adjustments. Intriguingly, Chapters 10 and 11 show that Sweden and the UK, though with different national contexts, have used their non-membership to anticipate Stage 3 adjustment and both can be now regarded as viable members of the euro area, even if their continuing doubts about joining mean that they will stay out for some time. Indeed, the Swedish and UK cases suggest that in constructing alternative macroeconomic frameworks, both countries have innovated in developing methods of adjustment that seem to work better, and possibly hold lessons for the evolution of the euro area policy model. It can also be argued that the 2005 reform of the SGP reflects some of the advantages of the Swedish and UK approaches.

It is in the nature of structural problems that they can accumulate, leading to a slow but inexorable deterioration, yet often be placed in the 'too difficult' box until a crunch point is reached. Stagnation in Japan since the early 1990s coupled with reluctance (or, perhaps, political timidity) until very recently to confront the hard choices that were required – especially in the financial system – illustrates the dilemmas. Italy was able to push through substantial changes, for example to the social protection system and to the efficacy of tax collection during Stage 2, but has suffered something of a hangover in Stage 3, the implication being that maintaining the pace of reform is also a challenge. In France, even Nicolas Sarkozy – a charismatic and dynamic character with a radical agenda – hesitated to push through harsh reforms during his – admittedly brief – tenure as finance minister. Although there appears to be a growing awareness in France about the need for change, the particular political economy constellation in that country – notably the weight accorded to special interest groups – suggests that it will be a hard-fought process.

The analysis in Chapter 7 demonstrates that Germany, especially, now appears to face a different need for adjustment insofar as its well-publicised problems in achieving structural reforms point to an EMU-related difficulty. It is a moot point whether monetary union has caused these problems or exacerbated them, or whether, instead, it provides an impetus for reforms that might otherwise have been put off. What is clear is that the travails of the German economy exert a substantial negative spillover on other euro area members. Agenda 2010 and the political costs of being seen to fail both by peers and by domestic actors may presage improvements, but it is hard to avoid the conclusion that Germany faces a difficult period. However, on balance, it is less a problem of adjusting to EMU than of dealing with structural problems that would have had to be confronted regardless, aggravated by policy mistakes in the unification process (at least from an economic standpoint, though the political imperatives have to be acknowledged).

Ireland and Estonia though very different in some respects, as Chapters 8 and 12 show, are small open economies that, while benefiting from the pooling of monetary policy in line with the contribution of McKinnon (1963) to OCA theory, might be more vulnerable to asymmetric shocks. Yet the indications are that they have been able to give more weight to other adjustment mechanisms and have dealt with potentially destabilising circumstances (the asset price boom in Ireland and the 1998 Russian crisis for Estonia) with comparative ease. The key has been that adjustment took place fairly rapidly.

The research has identified some factors that appear to increase the probability that a Member State will find it easy to live with Stage 3 of EMU, but also revealed some of the pitfalls. Prior adjustment – perhaps counter-intuitively in the light of the economist:monetarist debates of the 1980s – is not foolproof, as the experience of some Member States shows. Indeed, it may have induced a sense of complacency in countries which only had to adjust marginally in Stage 2, but are now finding that structural problems that had been swept under the carpet have resurfaced and require more, not less urgent attention.

Given that the switch to the new policy regime represented a far bigger change for some countries than others, the manner in which they have embraced and consolidated the EMU macroeconomic framework has proved to be critical. Thus, three small countries (Finland, Ireland and Estonia, the last de facto in the euro because of the currency board) took early steps to put in place a macroeconomic policy framework that allowed them to deal effectively with the challenges of EMU. By contrast, Germany has been unable to keep its fiscal deficit within the 3% limit since 2001, and finds itself without room for manoeuvre in responding to the continuing stagnation of the economy. Moreover, holding down wage inflation in Germany may well be having the perverse effect of restraining domestic consumer demand at precisely the time it is needed. Germany has also faced comparatively high real interest rates and while its robust current account surplus can be taken as a sign of external competitiveness, one school of thought is, nevertheless, that Germany entered Stage 3 at an overvalued exchange rate.

13.2 Whither reform?

Our research bears on a number of features that have emerged in the early years of EMU as contentious and which are likely to be subject to calls for reform. Some can be regarded as flaws that diminish the capacity of EMU to deliver the non-inflationary growth that is, after all, its raison d'être. In considering possible reforms it is, however, important to focus on the structures and strategic choices for policy formulation rather than on possible errors in policy implementation. The latter are bound to arise in any policy regime, though it can be argued that an effective system will minimise the scope for such errors. In any case, the record on monetary policy on the limited evidence so far is positive, while on fiscal policy there has, so far, been no recurrence of the excesses of the 1980s and early 1990s.

13.2.1 The conduct of monetary policy

One of the main criticisms of monetary policy has been that the ECB has not followed best practice by adopting an inflation-targeting approach, preferring its own two-pillar approach, as explained in Chapter 2. Yet it is questionable whether there is much difference in practice.

A second issue has been that the reference value adopted for price stability has been too tight with the corollary that policy may have hindered growth. A related criticism is that the 2% reference value is an upper limit and that less attention has been paid to a lower limit, a stance that may have courted deflation in those Member States with the least propensities to inflation. Recent clarifications from the ECB have signalled that 2% actually means 'close to 2%', while the actual conduct of policy has, if anything, signalled that the ECB has taken a pretty relaxed view of the 2% figure.

One consequence of the two pillars and the 2% reference value is that professional economists still do not seem to have a good understanding of ECB policy, raising concerns about transparency and communication (de Haan, Amtenbrink and Waller, 2004: 788). Transparency in other words is as much about clarity of explanation as it is about making the details of policy available. Even though the Bank scores fairly highly on transparency and has improved its rating (Eijffinger and Geraats, 2005) the clarity of its policies remains problematic, even allowing for how intermediaries like the financial press interpret and present those policies. In the US, Fed watchers in the specialist press and the financial markets have refined the art of interpreting Greenspan's every twitch – to their mutual benefit – but the impression is that in the euro area, the equivalent signalling mechanisms are still being developed.

13.2.2 Reforming fiscal policy co-ordination

The 'suspension' of the SGP in November 2003, when Ecofin chose to take no action against France and Germany even though it was agreed that both were in breach of the rules on excessive deficits, brought to a head many of the concerns about co-ordination of fiscal policy identified in Chapters 3 and 4. Four main categories of problem had become apparent:

1. First, the SGP rules – long criticised by a number of prominent economists – were being increasingly called into question. In particular, their pro-cyclical nature was proving to be politically unacceptable in the face of the continuing stagnation of the core economies. The SGP was also criticised for its failure to enforce an adequate degree of budgetary consolidation during conditions of favourable growth in 1999 and 2000 and for its failure to distinguish between the quality and sustainability of public finances across Member States.
2. A second difficulty is the ambivalent role assigned to the BEPGs. In principle, these guidelines are supposed to set the overarching framework for policy and, implicitly, to establish the basis for an appropriate policy mix by co-ordination, yet their effectiveness has been limited by the failure of peer pressure to bite and by the accumulation of too many policy objectives.
3. Third, the one-size-fits-all character of the fiscal prescription has looked increasingly untenable and will be further challenged by the accession of new members. A core purpose of fiscal rules is to assure the sustainability of public finances, so that limits on deficits that make sense for a country with a high public debt and growing pension liabilities may be wholly unsuitable for a country with substantial immediate infrastructure needs or negligible debt.
4. Perhaps the most pressing concern is the willingness of the larger Member States simply to disregard the rules when they become uncomfortable. The problem here is not so much economic as institutional/political. The slippage in the deficit ratios of France and Germany has been small enough to be of little consequence for the conduct of monetary policy: indeed, the fiscal stimulus would be regarded by many as an appropriate response to economic stagnation. But the risk is that the breakdown of fiscal discipline will be contagious, stoking up future problems.

Pressures to reform the SGP grew during 2002 and 2003, partly because the experience of the slowdown in 2001 had exposed problems in conforming to the letter of the rules, but partly also because several Member States had come to question the rationale for the rules themselves, notably the medium-term aim of balancing the books. Moreover, the underlying purpose of fiscal restraint – sound public finances – is not easily captured in simple rules. As Pisani-Ferry (2002) points out, 'there is wide agreement on the need for fiscal discipline in a monetary union, but there are several problems with our current definition of it'. He refers especially to the use of current rather than cyclically adjusted ratios, the neglect of public debt and of off balance-sheet public liabilities. In addition, the Commission comment that 'the process of budgetary consolidation has ground to a halt since 1999, and in some cases has reversed' (Commission, 2002b) is symptomatic of a broader concern that the Pact does not (and cannot) promote fiscal discipline effectively. Indeed, the French government went so far as to state, unilaterally, that it would not implement policies to achieve balance by 2004, but would instead do so when it judged the time would be ripe, and not before 2006.

The Commission put forward five proposals designed to reconcile the importance of sound public finances with the need for a more flexible interpretation of the SGP (Hodson and Maher, 2004: 809). First, the medium-term balance rule should be interpreted with respect to the economic cycle, according to an agreed methodology. Second, Member States which are in breach of the medium-term balance rule should, as a principle, be required to consolidate their public finances by at least 0.5% of GDP per year until the situation is rectified. Third, the SGP should work symmetrically so as to avoid a pro-cyclical budgetary position during periods of economic upswing. Fourth, it is recognised that the SGP should cater for 'the inter-temporal budgetary impact of large structural reforms' that boost growth or employment and improve the overall health of public finances. In practice, this would permit Member States which have already achieved a healthy budgetary position and a low level of public debt to run a deliberate but temporary deficit, providing that the additional resources generate economic and budgetary benefits. Finally, Member States should adopt the sustainability of public finances as a 'core policy objective' and thus pay closer attention to debt ratios and the challenge of ageing populations in the process of economic policy co-ordination.

These reforms were largely accepted by the Ecofin (2003b) and further reform was agreed in March 2005, following the decision of the European Court of Justice (C-27/04, 13 July 2004, nyr). The Court annulled the conclusions of the Council which attempted to by-pass the Commission recommendation to trigger the legally binding part of the EDP against France and Germany. At the same time, the Court acknowledged that in the absence of a qualified majority willing to adopt the recommendation the procedure is put into de facto abeyance. Thus the Court confirmed the agenda-setting position of the Commission and the ability of the Council to veto Commission recommendations (Maher, 2004). The seven-month gap between the Ecofin meeting and the judgment allowed for a cooler assessment by all parties of what is required for further reform. Although there was some tough haggling at the last minute about how to define exceptional circumstances, the reforms agreed in 2005 do not require Treaty change. The proposals imply a shift in emphasis from *ex-post* disciplinary action – as encapsulated in the EDP – to ex ante prevention of deficits (Begg and Schelkle, 2004b). This in effect is a reassertion of the original purpose of the Pact which sought to underline the early warning system of multilateral surveillance which in turn rests on the BEPGs.

The Commission has suggested that more focus be placed on debt and sustainability, combined with a shift away from the generally inappropriate one-size-fits-all approach to fiscal policy. Instead, there should be a greater emphasis on individual country circumstances when evaluating MTO and indeed when determining the duration and nature of a Member State's adjustment path when it has breached the budget deficit rule, acknowledging that the time limits of about a year set down in the Pact may not be appropriate. The greater emphasis on multilateral surveillance and peer pressure creates the risk of deals behind doors which raise doubts about the legitimacy of the system and allows for the rules themselves – and the peer pressure underpinning them – to be neutered or at least undermined. For this reason the Commission emphasises the need for simplicity and transparency if and when the EDP is triggered. The need for transparency means it remains committed to the 3% threshold as a clear indicator even though the figure has been much criticised as too crude and too rigid for the purposes of fiscal policy co-ordination.

As part of this commitment to greater transparency but also as an important strategy in improving political ownership of the fiscal coordination by the states of the SGP, the Commission suggests that the economic cycle should be organised so that the BEPGs could be taken into account in planning the national budget. This would ensure that the BEPGs became part of national economic planning to a greater degree. It would also involve national Parliaments more in the planning and review of national performance in the light of the BEPGs. Such involvement would bolster legitimacy by extending the (currently extremely narrow) net of accountability, allowing for domestic political pressure to be brought to bear in encouraging compliance with the BEPGs. This emphasis on national ownership of the process and transparency are themes echoed in the Kok report (2004: ch. 3) in relation to the effective operation of the Lisbon Strategy. In theory, both the re-launched Lisbon strategy and the reformed SGP are, in future, to engage national Parliaments and be more open to national discourse.

The EDP – with its threat of a fine – remains part of the Treaty. One suggestion is that if a fining mechanism is to remain, it should be changed so that a fine would be imposed not as a result of a deficit arising (thereby exacerbating) the budget deficit, but when a state fails to reduce a deficit during times of prosperity (Editorial, 2004). This would require a Treaty amendment so that while it would help to diminish the pro-cyclical impact of the SGP, it is unlikely in the immediate term.

13.2.3 Further participants in Stage 3

From the perspective of the architects of European integration, the fact that full participants in Stage 3 are now – just – in a minority is troubling. Incomplete membership poses problems of governance, notably when institutions such as Ecofin include non-participants. The creation of the Eurogroup as an *ad hoc* response is not an enduring solution, even though it has been shown to function rather effectively, as we demonstrated in part I. The obvious way forward is for non-members to sign up but there will be continuing difficulties if a number of states decide they do not want to proceed to Stage 3. Then, institutional reform would become necessary in order to balance the level of participation in decision-making by non-members with their participation in EMU. The political risks with this are that it would equate EMU with something akin to enhanced co-operation, rather than a core element of the Union, re-activating old ideas of Europe à la carte. Problems of governance, in part due to the large number of states, had become increasingly evident in the EU in a variety of domains. The Treaty of Nice only resolved some of them prior to enlargement, while the uncertainty over ratification of the Treaty Establishing a Constitution for Europe means that a more comprehensive solution remains in abeyance. Many governance problems are, however, as much about the unwillingness and/or incapacity of some of the larger states already in EMU to conform to existing commitments and rules, and thus a political challenge, as about the necessity of institutional change.

Only Denmark and the UK have formal agreements permitting them *not* to join, and in both cases the opt-out was concocted as a means of circumventing awkward domestic political problems when the Maastricht Treaty was being agreed and ratified, rather than being seen as an enduring characteristic of EMU. Consequently, the expectation is still that they will join when the 'time is ripe' rather than never. Sweden has no opt-out, yet it has shown that in practice the distinction counts for little although it may be construed as an (unenforceable) breach of its obligations under the Treaty (Louis, 2004: 605). Sweden and the UK have followed their own courses in monetary policy since 1999, with ramifications for their exchanges rates, while Denmark has effectively shadowed the euro and has, consequently, had a monetary policy almost identical to that of the euro area. As a result, it would not need to adjust much to become a full member.

For the ten new members that acceded to the EU in May 2004, the expectation is that they will join rapidly and, as for Sweden, there is no legal provision for them not to. The issue they have to confront is whether early participation entails adjustment costs that would be intolerable. This boils down to a trade-off between the flexibility of retaining the option to vary the exchange rate and the credibility or stability gains that flow from being part of EMU. There cannot be a blanket answer. For the small open economies, the balance of costs and benefits will tend to favour entering Stage 3 as quickly as possible. The evidence on Estonia is persuasive in this regard, since it shows that a country that started from an inauspicious position has been able not only to adapt its macroeconomic variables rapidly, but has also seen a recasting of its supply-side. The beacon of the EU, in short, has led the economy in what, so far, appears to be a virtuous direction. But others are hesitating as can be seen by the target accession date for Hungary quietly being postponed from 2008 to 2010, not to mention the more overt hostility to early accession of the Czechs.

For other new members, such as Poland, the findings of this study point to a more mixed outlook. In population terms, Spain is a close parallel and it is worth recalling that Spain, too, has been through a successful transition, albeit from a different form of totalitarianism. Like Poland, Spain saw a rapid rise in unemployment and had to contend with a sharply declining rural economy. The time span was longer and the distance that had to be travelled shorter, but the fact that Spain, as seen in 1991/1992, let alone 1986 or 1975, has gone from being a marginal candidate for full participation in EMU to one of the more successful economies ought to be a source of encouragement for countries like Poland. But the difficulties encountered by Italy point in the other direction. For Italy, being a founder member of Stage 3 was, politically, of paramount importance. Yet the costs have been evident. Compared with its heyday in the 1960s and 1970s, the Italian economy has been through a prolonged period of slower growth as it has adjusted to the rigours of the stability orientated macroeconomic model underpinning EMU. Poland's approach and background has, thus far, been more akin to that of Spain than of Italy, giving grounds for optimism, although the prospects will depend critically on policy choices in the early years of EU membership.

13.3 Economic governance

Any system of economic management has to balance competing aims and a continuing worry about the proposals for reform of the ECB and the SGP is that they are too tame. Stability remains the focus, with little concession to growth imperatives such as the acknowledged need to accelerate and support structural reforms. In addition, the reforms would still not allow for optimising the policy mix, whether by co-ordinating national fiscal positions or providing a means of integrating fiscal, monetary and supply-side policies. Even so, a cursory look at how policy is being co-ordinated in the EU shows not only that there is much of it going on, but also that it is being done through an eclectic range of approaches. The underlying question, however, is whether current arrangements provide a policy framework that is robust enough for what EMU will become five, ten or twenty years hence. The Sapir report argues that reform is needed:

> For the EU to achieve higher sustained growth in a macroeconomically stable and cohesive Union it is not only necessary to reassess carefully the trade-offs and complementarities among the various objectives and efficiently align the various policy instruments towards the pursuit of such goals. In addition . . . it will be necessary to revise the methods of governance to ensure both that the various instruments are allocated to the appropriate decision levels and that the latter behave coherently with the ultimate aims of the EU economic system (Commission, 2003e: 74).

In the light of the discussion in Chapters 4 and 5, a particular question is whether the present reliance on the OMC for so many important areas of supply-side policy can be sustained? On this, the jury is out, but there are other facets of policy co-ordination that also warrant more thought. At the heart of the matter is what the EU has become, or is moving towards, as a system for economic governance. If the *finalité économique* is to be a substantially integrated European economy as is implicit in Article 2 of the Treaty, not to mention the rhetoric surrounding the single market and the necessity for it of a single currency, then Member State economic policies will have to be more closely aligned. If they are not, tensions in the system will inevitably grow, making it more difficult to maintain the integrity of the single market, let alone the EU itself.

As the Sapir report – *inter alia* – has made clear, the problems of governance are principally in the policy framework. Five main strands of criticism can be enumerated:

1. First, both monetary policy and fiscal policy are considered to be too focused on stability and not enough on growth. This is, in part, the result of the dominance of a single 'model' of how the economy works, but it also reflects the institutional separation of policy-making and the dominant position of the single monetary policy vis-à-vis fragmented fiscal policy, and is compounded by uncertainty about what macroeconomic policy should try to do.
2. Second, the policy machinery relies too much on rules that are often perceived politically to have no evident economic logic to them, so that the underlying objectives become blurred. A related question is whether the same rule makes sense for all Member States. The reference value for monetary policy and the use of concurrent fiscal ratios irrespective of the point in the cycle can be considered too crude, and conceivably lead to ill-judged responses. The former seems to be quietly moving further away from the limelight in the face of difficulties in its use, but many of the fiscal rules remain problematic. Manifestly, a heavily indebted country that runs a deficit is at much greater risk of fiscal instability or indeed solvency problems. The reformed SGP will make some attempt to allow

for the cycle, but more thought is needed about how to adapt the rules to ensure adequate public investment.

3. Third, it is evident that demand-side and supply-side policies are inadequately integrated, and also that there are gaps within the supply-side 'processes'. The three dimensions (economic growth and competitiveness, the social model and environmental sustainability) of the Lisbon/Gothenburg agenda are also much less coherent than they should be if they are to revitalise the EU economy. Moreover, the March 2005 re-launch of the Lisbon strategy appears to have backtracked in this regard by playing down the social and environmental pillars. Yet, paradoxically, there is also a problem of institutional complexity.
4. Fourth, the ease with which some (especially larger) Member States have been able to flout (or at least appear to flout) the rules in various domains undermines their credibility. The reluctance to comply is exacerbated by the nature of the enforcement mechanisms and sanctions. Giving Ecofin discretion to determine when early warnings under the EDP should be issued – and ducking the hard choice at virtually the first time of asking – suggests that asking a peer group to judge a potentially delinquent Member State is unlikely to work. Evidence suggests, moreover, that the institutional configuration within Member States matters, especially how powerful the finance ministry is (Buti and Pench, 2004). A major issue is therefore how to reconcile hard and soft rules, and, depending on the resulting policy structures, how to improve compliance.
5. Finally, there is a problem of delivery and responsibilities, evoking memories of the Clinton election aphorism: 'it's the economy, stupid'. Poor economic performance prompts questions about who or what to blame, but neither the Member States nor the EU level can provide the answers. The latter, especially, lacks budgetary means, is often obstructed by Member States and has found its legitimacy called into question, yet faces increasing demands to act. Some of the issues are highlighted in the Sapir report (Commission, 2003e: 85) which notes that 'EMU thus represented a step change in the governance methods of the EU system and while successful, it has raised new challenges, which have not been fully surmounted'.

These problems point to a number of obvious potential directions for a rethinking of the system of economic governance rather than the rules themselves. They highlight the importance of optimising between hard and soft approaches in fostering development of the system in a manner that will simultaneously allow genuine choice in policy-making while keeping policy excesses in check. They also hint at a major constitutional choice that was largely absent from the debate on economic governance during the Convention on the Future of Europe and the subsequent negotiations on the Constitutional Treaty, namely should there be a politically constituted centre of economic (as opposed to monetary) policy-making. While the Convention had a mandate to strengthen economic co-ordination, in fact it did little more than tinker with the existing framework.

13.3.1 Constitutionalisation

As shown in Chapter 3, EMU has a particular constitutional form. There was extreme caution to preserve the independence of the ECB in the Constitutional Treaty and the discussions that led up to it. That independence was in fact bolstered by the proposal to grant the ECB the status of an EU institution. It is not clear whether this reclassification of the status of the Bank will have any effect on the operation of what the ECB refers to as the Eurosystem, namely, those parts of the ECB and the twelve participating central banks that relate to the euro area and its management. Under EMU, there is a cross-border system of central banks rather than a central banking system, that is the system reflects institutionally the principle of subsidiarity, but that principle is, as Louis points out, a two-way street (Louis, 2004: 591). Thus he sees a clear bias towards decentralisation in the ECB Statute but one qualified by the principle of effectiveness, with the ECB organs deciding on the extent of centralisation or decentralisation. While the formal institutionalisation of the ECB in the Constitutional Treaty could be seen as allowing for greater centralisation, Louis suggests that as there has been no change in the Statute, the formalisation is one of clarification rather than substantive change (Louis, 2004: 603).

The Governing Council has already taken advantage of the 'enabling clause' in the Nice Treaty to limit voting rights when its membership exceeds 21. Clearly it can also take operational decisions to work in a more (or less) centralised manner in the light of practical experience without any Treaty-based compulsion to do so. Indeed the integration of financial markets is itself leading to centralisation in areas such as the payment system.

The Commission's position would be marginally strengthened so as to allow it to act alone in issuing warnings under multilateral surveillance and to give an opinion rather than a recommendation under the EDP. These changes are, as Louis suggests, not meaningless, but still very limited (2004: 583). Even on economic co-ordination, the focus was on shifting the balance as between the 'ins' (now in a minority) and the 'outs' in Council so as to allow some BEPGs to refer specifically to the euro area only. Article III-88(1) allows Ecofin to take decisions where only the 'ins' vote but the scope of this closer co-operation is limited by the terms of the constitution itself such that modifications must not change any treaty provision unless expressly allowed to do so. This does allow for some change of the protocol on the EDP. With the Eurogroup being acknowledged only via a protocol, it remains politically a powerful body but one that has been juridified only to a very limited degree such that it remains on the margins of the Treaty, with an uncertain status and no formal decision-making powers, although its existence will be apparent within the constitutional structure of EMU. Political sensitivities have influenced the timing and content of reforms, though in the wake of the 2003 Sapir and 2004 Kok reports, there does seem to have been some willingness by the Barosso Commission to push forward in improving economic governance.

In a sense the EMU constitution is marked out from the rest of the Constitutional Treaty, with the economic context perhaps having greater weight than the political/legal aspirations inherent in the whole convention. The lack of urgency also applies as membership of the EU does not automatically or immediately lead to membership of the euro area, giving more breathing space to effect reform of the EMU system. The 2005 agreements on the SGP and Lisbon have, plainly, set the ball rolling, but are surely not the end of the process. There seems to be a consensus that rules play an important role (Louis, 2004: 579) and cannot be eschewed entirely. What remains to be decided is the balance between hard and soft norms, with the recent judgment of the European Court making it clear that even highly discretionary procedures, such as the early stages of the EDP, are still nested within the legal domain.

13.3.2 *Gouvernment économique*: A possible answer?

Three different arguments can be adduced in support of *gouvernement économique*. The first is that there is simply an imbalance in power that could result in too great a weight being assigned to narrowly monetary objectives, and not enough to the real economy, although some would argue that a low inflation environment is, itself, a precondition for raising the sustainable growth rate (Alesina *et al.*, 2001). Second, some form of centralised economic power may be necessary to co-ordinate and agree the conduct of policy, with the implication that the existing co-ordination machinery is not sufficient for this purpose. This second argument has mainly been articulated in relation to fiscal policy, but could, as discussed above, conceivably be extended to embrace the supply-side policies. In this regard, Pisani-Ferry (2002) advocates starting with at least a dialogue between the ECB and the Eurogroup on the interaction between structural reform and macroeconomic policy.

A third factor is that unless there is scope for political input in arriving at agreed decisions, policy-making will take place within a normative vacuum. A closely related question is whether there is a single 'true model' of the contemporary capitalist economy towards which all but the misguided will want to converge. In appraising the case for *gouvernement économique* an important consideration is whether much of economic policy can ultimately be reduced to technical choices or has such significant distributive consequences that the political dimension must inevitably be paramount. The EMU system is, on the whole, in the former camp. An independent central bank, fiscal policy constrained by rules and attempts to chart a common way forward on the supply-side all point towards both the technical paradigm and the existence of an agreed model. Yet even the apparently minor spat in 2001 between the Commission and the Irish government over how big a budgetary surplus Ireland should run revealed not just conflicting views on the underlying economics, but also the relevance of political aims.

To sum up, the case for a *gouvernement économique* looks compelling in some respects, yet remains paper-thin in others, and may in any case fall foul of the principle of subsidiarity, implying that it is beyond political credibility at present. However, the history of European integration is replete with examples of institutional developments that seemed implausible just a few years beforehand – consider EMU itself, let alone how far common defence has moved – so that the political obstacles could easily fade.

Even if the current framework does not need modifying *per se* to achieve improved economic outcomes, there are arguments that the way it is being operated might be leading to an unnecessarily poor equilibrium. Because the monetary authority is uncertain about what the fiscal authorities may do, it is quick to point out the downside of actions that may be potentially inflationary. The ECB has found itself pushed into being a strong supporter of the letter of the SGP and of the Commission in its proposals, as that is the only way it can pin its remarks on rules rather than opinions. In the same way, led by the particular economic evolution of the period since 1999, governments have tended to criticise the ECB for harshness. This asymmetric atmosphere of complaint may spill over into caution elsewhere and hence a degree of self-fulfilling expectations of a more pessimistic future. It may also be spilling over into action, with the ECB being more reluctant to change in the face of promises it views with suspicion, and governments more ready to act in the expectation that the ECB will exercise just that caution.

The tradition of central bank councils being critical of governments and vice versa applies only in some countries, Germany being a good example. Observers of the more measured debate in the US may be forgiven for feeling that the extent and passion of any such (dis)agreements are different. The deficit in the US would have clearly triggered an excessive deficit procedure in the EU. It may simply be that the expression of the extent of disagreement is different according to tradition. While a period of more favourable economic circumstances may both dampen the rhetoric and permit actions that increase mutual trust, it may take an actual change in the framework to alter expectations and persuade observers that the future macroeconomic policy interaction will be different.

13.4 Specific policy recommendations

It is the 'E' in EMU which has given rise to most of the concerns under EMU, rather than monetary union as such. The ECB is generally seen as having got it right, though it probably needs to do more to ensure that transparency, in the widest sense, is built on so that its policies are clear to both expert and wider communities. Insofar as it adopts a somewhat unconventional approach to central banking, it needs to take full account of the fact that it is seen as unconventional and thus requires additional care and effort when explaining its approach and policies.

The European Court of Justice, by clarifying the scope of discretion available to the Council and the extent to which it is contained by the initial recommendations of the Commission, has both created an impetus to further reform and removed any notion that economic policy formation can occur exclusively within the political realm without any regard to law. The implication is that, soft law is more than the exercise of political discretion, and is shaped by the constitutional context in which it occurs in particular, the role of the institutions and other actors involved. As we explained in Part 1, the way hard and soft law are combined is one of the key institutional issues. We concur with the IMF (2004) in suggesting that there is a need to harden the soft law dimensions of the Pact and to soften the hard law dimensions. For the early warning system, this implies a need to prevent hi-jacking of the process by the Council and to ensure adequate transparency and peer pressure (both top–down and bottom–up). The uncertain status of such a warning shows the ambiguous commitment of the states to giving the Commission a role – allowing recalcitrant states some licence to challenge/ignore/fudge any such warning. It would be better at a minimum if it were a recommendation – a form of soft law widely used and generally recognised in the Union.

Most importantly, the multi-level governance nature of economic policy in the EU needs to be taken into account, especially when considering the balance of hard and soft law measures at the Union level. We therefore welcome the changes to the SGP agreed in March 2005. The severity of sanctions under the old procedure were such that they were undermined by the attempts of the Council to avoid triggering them, leaving it without credibility. At the same time, smaller states that have tended to meet the requirements of the Pact can rightly be concerned that they have less scope to evade the rules as they may not be able to muster the blocking votes needed. For credibility, the rules need to be consistently applied, with any get outs or exceptions transparent and up front. This implies that circumstances ought to be defined under which a breach of the thresholds will not be triggered. The March 2005 agreement appears to have moved in this direction, but it will be the detail and practice that matters in rendering the procedure more credible and hence more legitimate, as well as giving it greater relevance.

Some regard – or even guidance – needs to be given to the institutional framework at the national level: for example the IMF suggests (citing Gros, Mayer and Ubide, 2003) that the relevant Member State minister should have to account to Parliament when the country is the subject of a negative

Commission report. This simultaneously increases accountability, transparency and, hence, legitimacy. While prescription as to governance models at the national level may not be politically possible or desirable, some linkage between governance and policy outcomes could be achieved indirectly. A good illustration would be greater transparency in the follow-up from the BEPGs (as well as other policy processes, such as the National Reform Plans agreed as part of the 2005 re-launch of the Lisbon strategy) through to implementation at the national level and the feedback loop up to the EU. In other words, policy learning calls for regard to be had as to how institutions (broadly defined) affect outcomes as well as what those policy outcomes are or should be.

The difficulty the system faces – as the evidence presented in Part II of this book shows – is that some states are much closer to the boundaries of sustainable policy than others. It is those states, and not the general run of behaviour, that are likely to test the system first. While making exit or default unpleasant and expensive is a good form of discipline, making them unthinkable can lead to outliers causing more harm to the whole. Consequently the challenge is how to engineer reform that is both outcome-focussed – more countries meeting the targets set, and process-focussed – meeting those targets will be more likely if states can own the system because it is credible and legitimate. It is a demanding agenda, but not an impossible one.

Notes

1 Introduction

1. A typical demand-side policy is increased government expenditure or tax cuts aimed at providing a stimulus to aggregate demand.
2. An example of a supply-side policy is a reform of employment protection legislation with the aim of increasing labour market flexibility.
3. See, for example, the model developed in Artis and Buti (2000) and some of the contributions in Brunila *et al.* (2001) and Buti *et al.* (2002).
4. The request to the European Court of Justice by the Commission for review of the legality of the Ecofin conclusions on 25 November 2003 effectively to suspend the SGP was designed to clarify the nature of Ecofin discretion, see Case *C-27/04 Commission* v. *Council* 13 July 2004, nyr.

2 Macroeconomic policy in EMU

1. No data were available for Luxembourg, so the results refer to the remaining 14 countries and cover the period 1961 to 1999 although some results relate to the shorter period of 1972–1999.
2. While the asymmetry is clear for almost every country, there are some perverse signs and a number of rather insignificant coefficients. Moreover, the results for the individual countries vary substantially as well, showing that although the nature of the asymmetry may be common, its extent and the extent of the use of fiscal policy across the cycle vary markedly.
3. The US, Canada, Japan, New Zealand and Australia are also considered in Mayes and Virén (2003) with similar results. The size of the public sector is measured by employment and the private sector by output. The threshold variable is the share of government consumption in GDP. Variables are expressed in differences of logs and the equation also includes one lag on private sector variable. Koskela and Virén (2000) in developing the original analysis also consider labour shares and consumption shares but the pattern is qualitatively the same.
4. Estimation uses a GAUSS routine available from Bruce Hansen on http://www.ssc.wisc.edu/.
5. We use a more complex lag structure in estimation.
6. These models follow the common convention of using the output gap rather than unemployment.
7. Encompassing tests give a similar conclusion but the reformulation to put the two models in a common framework generates a number of perverse coefficients.
8. The data periods used are necessarily short, not just to avoid regime changes in monetary policy but also because it has been very difficult to obtain long data series for house prices. Even in the short data period only the prices for Denmark, Finland, Norway, Sweden and the UK are direct measures of house prices. Mayes and Virén (2002e) however also includes results using a much longer data set provided by Iacoviello, stretching back to 1972 for Germany, Italy, Spain, Sweden and the UK. The results are very similar.

9. This is one area where the reform of the SGP is hoping to make progress by tightening up on accounting and projection standards.
10. As HMT (2003h) points out, such consumption smoothing is only likely to be partial (Mankiw, 2000). What is at issue here is its extent and the degree to which membership of a monetary union may affect it.
11. There is a concern that at some point monetary policy may become unduly restrictive because it requires a wide range of prices and more particularly nominal wages to fall if average inflation is to be low enough. There may be a resistance to actual wage cuts. The existence of this rigidity in practice has been disputed (Cassino, 1995; Yates, 1998). Furthermore monetary policy itself encounters a bound when nominal interest rates reach zero and monetary policy has to operate through the exchange rate and further along the yield curve, thus hindering its ability to revive the economy. A result also disputed (Bernanke, 2003).
12. This is not the only form of solution and in Mayes and Virén (2003) we suggest creating twin markets for public debt in the EU, a first tranche that is in a sense at the European level and backed by the other Member States (we suggest up to 30% of GDP as an illustration) and a second tranche above that which is fully open to the threat of default might act as a disciplining device on the more profligate Member States.

3 The EMU constitution

1. 'Pact ruling euro nations is stupid, says Prodi', S. Castle, *The Independent*, 18 October 2002.
2. Article 105(1) EC.
3. Article 110(3) EC. It can issue regulations and decisions as well as non-binding recommendations and opinions.
4. Article 105(4) EC. For limitations on this privilege, see Case C-11/00 *Commission* v. *ECB* [2003] ECR I-7147, paragraph 110–11.
5. Article 106 EC.
6. Article 105(2) EC. There is also a limited role in respect of financial stability, see Article 105(6) EC.
7. Article 111 EC.
8. Denmark, Sweden, the United Kingdom and the ten new members that acceded to the EU in 2004 are not members.
9. Article 112(1) EC and statute of the ECB Article 11(1).
10. Article 121 EC.
11. Article 107 EC.
12. 2003/223/EC: Decision of the Council, meeting in the composition of the Heads of State or Government on 21 March 2003 on an amendment to Article 10.2 of the Statute of the European System of Central Banks and of the ECB OJ L 83, 1.4.03, pp. 66–8.
13. Article 112(2)(b) EC.
14. Article 123 EC.
15. Article 11.4, protocol on the statute of the ECB and the European System of Central Banks (1992) OJ C 191/78, 29 July 1992.
16. Article 113(1) EC. The President can also submit a motion for discussion.
17. Article 99 EC and Council Regulation 1466/97 OJ L 209, 2.8.97, p. 1. To be amended by the March 2005 council proposals, see ch. 13.
18. Article 99(4) EC.

19. Article 104 EC and Regulation 1467/97 OJ L 209, 2.8.97, p. 6. To be amended by the March 2005 council proposals, see ch. 13.
20. Article 104(13).
21. Case C-27/04 *Commission* v. *Council* OJ 2004 C 35/5.
22. Ibid. 13 July 2004, not yet reported.
23. Article 114(2) EC and Council Decision 1998/743/EC on composition OJ L 358, 31.12.1998, p. 109, and Council Decision 1999/8/EC on the EFC statute OJ L 5, 9.1.99, p. 71.
24. Article 114(1) EC.
25. Article 114(4) EC.
26. Resolution of the EC on the Stability and Growth Pact, OJ C 236, 2.8.97, p. 1.
27. Decision 1974/122/EEC OJ L 63, 5.3.74 as amended by Council Decision 2000/604/EC OJ L 158, 27.6.03, p. 55.
28. Council Decision 2000/604/EC of 11.10.00 on the composition and the statutes of the EPC OJ L 257, p. 30.
29. Article 130 EC. Council Decision 2000/98/EC OJ L 29, 24.1.00, p. 21.
30. Council Decision 2000/436/EC OJ L 172/26, 12.7.00.
31. Article 144 EC.
32. Article 99(3) EC.
33. Article 99(2) EC.
34. Article 5(2) for stabilisation programmes and Article 9(2) for convergence programmes Regulation 1466/97, n. 19.
35. Article 99(4) EC.
36. Article 104(3) EC.
37. Article 115 EC and Resolution of the EC on the Stability and Growth Pact, n. 26.
38. Article 108 EC and Article 7(1) Statute. The personnel of both the ECB and national central banks cannot take instruction from any EC institution or body, from Member State governments or from any other body.
39. The statute itself contains exceptions to this general rule, see Article 41(1).
40. Article 113(3) EC.
41. Article 113(1) EC. The President can also submit a motion for discussion.
42. Case C-11/00 *Commission* v. *ECB*, [2003] ECR I-7147, para. 130 et seg.
43. Article 99(2) EC.
44. Article 99(4) EC.
45. Article 104(11) EC.
46. See e.g. case T-333/99 X v. European Central Bank, ECR-SC [2001] I-A-199 and II-921.
47. Case C-11/00 *Commission* v. *ECB*, [2003] ECR I-7147.
48. Article 104(10) EC.
49. Article 10 EC.

4 Policy co-ordination under EMU

1. In 1997, Pierre Werner made the acerbic comment in conversation with one of the present authors that the start of Stage 3 would arrive a full thirty years after his first report on how to achieve it.
2. This is rather different from the normal meaning of legalisation as rendering something that was previously illegal as legal.
3. Case 22/70 *EC Commission* v. *EC Council*: Re European Road Transport Agreement (1971) ECR 263.

4. The constitutional treaty formalises the status of the Eurogroup and makes an explicit distinction in a number of areas between the members of the euro area and the other Member States who do not (yet) participate fully in Stage 3 of EMU.
5. Interviews carried out by the authors as part of ESRC project L213252034.

5 Structural policies as means of adjusting under EMU

1. Strictly, the Luxembourg process is only part of the EES, but the terms are used inter-changeably throughout to refer to employment and labour market initiatives agreed in recent years. It is important to note, however, that wage policies are covered in the BEPGs in the EU system, but are not explicitly addressed in the EES, nor in labour market deregulation.
2. IDT – International Data Corporation, EITO – European Information Technology Observatory, quoted in Commission (2002f), p. 28.
3. From 2003 onwards, however, the process changed from an annual to a medium-term exercise following the agreement to have more streamlined co-ordination.
4. Interviews with participants in the process.
5. Member States implement policies and can, and do, spend substantially on their employment polices. Some EU funding may be used insofar as the European Social Fund contributes to such policies, but in so doing it is not strictly as part of the EES.

6 The early years of EMU: Convergence, but uneven adjustment?

1. Crowley *et al.* (2005) use two forms of wavelet analysis to separate out the fluctuations in the economies at different frequencies. They lead to similar conclusions.
2. The 1992/1993 crisis led to a widening of the margins of fluctuation in the EMS and were followed by wide exchange rate fluctuations. But France maintained its central rate and the market rate returned to it in 1998. These problems were therefore more about the vagaries of the foreign exchange market than any deviation from the effective monetary union.
3. For 1961–1998 the correlation was 0.91415. It was marginally higher over the period 1983–1998, 0.93772, than it was from 1961–1983, 0.92389.
4. Such as the takeover of Nissan by Renault.
5. The explanation is that the Dutch price level will fall because of a technical adjustment, but a mechanical application of the formula would, nevertheless, mean a reference value much below the euro area average.
6. In a presentation to the ETUC conference on 'Delivering the Lisbon goals: The key role of macro economic policy making', held in Brussels on the 1st and 2nd of March 2005.

7 Germany: Painfully adjusting to EMU?

1. There has been considerable academic discussion of German dominance in the system. Although the influence of German monetary policy on other countries in the EMS was pervasive, German monetary policy was also to an extent influenced by conditions in other EMS countries (Gros and Thygesen, 1998).
2. Or whether Germany *should* be an EMU member.

3. With several countries falling towards to the bottom of their fluctuation margins within the parity grid against the Deutschmark, the onus for action would fall on these countries rather than Germany. Under the same circumstances, but with exchange rates fixed against the ECU, it would be the Deutschmark that would be out of line and therefore expected to take action. This would have undermined the Bundesbank's ability to manage inflation and so was not acceptable to Germany.
4. There were of course other problems such as misaligned exchange rates.
5. The margins of exchange rate fluctuation were widened from ±2.25% to ±15%.
6. In 2001 intra-EU exports of goods accounted for 16.4% of German GDP, compared with 13.4% for France and 12.0% for Italy (Commission, 2003f, Table 38).
7. Strictly the aggregation of the 15 separate national labour markets, since there is not really a single market for labour in the EU.
8. Coordination can be achieved by centralised bargaining or by institutional features, as in Germany.
9. 'Alliance for Jobs', which is currently suspended.
10. Except Sweden.
11. The Beveridge curve in this case is estimated using EC business survey data, which gives complete coverage of the 12 Member States. The percentage of manufacturing firms reporting labour shortages as the main factor limiting production is used instead of vacancies.
12. This implies that inactivity is rising, but if these individuals were not really actively engaged in the labour market, it is not really additional hidden unemployment.
13. 18 months for people aged 55 years and over, down from 32 months.
14. The significance is another matter 'this may not do much more than prevent a rise in non-wage labour costs for the moment and perhaps reduce them by 1 to 2%... and even then only from 2006 or 2007' (Schröder and Walter, 2003).
15. Up to €50,000.
16. In 6 of the 41 trades, the Meisterbrief is still required.
17. Associated with declining immigration.
18. An important factor behind the problems with the SGP.
19. Sinn and Reuter's estimate for Ireland is 2.3% because the effect of total factor productivity growth on prices is assumed to be greater.
20. Completely in the case of Ireland.
21. GNI is used to avoid the 'Irish problem' where, because of the substantial multinational firm presence in the economy, GNP is substantially smaller than GDP because of interest, profit and dividends paid overseas.
22. The increase in euro area inflation (0.137%) divided by the share of euro area output accounted for by the remaining countries (86.3%).

9 Finland: Membership to encourage change

1. The authors guessed wrongly that Italy and perhaps Spain and Portugal, in addition to Greece, would also not be in the first wave. When the report came out, in Swedish, in November 1996, that would have been a widely shared view. It is unlikely that this one item would have tipped the balance. The Finnish Commission was not appointed until after the Swedish report was published, although they completed their work by May of 1997. Even over that period there was little change in general sentiment over the likely outcome of the convergence process (or over EMU for that matter).

10 Sweden: Not now or not ever?

1. It may also be helped by the national economic association (Nationalekonomiska Föreningen) which has had a far more effective focus and debate on contemporary issues of economic policy than its counterpart professional associations in other countries (Henriksson, 2001).
2. There were marginal differences in the inflation target between the two countries. Sweden aimed, and still aims, for 2% inflation with a 1% tolerance either side, while Finland aimed not to exceed 2% but with phraseology that implied that the desired outcome was also around that level. This somewhat ambiguous and asymmetric approach has been adopted by the ECB. Hence the transition for Finland was smooth. For Sweden there could be a problem if inflation were near the top of the tolerated range though in practice rates inside the euro countries' range have been achieved consistently.
3. There is considerable debate over the appropriate measurement of the length of crises (Mayes and Liuksila, 2003, ch. 1) and Jonung and Hagberg's definition of when the growth rate returns to trend results in considerably smaller estimates than from calculations based on when the level of real income returns to its trend path.
4. The discussion of the Calmfors Commission included in Chapter 9 is not repeated here.
5. The report is careful to differentiate between new labour market mechanisms, such as those relating to the encouragement of mobility and retraining, that should be applied whether or not Sweden opts for Stage 3 of EMU, and those which are only required if entry does occur.
6. Currently the 'normal' automatic response is estimated to be up to 2% of GDP.
7. The FRA in New Zealand has a further requirement for the public sector to have non-negative net worth. This is rather different from the golden rule. The government is not simply constrained in its borrowing to ensure that there is an adequate rate of return on a project basis to justify an investment, it can take into account more long-lasting assets, such as real estate, which may have been acquired at almost no cost. The important issue remains that in some sense the fiscal position is sustainable. Thus in the New Zealand case it would be possible to pay-off all the debt holders in the long run, with current tax and spending plans if the public sector's assets were to be sold. Quite how this would enable government to continue thereafter is not of course addressed. The point is that the debt-holders need to have adequate confidence in the future value of their assets for the risk margin to be kept down to acceptable levels. Given that governments are sovereign, they can always change the rules in the future and that ability will in itself impart some risk.
8. According to evidence assembled by the OECD (1998) this compression will also tend to discourage the development of new enterprises. It is difficult either to undercut or attract staff away from the incumbents.

11 The United Kingdom: Prospering outside the euro area?

1. Protocol (25) on certain provisions relating to the United Kingdom of Great Britain and Northern Ireland (1992) of the consolidated Treaty (Commission, 2002a).
2. All Member States were members of the EMS but the operational part of the system which involved fixed exchange rates was the ERM.

3. Two ironies characterise the present framework. First, the Labour government, for reasons of political spin, has taken to referring to all public expenditure as 'investments' in public services. Second, a much repeated promise by Chancellor Gordon Brown was to abolish boom and bust (i.e. the economic cycle).
4. The government could have offset these effects with a tighter fiscal policy.
5. Based on a broad sample of partner countries and on consumer prices.
6. Calculations using data from OECD (2004).
7. A Member State has to respect the normal fluctuation margins provided for by the Exchange Rate Mechanism of the European Monetary System without severe tensions for at least the last two years before the examination. In particular, the Member State shall not have devalued its currency's bilateral central rate against any other Member State's currency on its own initiative for the same period.
8. The minimum so far has been Italy for 15 months before the examination. All the other current members completed two years in the ERM before becoming full members of EMU.
9. Volatility also makes it more difficult to recognise misalignment.
10. 1974–1993 UK average annual growth was 1.7%. The only EU-15 countries with lower growth were Denmark 1.3%, Greece 1.5% and Sweden 1.6% (Commission, 2004a).
11. Measured by the coefficient of variation.
12. The other exceptions were Austria, Italy and Greece.
13. Strictly the aggregation of the 15 separate national labour markets, since there is not really a single market for labour in the EU.
14. ILO unemployment measures unemployment on the basis of survey evidence as those looking for work.
15. Except Sweden.
16. The Beveridge curve in this case is estimated using EC business survey data, which gives complete coverage of the 12 Member States. The percentage of manufacturing firms reporting labour shortages as the main factor limiting production is used instead of vacancies.
17. It has also been looser than in France and Germany on a cyclically corrected basis.

12 The new members: Big bang or slow transition to Stage 3?

1. Speech to the 11th European Banking Congress in Frankfurt, 23 November 2001.
2. These figures are measured in PPS. They have to be treated with some caution because of intra-country disparities in price levels and the incidence of undeclared activity.
3. Greece's deficit has remained at around 25% of exports.
4. Nor indeed have many euro area Member States.
5. The gap had been sufficiently high that, even with the strict limitation on duty-free quantities, it was possible to save more than the costs of the boat fare to Estonia with the difference in duty charged. Although duty is applied after membership, the increased quantities that could be imported could have resulted in a major diversion of activity. As it is, alcohol tax revenue has risen in Finland despite the size of the cuts in the rate – possibly not one of the more intended gains from EU enlargement.
6. To a significant extent Estonia is already having to adjust to euro area conditions because, with the currency board, the exchange rate is fixed. Membership would in addition imply a monetary policy geared to average euro area conditions rather than to maintaining the exchange rate parity.

7. Source: UNCTAD (2004); statistics for the Czech Republic were not available.
8. Levels of FDI were lower in the 1980s.
9. There is also a concern about becoming dependent upon Russia for energy.
10. Many of the smokestack industries were concentrated in the Russian-dominated areas of Estonia. The combination of a history of large-scale economic activity and a Russian cultural and language tradition have not been favourable to entrepreneurship. In some areas up to 80% of the population can be Russian-speaking.

Bibliography

Abbott, K.W., Keohane, R.O., Moravcsik, A., Slaughter, A.-M. and Snidal, D. (2000) 'The Concept of Legalization', *International Organization*, vol. 54, pp. 401–19.

Abbott, K.W. and Snidal, D. (2000) 'Hard and Soft Law in International Governance', *International Organization*, vol. 54, pp. 421–56.

Abel, A.B. and Eberly, J.C. (1999) 'The Effects of Irreversibility and Uncertainty on Capital Accumulation', *Journal of Monetary Economics*, vol. 44, pp. 339–77.

Addison, J. and Grosso, J.-L. (1996) 'Job Security Provisions and Unemployment: Revised Estimates', *Industrial Relations*, vol. 35, pp. 585–603.

Agell, J., Calmfors, L. and Jonsson, G. (1996) 'Fiscal Policy when Monetary Policy is Tied to the Mast', *European Economic Review*, vol. 40, pp. 1413–40.

Agenda 2000 – Commission Opinion on Estonia's Application for Membership of the European Union – 15 July 1997, DOC/97/12.

Aiginger, K. and Leitner, W. (2001) 'Regional Concentration in the USA and Europe: Who Follows Whom?', http://www.wifo.ac.at/Karl.Aiginger/publications/2001/Regconc.pdf.

Aizenman, J. (1992) 'Exchange Rate Flexibility, Volatility and Patterns of Domestic and Foreign Direct Investment', *IMF Staff Papers*, vol. 39, pp. 890–922.

Aizenman, J. (1994) 'On the Need for Fiscal Discipline in an Union', *National Bureau of Economic Research Working Paper*, W4656.

Akerlof, G., Dickens, A., Perry, W. and George, L. (2000) 'Near Rational Wage Price Setting and Long-run Phillips Curve', *Brookings Papers on Economic Activity*' vol. 30(1), pp. 1–44.

Alberola, E., Cervero, S.G., Lopez, H. and Ubide, A. (1999) 'Global Equilibrium Exchange Rates: Euro, Dollar, "Ins", "Outs" and other Majority Currencies in a Panel Cointegration Framework', *IMF Working Paper*, No. 99/175, Washington: International Monetary Fund.

Alesina, A., Blanchard, O., Gali, J., Giavazzi, F. and Uhlig, H. (2001) *Defining a Macroeconomic Framework for the Euro Area*, Monitoring the European Central Bank 3, London: Centre for Economic Policy Research.

Algoé Consultants in conjunction with Alphametrics Limited (2002) 'The Construction of an Index of Labour Market Adaptability for EU Member States', report for the European Commission.

Allsopp, C. and Vines, D. (1996) 'Fiscal Policy and EMU', *National Institute Economic Review*, vol. 158, pp. 91–107.

Allsopp, C.J. (2002) 'The Future of Macroeconomic Policy in the Euro Area', Presented to the Austrian Institute of Economic Research (WIFO), February 2002. Available as Discussion Paper 7. External MPC Discussion Paper Series, Bank of England.

Allsopp, C.J. and Artis, M.J. (2003) 'The Assessment: EMU, Four Years On', *Oxford Reivew of Economic Policy*, vol. 19(1), pp. 1–29.

Amtenbrink, F. (1999) *The Democratic Accountability of Central Banks: A Comparative Study of the European Central Bank*, Oxford: Hart.

Amtenbrink, F. and de Haan, J. (2003) 'Economic Governance in the European Union: Fiscal Policy Discipline versus Flexibility', *Common Market Law Review*, vol. 40, pp. 1075–106.

Andersen, J.V. and Rasmussen, J.H. (1999) 'Solving the Unemployment Puzzle in Europe', *EIB Papers*, vol. 4(2), pp. 50–9.

Angeloni, I., Kashyap, A., Mojon, B. and Terlizzeese, D. (2002) 'Monetary Transmission in the Euro Area: Where Do We Stand?', *ECB Working Paper*, No. 114.

Ardy, B. (2004) *Employment and Unemployment in Germany and the UK and the European Employment Strategy*, London and Berlin: Anglo German Foundation.

Ardy, B., Begg, I., Schelkle, W. and Torres, F. (2002) *EMU and Cohesion: Theory and Policy*, in S. Joao do Estoril – Cascais: Principia.

Ardy, B. and Umbach, G. (2004) *The European Employment Strategy and Employment Policy in the UK and Germany*, London and Berlin: Anglo-German Foundation.

Arestis, P. and Sawyer, M. (2003) 'Macroeconomic Policies of the Economic Monetary Union: Theoretical Underpinnings and Challenges', *Levy Institute Working Paper 385*, July.

Arrowsmith, J., Barrell, R., Pain, N., Young, G. and Wlodek, K. (1997) *Capital Market Liberalisation in Europe*, London: Kogan Page.

Artis, M. (2003) 'Analysis of European and UK Business Cycles and Shocks', HM Treasury, EMU Study, London: HMSO.

Artis, M. and Buti, M. (2000) ' "Close to Balance or in Surplus": A Policy-maker's Guide to the Implementation of the Stability and Growth Pact', *Journal of Common Market Studies*, vol. 38, pp. 563–91.

Artis, M. and Ehrmann, M. (2000) 'The Exchange Rate. A Shock Absorber or a Source of Shocks? A Study of Four Open Economies', *EUI Working Papers*, RSC No. 2000/38.

Artis, M. and Zhang, W. (1999) 'Further Evidence on the International Business Cycle and the ERM: Is there a European Business Cycle?', *Oxford Economic Papers*, No. 51, pp. 120–32.

Artis, M. Krolzig, H.-M. and Toro, J. (1999) 'The European Business Cycle', *European Institute – EUI Working Papers in Economics*, No. 99/24, European Institute – European Forum.

Asdrubali, P., Sorensen, B. and Yosha, O. (1996) 'Channels of Interstate Risk Sharing: United States 1963–1990', *Quarterly Journal of Economics*, vol. 111 (November), pp. 1081–110.

Astley, M.S. and Garratt, A. (1998) 'Exchange Rates and Prices: Sources of Sterling Real Exchange Rate Fluctuations 1979–94', *Bank of England Working Paper*, No. 85.

Bacarro, L. and Simoni, M. (2004) 'The Irish Social Partnership and the "celtic tiger" Phenomenon', *International Labour Organisation, Discussion Paper*, DP/154/2004.

Baker, T., Fitzgerald, J. and Honohan, P. (eds) (1996) *Economic Implications for Ireland of EMU*, Dublin: Economic and Social Research Institute.

Baldwin, R. (1995) *Rules and Government*, Oxford: Clarendon Press.

Balmaseda, M., Sebastián, M. and Tello, P. (2002) 'Spain Accession to the EMU: A Long and Hilly Road', *The Economic and Social Review*, vol. 33(2), pp. 195–222.

Bandilla, R. (2004) 'The Excessive Deficit Procedure and the Result of the Ecofin Council of 25 November 2003 – Some Preliminary Comments', Centre for European Policy Studies, Brussels, http://www.ceps.be/Article.php?article_id=290.

Bank of Estonia (Eesti Pank) (1993) 'Law on the Central Bank of the Republic of Estonia', http://www.ee.epbe/norm/index.html.en.

Bank of Finland (2000) 'The Bank of Finland's Macroeconomic Forecast 2000–2002', *Bulletin*, vol. 74(2), pp. 2–17.

Bank of Finland (2001) 'The Bank of Finland's Macroeconomic Forecast 2001–2003', *Bulletin*, vol. 75(2), pp. 1–16.

Bank of Finland (2003) 'The Bank of Finland's Macroeconomic Forecast 2003–2005', *Bulletin*, vol. 77(3), pp. 1–16.

Banque de France (1998) 'Statute of the Bank of France', http://www.banque-france.fr/gb/banque/main.htm.

Barnard, C. (2002) 'The Social Partners and the Governance Agenda', *European Law Journal*, vol. 8(1), pp. 80–101.

Barrell, R. (ed.) (1992) *Economic Convergence and Monetary Union in Europe*, London: Sage Publications.

Barrell, R. (2002) 'The UK and EMU: Choosing the Regime', *National Institute Economic Review*, No. 180, April, pp. 54–71.

Barrell, R., Darby, J. and Donaldson, C. (1992) 'Structural Stability in European Wage and Price Systems', *NIESR Discussion Paper*, No. 188.

Barrett, A. and Trace, F. (1998) 'Who is Coming Back? The Educational Profile of Returning Migrants in the 1990s', *Irish Banking Review*, Summer, pp. 38–52.

Barro, R.J. (1990) 'Government Spending in Simple Model of Economic Growth', *Journal of Political Economy*, vol. 98, pp. 103–25.

Barry, F. (ed.) (1999) *Understanding Ireland's Economic Growth*, Basingstoke: Macmillan.

Barry, F. (2003) 'Economic Integration and Convergence Processes in the EU Cohesion Countries', *Journal of Common Market Studies*, vol. 41(5), pp. 897–921.

Battocchi, M. (2003) 'Italy's Admission to the Third Stage of the European Monetary Union: A Case Study on the Diplomacy of European Integration', Woodrow Wilson School Case 01/03, Princeton University, http://www.wws.princeton.edu/~cases/papers/italy.pdf.

Bayoumi, T. and Eichengreen, B. (1993) 'Shocking Aspects of European Monetary Unification', in F. Torres and F. Giavazzi (eds), *Adjustment and Growth in European Monetary Union*, Cambridge: Cambridge University Press.

Bayoumi, T. and Eichengreen, B. (1997) 'Ever Close to Heaven? An Optimum-Currency-Area Index for European Countries', *European Economic Review*, vol. 41, pp. 761–70.

Bayoumi, T. and Masson, P. (1995) 'Fiscal Flows in the United States and Canada: Lessons for Monetary Union in Europe', *European Economic Review*, vol. 39, pp. 253–74.

Beatty, C., Fothergill, S., Gore, T. and Green, A. (2002) 'The Real Level of Unemployment 2002', Centre for Regional Economic and Social Research, Sheffield Hallam University.

Beaumont, P. and Walker, N. (eds) (1999) 'The Euro and the European Legal Order', *Legal Framework of the Single European Currency*, Oxford: Hart.

Beetsma, R. and Bovenberg, A. (1999) 'The Interaction of Fiscal Policy and Monetary Policy in a Monetary Union: Balancing Credibility and Flexibility', in A. Razin and E. Sadka (eds), *The Economics of Globalization: Policy Perspectives from Public Economics*, Cambridge, New York and Melbourne: Cambridge University Press, pp. 373–405.

Beetsma, R. and Uhlig, H. (1999) 'An Analysis of the Stability and Growth Pact', *Economic Journal*, vol. 109(458), October 1999, pp. 546–71.

Begg, D., Canova, F., De Grauwe, P., Fatas, A. and Lane, P. (2002) *Surviving the Slowdown*, Monitoring the European Central Bank 4, London: CEPR.

Begg, D., Halpern, L. and Wypolsz, C. (1999) 'Monetary and Exchange Rate Policies', EMU and Central and Eastern Europe, CEPR, New York: London Eastwest Institute.

Begg, I. (2002a) 'Running EMU: The Challenges of Policy Co-ordination', in Begg (2002b), pp. 13–28.

Begg, I. (ed.) (2002b) *Europe, Government and Money – Running EMU: The Challenges of Policy Co-ordination*, London: The Federal Trust.

Begg, I. (2003) 'Complementing EMU: Rethinking Cohesion Policy', *Oxford Review of Economic Policy*, vol. 19(1), pp. 161–79.

Begg, I. (2005) 'Do We Really Need a Lisbon Strategy?', *Intereconomics*, vol. 40, pp. 56–9.

Begg, I. and Berghman, J. (2002) 'Introduction: EU Social (Exclusion) Policy Revisited', *Journal of European Social Policy*, vol. 12, pp. 179–94.

Begg, I., Buti, M., Enderlein, H., Pench, L., Schelkle, W. and Weale, M.R. (2004) 'Symposium on Reform of Fiscal Policy Co-ordination', *Journal of Common Market Studies*, vol. 42, pp. 1023–60.

Begg, I. and Grimwade, N. (1998) *Paying for Europe*, Sheffield: Sheffield Academic Press.

Begg, I., Hodson, D. and Maher, I. (2003) 'Economic Policy Coordination in the European Union', *National Institute Economic Review*, No. 183, January, pp. 66–77.

Begg, I. and Mayes, D.G. (1991) *A New Strategy for Social and Economic Cohesion after 1992*, Luxembourg: European Parliament.

Begg, I. and Schelkle, W. (2004a) 'The Pact is Dead: Long Live the Pact', *National Institute Economic Review*, vol. 189.

Begg, I. and Schelkle, W. (2004b) 'Can Fiscal Policy Co-ordination be Made to Work Effectively?', *Journal of Common Market Studies*, vol. 42(5), pp. 1047–55.

Bentolila, S. and Bertola, G. (1990) 'Firing Costs and Labour Demand: How Bad is Euro Sclerosis?', *Review of Economic Studies*, vol. 57, pp. 381–402.

Bernanke, B. (2003) 'An Unwelcome Fall in Inflation?', *Economics Roundtable*, University of California, San Diego, La Jolla, California, July 23.

Bernanke, B.S. (1986) 'Alternative Explanations of the Money-Income Correlation', *Carnegie-Rochester Conference Series on Public Policy*, vol. 25, pp. 49–100.

Bini Smaghi, L. and Casini, C. (2000) 'Monetary and Fiscal Policy Co-operation in EMU', *Journal of Common Market Studies*, vol. 38(3), pp. 375–91.

Björksten, N. (2000) 'Real Convergence in the Enlarged Euro Area: A Coming Challenge for Monetary Policy', *Bank of Finland Working Paper*, No. 1/2000.

Blanchard, O. and Jimeno, J.F. (1999) 'Reducing Spanish Unemployment under the EMU', *Working Papers*, No. 99–02, FEDEA.

Blanchard, O.J. (2001) 'Country Adjustment within Euroland. Lessons after Two Years', mimeo, Department of Economics, Massachusetts Institute of Technology.

Blanchard, O.J. and Jimeno, J.F. (1995) 'Structural Unemployment: Spain versus Portugal', *American Economic Review*, vol. 85(2), pp. 212–18.

Blanchard, O.J. and Muet, P.A. (1993) 'Competitiveness through Disinflation: An Assessment of the French Macroeconomic Strategy', *Economic Policy*, vol. 16, April, pp. 11–56.

Blanchard, O.J. and Quah, D. (1989) 'The Dynamic Effects of Aggregate Demand and Supply Disturbances', *American Economic Review*, vol. 79, pp. 655–73.

Blanchard, O.J. and Watson, M.W. (1986) 'Are Business Cycles All Alike?', in R. Gordon (ed.), *The American Business Cycle: Continuity and Change*, Chicago: NBER and University of Chicago Press, pp. 123–56.

Blanchard, P. and Sevestre, P. (1989) 'L'indexation des salaires: quelle rupture en 1982?', *Economie et Prévision*, No. 87.

Blinder, A. (1997) 'Is Government too Political?', *Foreign Affairs*, November/ December, pp. 115–26.

Blinder, A.S. (1999) 'Central Bank Credibility: Why Do We Care? How Do We Build It?', *National Bureau of Economic Research Working Paper*, No. 7161.

Blomström, M. (2000) 'Internationalisation and Growth: Evidence from Sweden', *Swedish Economic Policy Review*, vol. 7, pp. 185–201.

Boissieu, C. de and Pisani-Ferry, J. (1995) The Political Economy of French Economic Policy and the Transition to EMU, CEPII, Document de travail No. 95–09.

Booth, A., Burda, M., Calmfors, L., Checchi, D., Naylor, R. and Visser, J. (2000) 'What do Unions do in Europe', *A Report for the Fondazione Rodolfo DeBendetti*, Milan, http://www.frdb.org/english/Labour/report1_17giugno00.pdf.

Bootle, R. (2001) *Britain's Trade with the EU and the Rest of the World: What Does our Current Account Really Look Like*?, London: New Europe, Online www.no-euro.com.

Bordes, C. and Giradin, E. (1992) 'The Achievements of the ERM and the Preconditions for Monetary Union: A French Perspective', in Barrell (ed.) (1992).

Borghijs, A. and Kuijs, L. (2004) 'Exchange Rates in Central Europe: A Blessing or a Curse', *IMF Working Paper* WP/04/2.

Bover, O., García-Perea, P. and Portugal, P. (2000) 'Iberian Labour Markets: Why Spain and Portugal are OECD Outliers', *Economic Policy*, No. 31, October, pp. 380–428.

Boyer, R. (sous la présidence) (1999) *Le gouvernement économique de la zone euro*, Paris: La documentation française.

Boyer, R. (2002) 'Co-ordination of Economic Policies in Europe: From Uncertainty to Apprenticeship', in Begg (2002b), pp. 39–54.

Braunerhjelm, P., Faini, R., Norman, R., Ruane, F. and Seabright, P. (2000) *Integration and the Regions of Europe: How the Right Policies can Prevent Polarization*, Monitoring Integration 10, London: Centre for Economic Policy Research.

Brewin, C. (1997) 'The External Impact', in D.G. Mayes (ed.), *The Evolution of the Single European Market*, Cheltenham: Edward Elgar.

Brunila, A., Buti, M. and Franco, D. (eds) (2001) *The Stability and Growth Pact: The Architecture of Fiscal Policy in EMU*, Basingstoke: Palgrave.

Buiter, W.H. (1999) 'Alice in Euroland', *Journal of Common Market Studies*, vol. 37(2), pp. 181–209.

Buiter, W.H. and Grafe, C. (2002) 'Anchor, Float or Abandon Ship: Exchange Rate Regimes for the Accession Countries', *Banca Nazionale Del Lavoro Quarterly Review*, No. 221, June 2002, pp. 1–32.

Buiter, W.H. and Grafe, C. (2003a) 'Patching up the Pact: Some Suggestions for Enhancing Fiscal Sustainability and Macroeconomic Stability in an Enlarged European Union', in Buti (ed.) (2003b), pp. 92–156.

Buiter, W.H. and Grafe, C. (2003b) 'Emu or Ostrich?', *Submissions on EMU from Leading Academics, EMU Study*, HM Treasury, London: HMSO.

Buiter, W.H., Corsetti, G. and Roubini, N. (1993) 'Excessive Deficits: Sense and Nonsense in the Treaty of Maastricht', *Economic Policy*, vol. 16, pp. 57–100.

Burgess, R., Fabrizio, S. and Xiao, Y. (2003) 'Competitiveness in the Baltics in the Run-Up to EU Accession', *IMF Country Report*, No. 03/114.

Bush, J. (ed.) (2001) *The Economic Case Against the Euro*, London: New Europe, Available, Online www.no-euro.com.

Buti, M. (2003a) 'Interactions and Coordination Between Monetary and Fiscal Policies in EMU: What are the Issues', in Buti (ed.) (2003b), pp. 1–25.

Buti, M. (ed.) (2003b) *Monetary and Fiscal Policies in EMU: Interactions and Coordination*, Cambridge: Cambridge University Press.

Buti, M. and Giudice, G. (2002) 'Maastricht's Fiscal Rules at 10: An Assessment', *Journal of Common Market Studies*, vol. 40(5), pp. 823–48.

Buti, M. and Pench, L. (2004) 'Why do Large Countries Flout the Stability Pact, and What Can Be Done about It?', *Journal of Common Market Studies*, vol. 42(5), pp. 1025–32.

Buti, M., Eijffinger, S. and Franco, D. (2003c) 'Revisiting EMU's Stability Pact: A Pragmatic Way Forward', *Oxford Review of Economic Policy*, vol. 19(1), pp. 100–11.

Buti, M., von Hagen, J. and Martinez-Mongay, C. (eds) (2002) *The Behaviour of Fiscal Authorities*, Basingstoke: Palgrave.

Buxton, A. and Mayes, D.G. (1986) 'The Persistence of Unemployment', *Quarterly Bulletin*, No. 88 (December) pp. 29–37.

Byrne, J.P. and Davis, E.P. (2002) 'A Comparison of Balance Sheet Structures in Major EU Countries', *National Institute Economic Review*, No. 180 (April), pp. 83–96.

Calmfors, L. (2001) 'Unemployment, Labor Market Reform, and Monetary Union', *Journal of Labor Economics*, vol. 19, pp. 265–89.

Calmfors, L. and Driffill, J. (1988) 'Bargaining Structure, Corporatism and Macroeconomic Performance', *Economic Policy*, No. 6, pp. 14–61.

Calmfors, L., Flam, H., Gottfries, N., Matlary, J.H., Jerneck, M., Lindahl, R., Berntsson, C.N., Rabinowicz, E. and Vredin, A. (1997) *EMU – A Swedish Perspective*, Dordrecht: Kluwer.

Campa, J.M. (1993) 'Entry by Foreign Firms in the United States Under Exchange Rate Uncertainty', *Review of Economics and Statistics*, vol. 75, pp. 614–22.

Canzoneri, M.B., Vallés, J. and Vinals, J. (1996) 'Do Exchange Rates Move to Address International Macroeconomic Imbalances?', *Centre for Economic Policy Research Discussion Paper*, No. 1498.

Carlin, W. and Glyn, A. (2003) 'British Exports, Cost Competitiveness and Exchange Rate Arrangements', *Submissions on EMU from leading academics, EMU Study*, HM Treasury, London: HMSO.

Carlin, W., Glyn, A. and Manning, M. (2002) 'Cost Competitiveness and Export Performance in OECD Economies: How Does the UK Compare?', *Paper Prepared for HM Treasury*, www.ucl.ac.uk/~uctpa36/CarlinGlynManning.pdf.

Carlin, W., Glyn, A. and Van Reenen, J. (2001) 'Export Market Performance of OECD Countries: An Empirical Examination of the Role of Cost Competitiveness', *Economic Journal*, vol. 111, January, pp. 128–62.

Carruth, A., Dickerson, A. and Henley, H. (2000) 'What Do We Know About Investment Under Uncertainty?', *Journal of Economic Surveys*, vol. 14, pp. 119–53.

Cassino, V. (1995) 'The Distribution of Price Shocks to the New Zealand Economy', Reserve Bank of New Zealand.

CEPS Macroeconomic Policy Group (2002) *The Euro at 25: Special Report on Enlargement*, Brussels: CEPS.

Chalmers, D. (1998) *European Union Law: Law and EU Government*, Aldershot: Dartmouth.

Chan, K.S. (1993) 'Consistency and Limiting Distribution of the Least Squares Estimator of the Threshold Autoregressive Model', *The Annals of Statistics*, vol. 21(1), pp. 520–33.

Chassard, Y. (2001) 'European Integration and Social Protection: From the Spaak Report to the Open Method of Co-ordination', in D.G. Mayes, J. Berghman and R. Salais (eds), *Social Exclusion and European Poverty*, Cheltenham: Edward Elgar, pp. 277–305.

Chiorazzo, V. and Spaventa, L. (1999) 'The prodigal son or a confidence trickster? How Italy got into EMU', in D. Cobham and G. Zis (eds), *From EMS to EMU: 1979 to 1999 and beyond*, Basingstoke: Macmillan.

Cihak, M. and Holub, T. (2003) 'Price Convergence to the EU: What do the 1999 ICP Data Tell us?', *Czech National Bank Working Paper*, No. 2/2003.

Cini, M. (2001) 'The Soft Law Approach: Commission Rule-Making in the EU's State Aid Regime', *Journal of European Public Policy*, vol. 8(2), pp. 192–207.

Coleman, A. (2001) 'Three Perspectives on an Australasian Monetary Union', in D. Gruen and J. Simon (eds), *Future Directions for Monetary Policy in East Asia*, Sydney: Reserve Bank of Australia, pp. 156–88.

Collignon, S. (2001) 'Economic Policy Co-ordination in EMU: Institutional and Political Requirements', Center for European Studies (CES), Harvard University, May 2001.

Commission and Council of the European Communities (1992) '*Treaty on European Union*', Protocol on the Statute of the ESCB and the ECB, Luxembourg: OOPEC.

Commission of the European Communities (1989) *Report of the Study Group on Economic and Monetary Union*, (the Delors Report) Brussels: Commission of the European Communities.

Commission of the European Communities (1995) 'Migration Statistics', Luxembourg: Office for the Official Publications of the European Communities.

Commission of the European Communities (1998) Euro 1999. 'Report on Progress towards Convergence and Recommendation with a View to the Transition to the Third Stage of Economic and Monetary Union', COM (98) 1999, Luxembourg: OOPEC.

Commission of the European Communities (1999a) *Employment Rates Report 1998*, Employment Performance in the Member States, DG Employment and Social Affairs.

Commission of the European Communities (1999b) 'Annual Economic Report for 1999', *European Economy*, No. 68.

Commission of the European Communities (2001a) 'Communication on Strengthening Economic Policy Co-ordination with the Euro Area', COM (2001) 82, final.

Commission of the European Communities (2001b) 'European Governance: A White Paper', COM (2001) 428, 25 July.

Commission of the European Communities (2002a) Commission Assesses the German Stability Programme (2001–2005) Press Release IP/02/164.

Commission of the European Communities (2002b) Communication from the Commission to the Council and the European Parliament: Strengthening the Co-ordination of Budgetary Policies COM (200) 668, final.

Commission of the European Communities (2002c) Public Finances in EMU, Brussels.

Commission of the European Communities (2002d), Communication from the Commission: A Project for the European Union, COM(2002) 247, final.

Commission of the European Communities (2002e) 'Co-ordination of Economic Policies in the EU: A Presentation of the Key Features of the Main Procedures', DG for Economic and Financial Affairs, *Euro Papers*, No. 45.

Commission of the European Communities (2002f) Communication from the Commission to the Council of Ministers and the European Parliament: Strengthening the Co-ordination of Budgetary Policies COM (2002) 668, final.

Commission of the European Communities (2002g) Consolidated Version of the treaty Establishing the European Community, *Official Journal C* 325, 24 December.

Commission of the European Communities (2002h) 'Germany's Growth Performance in the 1990s', DG Economic and Financial Affairs, *Economic Paper*, No. 170.

Commission of the European Communities (2002i) 'Impact Evaluation of the EES, Background Paper, Tax-Benefit Reforms and the Taxation of Labour', EMCO/23/060602/EN_REV 1, http://www.europa.eu.int/comm/employment_social/news/2002/may/tax_en.pdf.

Commission of the European Communities (2002j) *Industrial Relations in Europe 2002*, DG Employment, http://europa.eu.int/comm/employment_social/news/2002/ oct/indust_rels_europe_en.pdf.

Commission of the European Communities (2003a) Broad Guidelines of the Economic Policies of the Member States and the Community for 2003–05, COM (2003) 170.

Commission of the European Communities (2003b) Opinion on the Draft Council Decision on a Revision of the Statutes of the Economic and Financial Committee OJ C 130/9, 4 June.

Commission of the European Communities (2003c) Proposal for a Council Decision establishing a Social Protection Committee COM(2003) 305 final, 24 June.

Commission of the European Communities (2003d) 'From Accession to Adopting the Euro', Speech by Commissioner Pedro Solbes, Coordination in EMU and future participation of the Acceding Countries Conference, Warsaw, DN SPEEC/03/563, 21st November 2003.

Commission of the European Communities (2003e) *The Future of the European Employment Strategy (EES) 'A Strategy for Full Employment and Better Jobs for All'*, Communication from the Commission to the Council, the European Parliament, the Economic and Social Committee and the Committee of the Regions, COM(2003) 6 final.

Commission of the European Communities (2003f) Statistical Annexe of *European Economy*, No. 6, Autumn, DG Economic and Financial Affairs.

Commission of the European Communities (2003g) Statistical Annexe, Autumn 2003 Economic Forecasts, *European Economy*, No. 5/2003

Commission of the European Communities (2003h) *Eurobarometer*, 60, November, DG Press and Communication.

Commission of the European Communities (2003i) 'The Report on the Implementation of the 2002 Broad Economic Policy Guidelines (published as *European Economy*. No. 1 2003. Office for Official Publications of the EC. Luxembourg).

Commission of the European Communities (2003j) 'Spring 2003 Economic Forecasts' Directorate-General for Economic and Financial Affairs, Brussels.

Commission of the European Communities (2003k) 'Proposal for a Council Decision on Guidelines for the Employment Policies of the Member States', Brussels, 8 April.

Commission of the European Communities (2003l) Communication from the Commission to the Council, the European Parliament, the European Economic and Social Committee and the Committee of the Regions on 'Progress in implementing the Joint Assessment Papers on employment policies in acceding countries' (COM(2003) 663 final of 06/11/2003).

Commission of the European Communities (2003m) Comprehensive Monitoring Report on Estonia's Preparation for Membership available at: http://eng.euroopaliit.ee/docs/Monitoring%20Report%20on%20Estonia.doc.

Commission of the European Communities (2004a) 'Delivering Lisbon Reforms', Report from the Commission to the Spring European Council, COM (2004) 29 final/2, Brussels.

Commission of the European Communities (2004b) *3rd Cohesion Report*, Brussels.

Commission of the European Communities (2004c) Commission sets out Strategy for Economic Policy Coordination and Surveillance, Brussels IP/04/35.

Commission of the European Communities (2004d) 'AMECO Online Database', DG Economic and Financial Affairs, http://www.europa.eu.int/comm/economy_finance/indicators/annual_macro_economic_database/ameco_en.htm.

Commission of the European Communities (2004e) 'Commission Assesses the 2003 Update of the UK Convergence Programme', Press Release, IP/04/111, 28 January.

Commission of the European Communities (2004f) 'Communication from the Commission on the Implementation of the 2003–05 Broad Economic Policy Guidelines', COM (2004) 20.

Commission of the European Communities (2004g) 'Information Note to the Commission Implementation Report', Ecofin/392/03.

Commission of the European Communities (2004h) 'Convergence Report 2004', COM(2004) 690 final.

Commission of the European Communities (2004i) 'Communication from the Commission to the Council and the European Parliament: Strengthening Economic Governance and Clarifying the Implementation of the Stability and Growth Pact', COM(2004) 581(final).

Commission of the European Communities (2004j) 'Communication from the Commission to the Council and the European Parliament: The Situation of Germany and France in Relation to their Obligations under the Excessive Deficit Procedure following the Judgment of the Court of Justice', COM(2004) 813.

Commission of the European Communities (2005a) 'The Economy for the Euro Area, the European Union, and Candidate countries in 2004 – 2006: Economic Forecasts, Spring 2005', *European Economy*, No. 2.

Commission of the European Communities (2005b) 'Country Study: Spain in EMU: A virtuous Long-lasting Cycle?', *European Economy*, Occasional Papers, Brussels: European Commission.

Commission of the European Communities (various) *Employment in Europe*, Luxembourg: OOPEC.

Confais, E. and Muet, P.-A. (1994) 'Les Rigidités du Marché du Travail', in Muet, P.-A. (ed.), *'Le Chômage Persitant en Europe'*, Références/OFCE, Paris: Presses de la Fondation Nationale des Sciences Politiques.

Conseil d'Analyse Economique (2004) *Réformer la pacte de stabilité et de croissance*, Paris: La documentation française.

Coudert, V. and Couharde, C. (2002) 'Exchange Rate Regimes and Sustainable Parities for CEECs in the Run-Up to EMU Membership', *CEPII Working Paper*, No. 2002–15.

Council and Commission of the EC (1970) 'Report to the Council and the Commission on the Realisation by Stages of Economic and Monetary Union in the Community' – The Werner Report, *Bulletin of the EC* 7-1970, Supl.

Council of the EC (1988) Council Directive 88/361/EEC of 24 June 1988 for the implementation of Article 67 of the Treaty, OJ L 178 08.07.1988, p. 5.

Council of the EU (1998) Council decision of 3 May 1998 in accordance with Article 109j(4) of the Treaty (98/317/EC), *Official Journal L*, 139, 11.5.1998, p. 30.

Council of the EU (1999) 'Council Opinion of 15 March 1999 on the Stability Programme of France 1999 to 2002', *Official Journal C*, 124, 5/5/1999, p. 2.

Council of the EU (2000) 'Council Opinion of 13 March 2000 on the Updated Stability Programme of France 2000 to 2003', *Official Journal C*, 111, 18/4/2000, p. 1.

Council of Ministers (2002) 'Council Decision of 18th February 2002 on Guidelines for Member states' Employment Policies for the Year 2002', OJEC 1.2.2002.

Creel, J. and Sterdyniak, H. (1995) 'Les déficits Publics en Europe: Causes, Conséquences ou remèdes à la crise?', *Revue de l'OFCE*, n°54, July.

Creel, J., Latreille, T. and Le Cacheux, J. (2002) 'Le Pacte de stabilité et les politiques budgétaires dans l'Union européenne', *Revue de l'OFCE*, n°81, March.

Crowley, P.M., Marann, D. and Mayes, D.G. (2005) 'Analysing Growth in the Euro Area: Multivariate Spectral Analysis of Growth Cycles Using a CWT and Hilbert Wavelet Pairs', 'Growth and Cyclical Asymmetries in France, Germany and Italy' conference, Banque de France, 22–23 June.

Cukierman, A. (1992) *Central Bank Strategy, Credibility and Independence: Theory and Evidence*, Cambridge, MA: The MIT Press.

Danish Ministry of Finance (1999) *The Danish Economy: Medium Term Economic Survey*, Copenhagen: Ministry of Finance.

Danthine, J.-P. and Hunt, J. (1992) 'Wage Bargaining Structure, Employment and Economic Integration', *CEPR Discussion Papers*, No. 694, CEPR Discussion Papers.

Darby, J., Hughes-Hallett, A., Ireland, J. and Piscitelli, L. (1999) 'The Impact of the Exchange Rate on the Level of Investment', *Economic Journal*, vol. 109(454), March, pp. 55–67.

Decressin, J. and A. Fatàs (1995) 'Regional Labor Market Dynamics in Europe', *European Economic Review*, vol. 39, pp. 1627–55.

De Grauwe, P. (1988) 'Is the European Monetary System a DM-zone?', *CEPR Discussion Paper*, No. 297.

De Grauwe, P. (2000) *Economics of Monetary Union*, 4th edition, Oxford: Oxford University Press.

De Grauwe, P. (2002a) 'Central Banking: Art or Science? Lessons from the Fed and the ECB', *International Finance*, vol.5(1), pp.129–37.

De Grauwe, P. (2002b) 'Challenges for Monetary Policy in Euroland', *Journal of Common Market Studies*, vol. 40, pp. 693–718.

De Grauwe, P. (2003) *The Economics of Monetary Union: 5th Edition*, Oxford: Oxford University Press.

De Grauwe, P. and Sénégas, M-A. (2003) 'Common Monetary Policy with Transmission Asymmetry: Is there a Case for Using National Data in EMU?', Katholieke Universiteit Leuven, June.

De Gregorio, J. and Wolf, H. (1994) 'Terms of Trade, Productivity and the Real Exchange Rate', *NBER Working Paper*, No. 4807.

De la Porte, C. and Pochet, P. (eds) (2002) *Building Social Europe through the Open Method of Co-ordination*, Brussels: PIE Peter Lang.

Delors Report (1989) Committee for the Study of Economic and Monetary Union, *Report on Economic and Monetary Union in the European Community*, Luxembourg: OOPEC.

De Ménil, G. (1999) 'Real Capital Market Integration', *Economic Policy*, vol. 28, pp. 165–201.

Deroose, S., Langedijk, S. and Roeger, W. (2004) 'Reviewing Adjustment Dynamics in EMU: From Overheating to Overcooling', *European Economy, Economic Papers*, No. 198.

De Vincenti, C. (2001) 'Customer Markets, Inflation and Unemployment in a Dynamic Model with a Range of Equilibria', *Metroeconomica*, vol. 52(1), pp. 1–25.

Devereux, M. (2003) 'A Macroeconomic Analysis of EU Accession under Alternative Monetary Policies', *Journal of Common Market Studies*, vol. 41(5), pp. 941–64.

Dickens, R., Wadsworth, J. and Gregg, P. (2001) 'The State of Working Britain: Update 2001', LSE Centre for Economic Performance: London.

Diebold, F.X. and Rudebusch, G. (1999) *Business Cycles: Durations, Dynamics and Forecasting*, Princeton: Princeton University Press.

Dixit, A.K. and Pindyck, R.S. (1994) *Investment Under Uncertainty*, Princeton: Princeton University Press.

Doisy, N. and Hervé, K. (2003) 'Déficits Courants des PECO: Quelles Implications pour Leur Entrée dans l'Union Européenne et la Zone Euro?', *Economie Internationale*, No. 93.

Duguay, P. (1994) 'Empirical Evidence on the Strength of the Monetary Transmission Mechanism in Canada', *Journal of Monetary Economics*, vol. 33, pp. 39–61.

Dunning, J.H. (1997) 'The European Internal Market Programme and Inbound Foreign Direct Investment', *Journal of Common Market Studies*, vol. 35, pp. 1–30 and 189–224.

Dyson, K. (1994) *Elusive Union: The Process of Economic and Monetary Union in Europe*, London and New York: Longman.

Dyson, K. (2000) *The Politics of the Euro Area: Stability or Breakdown?*, Oxford: Oxford University Press.

Dyson, K. and Featherstone, K. (1999) *The Road to Maastricht: Negotiating Economic and Monetary Union*, Oxford: Oxford University Press.

EBRD (2003) *EBRD and Estonia*, available at: http://www.ebrd.com/country/country/estonia/index.htm.

EC Commission Working Group 4a on Governance (2001) *Involving Experts in the Process of National Policy Convergence*, June 2001, Brussels.

ECB (1999) 'Balassa–Samuelson Effect', *Monthly Bulletin*, October.

ECB (2002a) *Convergence Report*, Frankfurt.

ECB (2002b) 'Labour Market Mismatches in Euro Area Countries', March, http://www.ecb.int/pub/pdf/labourmarket2002.pdf.

ECB (2003a) 'The ECB's Monetary Policy Strategy', European Central Bank, Frankfurt, 8 May, http://www.ecb.int/press/03/pr030508_2en.htm.

ECB (2003b) 'Policy Position Of The Governing Council Of The European Central Bank On Exchange Rate Issues Relating To The Acceding Countries', Frankfurt: ECB.

ECB (2004) *The Monetary Policy of the ECB*, Frankfurt: ECB.

ECB (2005) *Statistics Pocketbook Database*, available for downloading at: http://www.ecb.int/stats/services/downloads/html/index.en.html.

Ecofin (1999) 2225 Council Meeting, 13456/99 (Presse 381) Brussels 29 November.

Ecofin (2001) 2329 Council meeting – Ecofin, Press Release: Brussels (12 February 2001) – Press: 35 – Nr: 5696/01, http://ue.eu.int/newsroom/main.cfm?LANG=1.

Ecofin (2002a) 2407 Council meeting, Press: 28 Nr: 6108/02, Brussels 12 February.

Ecofin (2002b) 'Council Decision of 5 November 2002 on the existence of an excessive deficit in Portugal – Application of Article 104(6) of the Treaty establishing the European Community', 2002/923/EC: Official Journal L 322, 27 November 2002, pp. 30–31.

Ecofin (2003a) The 2480th Economic and Finance Ministers Council Meeting, Press Release: Brussels (21 January), No. 6877/03.

Ecofin (2003b) The 2485th Economic and Finance Ministers Council Meeting, Press Release: Brussels (18 February), No. 6460/03.

Ecofin (2003c) 2546 Economic and Finance Ministers Council Meeting, Press Release: Brussels, (25 November), No. 14492/03.

Economist (2002) 'The EU Stability Pact: Promises, Promises, Fudge, Fudge. Germany Escapes an EU reprimand for its big budget deficit', *The Economist*.

Economist (2003a) 'Something Stirs', July 24.

Economist (2003b) 'Sick Man Walking', 18 December.

Editorial, (2004) 'Whither the Stability and Growth Pact?', 5 *Common Market Law Review*, 1193–1198.

Eichengreen, B. (1993) 'Labor Markets and European Monetary Unification', in P. Masson and M. Taylor (eds), *Policy Issues in the Operation of Currency Unions*, Cambridge: Cambridge University Press.

Eichengreen, B. and Wyplosz, C. (1998) 'The Stability and Growth Pact: More than a Minor Nuisance?', in D. Begg, J. von Hagen, C. Wyplosz and K.F. Zimmerman, (eds), *EMU: Prospects and Challenges for the Euro, Economic Policy: A European Forum*, Oxford: Basil Blackwell, pp. 65–114.

Eijffinger, S.C.W. and Geraats, P.M. (2005) 'How Transparent are Central Banks?', *Department of Economics Working Paper*, University of Cambridge.

EIRO (2002a) 'Industrial Relations in the EU Member States and Candidate Countries', European Industrial Relations Observatory Online, 30 September, http://www.eiro.eurofound.ie/2002/07/Feature/TN0207104F.html.

EIRO (2002b) 'Federal Employment Service to be Reformed', European Industrial Relations Observatory Online, 4 April, http://www.eiro.eurofound.ie/2002/03/feature/deo203204f.html.

Elgie, R. (2002) 'The Politics of the European Central Bank: Principal-Agent Theory and the Democratic Deficit', *Journal of European Public Policy*, vol. 9(2), pp. 186–200.

Elmeskov, J., Martin, J. and Scarpetta, S. (1998) 'Key Lessons for Labour Market Reforms: Evidence from OECD Countries' Experiences', *Swedish Economic Policy Review*, vol. 1, pp. 237–91.

EMAC (Economic and Monetary Affairs Committee of the European Parliament) (2003) Report on the Broad Guidelines of the Economic Policies of the Member States and the Community for 2003-05, A5–0142/2003, final.

EMCO (2002) 'Impact Evaluation of the EES', Background paper. 'Employment Policy Mix and Policy Making', EMCO/30/060602/EN_REV 1.

Employment Task Force (2003) *Jobs, Jobs, Jobs: Creating more Employment in Europe – the 'Kok' Report*, Brussels.

Erber, G. (2003). 'The Risk of Deflation in Germany and the Monetary Policy of the ECB', *CESifo Forum*, 3/2003; pp. 24–9.

Ernst and Young (2002) Ernst & Young's European Investment Monitor: 2002 report, Accessed 1 May 2002, Available, Online http://www.ey.com/global/gcr.nsf/International/European_Investment_Monitor_-_Real_Estate.

Esping-Andersen, G. (1999) *Social Foundations of Post-industrial Economies*, Oxford: Oxford University Press.

ETUC (2002) 'The Luxembourg Process – Where Next?', ETUC proposals, Brussels: ETUC.

European Convention (2003) Draft Treaty Establishing a Constitution for Europe CONV 850/03 Brussels, 18 July.

European Council (1997) 'Extraordinary Meeting on Employment: Presidency Conclusions', Press Release: Luxembourg (20 November 1997), No. SN300/97.

European Council (2000a) 'Lisbon European Council 23–24 March: Presidency Conclusions', Press Release: Luxembourg (24 March 2000), No. 100/1/00.

European Council (2000b) 'Nice European Council, 7–9 December: Presidency Conclusions', Press Release, Brussels (8 December 2000), No. 400/1/00.

European Council (2001a) 'Göteborg European Council 15–16 June: Presidency Conclusions', Press Release: Brussels (16 June), No. 200/1/01.

European Council (2001b) 'Laeken European Council 14–15 December: Presidency Conclusions', Press Release: Brussels (15 December 2001), No. 00300/1/01.

European Council (2002) 'Barcelona European Council 15–16 March: Presidency Conclusions', Press Release: Barcelona (16 March 2002), No. 100/02.

European Council (2003a) 'Presidency Conclusions, Brussels European Council, 20 and 21 March 2003', Brussels.

European Council (2003b) Brussels European Council 5 May 2003: Presidency Conclusions, Press Release: Brussels (5 May 2003), No. 8410/03.

European Monetary Institute (1998) 'Convergence Report: Report Required by Article 109j of the Treaty establishing the European Community', Frankfurt am Main: E.M.I.

European Union (2002) 'Consolidated Version of the Treaty Establishing the European Community', *Official Journal C*, 325, 33–184, 24 December 2002.

Eurostat (1999a) '*Eurostat Yearbook '98*'.

Eurostat (1999b) National Accounts ESA Detailed tables by branch, 1999 edition.

Eurostat (1999c) *External and intra-European Trade*, Monthly Statistics.
Eurostat (1999d) Annual Employment Statistics, www.rcade.dur.ac.uk.
Eurostat (1999e) *International Trade in Services EU, 1987–1999*, 1998 edition.
Eurostat (2000) National income and expenditure, http://europa.eu.int/en/comm/eurostat/facts/www.root/en/index.htm, 20 January 2000.
Eurostat (2002) 'Labour Force Survey', New Cronos Database.
Eurostat, (2003) Labour Costs Survey, 2000: EU Member States and Candidate Countries (A. Paternoster), http://epp.eurostat.cec.eu.int/cache/ITY_OFFPUB/KS-NK-03-018/EN/KS-NK-03-018-EN.PDF.
Fabiani, S. and Rodriguez-Palenzuela, D. (2001) 'Model-based Indicators of Labour Market Rigidity', *European Central Bank Working Paper*, No. 57.
Fatás, A. (1999) 'The Effects of EMU on the Spanish Business Cycle', in *The Euro and the Spanish Economy*, Fundacion Banco Bilbao Vizcaya Spain.
Favero, C., Freixas, X., Persson, T. and Wyplosz, C. (2000) *One Money, Many Countries: Monitoring the European Central Bank 2*, London: CEPR.
Favier, P. and Martin-Roland, M. (1990) *Le décennie Mitterrand*, Paris: Seuil.
Feldstein, M. (1997) 'The Political Economy of the European Economic and Monetary Union: Political Sources of an Economic Liability', *Journal of Economic Perspectives*, vol. 11, pp. 23–42.
Findlay, R., Jonung, L. and Lundahl, M. (eds) (2002) *Bertil Ohlin: A Centennial Celebration 1899–1999*, Cambridge, MA: MIT Press.
Fischer, C. (2002) 'Real Currency Appreciation in Accession Countries: Balassa–Samuelson and Investment Demand', *Economic Research Centre of the Deutsche Bundesbank Discussion Paper*, No. 19/02.
Fitoussi, J.P. (ed.) (2000) *Rapport sur l'état de l'Union européenne 2000*, Paris: Fayard and Presses de Sciences-Po.
Fitoussi, J.-P. and Creel, J. (2002) *How to Reform the European Central Bank*, London: Centre for European Reform.
Fitoussi, J. and Le Cacheux, J. (eds) (2005) *L'état de l'Union européenne 2005*, Paris: Fayard and Presses de Sciences Po.
Fitoussi, J.P., Passet, O., Freyssinet, J. (2000) Réduction du chômage: Les réussites en Europe, rapport du conseil d'analyse économique, n. 23, La documentation française, Paris.
FitzGerald, J. (2001) 'Managing an Economy Under EMU: The Case of Ireland', *The World Economy*, vol. 24(10), pp. 1353–71.
FitzGerald, J. and Honohan, P. (1997) 'EMU – Reaching a Narrow Verdict', *Irish Banking Review*, Spring, pp. 15–23.
Flanagan, R.J. (1999) 'Macroeconomic Performance and Collective Bargaining: An International Perspective', *Journal of Economic Literature*, vol. XXXVII, September, pp. 1150–75.
Flek, V., Markova, L. and Podpiera, J. (2002) 'Sectoral Productivity and Real Exchange Rate Appreciation: Much Ado about Nothing?', *Czech National Bank Working Papers Series*, No. 4.
Flores, E., Giudice, G. and Turrini, A. (2005) 'The Framework for Fiscal Policy in EMU: What Future after Five Years of Experience', *European Economy Economic Papers*, No. 223.
Forsman, P. (2000) 'The Electronic Industry and Finland's Transformation in to a High-Tech Economy', *Bank of Finland Bulletin*, vol. 75(3), pp. 11–16.
Frankel, J. and Rose, A. (1998) 'The Endogeneity of the Optimum Currency Area Criterion', *Economic Journal*, vol. 108 (449) (July), pp. 1009–25.

Frankel, J.A. and Rose, A.K. (1997) 'The Endogeneity of the Optimum Currency Area Criteria', *Swedish Economic Policy Review*, vol. 4(2), pp. 487–512.

Fratianni, M. and von Hagen, J. (1990) 'German Dominance in the EMS: The Empirical Evidence', *Open Economies Review*, vol. 1.

Friberg, R. and Vredin, A. (1997) 'Exchange Rate Uncertainty and Microeconomic Benefits from the EMU', *Swedish Economic Policy Review*, vol. 4 (2), pp. 547–94.

Fuhrer, J.C. and Moore, G.R. (1995) 'Inflation Persistence', *Quarterly Journal of Economics*, vol. 114, pp. 127–59.

Giudice, G., Turrini, A. and in't Veld, J. (2003) 'Can Fiscal Consolidations be Expansionary in the EU? Ex-post Evidence and Ex-ante Analysis', *European Commission Economic Papers*, No. 195.

Glick, R. and Rose, A. (2002) 'Does a Currency Union Affect Trade? The Time Series Evidence', *European Economic Review*, 46 (June), pp. 1125–51.

Goetschy, J. (1999) 'The European Employment Strategy: Genesis and Development', *European Journal of Industrial Relations*, vol. 5(2), pp. 117–37.

Goldberg, L. and Kolstad, C. (1995) 'Foreign Direct Investment, Exchange Rate Variability and Demand Uncertainty', *International Economic Review*, vol. 36, pp. 855–73.

Goldstein, J. and Martin, L.L. (2000) 'Legalization, Trade Liberalization and Domestic Politics: A Cautionary Note', *International Organization*, vol. 54(3), pp. 603–32.

Goodfriend, M. (1999) 'The Role of A Regional Bank in a System of Central Banks', *Federal Reserve Bank of Richmond Working Papers*, No. 99–4.

Goodhart, C.A.E. and Hofmann, B. (2000) 'Do Asset Prices Help to Predict Consumer Price Inflation?', *The Manchester School Supplement*, vol. 68, pp. 122–40.

Gordon, R. (1998) 'Foundations of the Goldilocks Economy: Supply Shocks and the Time-Varying NAIRU', *Brookings Papers on Economic Activity*, vol. 29(2), pp. 297–333.

Gray, A.W. (1997) (ed.) *International Perspectives on the Irish Economy*, Indecon Public Policy Series, October, Dublin: Indecon, Economic Consultants.

Gros, D. and Thygesen, N. (1998) *European Monetary Integration: From the European Monetary System to European Monetary Union*, London: Longman.

Gros, D., Mayer, T. and Ubide, A. (2003) 'The Nine Lives of the Stability Pact', Brussels: Centre for European Policy Studies.

Grubb, D. (1999) 'Making Work Pay: The Role of Eligibility Criteria for Unemployment Benefits', *OECD Economic Studies*, No. 31/II.

Gruen, N. (1997) 'Making Fiscal Policy Flexibly Independent of Government', *Agenda*, vol. 4 (3), pp. 297–307.

Gruen, N. (2000) *Greater Independence for Fiscal Institutions*, Paris: OECD.

Guiso, L., Kashyap, A.K., Panetta, F. and Terlizzese, D. (1999) 'Will a Common European Monetary Policy Have Asymmetric Effects?', Federal Reserve Bank of Chicago, *Economic Perspectives*, 4th Quarter, pp. 56–75.

Haan De, J. and Eijffinger, S.C.W. (2000) 'The Democratic Accountability of the European Central Bank', *Journal of Common Market Studies*, vol. 38(3), pp. 393–407.

Haan De, J., Amtenbrink F. and Waller S. (2004) 'The Transparency and Credibility of the European Central Bank', *Journal of Common Market Studies*, vol. 42(4), pp. 775–94.

Hadjiemmanuil, C. (2000) 'Democracy, Supranationality and Central Bank Independence', in J. Kleineman (ed.), *Central Bank Independence: The Economic Foundations, The Constitutional Implications and Democratic Accountability*, London: Kluwer.

Halko, M.-L. (2002) 'Buffer Funding of Unemployment Insurance in a Dynamic Labour Union Model', mimeo, European Central Bank Working Papers No. 188, October 2002.

Hall, P. (1988) 'L'Evolution de la Politique Economique sous Mitterrand', in S. Hoffman, and G. Ross (eds), *L'Expérience Mitterrand Continuité et Changement dans la France Contemporaine*, Paris: PUF.

Hallerberg, M. (2000) 'The Importance of Domestic Political Institutions: Why and How Belgium and Italy Qualified for EMU', Zentrumfür Europäische Integrationsforschung Center for European Integration Studies Rheinische Friedrich-Wilhelms-Universität Bonn, Working Paper B 10.

Halpern, L. and Wyplosz, C. (1997) 'Equilibrium Exchange Rates in Transition Economies', *International Monetary Fund Staff Papers*, vol. 44(4), pp. 430–61.

Halpern, L. and Wyplosz, C. (2001) 'Economic Transformation and Real Exchange Rates in the 2000s: The Balassa–Samuelson Connection', *UN Economic Commission for Europe: Economic Survey of Europe*, pp. 227–40.

Hancké, B. and Soskice, D. (2003) 'Wage-Setting and inflation targets in EMU', *Oxford Review of Economic Policy*, vol. 19(1), pp. 149–60.

Hanny, B. and Wessels, W. (1998) 'The Monetary Committee: A Significant though not Typical Case', in M.P.C.M. Van Schendelen (ed.), *EU Committees as Influential Policy Makers*, Aldershot: Ashgate.

Hansen, J. and Roeger, W. (2000) 'Estimation of Real Equilibrium Exchange Rates', DG Economic and Financial Affairs, *Economic Papers*, No. 144, ECFIN/534/00.

Harden, I. (1999) 'The Fiscal Constitution of EMU', in P. Beaumont and N. Walker, (eds), *Legal Framework of the Single European Currency*, Oxford: Hart.

Harden, I., von Hagen, J. and Brookes, R. (1999) 'The European Constitutional Framework for Member States' Public Finances', in M. Andenas, L. Gormley, C. Hadjiemmanuil and I. Harden (eds), *European Economic and Monetary Union: The Institutional Framework*, London: Kluwer.

Harris, R. and Silverstone, B. (1999) 'Asymmetric Adjustment of Unemployment and Output: Cross-country Estimates of Okun's Law', *University of Waikato Discussion Paper*, No. 99/2.

Helg, R., Manasse, P., Monacelli, T. and Rovelli, R. (1995) 'How Much (A)symmetry in Europe? Evidence from Industrial Sectors', *European Economic Review*, No. 39, pp. 1017–41.

Hemming, R., Mahfouz, S. and Schimmelpfennig, A. (2002) 'Fiscal Policy and Economic Activity during Recessions in Advanced Economies', *IMF Working Paper*, No. 02/87.

Henriksson, R.G.H. (2001) 'Nationalekonomiska Föreningen – A Central Forum for Economic Debate in Sweden', *Royal Economic Society Newsletter*, 102, pp. 11–15, 19.

Hinnosaar, M., Juks, R., Kaadu, H. and Uusküla, L. (2003) 'Estimating the Equilibrium Exchange Rate of the Estonian Kroon', *Bank of Estonia Research Department Working Paper*, No. 2.

HM Treasury (1997a) 'Chancellor's Statement on EMU: Monday 27 October 1997', HM Treasury News Release 126/97, www.treasury.gov.uk/press/1997/p126_97.html.

HM Treasury (1997b) 'UK Membership of the Single Currency: An Assessment of the Five Economic Tests', London: HMSO.

HM Treasury (2003a) 'UK Membership of the Single Currency: An Assessment of the Five Economic Tests', Cm 5776, London: HMSO.

HM Treasury (2003b) 'EMU and the Monetary Transmission Mechanism', EMU Study, London: HMSO.

HM Treasury (2003c) 'The Exchange Rate and Macroeconomic Adjustment', London: HM Treasury.

HM Treasury (2003d) 'EMU and Business Sectors', EMU Study, London: HMSO.

HM Treasury (2003e) 'EMU and the Cost of Capital', EMU Study, London: HMSO.

HM Treasury (2003f) 'Sustainable Public Finances: Convergence Programme for the UK Submitted in Line with the Stability and Growth Pact', December, London: HMSO.

HM Treasury (2003g) 'EMU and Labour Market Flexibility', London: HM Treasury.

HM Treasury (2003h) 'Fiscal Stabilisation and EMU', London: HM Treasury.

HM Treasury (2003i) *Meeting the Challenge: Economic Reform in Europe*, Norwich: HMSO.

HM Treasury (2004) *Advancing Long-Term Prosperity: Economic Reform in an Enlarged Europe*, Norwich: HMSO.

Hodson, D. (2003) 'The SVAR as an Adjustment Mechanism: An SVAR Approach to the Case of Ireland', *The Economic and Social Review*, vol. 34(2), pp. 151–72.

Hodson, D. and Maher, I. (2001) 'The Open Method as a New Mode of Governance: The Case of Soft Policy Co-ordination', *Journal of Common Market Studies*, vol. 39(4), pp. 719–45.

Hodson, D. and Maher, I. (2002) 'Economic and Monetary Union: Balancing Credibility and Legitimacy in an Asymmetric Policy-Mix', *Journal of European Public Policy*, vol. 9(3), pp. 391–407.

Hodson, D. and Maher, I. (2004) 'Soft Law and Sanctions: Economic Policy Coordination and Reform of the Stability and Growth Pact', *Journal of European Public Policy*, vol. 11(5).

Hoeller, P., Giorno, C. and de la Maisonneuve, C. (2004) 'One Money, One Cycle? Making Monetary Union a Smoother Ride', *OECD Economics department working paper*, No. 401, Paris: OECD.

Holzmann, H. (ed.) (1996) *Maastricht: Monetary Constitution Without a Fiscal Constitution?*, Baden-Baden: Nomos Verlag.

Honohan, P. (2001) 'Discussion' on: Persson, T. 'Currency Unions and Trade: How Large is the Treatment Effect?', *Economic Policy*, vol. 33, pp. 435–48.

Honkaphja, S. and Koskela, E. (1999) 'The Economic Crisis of the 1990s in Finland', *Economic Policy*, No. 29, pp. 401–36.

Honohan, P. and Flynn, J. (1986) 'Irish Inflation in EMS', *The Economic and Social Review*, vol. 17, No. 3, pp. 175–91, April.

Hooper, P. and Mann, C. (1989) 'Exchange Rate Pass-through in the 1980s: The Case of US Imports of Manufactures', *Brookings Papers on Economic Activity*, pp. 263–99.

House of Lords (2003) *The Stability and Growth Pact*, Report of the European Communities Select Committee.

Howell, C. (1996) 'French Socialism and the Transformation of Industrial Relations since 1981', in A. Daley (ed.), *'The Mitterrand Era: Policy Alternatives and Political Mobilization in France'*, New York: NYU Press.

Huang, A., Margaritis, D. and Mayes, D.G. (2001) 'Monetary Policy Rules in Practice: Evidence from New Zealand', *Multinational Finance Journal*, vol. 5(3), pp. 175–200.

Hughes Hallett, A., Lewis, J. and von Hagen, J. (2004) *Fiscal Policy in Europe, 1991–2003: An Evidence Based Analysis*, London: Centre for Economic Policy Research.

Hughes Hallett, A.J., Ma, Y. and Demertzis, M. (2000) 'The Single Currency and Labour Market Flexibility: A Necessary Partnership?', *Scottish Journal of Political Economy*, vol. 47, 141–55.

IAB (2003) 'Labour Market Statistics', www.iab.de.

IMF (2001) Staff Report for the UK 2000 Article IV Consultation, 2 February, *IMF Country Report*, No. 01/42.

IMF (2002a) 'Sweden: Selected Issues', *IMF country Report*, No. 02/160, Washington DC.

IMF (2002b) 'Germany Selected Issues', *IMF Country Report*, No. 02/2003.

IMF (2003a) 'United Kingdom: Selected Issues', *IMF Country Reports*, No. 03/47, February.

IMF (2003b) 'Deflation: Determinants, Risks, and Policy Options – Findings of an Interdepartmental Task Force', April 30. http://www.imf.org/external/pubs/ft/def/2003/eng/043003.htm.

IMF (2003c) 'Republic of Estonia: Selected Issues and Statistical Appendix', *IMF Country Report*, No. 03/331.

IMF (2004) 'Has Fiscal Behaviour Changed under the European Economic and Monetary Union?', *World Economic Outlook*, September, pp. 103–36.

Issing, O. (1999) 'The Eurosystem: Transparent and Accountable or "Willem in Euroland" ', *Journal of Common Market Studies*, vol. 37(3), pp. 503–19.

Issing, O. (2002) 'On Macroeconomic Policy Co-ordination in EMU', *Journal of Common Market Studies*, vol. 40, pp. 345–68.

Issing, O., Gaspar, V., Angeloni, I. and Tristani, O. (2001) *Monetary Policy in the Euro Area*, Cambridge: Cambridge University Press.

IW Institut der deutschen Wirtschaft Köln (2003) 'International Labour Costs in Manufacturing', cited by EIRO (2003) 'Manufacturing Labour Costs Still High by International Standards', eironline, http://www.eiro.eurofound.ie/2003/10/inbrief/de0310101n.html.

Jacobsson, K. (1999) 'Employment Policy in Europe – A New System of European Governance?', in *SCORE Rapportserie*, vol. 11, Stockholm.

Jacobsson, K. (2002) 'The Open Method of Coordination at Work: The Swedish Case', *paper presented at an Observatoire Social Européen conference*, 17 June, Brussels.

Jacquet, P. and Pisani-Ferry, J. (2001) *Economic Policy Co-ordination in the Euro-Zone: What has been Achieved? What Should be Done?*, London: Centre for European Reform.

Jansen, H. (2005) 'Domestic Gloom and Export Boom: A Look at German Competitiveness', *DG ECFIN Country Focus*, vol. 2(6), Brussels: DG Economic and Financial Affairs, European Commission.

Jansson, P. (1997) 'How Large is the Risk of Asymmetric Shocks for Sweden?', *Swedish Economic Policy Review*, vol. 4 (2), pp. 447–86.

Jarocinski, M. (2003) 'Nominal and Real Convergence in Spain, Portugal and Greece During Their Accession to the EMU', Centre for Social and Economic Research, Warsaw, *Working Paper*, No. 198.

Jayasuriya, K. (2001) 'Globalisation and the Changing Architecture of the State', *Journal of European Public Policy*, vol. 8(1), pp. 101–23.

Jobert, B. and Mueller, P. (1987) *L'Etat en Action: Politique Publiques et Corporatismes*, Paris: PUF.

Jobert, B. and Théret, B. (1994) 'France: La Consécration Républicaine du Néolibéralisme', in B. Thobert, (ed.), *Le Tournant Néolibéral en Europe*, Paris: L'Harmattant.

Joerges, C. (1996) 'Taking the Law Seriously: On Political Science and the Role of Law in the Process of European Integration', *European Law Journal*, vol. 2(2), pp. 105–35.

Johansson, B.K.Å. (2002) *Stabilisation Policy in the Monetary Union – a Summary of the Report*, Commission on Stabilisation Policy for Full Employment in the Event of Sweden Joining the Monetary Union, Stockholm.

Jonung, L. (2002) 'National or International Inflation Targeting? The Wicksellian dilemma of the euro-outs', *Journal of Public Policy*, vol. 22 (2), pp. 183–98.

Jonung, L. and Hagberg, T. (2002) 'How Costly was the Crisis of the 1990s? A Comparison of Finland's and Sweden's Deepest Economic Crises', conference on 'Sweden and Finland. Economic Interaction, Processes and Comparisons', Kauniainen, 6–7 September.

Kaminsky, G.L. and Reinhart, C.M. (1999) 'The Twin Crises: The Causes of Banking and Balance of Payments Problems', *American Economic Review*, vol. 89(3), pp. 473–500.

Karras, G. (1996) 'The Optimal Government Size: Further International Evidence on the Productivity of Government Services', *Economic Inquiry*, vol. 34, pp. 193–203.

Kenny, G. and McGettigan, D. (1996) 'Exchange Rate Pass-Through and Import Prices', *Central Bank of Ireland Technical Paper*, No. 6/RT/96.

Kieler, M. and Saarenheimo, T. (1998) 'Differences in Monetary Policy Transmission: A Case not Closed', European Commission, DG Ecofin, *Economic Paper*, No. 132.

Kilponen, J. and Mayes, D.G. (2003) 'Factor Mobility', ch. 18 in A.M. El-Agraa (ed.), London: Pearson.

Kilponen, J., Mayes, D. and Vilmunen, J. (2000) 'Labour Market Flexibility in the Euro Area', *European Business Journal*, vol. 12 (1), pp. 100–10.

Kingdom of Spain (2001) 'Stability Programme Update 2001–2005' (Madrid: Kingdom of Spain). Available at http://europa.eu.int/comm/economy_finance/about/activities/sgp/country/countryfiles/es/es20012002_en.pdf.

Kinnwall, M. (2000) 'Swedish Monetary Policy: On the Road to EMU?', pp. 146–65 in Miles (2000).

Knöbl, A. and Haas, R. (2003) 'IMF and the Baltics: A Decade of Cooperation', *IMF Working Paper*, WP/03/241.

Kok, W. (2004) Facing the Challenge: The Lisbon Strategy for Growth and Employment. Report from the high Level Group chaired by Wim Kok, November 2004, http://europa.eu.int/comm/lisbon_strategy/pdf/2004-1866-EN-complet.pdf.

Kontolemis, Z. and Samiei, H. (2000) 'The U.K. Business Cycle, Monetary Policy, and EMU Entry', *IMF Working Paper*, WP/00/210.

Koskela, E. and Virén, M. (2000) 'Is There a Laffer Curve Between Aggregate Output and Public Sector Employment?', *ETLA (the Research Institute for the Finnish Economy) Discussion Paper*, No. 737, October.

Kovács, M.A. (2002) 'On the Estimated Size of the Balassa–Samuelson Effect in Five Central and Eastern European Countries', *National Bank of Hungary Working Paper*, No. 5, Budapest.

Krugman, P. (1993) 'Lessons of Massachusetts for EMU', in F. Giavazzi and F. Torres (eds), *The Transition to Economic and Monetary Union in Europe*, Cambridge: Cambridge University Press.

Krugman, P.R. (1997) 'Good News for Ireland: A Geographical Perspective', in *International Perspectives on the Irish Economy*, edited by A.W. Gray, Dublin: Indecon Economic Consultants.

Krugman, P.R. (1998) 'What's New About the New Economic Geography?', *Oxford Review of Economic Policy*, vol. 14, pp. 7–17.

Krugman, P.R. and Venables A.J. (1996) 'Integration, Specialisation, Adjustment', *European Economic Review*, vol. 40, pp. 959–68.

Kydland, F.E. and Prescott, E.C. (1977) 'Rules Rather than Discretion: Time Inconsistency of Optimal Plans', *Journal of Political Economy*, vol. 85(3), pp. 473–92.

Landesmann, M. and Richter, S. (2003) 'Consequences of EU Accession: Economic Effects on CEECs', WIIW Research Report No. 299, Vienna: WIIW.

Layard, R., Nickell, S. and Jackman, R. (1991) *Unemployment: Macroeconomic Performance and the Labour Market*, Oxford: Oxford University Press.

Lazear, E. (1990) 'Job Security Provisions and Employment', *Quarterly Journal of Economics*, vol. 105, pp. 699–726.

Leach, G. (2001) 'UK Mortgages and the Euro', London: New Europe, http://www.no-euro.com.

Le Cacheux, J. (2004) 'Politique économique: Les inconvénients de la taille unique', in dossier 'Comment réveiller la croissance en Europe', *Sociétal*, n°43, 1er trimestre.

Lecointe, F., Przeborski, V. and Sterdyniak, H. (1989) 'Salaires, Prix et Répartition, ou Comment l'Inflation fut Vaincue', in Jeannneney, J.-M. (ed.), *L'Economie Française depuis 1967, la Traversée des Turbulences*, Pairs: Seuil.

Lemierre, J. (1999) 'Making Policy Co-operation Effective', in D. Currie, A. Donnelly, H. Flassbeck, B. Hall, J. Lemierre, T. Padoa-Schioppa and N. Wicks, *Will EMU lead to a European Economic Government?*, London: CER.

Lenschow, A. (2002) 'New Regulatory Approaches in "Greening" EU Policies', *European Law Journal*, vol. 8(1), pp. 19–35.

Levitt, M. and Lord, C. (2000) *The Political Economic of Monetary Union*, Basingstoke: Macmillan.

Levy, J.D. (1999) '*Tocqueville's Revenge: State, Society, and Economy in Contemporary France*', Cambridge, Massachusetts: Harvard University Press.

Lindahl, R. (2000) 'Swedish Public Opinion and the EU', in Miles (2000), pp. 97-126.

Lindbeck, A. (2000) 'Swedish Economic Growth in an International Perspective', *Swedish Economic Policy Review*, vol. 7, pp. 7–37.

Livi Bacci, M., Abbate, M., De Santis, G., Giovanelli, C. and Ricci, R. (1996) 'Mobilità e Territorio', in G. Galli (ed.), *La Mobilità nella Società Italiana*, SIPI: Roma, cited by Braunerhjelm *et al.* (2000; p. 48).

Lordon, F. (1997) *Les Quadratures de la Politique Economique*, Paris: Albin Michel.

Lordon, F. (1998) 'The Logic and Limits of Désinflation Compétitive', *Oxford Review of Economic Policy*, vol. 14, No. 1, pp. 96–113.

Louis, J.-V. (1998) 'A Legal and Institutional Approach for Building a Monetary Union', *Common Market Law Review*, vol. 35(1), pp. 33–76.

Louis J.-V. (ed.) (2002) *The Euro in the National Context*, London: The British Institute of International and Comparative Law.

Louis, J.-V. (2004) 'The Economic and Monetary Union: Law and Institutions', *Common Market Law Review*, vol. 41, pp. 575–608.

Ludlow, P. (1982) *The Making of the European Monetary System: A Case Study of the European Community*, London: Butterworth Scientific.

MacDougall, G.D.A. (1977) *Report of the Study Group on the Role of Public Finance in European Integration*, Luxembourg: EC Publications.

Maddison, A. (1991) *Dynamic Forces in Capitalist Development: A Long Run Comparative View*, Oxford: Oxford University Press.

Madsen, P.K., Munch-Madsen, P. and Langhoff-Ross, K. (2002) 'How Well Do European Employment Regimes Manage Social Exclusion', ch. 10 in R.J.A. Muffels, P. Tsakloglou and D.G. Mayes (eds), *Social Exclusion In European Welfare States*, Cheltenham: Edward Elgar.

Maduro, M. (1998) *We the Court: The European Court of Justice and the European Economic Constitution*, Oxford: Hart.

Maes, I. and Quaglia, L. (2003) 'The Process of European Monetary Integration: A Comparison of the Belgian and Italian Approaches', *Nationa Bank of Belgium Working Paper*, No. 40.

Maes, I. and Quaglia, L. (2004) 'France's and Italy's Policies on European Monetary Integration: A Comparison of "Strong" and "Weak" States', *Comparative European Politics*, vol. 2(1), pp. 51–72.

Maher, I. (1998) 'Community Law in the National Legal Order: A Systems Analysis', *Journal of Common Market Studies*, vol. 36, pp. 237–54.

Maher, I. (2004) 'Economic Policy Coordination and the European Court: Excessive Deficits and Ecofin Discretion', *European Law Review*, vol. 29(6), pp. 831–41.

Maher, I. (2004) 'Law and the Open Method of Coordination', *Zeitschrift für Staats- und Europawissenschaften* vol. 2(2).

Majone, G. (1998) 'Europe's "Democratic Deficit": The Question of Standards', *European Law Journal*, vol. 4(1), pp. 5–29.

Mankiw, N.G. (2000) 'The Savers-Spenders Theory of Fiscal Policy', *Harvard Institute of Economic Research Discussion Paper*, No. 1888, January.

Mayes, D.G. (2003) 'The Monetary Transmission Mechanism in the Baltic States', ch. 1 in *The Monetary Transmission Mechanism in the Baltic States*, Tallinn: Bank of Estonia, Bank of Lithuania, National Bank of Latvia.

Mayes, D.G. and Burridge, M. (1993) *The Impact of the Single Market Programme on European Economic Structure and Performance*, Brussels: European Parliament.

Mayes, D.G. and Liuksila, A. (2003) *Who Pays for Bank Insolvency?*, Basingstoke: Palgrave.

Mayes, D.G. and Suvanto, A. (2002) 'Beyond the Fringe: Finland and the choice of Currency', *Journal of Public Policy*, vol. 22(2), pp. 161–82.

Mayes, D.G. and Vilmunen, J. (1999) 'Labour Market Flexibility in a Small Open Economy', *Bank of Finland Discussion Paper*, No. 9/99.

Mayes, D.G. and Virén, M. (2000) 'The Exchange Rate and Monetary Conditions in the Euro Area', *Weltwirtschaftliches Archiv*, Band 136, Heft 2, pp. 199–231.

Mayes, D.G. and Virén, M. (2002a) 'Asymmetry and the Problem of Aggregation in the Euro Area', *Empirica*, vol. 29, pp. 47–73.

Mayes, D.G. and Virén, M. (2002b) 'Macroeconomic Factors, Policies and the Development of Social Exclusion', in R.J.A. Muffels, P. Tsakloglou and D.G. Mayes (eds), *Social Exclusion in European Welfare States*, Cheltenham: Edward Elgar, pp. 21–50.

Mayes, D.G. and Virén, M. (2002c) 'Policy Co-ordination and Economic Adjustment in EMU: Will it Work?', in A.M. El-Agraa (ed.), *The Euro and Britain*, London: Financial Times/Pearson, pp. 119–52.

Mayes, D.G. and Virén, M. (2002d) 'Financial Conditions Indexes', *Economia Internazionale*, vol. 55, pp. 1–30.

Mayes, D.G. and Virén, M. (2003) 'Pressures on the Stability and Growth Pact from Asymmetry in Policy', Bank of Finland (June), revised and shortened version forthcoming in *Journal of European Public Policy*.

Mayes, D.G. and Virén, M. (2004) 'Asymmetries in the Euro Area Economy', vol. 9(4), http://www.bof.fi/eng/6_julkaisut/6.1_Spn_julkaisut/6.1.5_Keskustelualoitteita/0409.pdf.

Mayes, D.G. and Webb, D. (1993) *The Effects of Exchange Rate Fluctuations on Public Purchasing*, Report for the European Commission, Brussels.

Mayes, D.G., Berghman, J. and Salais, R. (2001) *Social Exclusion and European Policy*, Cheltenham: Edward Elgar.

Mayes, D.G., Halme, L. and Liuksila, A. (2001) *Improving Banking Supervision*, Basingstoke: Palgrave.

McCallum, J. (1995) 'National Borders Matter: Canada-US Regional Trade Patterns', *American Economic Review*, vol. 85, pp. 615–23.

McCormick, J. (1981) 'Gaullism and Collective Bargaining: The Effect of the Fifth Republic on French Industrial Relations', in W. Andrews and Hoffmann (eds), *The Fifth Republic at Twenty*, Albany, New York: SUNY Press.

McCormick, N. (1993) 'Beyond the Sovereign State', *Modern Law Review*, vol. 56, pp. 1–18.

McKinnon, R. (1963) 'Optimum Currency Areas', *American Economic Review*, vol. 53, pp. 717–25.

McMorrow, K. and Roeger, W. (2000) 'Time-Varying Nairu/Nawru Estimates for the EU's Member States', DG Economic and Financial Affairs, *Economic Paper*, No. 145.

McMorrow, K. and Roeger, W. (2002) 'EU Pension Reform – An Overview of the Debate and an Empirical Assessment of the Main Policy Reform Options', DG Ecofin, *Economic Papers*, No. 163.

McNamara, K.R. (1999) 'Consensus and Constraints: Ideas and Capital Mobility in Monetary Integration', *Journal of Common Market Studies*, vol. 37(3), pp. 455–76.

Meen, G. (2003) 'UK Housing Markets and Monetary Union', *Submissions on EMU from Leading Academics, EMU Study*, HM Treasury, London: HMSO.

MEFI (1999) *Programme pluriannuel de finances publiques 1999–2002*, Ministère de l'Économie, des Finances et de l'Industrie.

MEFI (2000a) *Programme pluriannuel de finances publiques 2001–2003*, Ministère de l'Économie, des Finances et de l'Industrie.

MEFI (2000b) *Politique Economique 2000 – Edition de Printemps*, Ministère de l'Économie, des Finances et de l'Industrie.

Mélitz, J. and Zumer, F. (1999) 'Interregional and International Risk-sharing and Lessons for EMU', *Carnegie-Rochester Series on Public Policy*, vol. 51, pp. 149–88.

Melitz, J. and Zumer, F. (2002) 'Regional Redistribution and Stabilization by the Center in Canada, France, the UK and the US: A Reassessment and New Tests', *Journal of Public Economics*, vol. 86, pp. 263–86.

Midelfart-Knarvik, K.H., Overman, H.G., Redding, S.J. and Venables, A.J. (2000) 'The Location of European Industry', European Commission, DG for Economic and Financial Affairs, *Economic Paper*, No. 142.

Miles, L. (ed.) (2000) *Sweden and the European Union Evaluated*, London: Continuum.

Muellbauer, J. (2003) 'The UK and the Euro – The Role of Asymmetries in Housing and Credit Markets', *Submissions on EMU from Leading Academics, EMU Study*, HM Treasury, London: HMSO.

Muffels, R. and Fouarge, D. (2001) 'Social Exclusion and Poverty: Definition, Public Debate and Empirical Evidence in the Netherlands', ch. 5 in D.G. Mayes, J. Berghman and R. Salais (eds), *Social Exclusion and European Poverty*, Cheltenham: Edward Elgar.

Muffels, R., Tsakloglou, P. and Mayes, D.G. (2002) *Social Exclusion in European Welfare States*, Cheltenham: Edward Elgar.

Muffels, R.J.A. and Fouarge, D.J.A.G. (2002) 'Do European Welfare States Matter in Explaining Social Exclusion?', in R.J.A. Muffels, P. Tsakloglou and D.G. Mayes (eds), *Social Exclusion In European Welfare States*, Cheltenham: Edward Elgar, pp. 202–34.

Munchau, W. (2003) 'Why Schröder's Reforms are Bad Economics', *Financial Times*, 20 October.

Mundell, R. (1961) 'A Theory of Optimum Currency Areas', *American Economic Review*, vol. 51, September, pp. 657–65.

Muscatelli, A. and Trecroci, C. (2000) 'Monetary Policy Rules, Policy Preferences and Uncertainty: Recent Empirical Evidence', *Journal of Economic Surveys*, vol. 14, pp. 597–627.

National Institute of Economic Research (2000) *The Swedish Economy* (November), Stockholm: NIER.

Nickell, S. (1997). 'Unemployment and Labour Market Rigidities: Europe versus North America', *Journal of Economic Perspectives*, vol. 11, No. 3, Summer, pp. 55–74.

Nickell, S. and Layard, R. (1999) 'Labour Market Institutions and Economic Performance', in O. Ashenfelter and D. Card (eds), *Handbook of Labour Economics*, Vol. 3, Amsterdam: North Holland.

Nickell, S., Nunziata, L., Ochel, W. and Quintini, G. (2002) 'The Beveridge Curve, Unemployment and Wages in the OECD from the 1960s to the 1990s', LSE Centre for Economic Performance, http://cep.lse.ac.uk/pubs/download/dp0502.pdf accessed 6 October 2002.

Nicoletti, G., Scarpetta, S. and Boylaud, O. (2000) 'Summary Indicators of Product Market Regulation with an Extension to Employment Protection Legislation', *OECD Economic Department Working Paper*, No. 226.

Nitsch, V. (2000) 'National Borders and International Trade: Evidence from the European Union', *Canadian Journal of Economics*, vol. 33, pp. 1091–105.

Noorkoiv, R. Orazem, P.R., Purr, A. and Vodopivee, M. (1997) 'How Estonia's Economic Transition Affected Employment and Wages (1989–95)', *World Bank Policy Research Working Paper 1837*.

Norman, P. (2001) 'Italy's Budget Makes Mockery of Euro Zone Pact on Fiscal Policy', *Financial Times*, 13th July, p. 6.

North, D.C. and Weingast, B.R. (1989) 'Constitutions and Commitment: The Evolution of Institutions Governing Public Choice in Seventeenth-Century England', *Journal of Economic History*, vol. 49(4), pp. 803–32.

Novack, J. (2002) 'Finland and Sweden's Opposing Choices on EMU: Similarity in Difference', UACES conference on The Future of Europe, Queen's University, Belfast, September.

Nyberg, P. and Vihriälä, V. (1994) 'The Finnish Banking Crisis and its Handling', *Bank of Finland Discussion Paper*, No. 7/94.

Obstfeld, M. and Peri, G. (1998) 'Regional Nonadjustment and Fiscal Policy', *Economic Policy*, vol. 26, pp. 205–60

O'Connell, T. and Frain, J. (1989) 'Inflation and Exchange Rates: A Further Empirical Analysis', *Central Bank of Ireland Technical Paper*, No. 1/RT/89.

O'Donnell, R. (1998) 'Ireland's Economic Transformation: Industrial Policy, European Integration and Social Partnership', *Working Paper*, No. 2, Centre for Western European Studies: European Union Centre.

O'Donnell, R. (2001) 'Towards Post-corporatist Concertation in Europe?', in H. Wallace (ed.), *Interlocking Dimensions of European Integration*, London: Pinter Publishers.

OECD (1994) *OECD Economic Surveys: France 1993–1994*, Paris: OECD.

OECD (1997a) *OECD Economic Surveys France: 1997*, Paris: OECD.

OECD (1997b) *OECD Economic Outlook*, Paris: OECD.

OECD (1998) *Economic Survey of Sweden*, Paris: OECD.

OECD (1999a) *OECD Economic Outlook*, Paris: OECD.

OECD (1999b) *EMU: Facts, Challenges and Policies*, Paris: OECD.

OECD (1999c) *OECD Economic Surveys 1998–1999 France*, Paris: OECD.

OECD (2000a) *OECD Economic Outlook*, 67, June, Paris: OECD.

OECD (2000b) *OECD Employment Outlook*, June, Paris: OECD.

OECD (2000c) *EMU One Year On*, Paris: OECD.

OECD, (2001) *Economic Survey of Ireland: Assessments and Recommendations*, Paris: OECD

OECD (2002a). *Benefits and Wages: OECD Indicators*, 2002 edition, Paris: OECD.

OECD (2002b) *United Kingdom*, OECD Economic Surveys 2002/1, Paris: OECD.

OECD (2003) *France*, Paris: OECD.

OECD (2004) *OECD Main Economic Indicators*, accessed via www.mimas.ac.uk.

OECD (2005) *Economic Survey of Spain*, Paris: OECD.

Onofri, P. and Tomasini, S. (1992) 'France and Italy: A Tale of Two Adjustments', in Barrell (ed.) (1992).

ONS (2004) Time Series database, accessed via ESDS, http://www.esds.ac.uk/international/.

Organisation for Economic Cooperation and Development (2001) Economic Survey of Ireland: Assessments and Recommendations, Paris: OECD.

Oxford Economic Forecasting (2002) 'Scenarios on Behalf of the "No" Campaign', http://www.no-euro.com/factsfigures/pdf/oef.pdf accessed 1 May 2002, London: No Campaign.

Paczyński, W. (2003) 'ECB Decision-making and the Status of the Eurogroup in an Enlarged EMU', w/p 262, Warsaw: Center for Social and Economic Research.

Padoa-Schioppa, T. (1999) 'Europe's New Economic Policy Constitution', in D. Currie, A. Donnelly, H. Flassbeck, B. Hall, J. Lemierre, T. Padoa-Schioppa and N. Wicks, *Will EMU Lead to a European Economic Government?*, London: CER.

Padoa-Schioppa, T., Emerson, M., King, M., Milleron, J.C., Paelinck, J.H.P., Papademos, L.D., Pastor, A., and Scharpf, F.W. (1987) *Efficiency, Stability and Equity: A Strategy for the Evolution of the Economic System of the European Community*, Oxford: Oxford University Press.

Pain, N. (1997) 'Continental Drift: European Integration and the Location of UK Foreign Direct Investment', *The Manchester School Supplement*, vol. 65, pp. 94–117.

Paloviita, M. and Mayes, D.G. (2003) 'Asymmetry and Inflation Dynamics in Different Specifications of the Phillips Curve for the Euro Area', Bank of Finland.

Papell, D.H. (1984) 'Exchange Rates and Prices: An Empirical Analysis', *International Economic Review*, vol. 35(2), May, pp. 397–410.

Pekkarinen, J., Antola, E., Haaparanta, P., Honkapohja, S., Julkunen, R., Koskela, E., Loikkanen, H., Stenius, M. and Virén, M. (1997) *Monetary Union and Finland*, Helsinki: Council of State.

Pelkmans, J. (2001) 'Making Network Markets Competitive', *Oxford Review of Economic Policy*, vol. 17, pp. 432–56.

Pelkmans, J. and Hobza, A. (2002) 'A Sound Enlargement of Euroland', CEPS Briefing note, Brussels: CEPS.

Pelkmans, J., Gros, D. and Nünez Ferrer, J. (2000) 'Long-Run Economic Aspects of the European Union's Eastern Enlargement', WRR, Working Document W109, September, Scientific Council for Government Policy, The Hague.

Peutter, U. (2003) 'Informal Circles of Ministers: A Way Out of the EU's Institutional Dilemmas?', *European Law Journal*, vol. 9(1), pp. 109–24.

Pisani-Ferry, J. (2002) 'Fiscal Discipline and Policy Coordination in the Eurozone: Assessment and Proposals', Paper prepared for the European Commission President's Group of Economic Analysis.

Pollack, M.A. (1997) 'Delegation, Agency and Agenda-Setting in the European Community', *International Organisations*, vol. 51(1), pp. 99–134.

Poret, P. (1990) 'Les salaires dans les grands pays de l'OCDE au course des années quatre-vingt. Les comportements ont-ils changé?', *Economie et Statistique*, No. 235.

Posen, A.S. (2003a) 'Germany', *The International Economy*, Fall, pp. 15–17.

Posen, A.S. (2003b) 'Is Germany Turning Japanese?', *IIE Working Paper* 2–2003, Institute for International Economics, Washington, DC.

Ralle, P. and Toujas-Bernate, J. (1990) 'Indexation des salaires: La rupture de 1983', *Economie et Prévision*, No. 92–3.

Razzak, W. (2000) 'Are Inflation Targeting Regimes Credible? Econometric Evidence', *Reserve Bank of New Zealand Working Paper*.

Razzak, W. (2001) 'Money in the Era of Inflation Targeting', *Reserve Bank of New Zealand Discussion Paper*, No. 2001/02.

Ripatti, A. and Vilmunen, J. (2001) 'Declining Labour Share – Evidence of a Change in the Underlying Production Technology', *Bank of Finland Discussion Paper* 10/2001.

Rogoff, K. (1985a) 'The Optimum Degree of Commitment to a Monetary Target', *Quarterly Journal of Economics*, vol. 100, pp. 1169–90.

Rogoff, K. (1985b) 'Can International Monetary Policy Cooperation be Counterproductive?', *Journal of International Economics*, vol. 18, pp. 199–217.

Rollo, J. (2002) 'In or Out: The Choice for Britain', *Journal of Public Policy*, vol. 22(2), pp. 217–38.

Rose, A. (2000) 'One Money, One Market: The Effect of Common Currencies on Trade', *Economic Policy*, vol. 30, pp. 435–48.

Rose, A.K. (2001) 'Currency Unions and Trade: The Effect Is Large', *Economic Policy*, vol. 33, pp. 433–62.

Rose, A.K. (2003) 'The Potential Effects of EMU Entry on British Trade', *Submissions on EMU from Leading Academics, EMU Study*, HM Treasury, London: HMSO.

Rose, A.K. (2004) 'The Effect of Common Currencies on International Trade: Where Do We Stand?', in Volbert A., Melitz, J. and von Furstenberg G. (eds), *Monetary Union and Hard Pegs*, Oxford: Oxford University Press.

Ross, G. (1998) 'The Euro, The "French Model of Society", and French Politics', *French Politics and Society*, vol. 16(4), pp. 1–16.

Rostowski, J. (2003) 'When should the central Europeans join EMU?', *International Affairs*, 79, pp. 993–1008.

RWI (2002) 'Assessment of the Impact of National Policies in Connection with the European Employment Strategy', Essen/Cologne, Report for the European Commission, Brussels: DG Employment and Social Affairs.

SABL (Statistiche, Ämter des Bundes und der Länder) (2003) 'GDP at Constant 1995 Prices, 1991–2002', www.statistik-bw.de/VolkswPreise/ArbeitskreisVGR/.

Sachverständigenrat (German Council of Economic Experts) (2002) 'Jahregutachten 2002/2003, http://www.sachverstaendigenrat-wirtschaft.de/.

Sapir, A., Aghion, P., Bertola, G., Hellwig, M., Pisani-Ferry, J., Rosati, D., Viñals, J. and Wallace, H., with Buti, M., Nava, M. and Smith, P.M. (2004) *An Agenda for a Growing Europe*, Oxford: Oxford University Press.

Sargent, T. and Wallace, N. (1981) Some Unpleasant Monetarist Arithmetic, *Federal Reserve Bank of Minneapolis Quarterly Review*, Vol. 5, No. 3 (Fall), pp. 1–17.

Scharpf, F.W. (1999) *Governing in Europe: Effective and Democratic?*, Oxford: Oxford University Press.

Schembri, L. (2002) 'Living Around the Bloc: Lessons from Canada for Small Countries', *Journal of Public Policy*, vol. 22(2), pp. 119–42.

Schröder, U. and Walter, N. (2003) 'Agenda 2010 – A Giant Leap for German Politics – But One Small Step for the German Economy', *AIGS Advisor*, October 30, Washington, DC: American Institute for Contemporary German Studies.

Scott, C. (2000) 'Accountability in the Regulatory State', *Journal of Law and Society*, vol. 27(1), pp. 38–60.

Scott, C. (2002a) 'Governance of the European Union: The Potential for Multilevel Control', *European Law Journal*, vol. 8(1), pp. 80–101.

Scott, C. (2002b) 'Private Regulation of the Public Sector: A Neglected Facet of Contemporary Governance', *Journal of Law and Society*, vol. 29(1), pp. 56–76.

Servais, D. (1995) *A Single Financial Market*, Luxembourg: OOPEC.

Simmons, B.A. (2000) 'The Legalization of International Monetary Affairs', *International Organisation*, vol. 54(3), pp. 573–602.

Sinn, H.-W. (2003) 'The Laggard of Europe', *CESifo Special Report*, 1/2003.

Sinn, H.-W. and Reutter, M. (2000) 'The Minimum Inflation Rate for Euroland', *CESifo Working Paper*, No. 377, December, 2000, IFO, Munich.

Sinn, H.-W. and Reutter, M. (2001) 'The Minimum Inflation Rate for Euroland', *NBER Working Paper*, No. 7586.

Šmidkovà, K., Barrell, R. and Holland, D. (2002) 'Estimates of Fundamental Real Exchange Rates for the Five EU Pre-Accession Countries', *Czech National Bank, Working Paper Series*.

Snyder, F. (1995) 'The Effectiveness of European Community Law: Institutions, Processes, Tools and Techniques', in T. Daintith, (ed.), *Implementing EC Law in the United Kingdom: Structures for Indirect Rule*, Chichester: Wiley.

Solbes, P. (2002) 'Economic Policy Co-ordination – the Way Forward', Brussels Economic Forum, 2 May, mimeo.

Staiger, D., Stock, J. and Watson, M. (1997) 'The NAIRU, Unemployment and Monetary Policy', *Journal of Economic Perspectives*, vol. 11(1), pp. 33–50.

Statistics Finland and Bank of Finland (various) http://www.tekes.fi/eng/innovation/statistics/statistics.htm; http://www.stat.fi/tk/tp/tkesittely_lyhyesti_en.html; http://www.bof.fi/eng/index.htm.

Storesletten, K. and Zilibotti, F. (2000) 'Education, Educational Policy and Growth', *Swedish Economic Policy Review*, vol. 7, pp. 39–70.

Suardi, M. (2001) 'EMU and Asymmetries in Monetary Policy Transmission', DG Ecofin, *Economic Paper*, No. 157.

Summers, R. and Heston, A. (1991) 'The Penn World Table (Mark 5): An Expanded Set of International Comparisons, 1950–1958', *Quarterly Journal of Economics*, vol. 106(2), May, pp. 327–68.

Surico, P. (2003) 'Asymmetric Reaction Functions for the Euro Area', *Oxford Review of Economic Policy*, vol. 19(1), pp. 44–57.

Taylor, C. (2000) 'The Role and Status of the European Central Bank: Some Proposals for Accountability and Co-operation', in C. Crouch (ed.), *After the Euro: Shaping Institutions for Governance in the Wake of European Monetary Union*, Oxford: Oxford University Press.

Taylor, John B. (2000) 'Low Inflation, Pass-through and the Pricing Power of Firms', *European Economic Review*, vol. 44, pp. 1389–408.

Teague, P. (1999) 'Reshaping Employment Regimes in Europe: Policy Shifts Alongside Boundary Change', *Journal of Public Policy*, vol. 19(1), pp. 33–62.

TEPSA (2002) 'The Economic Outlook, European Parliament General Directorate for Research', *ECON Working Paper Series*, ECON 129, 2002.

Teubner, G. (1998) 'Legal Irritants: Good Faith in British Law or How Unifying Law Ends Up in New Cleavages', *Modern Law Review*, vol. 11, pp. 11–32.

Thom, R. and Walsh, B. (2002) 'The Effects of a Common Currency on Trade: Ireland before and after the Sterling Link', *European Economic Review*, vol. 46(6), pp. 1111–23.

Thomas, A. (1997) 'Is the Exchange Rate a Shock Absorber? The Case of Sweden', *IMF Working Paper*, WP/97/176.

Trichet, J.C. (1992) 'Dix ans de desinflation competitive en France', *Notes Bleues de Bercy*, October.

Turrini, A. (2004) 'Public Investment and the EU Fiscal Framework', *European Economy Economic Papers*, No. 202.

UNCTAD (Various) *World Investment Report*, United Nations, New York and Geneva.

Usher, J.A. (2000) *The Law of Money and Financial Services in the European Community*, Oxford: Oxford University Press.

Verdun, A. (1996) 'An "Asymmetrical" Economic and Monetary Union in the EU: Perceptions of Monetary Authorities and Social Partners', *Journal of European Integration*, vol. 20(1), pp. 59–81.

Verdun, A. (2000) 'Governing by Committee: The Case of Monetary Policy', in T. Christiansen and E. Kirchner, *Committee Governance in the European Union*, Manchester: Manchester University Press.

Vinals, J. and Jimeno, J.F. (1998) 'The Impact of EMU on Unemployment', *European Investment Bank Papers*, vol. 3, pp. 83–97.

Virén, M. (2001) 'Fiscal Policy, Automatic Stabilisers and Policy Coordination in EMU', in A. Brunila, M. Buti and M. Franco (eds), *The Growth and Stability Pact*, Basingstoke: Palgrave.

Visser, J. (2002) 'Is the European Employment Strategy the Answer?', paper presented at the NIG workshop, Utrecht, 26 April.

Von Hagen, J. and Harden, I. (1994) 'National Budget Processes and Fiscal Performance', *European Economy*, No. 3.

Wadhwani, S. (1999) 'British Unemployment and Monetary Policy', Speech delivered to the Society of Business Economists, 2 December, Available, Online www.bankofengland.co.uk (2 September 2001).

Walker, N. (1996) 'European Constitutionalism and European Integration', *Public Law*, pp. 266–90.

Wallace, H. (2000) 'The Policy Process', in H. Wallace and W. Wallace, *Policy-Making in the European Union*, Oxford: Oxford University Press.

Weber, R. and Taube, G. (1999) 'On the Fast Track to EU Accession: Macroeconomic Effects and Policy Challenges for Estonia', *IMF Working Paper*, No. 99/156 (Washington: International Monetary Fund).

Weiler, J.H.H. (1997) 'The Reformation of Constitutionalism', *Journal of Common Market Studies*, vol. 35, pp. 97–131.

Weiler, J.H.H. (1999) *The Constitution of Europe*, Cambridge: Cambridge University Press.

Wessels, W. (1997) 'Ever Closer Fusion? A Dynamic Macropolitical View on Integration Processes', *Journal of Common Market Studies*, vol. 35, pp. 267–99.

Wessels, W. and Linsenmann, I. (2002) 'EMU's Impact on National Institutions A Gouvernement Economique in the making: Towards Vertical and Horizontal Fusion?', in K. Dyson (ed.), *European States and the Euro: Playing the Semi-Sovereignty Game*, Oxford: Oxford University Press.

Westaway, P. (1997) 'What Determines the Natural Rate of Unemployment? And What Does Not?', *EUI Working Paper RSC*, No. 97/43.

Westaway, P. (2003) 'Modelling Shocks and Adjustment Mechanisms in EMU', HM Treasury.

Williamson, H. (2004) 'Entrepreneurs Held Back by German Trade Curbs', *Financial Times*, January 16.

Wood, G.E. (2003) 'Monetary Unions: Criteria, History and Prospects', Bank of Finland, August.

Working Group on Economic Governance (2002) Final Report of Working Group, CONV 357/02, WG 17, 21/10/02, Brussels.

Wren-Lewis, S. (2003) 'Estimates for the Equilibrium Exchange Rate for Sterling Against the Euro', EMU Study for HM Treasury.

Wren-Lewis, S. and Driver, R. (1998) *Real Exchange Rates for the Year 2000*, Washington, DC: Institute for International Economics.

Wynne, M. and Koo, J. (1997) 'Business Cycles under Monetary Union: EU and US Business Cycles Compared', *Federal Reserve Bank of Dallas Discussion Paper* 97–07.

Wyplosz, C. (1997) 'EMU: Why and How It Might Happen', *Journal of Economic Perspectives*, Vol. 11, No. 4, 3–22.

Wyplosz, C. (2002) 'Fiscal Policy: Institutions versus Rules', *CEPR Discussion Paper*, No. 3238.

Yates, A (1998) 'Downward Nominal Rigidity and Monetary Policy', *Bank of England Working Paper*, No. 82.

Zeitlin, J. and Pochet, P. (eds) with Magnusson, L. (2005) *The Open Method of Coordination in Action: The European Employment and Social Inclusion Strategies*, Brussels: PIE-Peter Lang.

Index